1492-1992: RE/DISCOVERING

COLONIAL WRITING

René Jara and Nicholas Spadaccini, Editors

HISPANIC ISSUES

1492-1992: RE/DISCOVERING COLONIAL WRITING

hispanic issues 4
edited and introduced by
René Jara and
Nicholas Spadaccini

University of Minnesota Press
Minneapolis   Oxford

The editors of this volume gratefully acknowledge assistance from the Program for Cultural Cooperation between Spain's Ministry of Culture and United States' Universities, as well as the College of Liberal Arts and the Department of Spanish and Portuguese Languages and Literatures, University of Minnesota.

Published by the University of Minnesota Press
2037 University Avenue Southeast, Minneapolis, MN 55414
Printed in the United States on acid-free paper
Second printing, 1991

COVER: Studio 87501, Santa Fe, New Mexico. Manuscript of Alfonso de la Torre, *Visión delectable de la philosophia e artes liberales*, Seville, Juan Cromberger, 1538. (Cromberger first introduced printing into America by starting a press at Mexico City in 1539: the first Hispanic issue.) Special thanks to Orlando Romero, History Library, Museum of New Mexico. *Galeones: Discovery of the West Indies by Christopher Columbus*, from a drawing dating from 1494 and attributed to Columbus himself. ("Epistolae Christofori Columbi," from photo of Lalance.) Special thanks to Laurence Hallewell.

Library of Congress Cataloging-in-Publication Data

1492-1992: re/discovering colonial writing/edited and introduced by René Jara and Nicholas Spadaccini.—1st ed.
    p. cm. —(Hispanic Issues, ISSN 0893-2395; #4)
  Includes bibliographies and index.
  ISBN 0-8166-2011-3
  1. Spanish American Literature—To 1800—History and Criticism.
2. Latin America in literature. I. Jara, René, 1941- . II. Spadaccini, Nicholas. III. Title: 1492-1992, rediscovering colonial writing. IV. Series: Hispanic issues; 4.
PQ7081.A15 1989.
809'.898—dc20   89-31361
                                      CIP

64995

Hispanic Issues

TABLE OF CONTENTS

INTRODUCTION:
ALLEGORIZING THE NEW WORLD

René Jara and Nicholas Spadaccini

The present volume deals with five hundred years of historical discourse. The initial phase of this writing comprises a variety of enunciative perspectives: that of the victors in the early military encounter; the one portraying evangelizing efforts directed toward the spiritual conquest and defense of native populations; the juridical and regulatory writing emanating from the Crown, the Church, and the newly established institutions in the Indies; the counter-narratives of epic disillusionment; the discourse of the Mestizo (person of mixed blood); the Indian view of conquest and colonization; and, the formulation of Creole writing as an expression of protonational feeling. These discourses did not become extinguished with the end of the Colonial period but are felt in a significant body of contemporary writing. The reason for their continued presence is that the shadow of Colonialism is still part of the reality of present-day Spanish America.

This volume's reexamination of Colonial writing involves the adoption of a bifocal perspective: that of our present experience of America and that of the time frame in which the conquest and colonization took place. What is clear is that the domination of the New World was ultimately achieved through writing which was the primary vehicle for the establishment, rationalization, and control of the overseas institutions of the Empire. Despite variations in historical setting, one can argue that this issue is still present today. The wars of independence at the beginning of the nineteenth century merely replaced the territorial domination of Spain with the economic pre-eminence of England, while the cultural influence of the Peninsula was substituted by that of France. Thereafter, in the twentieth century, the issue of colonialism was to become even more pressing due to the cultural, political and economic hegemony of the United States and the multinational corporations. In view of these historical shifts, Spanish-American writing has become more complex and has also sharpened its focus of political definition. In many places the so-called Indians still refuse to be considered nationals of a particular country and reclaim the right to preserve their ancient beliefs and cultural habits.

A Mestizo discourse which called into question the double European and native inheritance of Spanish America came to fruition by the middle of this century. Accordingly, the call for a reexamination of Spanish-American cultural roots is now at the very core of philosophical, literary, sociological, and anthropological writing. Elizabeth Burgos Debray registers the following statement by the Guatemalan Quiché Indian Rigoberta Menchú in 1983:

> And when the child gets to be around ten years old... is when s/he is made to remember that their forefathers were violated by the white colonialists. But they do not say how it is written except through the recommendations that have come from our grandparents and our forefathers. For the great majority of the

people do not know how to read or write nor that a
document exists for the Indian. But it is said that the
Spaniards violated the best children of our forefa-
thers, the most humble people and it is in their honor
that we must continue to keep our secrets. And no one
would be able to discover those secrets except for us
natives. (Burgos Debray 49-50 [our translation])[1]

Along the same lines, Michel De Certeau ("The Politics
of Silence: The Long March of the Indians" 225-233) quotes
from a speech by Francisco Servin before a Congress of Indians held in Paraguay in October, 1974: "We were once
the masters of the earth, but since the gringos arrived we
have become veritable pariahs....We have the hope that
the day will come when they realize that we are their roots
and that we must grow together like a great tree with its
branches and flowers". The French historian comments,
perceptively, " That day is dawning. The silhouette of that
tree, which in the past has signified revolutions based on
the liberty and solidarity of the people, seems to have returned with the Indian awakening and its parallels in
Western experiments and explorations"(231).

If until the middle of the 1600s writing was largely a
tool of colonization, thereafter it acquired an opposite
function —one which ran parallel to that of the
colonizer—while using many of the same rhetorical
strategies. This is precisely what is observable in the early
writings of Alonso de Ercilla y Zúñiga (1533-1594) and
Bartolomé de Las Casas (ca. 1474-1566), in those of the
Mestizo Garcilaso de la Vega, the Inca (1539-1616), in those
of Indian writers such as Guamán Poma de Ayala (d.1615)
and Fernando de Alva Ixtlilxochitl (ca.1578-1650), and
more decisively in the Creole discourse of Carlos de
Sigüenza y Góngora (1645-1700), Sor Juana Inés de la Cruz
(ca.1651-1695), and Fray Servando de Mier (1763-1827).

The Spanish Humanist Antonio de Nebrija (1441-1522),
an intellectual in the court of the Catholic Kings, was to
present to Queen Isabella his *Gramática Castellana*
("Castilian Grammar") in 1492. The presentation was
made with the understanding that language was a
necessary instrument for building and consolidating a new
Empire, in the same manner that Latin had functioned in

Roman times. Indeed, the project of colonization of the New World entailed the use of language for purposes of domination and exclusion. Within the framework of an early Modern State that seeks to exercise its hegemony over new territories, language becomes doubly important since it serves both purposes of inclusion and exclusion. Instructions, laws, geographic descriptions, territorial limits and, indeed, the very possession of land will be inscribed in the dominant language. Through the tyranny of the alphabet (see W. Mignolo in this volume), the native Amerindians are deprived of their basic natural rights and are subjected to enslavement. Through exclusive use of the official language, the native cultures were forced to surrender to the conqueror.

A grotesque example of the impact of the official language of the conquerors on the lives of the native population is the *requerimiento* (a pledge of submission), a document originally drawn up by the Spanish jurist Juan López de Palacios Rubios with the idea that Spanish officers would read it to the Indians before making war against them. Written in Spanish, the *requerimiento* entailed an acknowledgment by the Indians of the authority of the Church, the Pope, and the Spanish Kings over their lands (see A. Gómez-Moriana in this volume). One can imagine the bewilderment and fear of the Indians as they were confronted with a text hastily transmitted, in a language totally alien to them, as the Spaniards prepared to attack in their strange armors, with horses, barking dogs, and the clapping of weapons. Little wonder, then, that Las Casas did not know whether to laugh or weep upon reading the bizarre document.

Writing is the building block of the Empire and is an integral part of the Modern State's plan to administer its colonial possessions along rational lines. The very distance of the colonies from the Court meant that the bureaucracy acquired an even greater significance than it might have had otherwise. The implications of that distance were significant in the sense that power could not be exercised directly from the Metropolis but relied instead on an army of middlemen who acted in various capacities to bring the word of centralized authority to the colonial realm. Writing was, therefore, the only valid instrument for the transmission of the Crown's will to the colonies and, conversely, for the King to receive information from the Indies. Writing occasionally bypassed these middlemen and addressed itself directly to the King through physical presence. Such is the case with Hernán Cortés (1485-1547), Fray Antonio de Montesinos, and Fray Bartolomé de Las Casas who were forced to bring their messages to the Crown in person. This route was taken in order to avoid the potential problem entailed with any kind of mediation; it was a way of ensuring that the message reached the intended receiver.

Two administrative bodies were set up for the ruling of Spanish America from Spain. One was the *Casa de Contratación* (House of Trade) and the other was the *Consejo de Indias* (Council of the Indies). The first served to regulate and develop trade with the New World while the main function of the second was to advise the King in all American affairs. The House of Trade was founded in 1503 following Queen Isabella's appointment of Fray Juan de Fonseca to oversee Columbus's enterprise of the Indies. The jurisdiction of the Spanish House of Trade was mainly economic but in time it became a court of law for criminal and civil matters related to commerce with the colonies, thus becoming a treasure source of written documentation. One of the officers of the House was a *contador* or registrar who had to show in his books not only all people sailing to and returning from America but also records of exports and imports. The same institution counted since 1508 with a *piloto mayor* (master pilot) in order to register, research, and oversee all expeditions to the Indies.

The Council of the Indies instituted in 1524 was the supreme governing body of the Spanish colonies. It prepared the laws and ensured that they were enforced. The Council also functioned as a high court in order to judge infractions and was responsible for the interpretation of those laws. As an executive body, the Council supervised the treatment of the natives and arranged for the institutionalization of *Audiencias*, universities and bishoprics. It also granted permission for new expeditions of discovery, named civil and ecclesiastical officials of high rank, provided for the defense of the coasts, and determined when and how the *visitas* (official audits) of functionaries in the New World were to take place. It was also in charge of the *residencias*, a judicial procedure of evaluation that was to take place at the end of the tenure of every major crown official, from *alcalde* to viceroy. The Council had also supervising powers over Church matters under the Crown's privileges of *patronato real* (royal patronage). These institutions were to remain largely in place until the sweeping Bourbon reforms of the eighteenth century. One can well imagine the number of bureaucrats mobilized, the documentation generated, and the uncertain transport and delivery of written materials to and from America. One can also imagine the virtual impossibility of exercising direct power and control over distant subjects from the seat of the Crown. This explains the famous dictum attributed to Cortés: "I obey but cannot comply" ("obedezco pero no cumplo"). The profusion of written materials tended to diffuse the importance of the instructions and allowed for the creation of an interpretative space for the receiver. This same phenomenon can be seen in Spain and is registered by the *arbitrista* Sancho de Moncada and the diplomat and thinker Saavedra Fajardo who bemoans the excessive number of laws and attributes the lack of compliance to their proliferation: "the laws in Spain—says Saavedra Fajardo—exceed five thousand".

Language is never neutral and, in the particular case at hand, it was not simply a companion of the Empire. Rather it functioned as a double-edged sword, for just as it produced a great number of directives and laws, the noncompliance with those laws also fueled a protonational feeling in the New World. In its attempt to establish a hierarchy that privileged the peninsular Spaniards, it also managed to create a new hierarchy of influence in which the Creole will first parallel and later displace the former.

The first manifestation of the relationship of writing to power, order and control took the form of an accumulation and systematization of Indian cultures by the first wave of missionaries coming to the New World. Such is the case with Bernardino de Sahagún (ca.1499-1590), Fray

Toribio de Benavente, also known as Motolinía (d.1569), and Fray Juan de Torquemada (1562-1624) among others. This is the point where power, writing, and knowledge coincide. But it is also the point in which knowledge creates the power of alterity. Fray Juan de Torquemada in his *Monarquía Indiana* ("Indian Monarchy," 1615) diagnoses this problem in recognizing the total appropriation of the writing of history on the part of the Europeans who had managed to obliterate the voices of those Indian chroniclers who would have been able to bring a more accurate and balanced view of the events surrounding the conquest and colonization. Torquemada goes on to appreciate the rhetorical and informational value of indigenous writing saying that he would have been pleased to have been able to render them into Castilian Spanish with the same elegance and grace of the Mexican original (León Portilla, "La conquista de México: Visión de los vencidos" 19-42).

It is important to recall here that most of the colonial texts had an epic character in the sense that writing was used to control the domain of the Other. The description of space became the first political projection of colonialism. Columbus's *Diario*, Cortés's *Cartas de relación*, and the historical account of Bernal Díaz del Castillo (1492-1581) have in common the control of property through representation. Discoverers and conquerors create a phantasmagoric space which seeks to introduce the lands of the New World to the European in order to justify commercial interests. This semiotic operation which also brought about the falsification of the American environment for its commodification entailed a deprivation of identity (see respectively A. Gómez-Moriana and B. Pastor in this volume).

It should not surprise us that all colonial writing had hegemonic and propagandistic intentions, for the idea behind such writing was to foster the establishment of the institutions of the Empire. Moreover it was also a question of promoting commercial relations and the project of evangelization. These dominant features of colonial writing help explain the scarce description of people and geographical spaces. The early chronicles, and the epic in general, did not have an anthropological bent; they followed instead the conventions of military discourse as they dealt with the appropriation of geographical locations through military means. For these reasons details are generated not to represent physical space but to recreate the field of battle.

Representation was not an easy task for it involved the construction of a New World through a language whose conventions and formulae did not always meet the needs for depicting the unknown. Thus when Cortés writes of a Mexican market, and of the abundance of diverse objects to be found there, he also argues that it is impossible to name and describe all of them. Similarly, when Gonzalo Fernández de Oviedo (1479-1557) attempts to depict the variety of languages, habits, animals, and types of vegetation he bemoans the insufficiency of language for an adequate representation and understanding of the new (see S. Merrim in this volume). The frequency with which Columbus (ca.1451-1505), Cortés, and Bernal Díaz, among others, use expressions such as "no one would be able to describe" ("nadie podría describir"), or "something that I cannot describe" ("algo que no puedo describir"), or can only describe following the conventions of the romances of chivalry that had entered the European imaginary, reveals a linguistic impotence that opens up new spaces in the colonial construction of reality. First, the conqueror and colonizer is forced to recognize alterity and, in doing so, to accept it as a necessary component of his world. Second, the adaptation of the modes of representation familiar to the native languages of America become a rhetorical necessity, thereby clearing the way for Mestizo and Indian inscriptions of the Spanish and Amerindian cultural environments. Finally, a space is opened for an understanding of cultural independence through the mastery of knowledge and power as it is evident later in Carlos de Sigüenza y Góngora and Sor Juana Inés de la Cruz.

Within ten years of Columbus's first voyage to the New World, the Crown recognized the need to consolidate and organize the Admiral's discoveries. This charge was given to Nicolás de Ovando who was sent to the New World with 2500 people in 1502 with the express purpose of reorganizing the economy and of rationalizing the relations with the Indians. In order to guarantee a constant supply of native labor, Ovando, following the instructions contained in a royal decree of 1503, replaced the *repartimiento* system with that of the *encomienda*.

The *repartimiento* (partition or distribution) was in operation as early as 1499 and provided for the apportionment of Indians to the colonists and the local government for the latter's use. Indians were supposed to work for a given period of time and in specific tasks, and once the job was done they were to be freed and returned to their villages. They were also supposed to be paid for their labor. The ideological justification for the *repartimiento* was that if the Indians were not kept in contact with the Spaniards the works of Christianization would be difficult to achieve.

The *encomienda* system as legally defined in 1503 consisted of a grant of Indians to a conquistador who would receive tribute and labor from his subjects in exchange for the teachings of the Christian faith. Although the *encomienda* did not include grants of land, the grantee managed to gain control over them. Both systems—*repartimiento* and *encomienda*—brought about abuses which translated into the enslavement and personal servitude of the Indians. Cortés, for example, allotted himself an *encomienda* of 100,000 Mexican natives.

The decimation of the native population of the Antilles which was provoked by pestilence, by their eradication from their lands, by the inhumanity of forced labor, especially in mines, and by their demoralization which in some cases led to collective suicide, coupled with the emergence of a new system of lordship that threatened to become an aristocracy in opposition to that of Spain, was to awaken the defense mechanisms of the Crown. The Laws of Burgos (1512) and later the New Laws (1542) were promulgated as reactions to these exploitative and abusive practices which concentrated too much power in the hands of the colonists. Significantly, both bodies of laws were defeated by the colonists' opposition, although the institution of *encomienda* was partially tamed by the efforts of the Church and the Crown by the middle of the century. The weakening of this system of forced labor was, to a large extent, the result of the activities of the Dominican friar Bartolomé de Las Casas whose victory over the *encomenderos'* spokesman—the jurist Juan Ginés de Sepúlveda—made it clear that natives were free persons and vassals of the Crown. The New Laws forbade new entrustments of Indians to colonists and abolished the rights of inheritance of previous entrustments.

The reforms proposed by Las Casas, which eventually shaped the Laws of 1542, were part of a utopian project meant to be realized not through transcendental means but through human actions and for human ends—social as well as economic—within the colonial context (see J. Rabasa in this volume). One of the markers of his writing is the material definition of the objectives needed to address the political governance of the Indians; the system had to be both "temporal and reasonable" ("temporal y razonable") and had to strive toward the good, utility, prosperity, and development of the native populations (Maravall, "Libertad y derecho de ser hombre en el pensamiento lascasiano" 373-374).

One cannot disconnect Las Casas's utopian reforms with the providentialism of his view of world history, according to which the final step in the stages of human development was the conversion to Christianity. Thus while the Roman Empire preceded those of the Mexica and the Inca, the latter two anticipated the arrival of the Spaniards. This view of world history is said to have provided an explanation for the cultural distance between the Indians and the Europeans and even between the different Indian groups. Moreover, writes Anthony Pagden "it provided a justification for the conquest which suited the millenarian ambitions of the missionaries: If the "advanced" Indian groups had reached the limit of their evolutionary potential as pagans, then the evangelization of the Amerindian peoples could be interpreted as historically inevitable" (*The Fall of the Natural Man* 143).

While, paradoxically, the interpretation of Las Casas's writings may well have served to justify a conquest conducted under the shield of evangelization, the primary objective of his writings seemed to be a concern for the economic and social welfare of the Indians. The political construction of a new society, for example, appears based on presuppositions related to the notions of liberty and private property. Yet, the defense of private property in Las Casas does not purport to defend the accumulation of wealth in the hands of the rich and powerful but is clearly limited to the rights of Indians and small farmers who had settled on the new continent. In Las Casas's thinking God had created things for use by all people and, therefore, the mere occupation of land was enough to provide legitimate title of property. It followed that the Indians and the first workers who arrived in the New World were deemed to be the owners of the land; thus all sales, donations and *encomiendas* emanating from the Spanish Crown and affecting the property of the natives lacked legitimacy and needed to be made invalid. Indians were free and ought to be treated accordingly and, therefore, could not be deprived of what belonged to them by natural law.

The principle of liberty in the context of the natural rights of human beings has important ramifications for the political order as neither a government nor a religion can be imposed without a group's willingness to accept it. José Antonio Maravall argues that in *Del único modo de atraer a los pueblos a la verdadera religión* ("The Only Way of Attracting People to the True Religion"), Las Casas's thinking goes beyond the notion of tolerance and edges close to the concept of freedom of conscience, at least in reference to Spain's recognized minorities, the Jews and the Moslems, implying that heavy-handed evangelization and forced conversions could not be imposed on a community: "If, as in the case of the Indians, the entire republic, by common consent of all the subjects, does not wish to hear us, but retain the rituals of their lands, where there had never been Christians, in such a case we cannot wage war against them." ("Si toda la república, de común consentimiento de todos los particulares, no quisiesen oirnos, sino estarse con sus ritos en sus tierras, donde nunca había habido cristianos, como son los indios, en tal caso no les podemos hacer guerra" [cited by Maravall, "Libertad y derecho" 379]).

The Lascasian notion of liberty has severe implications on the level of governance as it connects with the idea that power emanates directly from the people. At the same time, it allows Las Casas to distance himself from a line of thinking that will later evolve toward monarchical absolutism, a form of governance which, according to him, could only be justified if it was "based on the consent of the subjects for it brings with it neither the strengths of natural law nor absolute necessity" [cited by Maravall, Ibidem 380]. ("Se funda sobre el consentimiento de los súbditos y por tanto no trae consigo natural fuerza ni absoluta necesidad"). The consent of the subjects, however, does not translate into an abrogation of their freedom. The principle of legitimacy that accrues through the free consent of the people also carries with it the right of resistance which though rarely admissible under the absolutist monarchies of Europe, had ample justification in a world in which social injustice and absence of freedom had provoked Indian unrest and open rebellion.

Las Casas's defense of the Indians also entails a demonstration of their capacity to maintain a political order and authority. Anthony Pagden (*The Fall of the Natural Man*) reminds us that the Mexica and the Inca chieftains guided their peoples like elder relatives and fathers in a family, ruling according to customs and law. Since the family is the origin of the State, their regime and government were most natural and, although primitive, they were legitimate. Las Casas stresses the Indians' humanity and their unity with the other peoples of the world. Thus, in the preface to his *Historia de las Indias* ("History of the Indies") he insists on the sameness of humankind: "as all of the people of the world are united and bonded among themselves in a type of brotherhood and kinship of nature and, therefore, are reduced as if they were all together looking at themselves" [cited by Maravall, Ibidem, 384]. ("como todos los hombres del mundo sean unidos y ligados entre sí con una cierta hermandad y parentesco de naturaleza y, por consiguiente, se reducen como si todos juntos estuviesen mirándose"). The contemporary notion of alterity is displaced by Las Casas as he eliminates the connotations of monstrosity, irrationality and evilness in favor of a comprehensive view of humanity which saw the possibility of Christian salvation for the Indians as an asset rather than as an absolute necessity.

It is important to recall here that Las Casas's position on the conquest of the New World and, indeed, his arguments in favor of a common bond among all men, was seriously challenged in his own time. The high point of this challenge were the famous debates between the Dominican friar and Ginés de Sepúlveda in Valladolid (1550). Sepúlveda, a Humanist who was steeped in the classics, who had studied theology at Alcalá and philosophy at Bologna with the Aristotelian scholar Pomponazzi, and who was an official chronicler of Charles V, was espousing the idea of the just war, an idea anchored in a number of arguments, including one which alleged that some beings were by nature inferior to others. Sepúlveda's *Democrates Secundus* converges on three essential propositions: "That the Indians are culturally inferior and require tuition; that their unnatural crimes deprive them of their right of dominium; and that the bulls of donation are a valid charter for the Spanish conquest" (Pagden 118). Pagden correctly suggests that, ultimately, the notion "that Indians might be slaves by nature... was first advanced as a solution to a political dilemma; by what right the Crown of Castile occupied and enslaved the inhabitants of territories to which it could make no prior claims based on history" (Pagden 27).

In trying to advance this type of political agenda, Sepúlveda established comparisons between the respective cultures of Spaniards and Indians. He compares, for example, the cleverness of Cortés with the feeble-mindedness of the flabbergasted Moctezuma; the mental ability, prudence and common sense of the conquistador and his followers with the docility and paralysis of the conquered: "Can there be a greater or clearer testimony of the advantage which some men have over others in intelligence, ability, strength of soul and virtue? Is it not proof that they are servants by nature? For the fact that some of them seem to have intelligence for some mechanical things is not an argument for greater human prudence, for we see how certain small animals such as bees and spiders do things which no human mind could devise" (*Demócrates Segundo*, Ed. Angel Losada 36).[2]

Lewis Hanke (*La lucha por la justicia en la conquista de América* 336+) has shown how Las Casas takes Sepúlveda to task for misunderstanding Aristotle and points out that, in any case, Las Casas's position prevailed because of his first-hand knowledge of the New World and the reliance of the Spanish Monarchs on the Dominican's thinking on these issues. It is well known that Sepúlveda's doctrines did not find acceptance within the official centers of power and that, in fact, his books were not published until the eighteenth century. But despite their lack of official acceptance, his position had some resonance among the conquistadors of his time and, needless to say, has continued to have echoes in the aspirations of the political right and in that line of Spanish historiography which until recent times has tried to advance a messianic vision of Spain: "For there are certain virtues that can be seen in nearly all stations; such is the case with valor, which the Spanish legions displayed beyond belief throughout history, as happened in past times in the war of Numancia...; in the times of our fathers under the leadership of the Gran Capitán Gonzalo [de Cordoba]; and in our time under the auspices of the Caesar, Charles [V] in Milan and Naples, and Tunis in Africa under the personal direction of Charles himself; and not too long ago in the campaigns of Belgium and France; and recently in those of Germany where the Lutheran heretics were defeated with great glory [accruing] to our Emperor." (*Demócrates Segundo* 34).[3]

Sepúlveda's writings may not have circulated widely in his own time but they did express broadly-held beliefs regarding the cultural and intellectual world of the Indian. It was against those images that Las Casas fought, doing so through the use of the empirical data which his enemies had either ignored or misrepresented (Cf. Pagden 145).

On the other side of the Pyrenees Montaigne will implicitly take issue with the Spanish jurist by highlighting the so-called savages' punishment of those priests who abuse language in order to speak of the unknowable. He also called attention to their symbolic placing of the dead in which "the worthy go to the East where the New World is dawning, and the damned go to the West, where a world is coming to its end". This proves, according to Michel de Certeau "that the savage body obeys a law, the law of faithful and verifiable speech" (Michel de Certeau, "Montaigne's 'Of Cannibals'" 75). The attention drawn by Montaigne to the materiality of the native discourse (see T. Conley in this volume) anticipates features that will characterize Creole writing during the seventeenth century. Sepúlveda's rejection of Indian values and humanity was not shared by all learned Europeans as we have already seen in the writings of Las Casas and Montaigne. The defense and recognition of Indian values and culture took different forms of expression. An interesting case, for example, is that of the Spanish aristocrat and soldier named Alonso de Ercilla y Zúñiga (1533-1594).

There is no doubt that Ercilla did not share Las Casas's ideas regarding the recognition of Indian values. Ercilla believed in the assimilation of the vanquished, in the necessity of imprinting in their souls an identity of values, feelings, and beliefs. This was the basis for equality. Ercilla's own experiences were to teach him that their values were after all not so different from those which he esteemed. Along these lines the justification for the conquest was limited to matters of religion and evangelization. For Las Casas, on the other hand, equality did not require sameness so that the Indians could conceive of God according to their own traditions.

Ercilla was to travel to the New World in 1543 following the authorization received from the future Philip II for the purpose of joining the forces of the newly appointed Viceroy of Peru, Andrés Hurtado de Mendoza and the new Governor of Chile, Jerónimo de Alderete. They were to combat the insurrection of Francisco Hernández Girón in Peru and the revolt of the Araucanian Indians in Chile who had executed the conqueror Pedro de Valdivia. Alderete's death in 1556 prompted the naming of the Viceroy's son, Don García, as Governor of Chile, and Ercilla was to join his expedition against the Araucanian Indians. The writing of Ercilla's epic poem *La Araucana* ("The Araucaniad," 1569, 1578, 1589) was begun within this historical context.

La Araucana initiates a discourse that counters from within that of the Empire by subverting its basic contentions. To Ercilla's surprise, the barbarous world of the Araucanian Indians was not unlike that of his native Spain in terms of values such as patriotism, liberty, and the worth assigned to courage and pride. Ercilla also realized that in order to translate what he had seen and heard in the New World he needed to render it into the language of his own Europe.

More than a history of conquest, *La Araucana* is a song to war that focuses not so much on the military encounter between the antagonists as it does on the ideological conflict between the values of the Empire and those of the inhabitants of the land. Structurally this is expressed, on the one hand, through the confrontation of the exordia and conclusions, which manifest the Christian attitudes of the narrator, and, on the other, through the harangues of the Indian chieftains regarding their conceptions of land and liberty. The parallel structure of episodes and characters is a central mark of the poem and reflects a balanced perspective regarding the confrontation between Spaniards and Indians.

Despite Ercilla's attempt at balancing, one sees a subtle tilting toward the discourse of the Empire. In his descriptive moments the author observes in the aborigines an attitude that the reader can interpret as religious Titanism. Such an attitude privileges faith in man, pride, love of land and materiality over the transcendental values of Christianity (Sor Juana is to make the same observation later in the *Loa* to her sacramental play, *El Divino Narciso* ["Divine Narcissus"]). The narrator rejects the beliefs of the aborigines qualifying them as a satanical attitude directed like that of Lucifer against the Creator.

The hermeneutical operation of Ercilla regarding an understanding and an explanation of the Other has the image of Lucifer as a point of departure. The metaphor of the fallen angel means both a fatal condemnation to submission and a behavior and world view that is characterized by resentment. Thus it happens that in *La Araucana* the festivals of war are transformed by Ercilla's perspective into an insult against the Christian God of the Spaniards.

The religion of the enemy is translated into a perverse ritual; the celebration of victory becomes a demoniacal
witches' Sabbath; and the Native's defense of land and
property is converted into an exhibition of brute force.

Ercilla's criticism of Indian religious values is matched
by his critical vision of the Empire. Significantly his analysis of Spanish decadence is constructed around the symbols of Spain's imperial greatness: the battles of San Quintín and Lepanto and, to some extent, around the unification of the Peninsula under Philip II. Against the canonical views of Ercilla's epic as a disconnected text we see the
inclusion of these episodes and, in particular, of that of
Dido, as being essential to the structure and function of the
work.

Ercilla's epic poem is both a statement of imperial disil-
lusion and a recognition of the values of the Other. One
can see this in the structural arrangement of the text. Thus
the victory of the Spaniards in San Quintín over the
French is placed in a tactical relation to the Araucanians'
siege of the then recently constructed fortress of Penco. Let
us recall that the victory at San Quintín marked the zenith
of Spanish hegemony. Philip II had humiliated France
which was then one of the major world powers. Yet, a
mere twenty years after Spain's momentous victory at San
Quintín the Spaniards found themselves under siege in
distant Chile at the hands of a barbarous, Godless horde.
Ercilla's poem incorporates an internal polemic that ultimately questions the very destiny of the Empire. That is,
between the date of the battle of San Quintín (1557) and
the publication of the second part of La Araucana (1578)
the glorious victory had become a mere nostalgic event.
Spain was beginning to lose sight of its destiny.

The same strategy is adopted through the introduction
in the text of Spain's victory in the Gulf of Lepanto against
the Ottoman Empire. Let us recall that in 1571 the Christian fleet commanded by Juan de Austria sought to end
piracy in the Mediterranean as well as the trade of Christian slaves in Africa. The Spanish victory was thus seen as
the final triumph of Christianity over the infidels, and
that victory, together with its earlier defeat of France created a perception of invincibility. That perception was not

shared by Ercilla whose reading of these events is inscribed in *La Araucana* by structurally highlighting historical intertextuality. Thus the battle of Lepanto is placed next to a fiery speech by the rebellious chieftain Galvarino and Fitón's magic which gives Ercilla legitimacy as a chronicler.

The linking of Lepanto with Galvarino's speech allows Ercilla to question those Christian principles which supported and gave credence to the conquest. Ercilla questioned their use in a war fought largely for the private gain of the conquistadors who, despite being Christians, corrupted the values of religion and infringed upon the law. Ercilla was well acquainted with the crimes committed against the Indians by Spanish Governors such as Rodrigo de Quezada (1565-1567; 1575-1580) and Bravo de Saravia (1567-1575). Yet he also realized that those crimes were not any different from those perpetrated by the Turks against the Christians in the Mediterranean and in Africa. This can be inferred in the poem as Ercilla's respect for Christian values as well as for those related to authenticity and freedom allow for an understanding and recognition of the Other.

The third part of *La Araucana* is published in 1589, one year after the destruction of the Spanish Armada. In this section of the poem there is more emphasis on theoretical reflection than on the representation of war. Ercilla's epic song is one of hope and concern as the poet and his comrades in arms meet friendly Indians in the extreme south of Chile. At the same time that the narrator is affected by a new experience with the Indians he becomes increasingly concerned for them: civilization brings with it corruption, greed, injustice, and other ills. He realizes that the ideal of a Christian conquest has become a nightmare, a distorted reflection of Thomas More's utopia.

Ercilla's attitude toward war implies both a justification and a rejection of war. War might be justified when it is declared by a just sovereign whose actions are prompted by a quest for peace and for the benefit of the subjects. Such is the case with the unification of the Iberian Peninsula under Philip II which is discussed in the last chapter of *La Araucana*. On the other hand there is in Ercilla a rejection of war when it is waged indiscriminately for reasons of personal gain. Such had been the case in Chile where the natives had been mistreated in the name of a predominating search for wealth. The Indians had fought back to defend their territories and their freedom.

In Ercilla's subtext the attitude of the Indians resembled a love intrigue in which the natives are suitors and defenders of their loved land. It is this attitude which justifies structurally the introduction of the Dido story in the text. It is a story that relies on a heterogeneous reading of the Dido legend rather than on the canonical appropriation of Virgil. The latter version focuses on a self-consuming passion that leads to the suicide of the protagonist. The Christian version preferred by Ercilla stresses the sacrifice of the character in order to preserve the dignity and memory of the dead husband. Such is the case with Elisa-Dido, the Queen of Carthage, who resists the matrimonial advances by Yarbas, the tyrant of Lybia, as well as the pressures of her fellow citizens who fear for the destruction of the city. Her death might be read as a victory over selfishness and betrayal.

The recollection of this story is surprising because at the beginning of the poem the narrator had promised not to relate a love intrigue, but to focus on the Araucanian war. When one looks at the text closely, it becomes clear that Ercilla has kept his promise, for the love stories he represents are always entangled with the trials of war, which are recounted from the perspective of both the Spanish and the Araucanian combatants. This is again the function of the intertext which relies on a dialog that is ultimately tilted toward the imperial world view. The introduction of the Dido legend allows for a kind of symbolic intertextuality according to which the virtuous Queen replicates the values attributed by the Araucanians to their land. Just as Yarbas becomes a symbolic double for the Spanish army ready to invade the land of Arauco, so, too, the Araucanians and the Indians of the Southern part of the territory seem to press the motherland to repel aggression. Ercilla's double for Dido, however, does not commit suicide, as the war will continue.

The Americanization of the Dido legend is brought about through the creation of the fictive Glaura, a beautiful Indian woman who wonders through forests, mountains, and encampments in search of her husband, Cariolano. She also wanders throughout the poem in search of consolation. Eventually she is found by Ercilla, the poet—and sentry—who returns her to her husband, a man whom he has captured in order to save him from the Spanish soldiers. The Spanish captain Ercilla is no less generous than Cariolano who had come to the Spanish camp to prevent Ercilla from being killed in an Indian ambush.

La Araucana is an answer to the discourse of the Empire; it encompasses the traditions of a people in accordance with values such as justice, love, liberty, and truth. If there is a victory in *La Araucana* it is that of love over death; it is the victory of peace over war; of poetry, which affirms its existential vitality, over the destruction of the conquest. It is perhaps for these reasons that the war against the Araucanians was the most common epic theme of the Colonial period, followed closely by the deeds of Cortés. Ercilla's pattern of discourse was constructed upon the notion that the acceptance of the Other was inevitable. This was to be the great topos of the writings dealing with the conquest of America. The texture of its representation will alter the character of the discourse of the Empire in the last quarter of the sixteenth century. Imperial writing was soon going to be countered from within by the traces of native American and Mestizo discourses (R. Jara, *El revés de la arpillera*).

Whereas Ercilla and others had gone to the Indies and had written their narratives from the standpoint of their American experiences for a Spanish audience, there were native Amerindians who traveled to Spain to confront the language of the Empire with the written mold of their own traditions. Such is the case with Garcilaso, the Inca (1534-1616) and Guamán Poma de Ayala whose date of birth is unknown and who died around 1615.

Born Gómez Suárez de Figueroa, Garcilaso was the son of a conquistador, Garcilaso de la Vega, and of an Indian princess (Palla) named Isabel Chimpu Ocllo. He was later to assume the name of his father without forgetting his native origin. Hence he called himself Garcilaso de la Vega, el Inca. On his father's side he was related to a family that had produced one of the great poets of the Spanish Renaissance while on his mother's side he was a descendent of Tupac Yupanqui, the penultimate Inca Emperor. Although Quechua was his native language he became perfectly bilingual as he lived with the first generation of Creoles and Mestizos in the city of Cuzco. After his father's death in 1560 he went to Spain to claim his inheritance and stayed there until he died in 1616. It was in Spain that he produced all of his writing, including the history of his native Peru. His *Comentarios reales* ("Royal Commentaries") not only offered a chronology of Inca rule, from its origin until the arrival of the Spaniards but also an extensive anthropological commentary on language, on religious and social customs, on the means of communication, and on royal protocol. In his *Historia general del Perú* ("General History of Peru") he deals with the civil wars during the first phase of Spanish occupation until the beginning of the administration of Viceroy Francisco de Toledo in 1669.

Garcilaso's *Historia general del Perú* was a sort of generational testimony of fables and legends, the representation of an ideological and mental space that could only be defined in terms of its Otherness vis-à-vis the European. In fact, Garcilaso understood the European conquest as a Providential mandate toward the expansion of Christianity throughout the world. This is corroborated by the apparitions in the text of the Virgin and of Saint James, the Moorslayer, who is converted into an Indianslayer during the siege of Cuzco. Garcilaso also assigned to the rule of the Incas the same sort of manifest destiny since prior to the Incas everything had been barbarism and ignorance. The civilizing work of the Incas had thus paved the way for the rooting of Christianity in Peru.

Garcilaso's discourse assumes the characteristics of an antilanguage that opposed the official history which renounced Inca culture as barbaric and tyrannical while reserving for Spain the niceties of civilization, virtue, and victory. His recuperation of Indian traditions from a Hispanic point of view differs from the type of affirmative antidiscourse that one observes in Felipe Guamán Poma de Ayala whose *Primer nueva coronica y buen gobierno* ("First New Chronicle and Good Government," 1615) focuses on the vision of the vanquished. Although Garcilaso's writing is not as virulent as Guamán Poma's, his critical vision of the Spanish conquest coupled with his constant exultation of his faraway motherland were to make him suspect within the centers of power. Toward the end of the eighteenth century, at the time of the violent execution of the rebellious Inca Tupac Amaru III (José Gabriel Condorcanqui), the Spanish Crown sought to collect all copies of the *Comentarios reales* that were still in circulation. The tensions connected with a territorial definition and the undercurrent of a protonational feeling displaces this writing from its historical inception to become an early inscription of the desire for Spanish-American independence. A sign of the importance of the *Comentarios reales* is that San Martín, the Liberator of the South, sought to reedit the book as a symbol of patriotic fervor.

While Garcilaso's *Comentarios reales* had an impact on the reading public since its appearance in 1609, Guamán Poma's *Primer nueva coronica y buen gobierno*—written between 1585 and 1615—was to meet with a different destiny. The book was lost for three centuries until its discovery in the 1920s, at the time when the new American nations were in the process of defining their identities through the rediscovery of a tradition that went back not only to the early years of colonization but also to the values existent in ancient civilizations. That rediscovery included cultures such as those of the Yarowilca in Peru or the Maya in the plains of Mexico and Guatemala.

As we have indicated above, Guamán Poma undertakes the writing of a counter-narrative in which the conqueror is interpreted in his own language. Writing in a somewhat stilted Spanish prose that was enriched with words and expressions in Quechua and Aymara, he argues that Spain's fortunes were due to the encounter and exploitation of the Andean natives.

His writing is directed to Philip III whom he addresses as an equal. He claims to be a descendant of the Incas and Yarowilcas and, to substantiate that claim, he manages to incorporate into his name the heraldic figures of his ancestors: the puma and the falcon. That genealogy authorized him to validate the Indians as lords of their land and the Spaniards as intruders. Guamán Poma's writing oscillates between orality and alphabetic inscription. The use of pictographic writing in the Chronicle produces an alternate text that is derived from the ecclesiastical forms of the *regimime principum* which was used since the Middle Ages to expand the possibility of communication by making a text comprehensible even to those who were illiterate.

Pictographic writing allowed Guamán Poma to bypass the European patterns of representation. The emblem makes the depiction of the native world more poignant and immediate. Thus, for example, the image of an agonizing Inca in a wooden cabin surrounded by a fire set by Pizarro makes a striking representation of the anguish of the native chieftain who is forced to hand over possessions and riches to the violence and greed of the conqueror. Pictographic writing would thus represent with greater efficacy the social and political conditions of the environment. Only in this manner could the indigenous world be recognized in the European cultural sphere as a world placed upside down (*pachacuti*) through the effects of the envy and vices of the Spaniards (see W. Mignolo in this volume).

Guamán's strategy was to model his program of "good government" through the rhetoric and ethical principles of Christianity. In her *Guamán Poma. Writing and Resistance in Colonial Peru*, Rolena Adorno argues that through the use of religious language "Guamán Poma moves the political problem and its solution into the spiritual arena" (79), an arena that is ultimately ineffective for the defense of his people. This same strategy also allowed Guamán to affirm his own nobility within the Andean society, thus paving the way for his address to His Majesty, the King of Spain, on equal terms both as chronicler and messenger of a society that had disappeared, and as a witness of the Colonial system's brutality and horror.

For Guamán Poma, the Indian was capable of conceiving and organizing his own political structures, yet he had been deprived of such a right by the European intrusion despite having possessed the conditions necessary for conversion to Christianity and for becoming a free vassal of the Spanish Crown. Guamán Poma introduced the Indian view of the world into the interior realm of Christianity because the phenomena of Christianization had taken place in both worlds. The Peruvian Indians had received Christianity through the early teachings of Saint Bartholomew who had made them into rational and moral beings. A similar claim was to be made later by the Mexican Creole Sigüenza y Góngora and was used by Fray Servando de Mier to claim independence from Spain (see R. Jara in this volume). Within Guamán Poma's frame of mind, miscegenation (*mestizaje*) was·a historical error for without it the aborigines would have been able to maintain their pristine condition. The person of mixed blood (*mestizo*) was for him the agent of exploitation of the Indians and was responsible for the imposition of mercantilism as an economic model. For Guamán Poma the solution to the problem was to be sought in the Christianization of the Spaniards.

When the Inca Garcilaso and Guamán Poma take us in their writings to the turn of the seventeenth century, the inscription of the New World has changed. Let us recall briefly what had transpired before the time of their writing and anticipate the later emergence of a decisive protonational feeling which will eventually lead to independence. The pivotal figures are those of Sor Juana Inés de la Cruz and Carlos de Siguenza y Góngora.

Columbus's discussion of his experience of the New World went beyond the textual inscription. There was an underlying second argument in his discourse: that of the strategies of economic exchange and market building which he deemed necessary for the appropriation of the lands just encountered. Columbus's allegory is, in turn, allegorized by the narratives of the conquest which continued the process and take it to a point of apparent closure when colonization seems to have been stabilized by the end of the sixteenth century. Such is the case with the discourses of Cortés, Fernández de Oviedo and Alvar Núñez which, with different inflections, bring this development to a military, legal, and clerical completion.

There soon surfaces a counter-discourse which produces a negative allegory that denies validity to the one already described. This, for example, is what happens in the writings of Las Casas which focus on the presence and human value of the indigenous Other, thus displacing the locus of alterity to the European world. The writings of Ercilla, Alva Ixtilxochitl and the like reinforce Las Casas's position regarding the presence of the native American in the very process of conquest and colonization. Soon thereafter, at the height of the crisis of the Spanish Baroque, Garcilaso, the Inca, a writer of mixed blood (*mestizo*), manages to represent the values of the native American culture on a par with that of the conquerors. At approximately the same time, Guamán Poma de Ayala, a Peruvian Indian, forcefully translates his experiences into the language of the Other, all the while corroborating and/or contradicting the written text through the use of pictographic writing. A distillation of all of these discourses will be seen in the Creole writings of Sor Juana and Siguenza y Góngora.

Sor Juana Inés de la Cruz (Juana de Asbaje y Ramírez de Santillana [1651-1695]) was an illegitimate child born of Creole parents. Her passion for knowledge and her rancor toward a world built for men lead her to abandon the court of the Viceroy and opt for a life in a convent. These motives, coupled with the jealousies that were prompted by her brilliant intellect, are prevalent topics in her poetry and prose as well as a symptomatic feature of the first phase of a Creole consciousness that is beset by feelings of persecution and guilt. Sor Juana's proclivity toward experimentation, her understanding of natural laws as a result of quantitative measurement, her rejection of the Aristotelian principles of classification, nomination, and taxonomy surrounded her activity with shadows of heresy and disobedience. In her *Respuesta a Sor Filotea de la Cruz* ("Response to Sor Filotea de la Cruz," 1691) we see how

Sor Juana's mistrust of Scholasticism and of the efficiency of pure verbal rationalization are coupled with a penchant for analysis, observation, and a direct reading of natural phenomena. In Sor Juana wisdom is equated with good judgement: " Knowledge—writes Sor Juana—is not the ability to make subtle speeches, for knowledge consists only in the election of what is most sensible" ("No es saber, saber hacer/ discursos sutiles vanos,/ que el saber consiste sólo/ en elegir lo más sano"). Sor Juana here undermines the importance and power of official rhetoric, privileging the notion of freedom in the areas of perception and understanding. Such freedom extends to one's reading of the great text of the world which includes the sensorial and everything related to the quotidian. For Sor Juana knowledge is her "crown of thorns" and she is symbolically killed by her relentless passion for it.

In March of 1691 Sor Juana addressed her famous apology, the *Respuesta a Sor Filotea*, to the Archbishop of Puebla, Mexico. The idea of the letter was to defend herself against anonymous accusations which claimed that she was disregarding spiritual matters while privileging wordly pursuits. In the first place she justifies her writing as an act of obedience: "I have never written anything of my own volition, but rather to comply with requests and commands of others; so that I do not remember having written anything on my own initiative except a little paper called *El sueño*" ("Yo nunca he escrito cosa alguna por mi voluntad, sino por ruegos y preceptos ajenos; de tal manera, que no me acuerdo haber escrito por mi gusto sino un papelillo que llaman *El sueño*." [*Obras Completas de Sor Juana Inés de la Cruz*, IV, Ed. Alberto G. Salceda]).

While Sor Juana goes on to define the powerful inclination to letters as a natural impulse given to her by God, she argues that she has pleaded with her Creator to extinguish her light of understanding, except for what is required to follow His Law. She also reminds the implicit receiver of her letter—and not without a touch of irony— that, according to some people, women need not be blessed with the power that is needed to search for greater knowledge and understanding: "His Majesty...knows that I have asked Him to turn off the light of my understanding, leaving only what is needed to obey His Law, for the rest is superfluous in a woman, according to some: and there are also those who say that it is damaging. His Majesty also knows that not being able to achieve this, I have tried to bury both my knowledge and my name, and I have tried to sacrifice it only to the one who gave it to me." (Su Majestad... sabe que le he pedido que apague la luz de mi entendimiento dejando sólo lo que baste para guardar su Ley, pues lo demás sobra, según algunos, en una mujer: Y aún hay quien diga que daña. Sabe también Su Majestad que no consiguiendo ésto, he intentado sepultar con mi nombre mi entendimiento, y sacrificársele sólo a quien me le dió."(Ed. Salceda 445)

One can see how Sor Juana is perfectly aware of the extent to which social behavior is ruled by masculine conventions. She returns to this topic in her *Sátira filosófica* ("Philosophical Satire"): "Foolish men who accuse women without reason, without realizing that you are the cause of the very thing that you fault in them; if with unparalleled eagerness you seek their disdain can you expect them to act well if you incite them to evil?" ("Hombres necios que acusáis / a la mujer sin razón, /sin ver que sois la ocasión/ de lo mismo que culpáis:// Si con ansia sin igual / solicitáis su desdén,/ ¿por qué queréis que obren bien/ si las incitáis al mal?") (Sor Juana Inés de la Cruz, *Obras completas*, Ed. Monterde 109). Sor Juana's observation of cultural habits is consonant with the critical trend present in her *Respuesta a Sor Filotea*.

In the letter Sor Juana argues for the connectedness of knowledge as "all things [are] linked together one with another ("todas las cosas eslabonadas unas con otras"). Since knowledge emanates from God, human understanding is part of His plan: "All things emanate from God, who is at the same time the center and the circumference from whence they start and where all of the created lines end up." ("Todas las cosas salen de Dios, que es el centro a un tiempo y la circunferencia de donde salen y donde paran todas las líneas criadas."). Having framed her quest for knowledge as part of the Creator's plan, Sor Juana then speaks playfully about wanting to avoid problems with the Inquisition ("No quiero ruido con el Santo

Oficio") and as part of her strategy of self-defense, she treads cautiously in areas that could place her at odds with Church authorities. Nevertheless, her discourse on reading and writing, and her reflections on knowledge, serve a dual purpose: to sidetrack the official attempts to control her and, at the same time, to highlight the limitations of official power when it is not in consonance with an individual's will.

For Sor Juana reading is not a frivolous act; it is a mission implicated in the search for knowledge and truth. Yet, for the Church as an institution it is a practice deemed to be suspicious and, thus, in need of monitoring. Aware of these tensions, Sor Juana justifies her study of Logic, Rhetoric, Arithmetic, Geometry, Music, History, and other disciplines as a necessary preparation for her immersion in Theology, the Queen of the Sciences. Sor Juana displays a profound understanding of the potential relationship between various fields of knowledge and between different disciplines. It is this awareness which allows her to reflect on the reader's role in the construction and shaping of meaning: "What I do not understand in an author of one area [of knowledge] I usually grasp it from an author writing in another area that is very distant; and those very same, once explained, open up metaphorical examples from other arts." ("Lo que no entiendo en un autor de una facultad, lo suelo entender en otro de otra que parece muy distante; y esos propios, al explicarse, abren ejemplos metafóricos de otras artes.").

A Creole writer in search of an identity, Sor Juana is constantly defining herself through writing. That activity entails an interpretation of different cultural texts as she moves within the cultures of both the Old World and the New. In the *Respuesta a Sor Filotea* she claims to have been persecuted because of her love of knowledge, and recalls how, for a time, she was prohibited from reading. Yet, she also makes it clear that reading is not an activity limited to the apprehension of stories and discourses from printed texts but is connected to a wider search through the chain of knowledge. A reading of the great text of the world written by God also implies an analysis and interpretation of everyday life and experience, of "everything

that God created," including, one might say, the European
and Indian worlds, with their various traditions and cultures: "As far as not picking up a book was concerned, I
obeyed her, but as for not studying at all I could not do it,
since it does not fall within my power or authority, for
while I did not study through books, I studied through everything that God created." ("Yo la obedecí... en cuanto a
no tomar libro, que en cuanto a no estudiar absoluta-
mente, como no cae debajo de mi potestad, no lo pude
hacer, porque aunque no estudiaba en los libros, estudiaba
en todas las cosas que Dios crió.").

One must recall here that Sor Juana's letter is addressed
to a superior and she is thus forced to negotiate a space
through the affectation of many "I"s: "The autobiographical *yo* swings from outright insubordination, self
glorification and exaltation to utter subjugation, humility
and self denigration and what emerges, ultimately, is an 'I'
possessed by the compulsion to learn" (S. Merrim,
"Narciso desdoblado: Narcissistic Stratagems in *El Divino
Narciso* and the *Respuesta a Sor Filotea de la Cruz* 115).
What Sor Juana says in effect is that the prohibition of
reading does not foreclose the possibility of thinking,
imagining, and searching for truth. Access to knowledge
and truth involves a creative inquiry through an
imagination that is so powerful and relentless that it has
free reign in the sphere of the unconscious: "Not even my
dreams freed themselves of this continuous movement of
my imagination; rather, it usually operates even more
freely and openly in them" ("Ni aún el sueño se libró de
este continuo movimiento de mi imaginativa; antes suele
obrar en él más libre y desembarazada.").

Sor Juana does not equate writing—which she defines
as a natural impulse placed within her by God ("natural
impulso que Dios puso en mi")—with the consignment of
thoughts on paper or with their dissemination through
printing. For while this form of writing could be censored,
there was another that could not be denied. The latter belonged to the sphere of the productive imagination which,
for this Creole writer, entails a constant struggle to inscribe
and define herself and her world.

Sor Juana's *Primero sueño* ("First Dream," 1692) and *El Divino Narciso* ("Divine Narcissus," 1688) are also connected to this same search for knowledge. In these texts too the act of searching and discovering brings with it the possibility of transgression. *Primero sueño* suggests both the need for construction and interpretation. The poetic speaker presents herself alone in her search for knowledge. Hers is a journey without guidance; it is the Creole's anxious quest in search of codes that would allow one to articulate and organize one's world. In this poem the soul does not reach its desired goal for the body awakens with the advent of the sunrise. The introduction of the sun in this text brings to mind the Mexican solar rituals while, at the same time, the Christian vision of plenitude deconstructs itself and ends in a non-vision. This paradox might be interpreted as the need for religious and cultural syncretism such as what is proposed in the *Loa* to the sacramental play, *El Divino Narciso*. One also notices the absence of revelation in Sor Juana's dream, meaning that the human being is alone and that the supernatural realm has vanished. This brings to mind the native Amerindians' feeling of abandonment by their Gods and the failure of their efforts to understand the God of the conquerors. Sor Juana's dream is a voyage involving the will to knowledge and understanding.

The poem's powerful images underscore the materiality of the Creole's experience and knowledge of the world. Thus, the heart is equated to the machinery of a clock; the trachea is likened to an harquebus; and the lungs are compared to bellows. The frequency of medical and war images suggests a need to control, define, and appropriate the culture and reality of the world. Significantly there is no personification of God in the poem although the Author and first cause of the world is mentioned. As a Creole, Sor Juana is concerned with the search for power, truth, and freedom which are represented in the poem through the figure of the mythical Phaeton. Like the bastard son of Apollo who finds it necessary to drive a chariot through the Heavens in order to gain honor and fame, the Creole too will strive for recognition through power and knowledge which are the ingredients necessary to forge a national identity. The formulation of a Creole consciousness involves of necessity the idea of transgression and rebellion against established institutions of power and control. This can also be seen in the *Loa para el Auto-sacramental de El Divino Narciso.*

In the *Loa* the ideas advanced through the allegorical character of *América*—speaking to *Religión*—is that the repression of Amerindian culture cannot succeed entirely as long as there exists a will to preserve one's own past:

> *America:*
> If asking that my life be spared,
> and showing thyself compassionate,
> is done with the hope of conquering me
> with your loftiness,
> the way you did earlier with physical
> and later with intellectual
> arms, you are deceiving yourself;
> for though as a captive I lament
> the loss of my liberty, my will
> shall adore my Deities
> with even greater freedom.

> *América:*
> Si el pedir que yo no muera,
> y el mostrarte compasiva,
> es porque esperas de mí
> que me vencerás, altiva,
> como antes con corporales,
> después con intelectivas
> armas, estás engañada;
> pues aunque lloro cautiva
> mi libertad, ¡mi albedrío
> con libertad más crecida
> adorará mis Deidades!
> (Ed. Salceda, vv. 226-236)

The *Loa* insists on the idea that the violence and subjugation perpetrated upon the Indies—*Occidente* and *América*—is done in the name of God, even while the institutional discourses of the Church and the State are unintelligible to native Amerindians. In the *Loa*, the discourse of the Empire echoes through the allegorical voices of "Religión" and "Celo" who speak of conquering the Other and assimilating it into the Same. Theirs is a discourse of abstraction which tries to do away with the materiality of the native culture:

> *America*:
> ...If that is so,
> tell me: Will such a Deity
> be so propitious as to allow himself
> to be touched by my very hands,
> like the Idol that is fabricated
> here by my very hands
> with the seeds and innocent blood
> spilled only
> for this effect?

> *América*:
> ...Cuando eso así sea,
> dime: ¿Será tan propicia
> esa Deidad, que se deje
> tocar de mis manos mismas,
> como el Idolo que aquí
> mis propias manos fabrican
> de semillas y de sangre
> inocente, que vertida
> es sólo para este efecto?
> (Ed. Salceda, vv. 321-329)

As faith is basically rhetoric, there is a reliance on hearing over seing. Yet, *Religión* knows that it must adopt a strategy that is more conducive to the cooptation of the native subject. Such a strategy, conscious of the materiality of the native American world, has *Religión* speaking in metaphors while at the same time undertaking a representation of the story through visual images:

> *Religion:*
> Well let's see. For through an idea
> dressed up metaphorically
> with rhetorical colors,
> and representable to your eyes,
> I shall show it to you;
> for I know that you are inclined
> toward visible objects, more
> than toward what Faith advises you
> through hearing; so that
> it is important that you avail yourself
> of your eyes in order to

receive Faith through them.

Religión:
Pues vamos. Que en una idea
metafórica, vestida
de retóricos colores,
representable a tu vista,
te la mostraré; que ya
conozco que tú te inclinas
a objetos visibles, más
que a lo que la Fe te avisa
por el oído; y así,
es preciso que te sirvas
de los ojos, para que
por ellos la Fe recibas.
(Ed. Salceda, vv. 401-412)

Indeed, sacramental plays relied heavily on the spectacular; on the cooptation of its audience through rich visual images in order to mesmerize it and guide it toward a kind of passive, mass reception (see Maravall, *Culture of the Baroque;* Godzich and Spadaccini, "Popular Culture and Spanish Literary History"). Sor Juana is conscious of the power of the medium, of its potential for the manipulation of audiences for purposes of socio-political propaganda. Thus, regarding the propriety of representing the play in Madrid—the very center of monarcho-seigneurial power whose elites include the high aristocracy, Church authorities, and other bureaucrats—, it is the allegorical character named *Religión* that provides Sor Juana's own disclaimer: the writing of the sacramental play was an act of obedience; moreover what the characters say is more important than the identity of the speakers, for regardless of their identity the intended audience would be able to get at the very heart of the message.

The story of the Christian mystery of transubstantiation is to be told and made visible through the allegory of a sacramental play called *El Divino Narciso.* Yet, ironically, the play is to be represented not in the New World but in Madrid; not to an Amerindian audience that has shown a desire for knowledge but to a Spanish public characterized by predictable expectations. This very issue inscribed in the *Loa* functions as a (pre)text in which Sor Juana manages to distance herself from the propagandistic designs of the sacramental play, a genre which in line with a post-Tridentine ideology sought to reduce all Others to the Same.

Sor Juana returns insistently to the matter of the suppression of native cultures through evangelization and force of arms. A Creole writer with protonational feelings who must, nevertheless, navigate carefully within certain institutional constraints, she finds a space for the representation of conflicts between a New World marked by ancient values and traditions and an Old World that represses native cultures in its drive to impose a new political and religious order. Writing toward the end of the 1600s, and having reflected upon the consequences of colonization, Sor Juana goes back to ancient Aztec myth and rituals to rescue those obliterated voices. In earnest and in jest, within the parameters of conventional forms sanctioned by literary tradition and institutional authorities, she follows a quest that involves a search for knowledge—of the self and of the world around her. That quest is connected to writing which in Sor Juana always involves an act of will and transgression, one whose final manifestation will be her renunciation of writing and her embrace of a willful death at the service of her pestilence-ridden religious sisters.

With Sor Juana, as with Bartolomé de Las Casas in the first half of the sixteenth century, there is a reaffirmation of Neo-Thomistic Christian thought which distinguished the sphere of grace from that of nature. The consequences of such a distinction was a recognition of the autonomy of the natural world and the idea that the plurality of cultures found in the world was legitimate and therefore needed to be respected. In this line of thinking, natural rights could never be abrogated—not even in the name of the Church, the true religion, morality or a superior culture (Maravall, *La oposición política bajo los Austrias* 105-106).

It is precisely in the area of Neo-Thomism's recognition of cultural pluralism as natural phenomena that Sor Juana finds a space to problematize the reduction of the American Other to the European Same. It is within this frame that the *Loa* and the sacramental play that it accompanies, *El Divino Narciso*, become vehicles that provide an intellectual space for America. Such a space is found, on the one hand, in the reinscription of what used to be called "gentile" thought and, on the other, in the reinscription of Judaism. Thus, Echo and Narcissus represent two poles in the search for knowledge. Echo is America replicating Europe; it is an America that is both in love with Europe and in rebellion against it. That rebellion is responsible for Echo's temporary proscription and deprivation of language. Only when Narcissus dies is language recovered and America is rhetorically redeemed. The recovery of language implies, however, that it is going to be used to question the established voices of authority.

In *Divine Narcissus*, the allegorical character of Echo is also a metaphor for pre-Columbian America, a part of human nature that is originally despised by Narcissus who represents Christianity and conquering Europe. Narcissus falls in love with Human Nature and thus wants to be like her. Initially his monologic idea of human nature does not allow him to consider Echo a part of it, but he eventually changes his mind and ends up embracing what had been vilified by sin: Echo. The latter is ultimately redeemed through the cleansing of sins at the time of Narcissus's sacrifice: his death through love. With Narcissus's resurrection there is the disappearance of the old Echo, of absolute gentility. The new Echo has been brought, with the rest of human nature, under Narcissus's sphere.

In addition to Sor Juana's rewriting of the mystery of transubstantiation, we witness a subtle representation of the emergence of a new America, a Creole America that has acquired a new language and, with it, a new power to question and to contest. It is an America that will speak as it moves forward toward independence.

In 1695 one of Sor Juana's closest friends, the writer Carlos de Sigüenza y Góngora, was to give a formal eulogy on the occasion of her premature death. While the text of the panegyric has been lost, it is quite likely that some of the things he said about her had been inscribed earlier in his *Theatro de virtudes políticas* ("Theatre of Political Virtues," 1680): " No pen stands out as much as hers and none dares to profane her erudition. I should like to dispense with the praise with which I hold her, or with the veneration that she has gained with her works, in order to make manifest to the world her encyclopedic knowledge and the universality of her writing, so that it be known that Mexico enjoys in one individual what in previous centuries the Graces distributed to all of the learned women who were the astonishment of the venerable History....But I would not do justice to Sor Juana if I dared to compare her even with all of them together; because not even all of them seem to me sufficient to represent her..." (Sigüenza y Góngora 247).[4]

Carlos de Sigüenza y Góngora (1645-1700) was born in Mexico, the descendent of an aristocratic family that had migrated to the New World from Spain. He was a man of many interests and talents and was granted the Chair of Mathematics and Astrology at the University of Mexico in 1672. He soon became an expert on the pre-Columbian civilizations of Mexico, learning Indian languages, and accumulating codices, maps, relations, books and manuscripts. Among his acquisitions was an invaluable collection of documents that had belonged to the Indian chronicler Fernando de Alva Ixtilxochitl (1568-1648).

In 1680 Charles II of Spain was to name Sigüenza First Cosmographer of the Kingdom, the first Creole to have achieved such a distinction. Like Descartes in part VI of his *Discourse on Method* Sigüenza y Góngora was to realize that power and knowledge converged in discourse. Knowledge entailed for him all of the strategies of manipulation that the human being could exercise upon nature. This can be seen in his *Theatro de virtudes políticas que constituyen a un príncipe; advertidas en los monarcas antiguos del Mexicano Imperio* ("Theatre of Political Virtues that Constitute a Prince, Observed in the Monarchs of the Ancient Mexican Empire," 1680).

Sigüenza's *Theatro* underscores the irony and resentment of a Creole intellectual against the attempt of the Metropolis to impose cultural and political models at a time when those patterns have long ceased to be effective. Sigüenza had been charged with the task of organizing the reception of the new Viceroy, the Count of Paredes, and the festivities included the building of a triumphal arch.

The writer uses this occasion to subtly mock the ceremony, as he contended that triumphal arches were usually erected in celebration and recognition of great military deeds. That is, for Sigüenza the idea that a bureaucrat could be recognized as a Caesar was ludicrous and revealed the Empire for what it was: the empty mask of a paper tiger, a void that Sigüenza sought to fill with the memories of ancient Mexican warriors whom he contrasted with the bureaucrats who were sent by Madrid—those enchanted men who lived outside of the natural order of things. The Mexican intellectual's concern is to give materiality to Mexican history, which is contrasted to European inventions and fabulations. The models of virtue were to be sought in ancient Mexican history: " The beautiful love of virtue should not be sought in strange models; the praise of domestic [models] moves the people for it is preferable to know local triumphs" (El amor hermoso de la virtud no debe ser buscado en modelos extraños; la alabanza doméstica mueve los ánimos, y es mucho mejor conocer los triunfos en casa" (242).

Sigüenza y Góngora rejects the European models that are still being imposed on the New World and replaces them with concrete examples of virtue: those of Mexican Emperors. These, according to Sigüenza, were the models that the new Viceroy was supposed to emulate.

Sigüenza y Góngora's discourse goes on to incorporate in Prelude III of his *Theatro* Sor Juana Inés de la Cruz's *Neptuno Alegórico* ("Allegorical Neptune," 1680) which she had composed for the metropolitan Church on the same occasion of the arrival of the Viceroy, the Count of Paredes. For both writers the figure of Neptune was the "son of Misraim, grandson of Cham, great grandson of Noah, and progenitor of the Indians of the West" ("Hijo de Misraim, nieto de Cham, biznieto de Noé, y progenitor de los Indios Occidentales". Sigüenza, 247). As Sor Juana would indicate in her *Neptuno Alegórico*, most of the stories of the past "are based on true happenings; and what gentility called gods were really excellent princes to whom they attributed divinity either for their rare virtues or for having been inventors of things" ("...tienen su fundamento en sucesos verdaderos; y los que llamó dioses la gentilidad, fueron realmente príncipes excelentes, a quienes por sus raras virtudes atribuyeron divinidad, o por haber sido inventores de las cosas." Sor Juana, Ed. Monterde 780).

Sor Juana's penchant for universalization and abstraction finds its counterpart in Sigüenza. While she presents the Viceroy with the model of the American Neptune, the Creole mathematician seeks to impose upon him the patterns of a native tradition. For Sor Juana knowledge was the basis of power; it was what tied all of the virtues together. This knowledge was embodied in Neptune, the son of Isis, mother of the Gods and of the beasts. The new Viceroy was invited to emulate that model of virtue (Sor Juana, Ed. Monterde 781-784), and thus legitimize both the existence of America and his own position of authority. Neptune was after all a virtuous and powerful model who ruled over the oceans, which now comprised three-quarters of the world. Let us recall here that physiognomy of the world had changed after the rationalization of Columbus's discovery.

In contrast to Sor Juana's universalizing discourse, Sigüenza focuses on the hardships of the descendants of Neptune, the Indians of the West, who are referred to as "people who had been eradicated from their lands" ("gente arrancada de sus pueblos"). Neptune's descendants had experienced nothing but misery since the Spanish conquest: "People torn to pieces in the defense of their country and cut to shreds by their poverty; people that have suffered terribly and who are unequalled in their endurance of suffering; people who are always looking for a remedy to their miseries and who always find themselves stepped upon by all; [people] whose land experiences hardships through repeated floods" ("Gente despedazada por defender su patria y hecha pedazos por su pobreza; pueblo terrible en el sufrir y después del cual no se hallará otro tan paciente en el padecer, gente que siempre aguarda el remedio de sus miserias y siempre se halla pisada de todos, cuya tierra padece trabajos en repetidas inundaciones" 253).

Sigüenza y Góngora insists upon the insularity and particularity of native American people whom he characterizes as "gentem expectatem," people who awaited the coming of their own Lord. Clearly the new Viceroy does not meet the Creole expectations of forging institutions and, through them, the exercise of political power from within the New World. With a decidedly protonationalist bent, Sigüenza refers to the Creole Nation (255) and to the role of writing in its future shaping. For him the role of the intellectual in this endeavor was paramount as he indicates perceptively in his *Teatro*: "Even while we claim to be great lovers of our lands, what is known about them is due to the pens of foreigners" ("Cuando todos nos preciamos de ser tan amantes de nuestras patrias, lo que de ellas se sabe se debe a extranjeras plumas," 255). The intellectual is thus invested with a mission that entails the creation of a new political ideal: the Nation. In this respect Sigüenza y Góngora can be considered a pre-Enlightenment figure who anticipates along these lines the program of reforms that were to be discussed in Spain a century later. It may be worth noticing that while the writer of the Empire sought to categorize in minute detail the castes and people of the New World for purposes of discrimination (see I. Zavala in this volume), Creole intellectuals were attracted by the homogenizing task of collection works and manuscripts produced in America. This accumulation of knowledge was to serve as a basis for the invention of nationhood (see B. González in this volume).

For Sigüenza y Góngora the models of virtue for political governance are to be found not in the Old World but in the New: in the pre-Columbian world that the early discourse of colonization had sought to obliterate. The specific models which he holds up to the Count of Paredes are the Aztec Emperors with whom the founding of Mexico is connected. Their virtues are highlighted in contrast to a subtext which may be read in the *Theatro*: the abuses and injustices committed by the early conquistadors, by the *encomenderos*, and especially the new bureaucrats are set against the values of the pre-Christian rulers of Ancient Mexico. Those values were the following: love of knowledge, the obligation of the governor toward the governed, the importance of liberty and hope, the institution of laws and justice, the importance of prudence, the search for peace through a process of consultation, the capacity for love and friendship among citizens, and the necessity of pride and sacrifice. In the final analysis this was Sigüenza y Góngora's pointed allegory directed to the Viceroy in which the formal reception and welcome accorded to his authority goes through a number of displacements: there emerges a critical view of Spanish imperial power in America, a recuperation of the traditions of the Mexican past, and a clear call for the formulation of a nationhood that allows relations of power and authority to come from within.

Sigüenza y Góngora's discourse is that of a Creole who seeks to replace the Spanish aristocracy with that of his own class. The Creoles had felt displaced and powerless in their own land, and now sought to remedy their situation by asserting their independence from the Metropolis. One hundred years later, Fray Servando de Mier would articulate with perfect lucidity the overriding reasons for Creole independence (see R. Jara in this volume).

NOTES

[1] "Ya cuando el niño cumple sus diez años...es cuando se les hace recordar que nuestros antepasados fueron violados por medio de los blancos y de la colonia. Pero no lo dicen como está escrito sino a través de las recomendaciones que han venido dando nuestros abuelos y nuestros antepasados. Porque la mayor parte del pueblo no sabe leer ni escribir ni sabe que existe un documento para el indígena. Pero se dice que los españoles violaron a los mejores hijos de los antepasados, a las gentes más humildes y en honor a esas gentes más humildes nosotros tenemos que seguir guardando nuestros secretos. Y esos secretos nadie podrá descubrir más que nosotros los indígenas." (E. Burgos Debray, *Me llamo Rigoberta Menchú*, 49-50.)

[2] "¿Puede darse mayor o más claro testimonio de la ventaja que unos hombres tienen sobre otros en ingenio, habilidad, fortaleza de ánimo y virtud? ¿No es prueba de que ellos son siervos de naturaleza? Pues el hecho de que algunos de ellos parezcan tener ingenio para ciertas obras de artificio no es argumento de más humana prudencia, puesto que vemos

cómo ciertos animalitos, como las abejas y las arañas, hacen obras que ninguna humana habilidad logra imitar"

3 "Aunque hay ciertas virtudes que se aprecian casi en todas las clases [de nuestro pueblo]; así el valor, del que dieron a través de la historia las legiones españolas pruebas que exceden la humana credibilidad, como ocurrió en tiempos pasados en la guerra de Numancia...; en tiempo de nuestros padres a las órdenes del Gran Capitán Gonzalo, y en nuestro tiempo bajo los auspicios del César Carlos en Milán y Nápoles, y en Túnez de Africa bajo la dirección personal del propio Carlos, y no hace mucho en las campañas de Bélgica y Francia y recientemente en las de Alemania, donde fueron derrotados los herejes luteranos, con inmensa gloria del nuestro Emperador."

4 "No hay pluma que puede elevarse a la eminencia donde la suya descuella, cuanto y más atreverse a profanar la erudición que la adorna. Prescindir quisiera el aprecio con que la miro, de la veneración que con sus obras grangea, para manifestar al mundo cuánto es lo que atesora su capacidad en la enciclopedia y la universalidad de sus letras, para que se supiera que en un solo individuo goza México lo que, en los siglos anteriores, repartieron las Gracias a cuantas doctas mujeres son el asombro de la venerable historia....Pero le hiciera agravio a la Madre Juana si imaginara el compararla aún con todas; porque ni aún todas me parecen suficientes para idearla..."

WORKS CITED

Adorno, Rolena. *Guamán Poma. Writing and Resistance in Colonial Peru.* Austin: Univ. of Texas Press, 1988.

Burgos Debray, Elizabeth. *Me llamo Rigoberta Menchú.* Habana: Casa de las Américas, 1983.

Certeau, Michel de. "The Politics of Silence: The Long March of the Indians." *Heterologies. Discourse on the Other.* Minneapolis: Univ. of Minnesota Press, 1986.

—. "Montaigne's 'Of Cannibals': The Savage 'I'." *Heterologies. Discourse on the Other.* Minneapolis: Univ. of Minnesota Press, 1986.

Godzich, Wlad and Nicholas Spadaccini. "Popular Culture and Spanish Literary History." *Literature Among Discourses.* Minneapolis: Univ. of Minnesota Press, 1986.

Hanke, Lewis. *La lucha por la justicia en la conquista de América.* Trans. Ramón Iglesias. Buenos Aires: Editorial Sudamericana, 1949.

Jara, René. *El revés de la arpillera. Perfil literario de Chile.* Madrid: Hiperión, 1988.

Juana Inés de la Cruz, Sor. *Obras completas.* Ed. Alberto G. Salceda. México: Fondo de Cultura Económica, 1957.

—.*Obras completas.* Ed. Francisco Monterde. México: Porrúa, 1969.

León Portilla, Miguel. "La conquista de México: visión de los vencidos." *Historia 16,* Extra X (Junio 1979): 19-42.

Maravall, José Antonio. *Culture of the Baroque.* Trans. Terry Cochran. Minneapolis: Univ. of Minnesota Press, 1986.

—. "Libertad y derecho de ser hombre en el pensamiento lascasiano." *Utopía y reformismo en la España de los Austrias.* Madrid: Siglo XXI, 1982.

—.*La oposición política bajo los Austrias.* Barcelona: Ariel, 1972.

Merrim, Stephanie. "Narciso desdoblado: Narcissistic Stratagems in *El Divino Narciso* and the *Respuesta a Sor Filotea de la Cruz.* " Bulletin of Hispanic Studies 64, 2 (1987): 111-117.

Pagden, Anthony. *The Fall of the Natural Man.* London: Cambridge Univ. Press, 1984.

Sepúlveda, Ginés de. *Demócrates Segundo.* Ed. Angel Losada. Madrid: Consejo Superior de Investigaciones Científicas, 1984.

Sigüenza y Góngora, Carlos de. *Obras históricas.* 2nd. ed. Ed. José Rojas Garcidueñas. México: Porrúa, 1960.

CHAPTER 1:
LITERACY AND COLONIZATION:
THE NEW WORLD EXPERIENCE

Walter D. Mignolo

UNDERSTANDING THE PAST AND SPEAKING THE PRESENT

Understanding the past could hardly be a solitary and monologic enterprise. Understanding is, on the contrary, a communal and dialogic venture. As long as my understanding of the past has to be communicated it cannot be rendered in a neutral language or discourse. It is relative to an audience and to a context of description (e.g., the context I have chosen to make the past event or object meaningful). Understanding the past cannot be detached from speaking the present, just us the need of speaking the present is what motivates me to understand the past. Contemporary concerns with literacy and the growing interest in re-reading the texts and events of the conquest and colonization of the New World are the parameters from which this essay has arisen. The "fusion of horizons," in hermeneutical parlance, could be interpreted as the encounter between our manner of speaking the present with the ways in which our ancestors spoke their present. The encounter should not necessarily be "friendly" (e.g., tracing back our own genealogy) but "critical" (e.g., detaching ourselves from a cultural or scholarly legacy). The links between the past which we strive to understand and the present which motivates us to speak do not always shine in front of our eyes. More often than not the links belong to the region that Ortega y Gasset identified as the underground of every act of saying. Thus the constant need for new interpretations, be they of texts, events, actions or ideas.

In this essay I shall explore, from a semiotic perspective, some consequences of Western literacy in the colonization of the New World at the time of the initial extensive contacts between Spanish and Amerindian cultures.[1] I am concerned primarily with the consequences of a communicative nature and I will focus, therefore, on communicative forms spanning cultural boundaries. Human communicative interactions cannot be divorced from factors of a socio-economic and psychological nature. However, my aim is to understand a specific aspect of communication, and which in light of the particular historical situation of the New World, I condense in the notion of "colonization" (Balandier 1951). It is my conviction that even today we hold some of the beliefs about the nature of language and its function in society which were held by the men of letters in charge of either educating the natives or justifying the education of the natives. Such a conception is related to our ideas about literacy and our belief that alphabetic writing is intrinsically superior to any other writing system. I will try to show, by examining communication forms across cultural boundaries, that the distinction between understanding the past and speaking the present implies also understanding how the present was spoken in the past. I shall focus on the voice of the colonizer and I will compare it, whenever possible and necessary, with the voice of the colonized. The comparison, which we can no longer avoid, will allow me to put in a regional context presuppositions about languages and cultures which became universals of human cultures in the pen of those who were able to write and be heard. When the fields of study are complex communicative forms and events, what interests the scholar is not so much what is being said as the presuppositions and strategies governing the saying. Thus, the colonizers' beliefs in their right to speak and write, their belief in the correspondence between their saying and the reality of the world, and the links between the system of belief and alphabetic literacy are at the center of my investigation. Furthermore, given that the natural difficulties of speaking and communicating in different languages are increased in a colonial situation (Balandier 1951) by the difficulties of the clash between different writing systems (Scharlau 1986: 94-156; 1987a, 1987b; Gruzinsky 1988: 15-99), literacy becomes a natural area of concern when communicative forms and events across cultural boundaries are at stake.

THE TYRANNY OF THE ALPHABET

Diego de Landa (in the Yucatan Peninsula) and Diego de Valadés (in Mexico) are two examples that enable us to understand the tyranny of the alphabet in sixteenth-century Europe and its implications for the colonization of the New World.

Two of the most spectacular performances of Diego de Landa in the Yucatan Peninsula were the burning of the Mayan's written records (which were called "books" in Castilian) and his attempt to translate Mayan hieroglyphs into the letters of the Roman alphabet (Landa 1566; 1941). While book-burning was not commonplace in the colonization of the New World, translating hieroglyphs into alphabetic units was, and this perhaps was one of the first efforts in Western civilization to use the letters of the alphabet as a means of conquest and colonization. Landa's assumption that hieroglyphs were a form of alphabetic writing was certainly amazing (Figure 1). Landa, as well as many contemporary educated persons, acted on the assumption that the history of writing in human culture is an ascending process moving from Sumerian cuneiform (proto)writing to the Greek alphabet (true writing). His assumption was based on the belief that "true" writing is any system of graphic signs which could be used as an alternative to oral discourse (Ong 1982: 84). Harris (1986:45) has observed, from a linguistic point of view, that "Landa's Maya alphabet stands as a kind of permanent folly in the history of linguistics. What it reveals is the depths of incomprehension which centuries of alphabetic culture can inculcate about the nature of writing."[2] From the point of view of the consequences of literacy in the colonization of the New World, Landa's example stands as a permanent folly and as a paradigmatic example of "communication" (e.g., interacting in different sign systems) between members of a literate community (e.g., in the restricted sense of having alphabetic writing, of having letters) with members of societies with different writing systems.

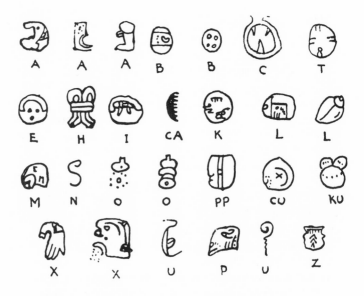

Fig. 1. Diego de Landa's "Maya Alphabet"

The second example, also very well known, is an early version of the mnemonic technique for learning the alphabet assembled by Diego de Valadés (1575). In the chapter devoted to different forms of exercising memory (a common preoccupation among rhetoricians [Yates 1966; Spence 1984]), Valadés developed a theory about the images of the "letter" based on the images of the sound and the graphic image. In the first mode, the images of the letters are formed by the sound of the voice and are illustrated with proper names: A, Antonio; B, Bartolomé, etc. This is most interesting, because the obvious graphic nature of any writing system is the image of the letter according to the figure it resembles. Valadés came up with a "translation" of the graphic images of the letters, in Ludovico Dolce's mnemonic alphabet, into figures common to the Aztec world (Figures 2 and 3). The introduction of alphabetic writing and the phonetic notation used for the transcription of native languages have been considered a decisive intellectual revolution (Ricard 1947; 1986: 378-379). And they were. Not only—and necessarily—toward the successful teaching of the Christian Doc-

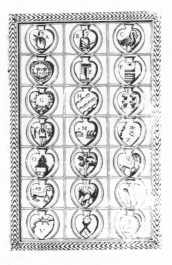

Fig. 2. Dolce's alphabet (*Dialogo nel qual si ragiona del modo de accrescere a conservar memoria*, Venice, 1562).

Fig. 3. Valadés's alphabet (*Rhetorica christiana*, Perusa, 1579).

trine, but also in the sense that a mixed nature of writing (Scharlau 1987a and 1987b) and of forms of communications (Gruzinsky 1988: 72-73) were among the first visible consequences of literacy in a colonial situation. The changes in communication forms could be understood by the description, provided by Valadés himself, of the communicative situation by means of pictographic and ideographic written signs which the Aztecs utilized. Valadés described the kind of communicative situation in which they had an extensive dialogue on the basis of some kind of graphic drawing. They sat, according to Valadés, on bended knee, squatting on their heels. He also observed that although the Aztec Lords would sit on three-legged stools or seats with back rests, they too would crouch down on their heels, especially when discussing business matters. One of the features of alphabetic writing—which we can guess was one taken for granted by Castilian men of letters—is that it permits us to communicate at a distance and to detach the "letter" (as image of the sound) from the body (Gumbrecht 1985; Mignolo 1987b).

These two examples illustrate at once the social construction and self-representation of communicative forms, and the social roles assigned to them which emanated from the communicative forms and situations shaped by alphabetic writing. I am not saying that alphabetic writing will, of necessity, originate under every circumstance the same kind of social construction and representation of communicative forms. It will take us too long, however, to explain the links between alphabetic writing, the program to expand the Christian Empire which began to emerge in fifteenth-century Italy (Roger 1962; Reinhard 1988),[3] the conjunction between religious motives, economic conditions and technical developments which converted the Book not only into a sacred object but also into the warranty of knowledge and truth (Skeat 1969; Clanchy 1983).[4] What Harris (1986: 46) had to say about the tyranny of the alphabet in the history of writing and culture is appropriate to the understanding of the consequences of literacy in the colonization of the New World.

The tyranny of the alphabet is part of that scriptist bias which is deeply rooted in European education. It fosters respect for the written word over the spoken, and respect for the book above all as a repository of both the language and the wisdom of the former ages.

"Western literacy" would be a better expression to refer to the issues I would like to address in this essay. It is apparent that the idea of speech and writing held by Castilian men of letters was of crucial importance in the colonization of the New World. Their conception of writing

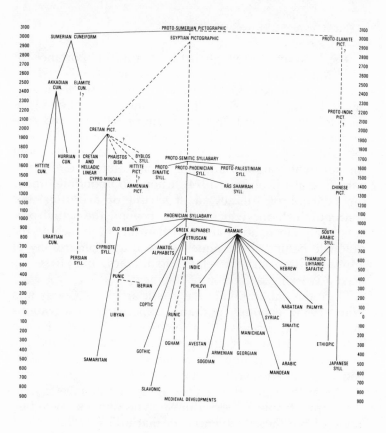

Fig. 4. The History of Writing (hypothetical) (From Gelb 1952).

was based on an evolutionary writing at the end of which
the alphabet was waiting. It obliterates the fact that the
history of writing should be perceived from a co-evolutionary point of view and that "literacy," properly speaking, is a conceptualization of writing based on the alphabet
and the concept of "letter" (Figure 4). The fact remains
that Castilians were able to build a pedagogical, administrative and philosophical apparatus based on their conception of language and of a hierarchy of human beings
with respect to their lack, or possession of, alphabetic
writing.

LITERACY: A WORKING DEFINITION

The tyranny of the alphabet is of crucial importance for
what Ricard called "the spiritual conquest" (1947) and, recently, Gruzinsky (1988) "the colonization of the imaginary." By the expression "literacy and colonization" I intend to bring to the fore a spectrum of activities and conceptualizations based on the experience of alphabetic writing which have already been exposed in narratives about
the spiritual conquest and the colonization of the imaginary (see also Kobayasi 1974). I hope to underline, under
the concept of literacy, a spectrum of activities and
conceptualizations which will go beyond the actual process of alphabetization and christianization, to include the
rationale behind the conquest as well as a philosophy of
administration strictly related to literacy. But, first, we
need a working definition of "literacy."

Since the publication of the classic article by Goody and
Watt (1963), echoing, perhaps, some early observations
made by Lévi-Strauss (1953: 264-65) in which the French
anthropologist was referring to writing (écriture) and not
to alphabetical writing, the debates over the "big divide"
between oral and written based societies have grown constantly at the same time that writing and alphabetic writing slipped toward an almost synonymous meaning.
Some of the theses advanced in that article were revised
and changed by Goody himself (1977: 36-51; 1987); others
have been challenged by more social and cognitive ori-

ented theories of literacy (Scribner and Cole 1981; Finnegan 1988). A review of the literature and the diverse issues in which the field of literacy research has grown (Chafe and Tannen: 1987)[5] does not concern me in this essay. I am interested, more particularly, in the consequences of literacy and the transformation of communicative forms in colonial situations in which a minority from a society which validates alphabetic writing interacts with members and institutions of a society with picto-ideographic writing systems. A working definition of literacy is required which will allow us to create a critical distance between the past that we construct and the present that we speak.

The term "literacy" has been and is being used in a wide variety of contexts (Graff 1981). From the straightforward competence in reading and writing to an educated knowledge about a given subject matter (cultural literacy), to a canonical knowledge of objects and cultural events (cultural literacy) to the challenge opened by the diversity of cultures and traditions (multicultural literacy). Scribner (1984) has reduced the notion of literacy to three metaphors: literacy as adaptation, literacy as power and literacy as a state of grace. In the first category she included the views according to which literacy helps the individual become integrated in the social domain and have a better adaptation to social life. The second category refers to those who emphasize the "relationship between literacy and group or community advancement." Scribner aligns in this view Freyre's (1970) philosophy of education, in which effective literacy education, in his view, "creates a critical consciousness through which a community can analyze its conditions of social existence and engage in effective action for a just society" (1984: 10). Finally, by literacy as a state of grace Scribner understands the long tradition of attributing special powers to those who are literate. And she adds: "In the perspective of Western humanism, literateness has come to be considered synonymous with being 'cultured', using the term in the old-fashioned sense to refer to a person who is knowledgeable about the content and techniques of the sciences, arts, and humanities as they have evolved historically" (1984:12). Scribner observes, furthermore, that the term sounds elitist and archaic, but insists that "the notion that participation in a literate—that is, bookish—tradition enlarges and develops a person's essential self is pervasive and still undergirds the concept of a liberal education." It is my contention, in this essay, that in order to have a critical understanding of the past (e.g., the colonization of the New World) we need to critically examine the ways we speak the present (e.g., our notion of literacy). Insofar as we are united with our ancestors by our beliefs in "literacy as a state of grace" we would have difficulties in understanding that the colonization process is not only enacted by those who believe in literacy as a state of grace but also by those who have a different writing system, an entirely different view of what speaking, writing, and education are all about (Gruzinsky 1988: 15-100). If it can be maintained, as I have already pointed out (Ricard (1947; 1986: 117-137; 378-379), that alphabetization in the New World was a true revolution, we should ask at the same time for whom such a statement holds its true value. We need, then, a working definition of "literacy" which will allow us to understand, on the one hand, the spectrum of activities that Castilians engaged in to implement a new technology (alphabetic writing) and, on the other, the whole domain of ideas and concepts they inferred from the values they placed on writing and literacy as a state of grace.

It is necessary, in the first place, to distinguish "literacy" from "Literacy." In a restricted sense "literacy" refers to the basic competence of reading and writing as well as to the domain of ideas and values that, in Western civilization, have been attributed to alphabetic writing and the book. In a general sense "Literacy" could be used to refer to any kind of graphic semio-linguistic interactions as well as to the respective conceptualization regulating the range of discursive practices of a given group or community (Pattison 1982: 10-15). While "literacy" refers to a regional writing practice and to its conceptualization elaborated by the practitioners, "Literacy" could be taken as a theoretical term referring to a field of study. Since "Literacy" has the inconvenience of being a term forged within the Western conceptualization of the written word ("Literacy" is derived from *littera*, a letter of the alphabet), it is perhaps advisable to have a different term to refer to different writing practices and their respective conceptualization in different cultures and traditions. Although an altogether new term will avoid misunderstanding and undue connotations, the fact remains that "writing" or "script" cannot be easily transformed to replace "literacy." I am happy, for the time being, in distinguishing a term that refers to a regional conceptualization of alphabetic writing ("literacy") from a term which designates a general field of study ("Literacy"). The first belongs to the community; the second is a disciplinary and theoretical concept. How much this distinction is needed (and perhaps a new term necessary) emerges from the fact that while "orality" can have a universal and non-problematic dimension "literacy," on the contrary, has the difficulties of universalizing a regional construction built around a given writing system and a set of communicative forms and interactions allowed by it. Before suggesting a term which will help us to distinguish the field of study from our own alphabetic habits, I would suggest distinguishing, on the one hand, speech and writing, and on the other, orality and literacy. I submit that such precautions are necessary since "literacy" is often used as synonymous with "writing" and sometimes with "alphabetic writing" thereby conveying the erroneous idea that literacy is a technology. In my working definition "literacy" is, once again, a name that captures the coexistence between a writing system and the conceptualization of its nature and social function.

The distinctions I have in mind are the following: 1) Human beings engage in oral and graphic communicative interactions; 2) Because of their recursive capacity, human beings are also able to conceptualize and refer to their own domain of interactions. "Speaking" and "writing" are the English terms which refer to both kinds of activities; 3) Finally, and because of their recursive capacity, human beings are able to conceptualize, refer to and describe the oral and written domain of interactions in terms of the oral and written practices of the group or community and the function of speech and writing in social life; to identify their practices in terms that authorize the difference from other practices and communities. Thus, while (in Castilian) *letrado* meant a cultivated person, *tlamatinime* (in Náhuatl) meant "he who has the wisdom of the word." While we can say, from an observer's point of view, that both conceptualizations have the same function, their respective natures are culture-relative. Levels 1 and 2 are covered by research on the relationship between spoken and written languages (Tannen 1982; Tannen and Chaffe 1987). Level 3 is, in my understanding, what has been opened up by the pioneering studies done by Goody and Watt (1963) and Goody (1977) in the context of cross-cultural communication, and by Havelock (1963, 1982) and Ong (1982) in the context of the history of Western civilization.

These preliminary distinctions require us to bear in mind that while the very conception of human beings presupposes speech, writing instead is not a necessary condition of humanness. A great time span separates the Homo Sapiens from the invention of writing (circa 3,000 years B.C.). On the other hand, we should keep in mind (as Figure 4 indicates) that the history of writing is not an evolutionary processes driving toward the alphabet, but rather a series of coevolutionary processes in which different writing systems followed their own transformations. This observation alerts us to the fact that the "lack of letters" that Castilians were ready to note in Amerindian cultures should be translated today as "having a picto-ideographic system of writing." It would be a useful thought-experiment, if nothing else, to think that the the Aztecs, for instance, could have noticed that Castilians "lacked the red ink and the black ink" as they used to refer to their own writing practices (Leon-Portilla 1961: 48-76).

As a consequence of what has been said, I will use orality and literacy to refer to a conscious conceptualizations of linguistic (oral and written) practices by those who participate in them. When we look, for instance, at the Aztecs' conceptualization of their different oral and written practices (Leon-Portilla 1961: 48-75; 1980: 15-35; 1985: 43-66); the sophisticated conceptualization of speech in Tzotzil's communities (Gossen 1974; 1985); the Dogon's categorization of their own oral practices (Calame-Griaule 1965: 21-92; 447-504); or how the Vai from Sierra Leone conceptualize their different written practices (Arab, English, Vai; Scribner and Cole 1979: 140-160), we soon realize that conceptualization of oral and graphic communication is a common feature of human communities. I would use "orality" to refer to the level of metalinguistic reflections and conceptualizations (expressed in speech or writing) of oral practices, and "literacy" to the level of metalinguistic reflections and conceptualization of written practices (expressed in speech or writing). While the former pair refers to communicative interactions accomplished through sounds and graphic marks respectively, the latter pair refers to the conceptualization of the social interactions by means of sounds or graphic marks. Neither should the tyranny of the alphabet obscure the fact that societies with primary oral means of communication have an equally sophisticated conceptualization of the nature and functions of language as societies with primary written forms of communication (Calame-Griaule 1965; Gossen 1974; 1985); nor should the fact that the natural differences between oral and written interactions and the differences between writing systems be automatically translated into cultural values (Gough 1968; Wood 1985: 1-20; 58-89; 117-124). In any event, it is not my intention to discuss here the consequence of literacy in the history of human culture, but rather to assess the consequences of the clash between alphabetic and picto-ideographic literacies in a colonial situation.

COMMUNICATION ACROSS CULTURAL BOUNDARIES

Beginnings are arbitrary and relative to a context of description (Said 1975: 27-78). If the origins or beginnings of Latin American culture are sought, it may be advisable to look to 1524 rather than 1492. The pertinent questions are what is a beginning, and for whom (Danto 1962; 1985: 285-98, 342-364; Said 1975: 50-52). The true communication across cultural boundaries and the beginning of a plurilingual and multicultural society in which a high number of native languages are still dominated by the language of the colonizers (Spanish, Portuguese and French, just to name the "Latin" ones), could be traced back to 1524 when the Franciscans began their alphabetization campaign and their millenarian kingdom (Phelan 1956; 1972: 65-116). I take the introduction of the alphabet as the beginning of a ramified history or a set of co-evolutionary histories (yet to be written) of what we understand today by "Latin America."

While Landa and Valadés were good examples illustrating the tyranny of the alphabet, the testerian "alphabet" is an excellent example of communication across cultural boundaries when what is at stake are not only different languages and cultures but also different writing systems. Testera has been celebrated for his "alphabet" (Figure 5), which was used to teach Christian prayers to the natives who did not know Spanish and were unable to read their own speech transcribed in alphabetic writing (León 1900). Mendieta calls it a "curiosity" (instead of a "folly"). The fact remains that the clash of different writing systems motivated, at the beginning, the

Fig. 5. The Testerian Catechism.

invention of graphic signs which would help the transition between picto-ideographic and alphabetic writing. Motolinía (1536-41: II, vi) reported how the natives confessed themselves by using figures (*figuras y caracteres*). He decided to confess only those who were able to "write" their sins in figures; those who knew how to paint and communicate by means of figures and were able to make themselves understood. Although Motolinía did not make any distinction between the conventional picto-ideograms painted by the professional *tlacuilo* and the figures drawn by those who needed to confess, it remains true that Motolinía, according to his description, participated in a conversation across cultural boundaries in which oral understanding was achieved by looking at graphic signs and by talking them out in conversation. The encounter between alphabetization (knowing how to read and write alphabetic writing) and literacy (learning the system of values attached to reading and writing) generated, during the sixteenth century, a dialogue across cultural boundaries in which the picto-ideographic writing system was overridden. Oral language and orality cannot be suppressed. Written language and its corresponding literacy can. Thus, we have today, on the one hand, scholars devoted to reading ancient codices in which the sign has remained but the knowledge about the sign (literacy) is gone, and, on the other, hundreds of native languages being spoken, while the alphabet is the only writing system in use.

The saga of the twelve mendicant friars from the instant the Pope authorized their mission to the moment they arrived in Mexico has been extensively reported (Motolinía 1536-41; Mendieta 1596, book III; Torquemada 1615, book XV) as well as studied (Ricard 1947; Kobayashi 1974, iv; Baudot 1976: 71-118; Duverger 1988: 153-227). This event was due to a petition from Cortés to Charles V who subsequently forwarded it to Pope Leo X. Mendieta reported that when Charles V requested help from the Pope to christianize the recently conquered people, he called a meeting of men of letters, theologians and jurists in order to inform himself about the correct procedures. Disregarding the fact that Mendieta is writing well after the debates about the legimitization of the conquest, what should catch our attention here is the fact that the King called a meeting of the most prominent men of letters, theologians and jurists ("hizo junta de letrados los más eminentes de sus reinos, teólogos y juristas"). The relevance of this move for understanding the consequences of literacy in a colonial situation could be seen, on the one hand, in the reports in which the process of alphabetization has been described and in the dialogues between the twelve friars and Aztec representatives (*principales*) transcribed in the well-known *Coloquios de 1524* (Sahagún 1564) and, on the other hand, in the use made of the alphabet by the natives to preserve traditions that were either being transmitted orally or were fixed in picto-ideographic writing.

The first example comes from Pedro de Gante in a letter to Philip II in which he reports the actions taken and the efforts made by the friars when they arrived in Mexico (Icazbalceta 1941). He underscored the friars' efforts in learning the native languages and commented on the difficulties involved in the task, since the natives were "people without writing, without letters, without written characters and without any kind of enlightenment" ("era gente sin escriptura, sin letras, sin caracteres y sin lumbre de cosa alguna," Icazbalceta 1941). The comparison between de Gante's report and Torquemada's observation about the difficulties of possessing a history when letters are lacking (see below) allows us to make some complementary comments. While Torquemada aligned the Aztecs' lack of letters with their lack of written histories, de Gante equated such an inadequacy with their deprived intelligence. The two correlations are not contradictory, by any means; they are perfectly complementary. In the first place, it made it seem natural that the Castilians were quickly self-appointed to write the history that the Aztecs needed but did not have. Secondly, it justified and legitimized the time and effort that the Religious Orders devoted to the introduction of literacy (e.g., to read and write as well as a given conception of the values implied in reading and writing) in order to enlighten the natives.

Values orient and support actions. Pedro de Gante reported in detail how they proceeded in order to transmit the "letter" to those who did not possess it. First, they assembled the children from the native nobility (*principales y señores*) in order to teach them God's Law, expecting (or instructing) them to transmit it to their parents as well as other relevant persons in their surroundings. Not long after the arrival of the twelve friars, de Gantes declares:

> At that time approximately one thousand children were gathered together, and we kept them locked up day and night in our house, and they were forbidden any conversation with their fathers and even less with their mothers, with the only exception of those who served them and brought them food; and the reason for this was so that they might neglect their excessive idolatries and their excessive sacrifices, from which the devil had served countless souls (Translated by Noel Fallows)

> Se juntaron luego poco más o menos mill mochachos, los cuales teníamos encerrados en nuestra casa de día y de noche, no les permitiendo ninguna conversación con sus padres, y menos con sus madres, salvo solamente con los que los servían y les traían de comer; y esto para que se olvidaran de sus excesivas idolatrías y excesivos sacrificios, donde el demonio se aprovechaba de innumerable cantidad de ánimas (Icazbalceta 1941: 204).

The interpretation of this paragraph shows that literacy is not instilled without violence. The violence, however, is not located in the fact that the youngsters have been assembled and enclosed day and night. It comes, rather, from the interdiction of having conversations with their parents, particularly with their mothers. In a primary oral society, in which virtually all knowledge is transmitted by means of conversation, the preservation of oral contact was contradictory with the effort to teach how to read and write. Forbidding conversations with the mother meant, basically, depriving the children of the living culture imbedded in the language and preserved and transmitted in speech.

The same underlying principle applies to the *Coloquios de 1524*. Mendieta offered a brief summary of the first dialogue in which, according to the author, after the friars informed the Aztec representatives about their goals and explained to them the Christian Doctrine, the *principales* readily accepted what the friars told them. When we read the *Coloquios* in Sahagún's version, we may conclude that Mendieta gave an accurate report of what happened. However, when the text is read in the Náhuatl version or in recent translations offered in Spanish (León Portilla 1986) or in English (Klor de Alva 1980)[6] what appears is a totally different picture (Mignolo 1988a). What are the consequences of literacy in these examples? After hearing the explanation of the Christian Doctrine, the Aztec *principales* asked the friars whether they had to abandon their own gods and traditions. To the affirmative reply of the friars, the Aztecs asked for a reason. To which the friars answered that everything they needed to know was written in the Divine Book. This simple answer revealed how much Castilians were involved in the tyranny of the alphabet since they had already forgotten the oral tradition of what they trusted as the Divine Book (Sanders 1985: 21-44; 1987: 175-192; Mignolo 1987b). The *Coloquios* are a clear example of the scriptist bias rooted in European education since the Renaissance (Pagden 1982: 185-90). The respect it fosters for the written word over the spoken is shared both by religious as well as academic communities (Ong 1982: 65-75). On the other hand, the written version of oral conversations which took place over an extended period of time (Klor de Alva 1982) in the year 1524, and which was reorganized by Sahagún (1564) to be printed at a later date (Pou y Martí 1924), is also an example of the versatility of alphabetic writing. Such writing makes it possible for what has been said to be fixed, and allows for the transmission of a text through time, losing, of course, the act of saying but keeping what has been said. This example shows that whatever may have taken place orally during the encounter between the twelve friars and the Aztec Lords, alphabetic writing gave control of the situation to the Castilians, for even if a version of the dialogue was written in Náhuatl, control of alphabetic writing and printing was in the hands of the colonizer.

But of course, not every step taken toward the alphabetization of the natives resulted in the desired effects which, from the friars' point of view, was for the good of the natives who would have the chance of changing their own "wrong" traditional and barbarous behavior to the "right" new and civilized one. Three examples illustrate the unexpected consequences of literacy in a colonial situation. The first has been reported by Mendieta and happened in Mexico; the second by Fray Francisco Ximénez and happened in the Yucatan; the third comes from colonial Peru, by comparing Garcilaso de la Vega with Guamán Poma de Ayala.

The children who, according to Pedro de Gante's letter to Philip II, were said to have been locked up in the monasteries, were not entirely from noble families. As is natural, the Aztec noble families had no reason to trust the friars' intentions and motives. Thus, instead of sending their own children, they sent the children of their vassals. Mendieta made it a point to report that those who were dishonest with the friars suffered consequences, for as the vassals learned how to read and write they ended up overruling their own superiors ("aquellos hijos de gente plebeya siendo alli doctrinado en la ley de Dios y en saber leer y escribir, salieron hombres hábiles, y vinieron después a ser alcaldes y gobernadores, y mandar a sus señores" (III, xv).[7]

It is within the context of unexpected consequences that native "books" from the Yucatan Peninsula such as the several *Books of Chilam Balam* or the *Popol Vuh* from the highlands of Guatemala, among others (Garza 1980; Edmonson 1985; Edmonson and Bricker 1985), could be explained. There is enough evidence to believe that the former (which were written in Yucatec and in European script), were transcriptions in alphabetic writing of the old hieroglyphic (or "painted") *códices*. Historians of the Yucatan Peninsula (Landa c.1566; Sánchez de Aguilar 1639; Avendaño y Loyola 1696: p.35r; López Cogolludo 1688) have had reactions to native writing systems and "books," similar to those of the historians of the Aztec civilization.

They have reported, for instance, that the natives would read the book in their assembly; that some of them were read following the rhythm of the drums; that others were sung, and still others were enacted. There is also evidence (Roy 1933: 5) that these "books" as we know them today were compiled not before the seventeenth or the eighteenth centuries. Consequently, what today is considered an "encyclopedia" or a mixture of genres (Tozzer 1921: 182-92; Roy 1933:3; Garza 1980: XXIX-XLI), presumably existed, before they were compiled in a single unit, as a diversity of genres common to pictographic writing (bookkeeping, time-reckoning) without parallel in oral genres. As time went on, the European script that the friars were so eager to transmit in order to be more effective in the christianization of the natives was used by the latter to stabilize their past, to adapt themselves to the present and to transmit their own traditions to future generations.

Rigoberta Menchú's recent narrative of the life and deeds of a Quiché community is an outstanding example of the "consequences" of literacy from the colonial period to the present. There are several moments, in raising a child, in which the adults talk to him or her about the importance of their tradition. Here is Menchú's report of the day the child turns ten years old:

> They tell them that they will be young men and women and that one day they will be fathers and mothers. This is actually when they tell the child that he must never abuse his dignity, in the same way his ancestors never abused their dignity. It's also when they remind them that our ancestors were dishonored by the White Man, by colonization. But they don't tell them the way that it is written down in books, because the majority of Indians can't read or write, and don't even know that they have their own texts. No, they learn it through oral recommendations, the way it has been handed down through the generations. They are told that the Spaniards dishonored our ancestors; finest sons, and the most humble of them. And it is to honor these humble people that we must keep our secrets. And no-one except we Indians must know (1984:13).

In colonial Peru, Garcilaso de la Vega was the perfect example of the adaptation (in order to criticize it) to Western literacy (González Echevarría 1987), while Guamán Poma epitomizes the use of alphabetic writing in order to resist the literacy of the colonizer (Adorno 1986). In fact, although Garcilaso was able to write as a Castilian native speaker and to assimilate their conceptualization of writing, history and the social role corresponding to writing activities (i.e., *letrado*), Guamán Poma also managed to have his message understood by a Spanish reader. In his "*coronica*" to King Philip III, Guamán Poma expressed his acute dissatisfaction through a counter-proposal for the administration and government of Peru, using alphabetical writing together with pictorial representation in order to convey his message. Thus, Guamán Poma was able to intermingle the literacy of his own ancestors with Western literacy, to make himself understood by his "others" without losing his own identity (Adorno 1988a). When compared with the *Popol Vuh* and the *Books of Chilam Balam*, Garcilaso and Guamán serve to illuminate several aspects of literacy in a colonial situation. They both preserved the authorial identity already linked to Western literacy; they used Castilian instead of their own native languages to convey their message to a Castilian audience (in spite of the obvious differences); they wrote for an audience that was detached from the act of writing and which would not have the need to crouch down and look at the pictures while listening to the authors narrations in order to understand the message. On the contrary, the "books" from the Yucatan Peninsula were anonymous and collective, written in the native languages and, consequently, addressed to a native audience, which preferred "listening" to an oral performance over "reading" the pages of a "book."

Examples of this sort enable us to reconstruct a wide spectrum of the consequences of (Western) literacy in the colonization of the New World. At one end of the spectrum we have the meeting between Charles V and the men of letters, and the friars' program to alphabetize the natives. At the other end we witness the uses of writing by natives in order to preserve and transmit what had until then been kept in memory and transmitted orally, as well as to interpret in alphabetic writing what had until then been recorded in painted images and interpreted orally. In the middle, so to speak, is Garcilaso who will fully embrace Western literacy in order to criticize the colonizer; and Guamán Poma who will use Western literacy in order to resist it. Even though script was secondary within native and marginal communities—as we can gather from Rigoberta Menchú's narrative, for not everybody knew how to read and write—the forms of communications in oral traditions dislocated the importance that alphabetic writing had in the European tradition. The fact remains that alphabetic writing used for purposes beyond the intention of those who planned and programmed the alphabetization of the colonized, as well as the silence to which the "illiterate" are reduced, reveal one of the major communicative paradoxes of a colonial situations, to which the New World experience is not an exception. While literacy is conveyed, initially, in order to govern and control the native population, it is prevented, ultimately, in order to have the same results (P. Freyre).

From the mendicant friars to Paulo Freyre, and from Guamán Poma to Rigoberta Menchú, the spectrum of communicative interactions across semiotic and cultural boundaries becomes a field open to investigation in our efforts to understand the past. But it also becomes a field of reflection once we accept that the romance languages in Latin America (Spanish, Portuguese, French) are surrounded by the plurality of the native languages. In this context, communication across cultural boundaries is not only a field of investigation to be explored in our understanding of the past but a domain of human interactions to be enacted in our speaking the present.

LITERACY AND SOCIAL ROLES

According to the working definition of orality and literacy, we human beings do not only speak and write. We also have opinions about what speech and writing are, their values, how they are relevant to society, and how societies characterize themselves according to the kind of communicative interactions they engage in. Although this definition is valid, in the context of my discussion, for Castilian as well as Amerindian cultures at the time of the conquest and colonization, in the pages that follow I will focus on the Castilian construction of literacy and on its implementation in the colonization of the New World.

A word of common use, *letrado*, summarized a complex network of meaning derived from the name of alphabetic units: *letra*. *Letrado* had two basic meanings which the *Diccionario de Autoridades* (DI) describes as follows: (a) *letrado* was applied to those having scientific knowledge, for scientific knowledge was matched to the written word (letters) ("es el docto en las ciencias que porque estas se llamaron letras, se le dio este nombre. Viene del latino *literatus*, que significa lo mismo"); (b) *letrado* was also applied to those expert in law (scribes, notaries, lawyers) rather than in sciences ("se llama comunmente al abogado. Lat. *Jurisperitus, Causidicus*").

Concerning the first case, it seems obvious that *letrado* came from *literatus*, although it is less obvious that it meant the same. Parkes (1973) notes that in the Middle Ages it was applied only to those who possessed knowledge of Latin and was sometimes related to learning. Maravall (1953) emphasized the reverse aspect: learning was mainly related to the knowledge of Greek and Latin. Clanchy (1979, 1981) reported that while toward the twelfth century "clericus meant literatus" and "laicus meant illiteratus," the synonymy was due to a semantic change by means of which *literatus* and *clericus* became interchangeable with terms meaning "learned" or "scholarly." Clanchy suggested that while the antithesis *clericus: laicus* was a Medieval creation, *literatus: illiteratus* had a Roman origin. The reference to the origin of the word *literatus* in DI seems to have a Roman rather than a Medieval background.

Concerning the second case, the meaning of the word began to reflect, toward the second half of the fifteenth century, a social change that could be described by inverting the hierarchical order which DI had registered in the eighteenth century. In fact, while a *letrado* in the sense of "a learned and scholarly person" may seem at first glance to have a more prominent social role than a *letrado* as "a person schooled in law and legal matters," certain differences may be perceived upon close inspection. Gil Fernández (1982: 231-298) has expanded on the classic study by Maravall (1953) devoted to the idea of knowledge in the Middle Ages and the corresponding symbolic representation of social roles related to it, by describing the distribution of social roles and functions of grammarians, men of letters (*letrados*) and humanists during the sixteenth century. While in the Middle Ages—according to Gil Fernández—the hierarchy of knowledge had the theologians as a superior caste in relation to the grammarians, lawyers and notaries, the situation began to change in Spain, toward the end of the fifteenth century. Experts in legal matters held positions of increasing importance (Maravall 1953; 1967: 334). As they gained in social status so the meaning of the word *letrado* shifted. They became a caste that detached itself from both the Medieval *clericus* and the Renaissance humanist.

In the context of the colonization of the New World the *letrados* (men of letters) will be in charge of the intellectual legitimization of the conquest, whereas the *letrados* (experts in law and legal matters) will take over everything concerning policy-making and administration. However, despite their different social roles and functions, both have taken their names from the word *littera*, a letter of the alphabet.

LITERACY AND THE LEGITIMIZATION OF THE CONQUEST

The arguments justifying the conquest and colonization could be divided into theological and rational categories. Theological arguments were mainly centered around the fight against the Devil who' was the cause of all the wrongdoings. The relationship with literacy is not obvious and I do not wish to force a possible connection. However, literacy has a crucial, although not always clear, role in the rational arguments justifying the conquest.

Some of the rational arguments are as follows (Garzón Valdéz 1988):

a) The conquest and colonization have a paternalistic character which is ethically justified.

b) The conquest and colonization have a liberating character which aspires to eliminate barbarism and introduce civilization.

c) The conquest and colonization have a commercial character which aspires to increase and promote the exchange among different countries.

Literacy is obvious in argument *b* and implied in *a* and *c*. Argument *b* is clearly related to the tyranny of the alphabet and the connections between civilization and alphabetic writing. The mediated connections with the theological argument can be inferred from here: if literacy brings civilization it is also necessary for christianization. And christianization is the best way to fight against the Devil since the Devil was, after all, an invention of Christianity.

But let us concentrate on argument *b*. The Valladolid debates are the best examples of the role played by the men of letters in the legitimization of the conquest. Based on what we know about the conceptualization of their social role, it is not surprising that they were able to conjugate a conception of literacy in which one of the distinctive features of the "barbarians" was their lack of alphabetic writing (Pagden 1982) with a campaign of alphabetization which led to a civilization crusade (Ricard 1947; Baudot 1976: 71-118; Duverger 1987: 127-152; 169-190).

As surprising as it may sound, the belief that not every human society necessarily had "developed" oral communication was still a criterion to distinguish the civilized from the barbarians. This theory loses ground when confronted with the New World experience. From the first Castilian report written by someone who spent some time living with the natives (Pané 1493), the lack of speech and language was never an issue. However, countless numbers of pages have been devoted to mention the fact that the Amerindians did not have alphabetic writing and to speculate on its consequences. Castilian historians and chroniclers deplored the fact that, because of their lack of alphabetic writing, Amerindians were un-equipped to keep exact records of their past or to build a coherent narrative of their origins (Mignolo 1981a; 1981b; 1986c). Thus, Fray Ramon Pané (1493) repeatedly pointed toward the contradictions in *tainos'* narratives which he sees as a direct consequence of the lack of alphabetic writing. Almost a century later, Torquemada (1615) had the same attitude toward what he considered were the neces-sary connections between having alphabetic writing and possessing a history. A few years before Torquemada, Fa-ther Acosta (Sandoval 1945: 80-83) reacted to Father To-var's report on the Indians of New Spain by asking a spe-cific question: how can they have history and beautiful figures of speech (as Father Tovar reported) if they did not have writing (Mignolo 1981a; 1981b; Pagden 1982: 185-90). A quote from Torquemada allows me to make my point clearer:

> One of the things which causes the most confusion in a republic and which greatly perplexes those who wish to discuss its causes, is the lack of precision with which they consider their history; for if his-tory is an account of events which are true and actu-ally happened and those who witnessed them and learned about them neglected to preserve the memory of them, it will require an effort to write them down after they have happened, and he who wishes to do so will grope in the dark when he tries, for he may spend his life collating the version which he is told only to find that at the end of it he still has not un-ravelled the truth. This (or something like this) is what happens in this history of New Spain, for just as the ancient inhabitants did not have letters, or were even familiar with them, so they neither left records of their history (translated by Noel Fallows)

> Una de las cosas que mayor confusión causan en una república y que más desatinados trae a los hombres que quieren tratar sus causas es la poca puntualidad que hay en considerar sus historias; porque si historia es una narración de cosas acaecidas y verdaderas y los que las vieron y supieron no las dejaron por memo-ria, sera fuerza al que después de acaecidas quiere escribirlas, que vaya a ciegas en el tratarlas, o que en cotejar las varias que se dicen, gasta la vida y quede

al fin de ella sin haber sacado verdad en limpio. Esto
(o casi esto) es lo que pasa en esta historia de la
Nueva España porque como los moradores antiguos no
tenían letras, ni las conocían, así tampoco no las
historiaban (Torquemada, 1615, I,xi)

Although he recognized that the Aztecs had some kind
of writing, it was not enough to replace the absence of letters (see also Acosta 1590: Book VI, Chapters 4 and 5). The
nuisance that Torquemada found in picture writing was
that a given case or event could be referred to or represented by only one figure ("una sola figura contenía la
major parte del caso sucedido") and, consequently, since
this manner of writing history was not common to all
known communities (was not, in other words, hegemonic), it was relatively easy to change the organization
of the event and, more often than not, to detach it from
the truth ("muy facil variar el modo de la historia y
muchas veces desarrimarla de la verdad y aun apartarla
del todo").

All the actions taken by the friars in the process of
alphabetization were supported by a sound conception of
the nature and function of language in human
communities and by the distinctions made between different kinds of human beings according to their forms of
communication and discursive interactions. Pagden (1982)
has traced the connections between the predominant
philosophy of language, the image of the barbarians and
the modifications forced upon existing ideas by the
"discovery" of the New World. It is interesting to point
out in connection with the topic of literacy and colonization, first, the attribution of "low" degrees of language development to human communities, and second, that human societies were ranked in the chain of being according
to their lack or possession of alphabetic writing. Covarrubias (*apud* Pagden) stated: "We call barbarians those
who are ignorant of letters, those who have bad customs
and who act badly, those who are wicked and will refuse
to communicate with other men of reason and live without [reason] and finally those who are without pity and
cruel." DI has *inculto* and *grosero* as features characteriz-
ing the barbarians and one of the examples is "barbaric

language." Thus, *barbarismo* has been used to refer to a figure of speech or writing going against the established conventions of grammatical rules. It should be emphasized that although the idea of the barbarian is not limited to language it is also true that language has played an important role in the characterization of the barbarian. This conception also has played an important role in the legitimation of the conquest and has determined the consequences of literacy in the colonization of the New World.

In Las Casas's world all knowledge (*scientia*) was textually dependent (Pagden 1982: 129) and it was consistent with the description of *letrado* as a man of letters and knowledge. Using this assumption as a point of departure, it is easy to construe the opposition between literates and barbarians and to anchor the opposition in the lack of or possession of alphabetic script. The ability to create a system of writing, and the access to the power and knowledge that such a system conferred, was the ultimate token of the superiority of the 'civil' man over the 'barbarian', who lived always as a slave to those with greater wisdom than himself. For Aquinas and his sixteenth-century followers, the written language belonged essentially to a different category from the spoken one, the difference being represented in most cases by the difference between the vernacular tongues and Latin (Pagden 1982: 130). In this context Las Casas was able to write:

> The second class of barbarians are those who lack a literary language (*qui literali sermone carent*) which corresponds to their maternal idiomatic language, as is Latin to us, and thus do not know how to express what they think (quoted by Pagden 1982:130)

I shall avoid the temptation of commenting on Las Casas's observation about Latin as a maternal language and shall limit myself to underlining the fact that a philosophy of language based on the tyranny of the alphabet and the superiority of knowledge secured by alphabetic writing, on the one hand, allowed the Castilians to justify the process of alphabetization and, on the other, is allowing us to understand the consequences of literacy in the process of colonization. When their justification is confronted with our understanding we realize, at the same time, that the Castilians' justification was their way of speaking the present in the context of a colonial expansion as our understanding is our way of speaking the present in the context of decolonization.

A comparison between the philosophy of education implied in the colonial period, on one hand, and in Freyre, on the other, would help in elucidating the last statement. Freyre has been credited with teaching and disseminating literacy in a country kept ignorant and silent by centuries of Portuguese colonization. In his philosophy of education, literacy is the road to liberation instead of to christianization. However, it could be argued that in the mind of Castilian men of letters, christianization was also liberation: liberation from the oppression of the Devil. The capitalistic regimes supported by military forces in Latin America took the place of the Devil in the New World. Freyre, like the mendicant friars, could be understood as fighting the same battle. There is a difference, however. In the sixteenth century the addressees of the literacy campaigns were the children of influential families in pre-Columbian cultures, because they were like gentlemen and noble persons. The friars have their goals clear. They knew that putting literacy into the hands of Indian children, without making a class distinction, would endanger the very results of the alphabetization campaign. And, indeed, some experiences have been reported during the first years, when the Aztec Lords did not send their own children but the children of their vassals (Icazbalceta 1941: 55-56). However, if there is a difference between the mendicants and Freyre's literacy campaigns, it could be cast in the following terms: While literacy in the Spanish colonization was justified by the tyranny of the alphabet and effected by the domestication of a small and controllable number of people, Freyre's campaign of teaching the oppressed in order to help their liberation is justified by the links between literacy, critical thinking and consciousness.

LITERACY AND THE ORGANIZATION OF THE NEW WORLD

Three aspects of alphabetic writing interest us here (Ricoeur 1971; Tannen 1982: 1-16; Finnegan 1988: 139-174). One is its capacity to communicate at a distance; second, the power of a writing system to be understood and employed by those able to read directly, without the need for an oral narrative interpreting what has been written; and, third, the depersonalized communicative situation in which conversation is no longer needed to "read" the graphic signs. When an oral interpreter is needed in order to transmit the meaning of a written text, the power of writing is limited (Goody 1986: 91). The difference between writing for record-keeping and time-reckoning and writing as an alternative to oral communication lies precisely in this fact. Alphabetic writing, however, extended the domain of the letter beyond the field limited to the voice and the body. The *letrados*-jurists, the *Ordenanzas de Indias* and the *Relaciones geográficas de Indias* are paradigmatic examples of the social roles in charge of the organization of the New World and of the close connections between a use and conceptualization of alphabetic writing (Western literacy) and colonization.[8]

I have already mentioned that in the sixteenth century the *letrado*-jurists began to play a role as important as or more important than the *letrado*-humanists. The Council of the Indies which corresponded to the supreme direction of the New World had executive, judicial and legislative functions. It passed through diverse stages, initially as part of the Council of Castile, until it finally began its independent life in 1524. It was made up of councilors "*de capa y espada*" and "*consejeros togados.*" The latter dominated the council through sheer force of numbers and through their experience in the affairs of the Indies, since many of them had been *oidores* in the *audiencias* or had filled government posts in the New World. All facets of life were subject to the jurisdiction of the Council, from high politics to detailed information on geography, political history, natural history, etc. (Malagón Barceló 1961:5). The *Ordenanzas de Indias* are a good example of this situation and, also, of the increasing role played by literacy in the colonization of the New World. In *Ordenanza* I, for example, a "philosophy" for the administration of the New World, is layed down, and it makes clear that if the members of the Council of the Indies had to be honest persons of noble stock and reputable lineage ("personas aprobadas en costumbres, nobleza, y limpieza de linajes") it is because they are selected according to their knowledge (letters) and prudence ("escogidos en letras y prudencia"). It is also specified that the Council of the Indies will be composed of the president and eight *Consejeros Letrados*. Such *consejeros* are not the kind of *letrados* related to *scientia* but to the law. *Ordenanza* XXVII is entirely devoted to emphasizing the importance of reading and writing letters. The colonizers were aware that the writing technology provided by the alphabet made it possible to effectively conduct business (like today with the telephone and electronic mail) and take control of the people and the land by compiling a massive set of regulations (*Ordenanzas*) and a questionnaire (*Instrucción y memoria*) which generated a massive amount of information (*Relaciones geográficas de Indias*). *Letrados* and cosmographers joined forces to trace the boundaries (in words and maps) of the newly acquired domains.

The Council of the Indies was responsible, then, for planning and implementing the massive information-gathering operation known as the *Instrucción y Memoria* and the written result of it known as the *Relaciones geográficas de Indias* (Cline 1964; 1972). While the *Ordenanzas* and the *Instrucción y Memoria* enjoyed the benefit of the printing press and could be printed by the thousands and distributed to the most remote corners of the Spanish Empire, the *Relaciones geográficas* were hand-written and hand-engraved and only began to be published toward the end of the nineteenth century (Figure 6). However, for those in control of the administration of the Spanish Empire in the New World, the *Relaciones geográficas* represented a powerful instrument for writing and mapping. The fifty questions of the *Instrucción y Memoria*, which were distributed by the Council of the Indies to representative persons in the Spanish administration, generally ended up on the desk of a public notary who would gather a representative number of Spanish and native people who would provide the answer to each question orally while the public notary fixed it in writing and sent it to his superior (Mignolo 1982: 70-73; Gruzinsky 1988: 101-138). After several steps of ascending order, and passing through the administrative hierarchy, the *Relación*, ended up in the hands of the Council (Mignolo 1987a: 456-62). What is relevant in this process is the fact that the oral report given by those who were invited to inform was written down by a *letrado* (public notary) who converted an oral situation into a written (alphabetic) report with administrative purposes.

Compared with the picto-ideographic writing system and mapping in pre-columbian Central Mexico, for instance, the *Relaciones geográficas* also illustrate the intervention of alphabetic literacy in picto-ideographic literacy. Alphabetic writing had not only made it possible to inscribe what had been said in a communicative situation (losing forever the act of saying and hearing in which

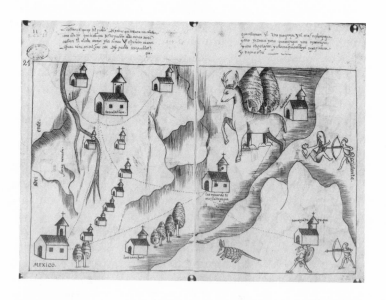

Fig. 6. Map from the Relación of Temazcaltepeque (Archivo de Indias).

the notary and the informant were involved) and to develop its own communicative strategies, but also allowed the detachment of alphabetic writing and mapping in a way that it is difficult to imagine for picto-ideographic writing and mapping (Teuber 1987).[8] In fact, when we look at the alphabetic written report and the map of the *Relaciones*, we perceive a distance between the two which is much closer in native writing systems and mapping (Figure 7). Pre-conquest maps (as well as post-conquest maps of the early years) were more than a representation of space and distances (Caso 1949). They "maintained a mythical, social, political and economic memory of the past" (Gruzinsky 1987: 48). On the other hand, and paradoxically enough, alphabetic writing and mapping were as linked from a material and physical point of view as they were detached conceptually. As Gruzinsky has also suggested (1987: 55; 1988: 65-66), "Spanish sketching and alphabetical writing can hardly be dissociated: they were nothing but two different modulations of the same stroke of the pen." Consequently, it is possible to think that the alphabetization of the Indian nobility has meant that, as a consequence, the *tlacuilo* became used to the "stroke of the pen" modifying, in the process, the traditional fashion of "mapping." That is, just as by the same modulation of the pens, the *tlacuilo* was able to unite writing and mapping, so he was also (conceptually) learning to identify the distance between the discursive aspect of alphabetic writing and the iconic aspects of mapping (Gruzinsky 1988: 65-80).

While mapping the new territories was systematically handled by the Council of the Indies by means of the *Instrucción y Memoria*, the oral reports and the maps provided by the Amerindians were absorbed and controlled by the administrative network and the fifty questions listed in the *Instrucción y Memoria*. Three of the questions requested a map. The assimilation of the writing conventions introduced by Castilians implied a deep transformation of the very nature of the social role of the *tlacuilo* as well as his function in the social structure. Thus, while the *letrado* and the cosmographer in Castilian social structure were people mastering two different (and

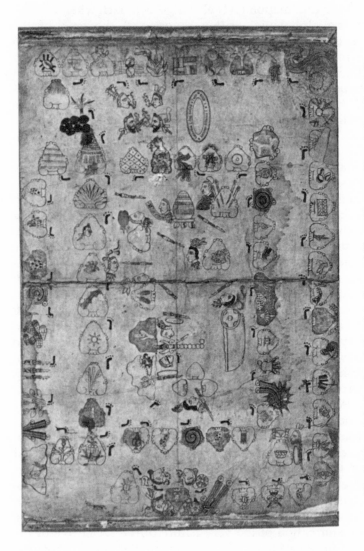

Fig. 7. Map of the border of Cuauhtinchan and Totomilhuacan (Boturini's collection).

interrelated) graphic conventions (writing letters and drawing maps) the *tlacuilo* in Aztec social structure were people mastering a code in which writing and mapping were not clearly distinguished.

Malagón Barceló (1961) has described the role of the *letrado* in the colonization of the New World in terms of what Goody (1986) subsequently, and coming from a different perspective, summarized in the expression "the logic of writing and the organization of the society." The *Relaciones geográficas de Indias* are a fitting example of the importance of writing in the organization of society as well as of the interrelations between writing and mapping in societies with different writing systems. Barceló has also observed that too much attention has been paid to the conquest of the New World and to the conquistadors while shadowing the role of literacy and the *letrados* ("the royal scribe, the judges, the *oidores*, in a word, the *letrados* or men of law") in the process of colonization (to colonize: to cultivate, to organize). As far as literacy—in the restricted sense—designates Western alphabetic writing and the system of values attributed to discursive practices, literacy is the basis for the justification of the conquest provided by the *letrado*-humanists and for the organization of society planned and carried out by the *letrado*-jurists. Their institutional locus was the Council of the Indies.

While Barceló has argued convincingly that the "Spanish empire was erected under the inspiration of the law" and its execution was in the hands of the *letrados*, I would like to emphasize that not only the law but also (mainly) the letter (e.g., alphabetic literacy), made possible the organization of the Spanish Empire in the Indies, of which the *Relaciones geográficas* are a spectacular example. Goody has made a similar point based on his knowledge of the African colonization. He has argued that "the advent of colonial regimes brought an extraordinary quantum jump apparent to anyone who has studied the documentary records of African scene over the last century" (Goody 113). The question is how to assess the relevance of literate activities in the political organization of society and of the Spanish Empire in particular. A part of the answer could be found in the history of unity and in the social function attributed to alphabetic writing in sixteenth-century Spain.

CONCLUDING REMARKS

I began by contrasting and relating understanding the past and speaking the present. I also referred to a "context of descriptions" from which neither understanding the past nor speaking the present could be detached. Two kinds of contexts of description guide our understanding and our saying. One is the context we construe as members of a given culture (e.g., tradition); the other is the context we construe as practitioners of a discipline. As members of a culture, our understanding of the past is guided by the social position (class, gender, generation, etc.) to which we belong. As practitioners of a discipline, our understanding of the past is guided by our theoretical and epistemological position in the disciplinary field. Both kinds of contexts of description are, of necessity, intermingled and a constant source of dispute, changing positions and self-analysis.

From a disciplinary point of view I have attempted to understand the past by framing it in the context of literacy; at the same time I have attempted to question some of our current ways of speaking about literacy by rethinking our understanding of the past. In the context of literacy and colonization, several of the presuppositions summarized under "The Tyranny of the Alphabet" allow me to perceive the close relationship between the Spanish colonizer's actions and justifications and current scholarship in which alphabetic writing is conceived as the end of a linear evolutionary process. By thinking of communicative forms and communicative situations, oral and graphic, we also detach ourselves from our culturally-based conception of literacy (and, consequently, of literature). In the context of my previous research and publications, the understanding some of the consequences of literacy in the colonization of the New World helped me to rethink both the field of literary studies and our conception of "colonial letters" (Mignolo 1986b; 1988a; Adorno 1988b).

As a member of Latin American culture I hope to have joined those who insist on conceiving Latin America as a plurilingual and multicultural society (Ballón Aguirre 1983; 1987, among others), in which the historical circumstances of "literacy and colonization" have contributed to the hegemonic role which is played today by the "Latin" component over the "Amerindian" traditions.

NOTES

* Research for this project has been partially supported by a Rackham School of Graduate Studies Grant (The University of Michigan) and a John Carter Library Grant. I wish to thank Noel Fallows for translating all quotations from Spanish into English.

[1] Literacy and colonization in the nineteenth century has been studied from a sociological perspective by Clammer (1976). The semiotic perspective I alluded to was laid down in Mignolo (1988a and forthcoming).

[2] See Clendinnen (1987: 112-128) for an overall view of the Franciscan mission in the Yucatan and the role played by Diego de Landa.

[3] I am thankful to Horst Pietschmann (Universität Hamburg) for bringing Reinhard's erudite and insightful article to my attention.

[4] Skeat (1969) has reported that recent findings make the knowledge we had about how the Bible was written and circulated obsolete. After tracing a brief history of the medium of writing (papyrus and parchment) to today's codex (or book), he surmises that in "the everyday world in which earliest Christians lived, we might have expected that they would adopt as the vehicle for their literature either the parchment scroll of contemporary Judaism, or the papyrus roll universal throughout the Gentile world, or both. But in fact they did neither of these things: in this, as in other matters, the men who 'turned the world upside down' had different ideas."

[5] Deborah Keller-Cohen (The University of Michigan) called this article to my attention.
[6] Duverger's (1988) French translation directly from the Spanish conveys Sahagún's point of view.

[7] The same event has been reported on several occasions. See, for instance, "El orden que los religiosos tienen en enseñar a los indios la doctrina, y otras cosas de policía cristiana" (Icazbalceta 1941: 55-56)

[8] I am indebted to Bernard Teuber (Universität München) for his willingness to explain to me his point of view on this topic and for letting me read the manuscript of this article. He has studied the Renaissance grammarians' (Nebrija, Oliveira) program for finding the correspondences between the voice and the graphic sign (which they applied later to non-European languages) and has pointed out the distance between the voice and the graphic sign in picto-ideographic writing systems perceived by Fray Alonso de Molina (*Vocabulario en lengua castellana y mexicana*, 1571).

WORKS CITED

Acosta, José de. 1590. *Historia natural y moral de las Indias*. Mexico: Fondo de Cultura Económica, 1940.

Adorno, Rolena. "Selections from the Symposium on 'Literacy, Reading and Power.'" *The Yale Journal of Criticism* 1 (1988a): 219-225.

—. "Nuevas perspectivas en los estudios literarios coloniales hispanoamericanos." *Revista de crítica literaria latinoamericana*. 28 (1988b): 11-27.

—. *Guamán Poma. Writing and Resistance in Colonial Peru*. Austin: Univ. of Texas Press, 1986.

Avendaño y Loyola, A. de. 1696. "Relación de las dos entradas que hice a la conversión de los géntiles ytzaes y cehaches." Manuscript in Newberry Library, Chicago.

Balandier, George. "La situation coloniale: approche théorique." *Cahiers internationaux de sociologie* XI (1951): 44-79.

Ballón Aguirre, Enrique. "Historiografía de la literatura en sociedades plurinacionales (Multilingues y pluriculturales)." *Filología* 2 (1987): 5-25.

—. "Multiglosia y poder de expresión en la sociedad peruana." Comp. A. Corbera. Educación y lingüística en la Amazonía Peruana. Lima:

Centro Amazónico de Antropología y Aplicación Práctica, 1983. 17-27.

Baudot, George. *Utopie et histoire au Mexique. Les premiers chroniqueurs de la civilisation mexicaine (1520-1569).* Toulouse: Privat, 1976.

Calame-Griaule, Genevieve. *Ethnologie et langage. La parole chez les Dogon.* Paris: Gallimard, 1965.

Caso, Alfonso. "El mapa de Teozacoalco." *Cuadernos Americanos* 8 (1949): 145-181.

Chafe, Wallace and Deborah Tannen. "The Relation Between Written and Spoken Language." *Annual Review of Anthropology* 16 (1987): 383-407.

Clammer, J.R. *Literacy and Social Change: A Case Study of Fiji.* Leiden: E.J. Brill, 1976.

Clanchy, Michael T. "Looking Back from the Invention of Printing." *Literacy in Historial Perspective.* Ed. Daniel P. Resnick. Washington: Library of Congress, 1983. 7-22.

—. *From Memory to Written Record. England 1066-1307.* London: Edward Arnold, 1979.

Clendinnen, Inga. *Ambivalent Conquest: Maya and Spaniard in Yucatan, 1517-1570.* Cambridge: Cambridge Univ. Press, 1987.

Cline, Howard F. "The *Relaciones geográficas* of the Spanish Indies, 1577-1588." *Handbook of Middle American Indians* 12 (1972): 183-242.

—. "The *Relaciones geográficas* of the Spanish Indies, 1577-1586." *Hispanic American Historical Review* XLIV, 3 (1964): 341-374.

Danto, Arthur. *Narration and Knowledge.* New York: Columbia Univ. Press, 1985.

—. "Narrative Sentences." *History and Theory* (1962): 146-179.

Davis, Rex. "Education for Awareness: A Talk with Paulo Freyre." Ed. Robert Mackie. *Literacy and Revolution: The Pedagogy of Paulo Freyre.* London: Pluto Press, 1980. 57-69.

Duverger, Christian. *La conversion des Indiens de Nouvelle-Espagne, avec les textes de Colloques des Douze de Bernardino de Sahagún* (1564). Paris: Editions du Seuil, 1987.

Edmonson, Munro S. "Quiche Literature." Ed., M. Edmonson. *Literatures. Supplement to the Handbook of Middle American Indians.* Austin: Univ. of Texas Press, 1985. 107-132.

— and Victoria Bricker. "Yucatecan Maya Literature." Ed. M. Edmonson. *Literatures. Supplement to the Handbook of Middle American Indians.* Austin: Univ. of Texas Press, 1985. 44-63.

Finnegan, Ruth. *Literacy and Orality: Studies in the Technology of Communication.* London: Basil Blackwell, 1988.

Foley, John Miles. "Oral Literature." *Choice* 18 (1980): 487-96.

Freyre, Paulo and Donaldo Macedo. *Literacy: Reading the Word and the World.* Foreword A.E. Berthoff. Introduction H.A. Giroux. Massachusetts: South Hadley, 1987.

—. *Pedagogy of the Oppressed.* New York: Seabury Press 1970.

Garza, Mercedes de la. "Prólogo." *Literatura Maya.* Caracas: Biblioteca Ayacucho, 1980. IX-LVII.

Garzón Valdés, Ernesto. "El problema de la justificación ética de la conquista." Paper presented at the conference Eroberung und Inbesitznahme Amerikas im 16. Jahrhundert Rechtertigung, Realitat und Literarische Reflexion. Eischstatt: Katholische Universitat, November 1988.

Gelb, I.J. *A Study of Writing. The Foundations of Grammatology.* Chicago: Univ. of Chicago Press, 1952.

Gil Fernández, Luis. *Panorama social del humanismo español (1500-1800).* Madrid: Alhambra, 1981.

González-Echevarría, Roberto. "The Law of the Letter: Garcilaso's Commentaries and the Origins of the Latin American Narrative." *The Yale Journal of Criticism,* 1, 1 (1987): 107-131.

Goody, Jack. *The Interface Between the Written and the Oral.* Cambridge: Cambridge Univ. Press, 1987.

—. *The Domestication of the Savage Mind.* Cambridge: Cambridge Univ. Press, 1977.

—. *The Logic of Writing and the Organization of Society.* Cambridge: Cambridge Univ. Press, 1986.

Goody, Jack and Ian Watt. "The Consequences of Literacy." *Comparative Studies in Society and History* 5 (1963): 304-45.

Gossen, Gary G. "Tzotzil Literature." Ed. M. Edmonson. *Literatures. Supplement to the Handbook of Middle American Indians.* Austin: Univ. of Texas Press, 1985. 64-106.

—. "To Speak with a Heated Heart: Chamula Canons of Style and Good Performance." Eds. R. Bauman and J. Sherzer. *Explorations in the Ethnography of Speaking.* London: Cambridge Univ. Press, 1974. 389-413.

Gough, Kathleen. "Implications of Literacy in Traditional China and India." Ed. Jack Goody. *Literacy in Traditional Societies.* New York: Cambridge Univ. Press, 1988.

Gruzinski, Serge. *La colonisation de l'imaginaire. Societés indigenes et occidentalisation dans le Mexique espagnole. XVIe - XVIIIe siecles.* Paris: Gallimard, 1968.

—. "Colonial Indian Maps in Sixteenth-Century Mexico." *Res* 13 (1987): 46-61.

Gumbrecht, Hans Ulrich. "The Body Versus the Printing Press: Media in the Early Modern Period, Mentalities in the Reign of Castile, and Another History of Literary Forms." *Poetics* 14 (1985): 209-227.

Harris, Roy. *The Origin of Writing.* Illinois: Open Court, 1986.

Havelock, Erick. *The Muse Learns to Write. Reflections on Orality and Literacy from Antiquity to the Present.* New Haven: Yale Univ. Press, 1986.

— *The Literate Revolution in Greece and Its Cultural Consequences.* Princeton: Princeton Univ. Press, 1982.

Icazbalceta, Joaquín Garcia. *Nueva colección de documentos para la historia de México. Códice Franciscano. Siglo XVI.* Mexico: Editorial Salvador Chavez Hayhoe, 1941.

Klor de Alva, Jorge. J. "Historicidad de los Coloquios de Sahagún." *Estudios de Cultura Náhuatl* 15 (1982): 147-184.

Kobayashi, José Maria. *La educación como conquista. Empresa franciscana en México.* Mexico: El Colegio de México, 1974.

Landa, Diego de. 1566. *Relación de las cosas de Yucatán*. Trans. A.M. Tozzer. Cambridge: Peabody Museum of American Archaeology and Ethnology, 1941.

León-Portilla, Miguel. "Náhuatl Literature." *Literatures. Supplement to the Handbook of Middle American Indians*. Ed. M. S. Edmonson. Austin: Univ. of Texas Press, 1985. 44-63.

León, Nicolas. "A Mazahua Catechism in Testera-Amerind Hieroglyphics." *American Anthropologist* 2 (1900): 723-740.

—. Toltecayotl. *Aspectos de la cultura náhuatl*. Mexico: Fondo de Cultura Económica, 1980.

— Miguel. *Los antiguos mexicanos a través de sus crónicas y cantares*. Mexico: Fondo de Cultura Económica, 1961.

Lévi-Strauss, Claude. *Tristes tropiques*. Paris: Plon, 1953.

López Cogolludo, Diego. 1688. *Historia de Yucatán*. Campeche: Comisión de Historia, 1954.

MacCormack, Sabine. "Atawallpa and the Book." Paper presented at the conference "The Book in the Americas." Providence: John Carter Brown Library, June 1987.

Malagón Barceló, Javier. "The Role of 'Letrado' in the Colonization of América." The Americas 18 (1961): 1-17.

Maravall, José Antonio. 1953 "Los 'hombres de saber' o letrados y la formación de la conciencia estamental." *Estudios de Historia del Pensamiento Español*. Madrid: Ediciones Cultura Hispánica, 1967. 345-380.

Menchú, Rigoberta. *I...Rigoberta Menchú. An Indian Woman in Guatemala*. Edited and introduced by E. Burgos-Debray. Translation A. Wright. London: Verso, 1984.

Mendieta, Fray Gerónimo de. 1596. *Historia Eclesiástica Indiana*. Mexico: Editorial Porrúa, S.A. 1971.

Mignolo, Walter. "Modeling the Letter. A Cross-Road between Semiotics and Literary Studies." *Semiotica* (Special issue on "Semiotic Modeling." Eds. M Anderson and F. Merrell), forthcoming.

—. "Anahuac y sus otros: la cuestión de la letra en el Nuevo Mundo." *Revista de Crítica Literaria Latinoamericana*, XIV, 28 (1988a): 29-54.

—. "La cuestión de la letra en la legitimación de la conquista." Paper presented at the conference Eroberung und Inbestznahme Americas im 16. Jahrhundert Rechtfertigung, Realitat und Literarische Reflexion. Eichstatt: Katolische Universitat, November 1988b.

—. "El mandato y la ofrenda: la descripción de la ciudad y provincia de Tlaxcala, de Diego Muñoz Camargo y las Relaciones de Indias." *Nueva Revista de Filología Hispánica*, XXXV, 2 (1987a): 451-484.

—. "Signs and their Transmission: The Question of the Book in the New World." Paper presented at the conference "The Book in the Americas." Providence: John Carter Brown Library, June 1987b.

—. "Historia, relaciones y tlatóllotl." *Filología* XXI, 2 (1986a) 154-177.

—. "La letra, la lengua, el territorio (o la crisis de los estudios literarios coloniales)." *Dispositio* 28-29 (1986b): 135-160.

—. "La escritura de la historia y la historia de la escritura." Paper presented at the Vigésimo Congreso del Instituto Internacional de Literatura Iberoamericana. Univ. of Texas, Austin, March 1981. Printed in *De la crónica a la nueva narrativa mexicana. Coloquio sobre literatura mexicana*. Eds., M. H. Forsters and J. Ortega. Mexico: Editorial Oasis, 1986c. 13-28.

—. "Cartas, crónicas y relaciones del descubrimiento y de la conquista." Coord. Luis Iñigo Madrigal. *Historia de la Literatura Hispanoamericana. Epoca Colonial*. Madrid: Cátedra, 1982. 56-125.

—. "El metatexto historiográfico y la historiografía indiana." *Modern Languages Notes* 96 (1981): 358-402).

Molina, Antonio de. *Vocabulario en lengua castellana y mexicana y mexicana y castellana*. Mexico: Santiago de Espinosa, 1571.

Motolinía (Fray Toribio de Benavente). *Epistolario* (1526-1555). Recopilado, paleografiado directamente de los originales y transcrito por el Lic. J.O. Aragón. Estudio preliminar, edición y notas de P. Lino Gómez Canedo. Mexico: Lauel, S.A., 1986.

—. 1541 *Historia de los Indios de Nueva España*. Ed. Fray Daniel Sánchez García. Barcelona: Herederos de Juan Gili, 1914.

Ong, Walter. *Orality and Literacy: The Technologizing of the Word*. New York: Methuen, 1982.

Pagden, Anthony. *The Fall of Natural Man. The American Indian and the Origins of Comparative Ethnology.* Cambridge: Cambridge Univ. Press, 1982.

Pané, Juan Ramón. *Relación acerca de las antigüedades de los indios. 1493.* Ed. Juan José Arrom. Mexico: Siglo XXI, 1974.

Parkes, M.B. "The Literacy of the Laity." Ed. D. Daiches and A. Thorlby. London: Aldous Books, 1973. 555-577.

Pattison, Robert. *On Literacy: The Politics of the Word from Homer to the Age of Rock.* New York: Oxford Univ. Press, 1982.

Phelan, John L. 1956. *El reino milenario de los franciscanos en el Nuevo Mundo.* Trad. J. Vázquez de Knauth. Mexico: UNAM, 1972.

Pou y Martí, José. "El libro perdido de las pláticas o coloquios de los doce primeros misioneros de México." *Estratto de la Miscellanea Fr. Ehrle III.* Roma: Tipografia del Senato, 1924.

Reinhard, Wolfgang. "Sprachbeherrschung und Weltherrqschaft. Sprache und Sprachwissenschaft in der europaischen Expansion." Ed. W. Reinhard. Humanismus und Neue Welt. Mitteilung XV der Kommission für Humanismusforschung. Acta Humaniora, 1988. 1-36.

Relación de Mezaltepeque. Diciembre de 1579. Archivo de Indias, Sevilla.

Relaciones de Teozacualco y Amoltepeque. Diciembre de 1580. Relaciones geográficas del siglo XVI: Antequera. Ed. René Acuña. Mexico: UNAM, 1984. 127-152.

Ricard, Robert. 1947. La conquista espiritual de México. *Ensayo sobre el apostolado y los métodos misioneros de las órdenes mendicantes en la Nueva España de 1523-1524 a 1572.* Trans. A.M. Garibay. Mexico: Fondo de Cultura Económica. 1986.

Ricoeur, Paul. "The Model of the Text: Meaningful Action Considered as a Text." *Social Research* 38 (1971): 529-562.

Robertson, Donald. *Mexican Manuscript Painting of the Colonial Period. The Metropolitan School.* New Haven: Yale Univ. Press, 1959.

Rogers, Francis M. *The Quest for Eastern Christians: Travels and Rumor in the Age of Discovery.* Minneapolis: Univ. of Minnesota Press, 1962.

Roys, Ralph L. *The Book of Chilam Balam of Chumayel*. Washington: Carnegie Foundation, 1933.

Sahagún, Bernardino de. 1564. *Los diálogos de 1524 según el texto de Fray Bernardino de Sahagún y sus colaboradores indígenas*. Edición facsimilar del manuscrito original. Paleografía, versión del Náhuatls, estudio y notas de Miguel León-Portilla. Mexico: UNAM, 1986.

—. 1564. "The Aztec-Spanish Dialogues of 1524." Trans. J.J. Klor de Alva. *Alcheringa/Ethnopoetics* 2 (1980): 52-195.

Said, Edward. *Beginnings. Intentions and Methods*. Baltimore: Johns Hopkins Univ. Press, 1975.

Sánchez de Aguilar, P. 1639. "Informe contra idolorum cultores del obispado de Yucatán." *Anales I*, 6 (1892): 13-122.

Sanders, James A. *Canon as Paradigm: From Sacred Story to Sacred Text*. Philadelphia: Fortress Press, 1987.

—. *Canon and Community. A Guide to Canonical Criticism*. Philadelphia: Fortress Press, 1984.

Sandoval, F.B. "Carta del P. Joseh de Acosta para el P. Joan de Tobar, de la Companía de Jesús"; "Respuesta del P. Joan de Tobar." Ed. Díaz-Thomé. *Estudios de historiografía de la Nueva España*. Mexico: El Colegio de Mexico, 1945.

Scharlau, Birgit. "Escrituras en contacto: el caso del México colonial." Actes du XVIIIeme. Congres International de Linguistique et Philologie Romanes, Hamburg, 1987a.

—. "The interaction of Aztec picture writing and European alphabetic writing in colonial Mexico." Manuscript, 1987b.

Scharlau B. and Munzel, M. Quellqay. *Mundliche Kultur und Schrifttradition bei Indianeren Lateinamerikas*. Frankfurt/Main: Campus Verlag, 1986.

Scribner, Sylvia and Michael Cole. *The Psychology of Literacy*. Cambridge: Harvard Univ. Press, 1981.

—. "Literacy in Three Metaphors." *American Journal of Education*. 93 (1984): 6-21.

Skeat, T.C. "Early Christian Book Production: Papyr and Manuscripts." Ed. G.N. Lame. *The Cambridge History of the Bible*. Vol. 2. New York: Cambridge Univ. Press, 1969. 54-79.

Spence, Jonathan D. *The Memory Palace of Matteo Ricci.* New York: Viking, 1984.

Tannen, Deborah. "The Oral/Literate Continuum in Discourse." Ed. D. Tannen. *Spoken and Written Language. Exploring Orality and Literacy.* New Jersey: Ablex Publishing, 1982. 1-17.

Teuber, Bernhard. "Europaisches und Amerikanisches im Fruhneuzeitlichen diskurs uber Stimme und Schrift." Paper presented at the Gehalten beim Deutschen Hispanistentag. Passau, February 1987 (mimeo).

Torquemada, Fray Juan de. 1615. *Monarquía Indiana.* Mexico: UNAM, 1975.

Tozzer, Alfred M. A. *Maya Grammar with Bibliography and Appraisement of the Works Noted.* Cambridge: Peabody Museum of American Archaeology and Ethnology, 1921. Vol IX.

Valadés, Fray Diego. *Rhetorica Christiana.* Perusa, 1579. Copy of the first edition at the John Carter Brown Library.

Wood, Ananda E. *Knowledge Before Printing and After: The Indian Tradition in Changing Kerala.* Delhi: Oxford Univ. Press, 1985.

Yates, Frances A. *The Art of Memory.* Chicago: Univ. of Chicago Press, 1966.

Yoneda, Keiko. *Los mapas de Cuhauhtinchan y la historia cartográfica prehispánica.* Mexico: Archivo General de la Nación, 1981.

CHAPTER 2:
NARRATION AND ARGUMENTATION
IN THE CHRONICLES OF THE
NEW WORLD

Antonio Gómez-Moriana

*(translated by Jane E. Gregg
and James V. Romano)*

In Spanish historiography, the year 1492 is doubly symbolic, for it coincides not only with the crowning of a long
process of national unification, but with the beginning of
Spain's territorial expansion on a global scale. National
unification was consummated with the armed conquest of
the last Islamic bastion in Iberian lands, the Arabic kingdom of Granada, and the expulsion of the Jews by decree.
The territorial expansion which would lead to the annexa-
tion of the earldoms of Rosellón and Cerdaña (1493), the
occupation of the kingdom of Naples (1503), the conquest
of Melilla (1497) and Orán (1509), and other incursions in
Africa and would later result in the religious wars in Europe with the subjugation of the Low Countries, began
with Christopher Columbus taking possession of the West
Indies in the name of the sovereigns of Castile and Aragón
on the twelfth of October 1492.

In this same year, the first Castilian or Spanish grammar was printed in Salamanca. Antonio de Nebrija dedicated it to Queen Isabella with words that demonstrated a
national conscience and an early interpretation of the past

and future of Spain, an entity which language would serve
as "companion of the empire." In the "Dedication," Nebrija indicated that "the scattered members and pieces of
Spain, which were spread about, were consolidated and
joined in a body and unity of kingdom." ("los miembros e
pedaços de España, que estauan por muchas partes derra-
madas, se reduxeron e aiuntaron en un cuerpo e unidad de
reino"). For Nebrija, this process, which was above all the
work of "divine goodness and providence," coincided with
the formation and development of the Castilian language
and would "reach the monarchy and peace that we enjoy."
It was also the outcome of the "industry, work and diligence" of the crown. Nebrija concludes:

> So that after purging the Christian religion, for
> which we are friends of God, or reconciled with Him;
> after the enemies of our faith have been vanquished
> through war and force of arms, from which our own
> received so much harm and feared even greater; after
> the justice and execution of the laws that unite us and
> allow us to live equally in this great company that
> we call the kingdom and republic of Castile; there is
> nothing left but the flowering of the arts of peace.
> Among the first ones is that which language teaches
> us.[1]

In *The Prince*, Machiavelli offers a historical interpretation similar to that of Nebrija, though putting much more
emphasis on the political dimension and thus unmasking
Ferdinand of Aragon's use of religion that turned him
into a "new prince":

> Nothing brings a prince more prestige than the ac-
> complishment of great deeds and giving uncommon
> examples of himself. In our time there is King Ferdi-
> nand of Aragon, the present king of Spain. The latter
> can practically be called a new prince for from being
> a weak king he has become, through fame and glory,
> the first king of the Christians; and if you consider
> his actions, you will find all of them to be great and
> some extraordinary. In the beginning of his reign he
> laid siege to Granada: and that undertaking was the
> foundation of his State [...] Besides this, in order to
> be able to undertake even greater campaigns, always
> making use of religion, he turned toward a pious cru-
> elty, expelling and eliminating the *marranos* from
> his Kingdom. There could not be a more pitiless or
> more uncommon example from the latter. Under the

> same mantle of religion he attacked Africa; he car-
> ried out the Italian Campaign; he recently attacked
> France; and in this manner he has always performed
> and carried out great projects which have always
> kept his subjects in a state of suspense and admiration
> and intent on their outcome. And these moves of his
> have followed so closely one upon another and in
> such a way that he has never allowed people time
> and opportunity in between those moves to be able to
> quietly counter them. (Machiavelli 119-120)

In order to understand this convergence of the linguistic, religious and political dimensions in the symbolic date
of 1492, one must go back to the moment when Spain was
"born" as a modern State and to the process of gestation of
this Nation-State around the last centuries of the so-called
"Reconquest." Only in this way can we understand the dynamic impulse that propelled the young Spanish State to
the American adventure as a "historical enterprise," one
that is realized under the sign of a "religious mission" entrusted to it by the Pope as the "Vicar of Christ [of *God*] on
earth."

The birthdate of the Spanish Nation-State can be fixed
as the eighteenth of October 1469 (another highly symbolic
date but much less cultivated in Spanish historiography).
Its place of birth is Valladolid, for it was there on that date
when the two great Christian kingdoms of Castile and
Aragón were united through the marriage of Isabella I of
Castile and Fernando V of Aragón. We are in the last
stages of the Middle Ages, a period that witnessed the rise
of many national European blocks as monarchies emanci-
pating themselves from the Roman Pontiff and the Christian Emperor.[2] Hence, to better understand the dynamics
that gives rise to the new State, it is important to analyze
the significance of the marriage that was arranged between
Isabella of Castile and Ferdinand of Aragón, as well as the
struggle undertaken immediately thereafter against the
Arabic kingdom of Granada.

Let us begin by focusing our attention, however briefly,
on that moment immediately prior to the constitution and
consolidation of the Spanish State, and examine the situation to which that marriage will respond, the same context
out of which the new State will emerge as a (future)
"project" conceived as a "historical mission." Once the
Arabs establish themselves on the Iberian peninsula, we
witness a fragmentation of those lands into small king-

doms, some Christian, others Islamic. These kingdoms live in a continuous struggle of territorial expansion, and establish their alliances according to the strategic convenience of the moment rather than through religious beliefs. In Toledo, we witness a major cultural undertaking in which the three great religions that live side by side during the Middle Ages in the Iberian peninsula—Judaism, Christianity and Islam—collaborate closely. Despite this collaboration, there is a moment when the Christian kingdoms begin to develop the "conscience" of a common "religious" mission and the expulsion of the Moslems from Iberian lands is conceived as a type of "Christian crusade" against the "infidels." This idea is launched by Pope Innocent III when he gives the designation of "Christian cause" with corresponding Crusade bulls to the wars that Alfonso VIII, king of Castile, was preparing against the Arabs. In that enterprise, Castile was joined by the kingdoms of Navarra, León and Aragón as well as the other kingdoms of Christian Europe that sent troops in a common undertaking that would be crowned by a victory at Las Navas de Tolosa (1212). The rich booty obtained there and the ever-more-present idea of a "holy war" instigate a series of military alliances and marriages that contribute to the progressive unification of the Christian kingdoms. In that manner the multitude of Christian kingdoms (Galicia, Asturias, León, Navarra, Castile, Aragón, Catalonia and Portugal) slowly begin to contract until there emerges two great blocks, Castile and Aragón, united in 1469 by the marriage of Ferdinand and Isabella on the one hand, and Portugal on the other. The formation of the Spanish State and its victory in Granada can thus be seen as the crowning of a secular undertaking stemming from the Papal bull granted by Innocent III to launch the idea of the Castilian conquest as a "Christian cause," as a Crusade.[3]

The idea of the Reconquest thus constitutes the bonding element of the various Christian kingdoms of the Iberian peninsula in a dynamic process that would lead to the union of Castile (which had fused under its crown the old kingdoms of Galicia, Asturias, León and Castile) and Aragón (which for its part had united Navarra, Aragón and Catalonia). The idea of the Reconquest also generates the political and religious ideal that turns those same kings who had earlier called themselves "emperors"—in order to encompass under their crowns Christians, Jews and Moslems—into chieftains (*caudillos*) of the "crusade against the infidels." Their ideal becomes one of "purity of faith" in their territories, and their expansionist drive is confused (ideologically) with the expansion of Christianity precisely at a time when it was witnessing a "decline" in Europe.

During the first centuries of the period that Spanish historiography designates in general terms as the Reconquest, Jews, Christians and Moslems lived side by side in each of the kingdoms established on Iberian lands, and temples were erected for the three faiths. Yet, from the moment of the idea of the "crusade against the infidels," the Moslems and Jews living in "Christian territory" will have no other alternative but to convert to Christianity or escape. Under such circumstances, "false conversions" proliferate. In 1478, the Catholic kings create inquisitional tribunals charged with the difficult task of combatting false conversions and watching over "the religious and social unity" of the new State. A political-religious institution now espouses the domestic politics of those kings who considered themselves guarantors of their subjects' "purity of faith." Freed from the "inner enemies" of the Faith through the vigilance of those tribunals, it is not surprising that they later seek its expansion, thus complying to the letter with the religious mission that had been assigned to them by the Pope, the "Vicar of Christ on earth."

Proof of the interest shown by Rome in the total elimination of the Arab presence in the Spanish territories is a series of Crusade bulls that precede and inspire the conquest of Granada. Already on November 13, 1479 (ten years after national unification), Pope Sixtus IV promulgates the first bull. That gesture is repeated with the concession of new privileges and new indulgences in 1482, 1485, 1487, 1489 and 1491. The chroniclers relate that when news of the capitulation of the kingdom of Granada to the Catholic kings reached Rome, bells tolled and the "Christian triumph" was celebrated with religious and secular feasts lasting several days.

Having followed the genesis of the Spanish Nation and its organization as a State in the modern sense, we may better understand the project that the new nation proposes to carry out. We recall that the nation was formed under the sign of a "religious struggle," a crusade against the "infidels" who had settled in its territories, and we have seen the attainment of territorial-religious unification of the nascent State's external and internal borders. It seems as if the *homo hispanus* had identified himself to such an extent with the chivalric ideal of the crusade that, after having achieved an interior "purity of faith," he would seek to impose it the world over (see Bataillon, especially 55-65).

Immediately after the conquest of Granada there are military expeditions to the north of Africa, where between 1497 and 1512 the Spaniards conquer fortified towns such as Melilla, Alcazaquivir, Oran, Tripoli, and others. As a result of these expeditions, military bases for Spanish fleets are established for their defense and expansion into southern Italy, thus guaranteeing Spanish domination of the Mediterranean ("Mare nostrum" ["Our sea"]), all under the pretext of the "Turkish peril" to Christianity. When the Protestant Reformation surfaces, Charles V fights it with the same zeal with which his predecessors had fought against the Crescent in and outside of Spain. The same policies continue with Philip II, who manages to ruin the Spanish economy in the religious wars in Europe and in the expedition against the Turks—which ends with a victory in Lepanto (1571). The struggle of the Spanish infantry in the Low Countries and the "Invincible Armada" sent against England are also military expeditions undertaken under the sign of a frustrated religious-political expansion of the great "Catholic power," a power that the Hapsburgs used to oppose the Protestant Reformation.

But it is in the conquest and colonization of the New World where the ideological identification of the Spanish policy of expansion is identified most clearly with the Catholic Church's ideals of an evangelizing expansion. Just over six months after Columbus steps into the "New World," the Spaniards are granted a bull "Inter cœtera" by the (Spanish) Pope Alexander VI for the purpose of "setting up missions" in the "discovered" territories. It was a kind of *missio canonica* which charged the Spanish Kings with preaching the gospel and converting the so-called "Indians" to the Catholic faith. The extent to which the Catholic Kings assumed literally the "religious" mission granted to it by Rome can be seen in the title designating their role in this "Christian cause": Royal Apostolic Vicar (*Regio Vicariato Apostólico*), a purely religious title through which the Kings assume a religious mission as "vicars" delegated by Rome. If one considers the Church's development and expansion in the New World by the early seventeenth century, one also sees how closely the Catholic Kings followed the charge received from Rome. A little over a century of "missionary" work had seen the establishment of five metropolitan Holy Sees, with twenty-nine subordinate episcopates; the number of missionaries that accompanied conquistadors, settlers, adventurers and gold-seekers in the New World had also reached many thousand, while the number of churches, convents and cathedrals erected was considerable.[4]

I will not dwell here on the well-known series of abuses committed in the exercise of this "religious mission." More presently significant is the division of opinions and property claims of the West Indies based on the historical mission.

Thus, for Father Bartolomé de Las Casas and for Pedro Mártir de Anglería, the Indians were subjected to horrible slavery in the name of God and the gospel. For Bartolomé de Las Casas what the Spaniards bring to the heart of Indians is not God's law but greed, envy and anger. In Columbus's description that recalls Ovid's *Metamorphoses*, the Indians live in a purely natural state.[5]

For other authors such as Francisco López de Gómara, the chronicler of Cortés, the colonization of America signifies the epic of "the redemption of the most primitive people on earth" ("la redención de los pueblos más primitivos de la tierra") who until then had lived with "cannibalism, poligamy, polytheism, not free of cruel human sacrifices" ("canibalismo, poligamia, politeísmo no libre de cruentos sacrificios humanos"). With Biblical quotes, the conquest of America is described as "the liberation of the Indians from the slavery of Egypt" ("la liberación de los indios de la esclavitud de Egipto") and it is likened to the "conquering of the vineyard of the Lord" ("conquista de la vid del Señor") and to the "conquest of the promised land" ("toma de posesión de la tierra prometida") by the "chosen people of God" ("pueblo elegido de Dios") (see López de Gómara's *Historia general de las Indias*). In one of his descriptions of the military strategy of the conquistadors, Martín Fernández Enciso takes literally the Biblical text of the conquest of Jericho, thus underscoring the "divine election" ("elección divina") of the Spanish people:

> And then Joshua commanded those [officers] of the
> first city, which was Jericho, to take possession of
> the land which the Lord God had given them to pos-
> sess.

> E después envió Josué a requerir a los de la primera
> ciudad, que era Jericó, que le dejasen e diesen aquella
> tierra, pues era suya porque se la había dado Dios.
> (see *Suma de Geografía*)

Indeed, before being engaged in battle the Indians were
read a *requerimiento* (requisition or injunction), a theological treatise that evoked "the history of Man's health,"
from the creation of the world and the first sin to his redemption through Christ and the founding of the Church,
depository of such redemption and of the authority of
Christ. The Pope as Vicar of Christ and as head of that
Church had entrusted those lands to the King and Queen
of Castile so that the acceptance of baptism on the part of
the inhabitants and the acknowledgment of the authority
of the Spaniards above them was exacted in their name
and authority. The answer received by the missionaries
and conquistadors from the people of the Sinú region (of
present day Colombia) is well known. Gonzalo Fernández
de Oviedo recalls their reaction upon hearing the *requerimiento* that they recognize the authority that the Pope
had given the Kings of Castile over them and that they accept Christian baptism:

> those Indians agreed that there was only one God,
> but as to the claim that the Pope was the master of
> the universe, and that he had granted those lands to
> the Kings of Castile, they said that the Pope must
> have been drunk when he did so, for he was giving
> what did not belong to him. And that the King who
> asked for and accepted such favor must be crazy, for
> he asked for what belonged to others.

> Estaban de acuerdo aquellos indios en que no havía
> sino un Dios; pero en lo que decía que el Papa era señor
> del Universo y que él había fecho merced de aquellas
> tierras a los reyes de Castilla, dixeron que el Papa
> debiera estar borracho cuando lo fizo, pues daba lo
> que no era suyo. Y que el rey que pedía y que tomaba
> tal merced debía ser algún loco, pues pedía lo que era
> de otros[6]

The disputed vision of the conquest, such as the controversy instigated by the texts of Father Bartolomé de Las Casas at the University of Salamanca around the *títulos de dominio* (titles of domain) that legitimize the presence of the Spaniards in the New World and the controversy between Father Las Casas and Father Sepúlveda over the nature of the Indian, demonstrates a shared mentality: the existence of a "religious mission" in the New World, be it well or poorly carried out on the part of the Spaniards, and a description of its inhabitants that insists on its differences vis-à-vis the Spanish model (either to idealize them as *bon sauvage* or to condemn them for their "barbarism"). Their positions therefore do not differ in the basic assumptions with respect to the Indians. They only differ in the selection of the "facts" narrated in accordance with an interpretative argumentation of a conquest whose legitimacy no one doubts, not even those who insist on highlighting its disastrous effects. An analysis that limits itself to the study of the narrative contents of this textual corpus can only contribute to the dualist, Manichaean position which has dominated for centuries the historiography dealing with the Spanish presence in America.[7]

Based on discursive analysis, I shall now attempt to outline the change of mentality that takes place in Spain, a mentality that produces and consumes these texts. To do so, we shall pay more attention to the organization of the narrative than to that which is narrated. Only in this manner can we go beyond the explicit "information" selected by the text, to the implicit that the same text conceals more or less consciously (intentionally). Ultimately, it is a question of searching for that collective unconscious repressed by the active presence of a super ego imposing an ideology at the service of the interests of hegemonic groups of imperial Spain, and which, because of the inertia characteristic of ideologies, continues until our day.

Les us take as an example the first vision of the Indian as described by Columbus in his *Diario* ("Diary"). With few variants, this text, whose original has not been conserved, has been transmitted to us both in the compilation of Father Bartolomé de Las Casas[8] and in the reelaboration of Hernando Colón, who uses it as a base for much of the biography that he wrote of his father under the title of *Historia del almirante* ("History of the Admiral").[9] The entry dated Thursday, October 11, 1492, in which the happenings of the 12th are also related without transition, ends in the following manner:

> The words that follow are the formal words of the Admiral, in the book of his first voyage and discovery of these Indies. "I [says he], to gain great friendship, for I realized that they were people who could be freed and converted to our Sacred Faith better with love than by force, gave some of them colored caps and some glass beads which they put around their necks, and other things of little value which gave them much pleasure and they ended up being ours to an amazing extent. Thereafter, they came swimming to the boats of the ships where we were and they brought us parrots and balls of cotton thread and spears and many other things and exchanged them for other things which we gave them such as little glass beads and bells. Finally, they took everything we offered and gave of what they had willingly. But I thought that they were poor people who lacked so much; they were all as naked as their mothers made them, even the women, although I only saw a very young one and all I saw were all lads for I did not see any older than thirty. They were well made, with very beautiful bodies and very beautiful faces; their hair was short and almost as thick as the bristles in a horse's tail; their hair comes down to their eyebrows, except for a few strands in the back, which are long, and which they never cut; some of them painted themselves blackish and they are of the color of canaries, neither black nor white, and some of them paint themselves white and some red, and some in whatever they find, and some paint their faces, and some their whole body, and some only their eyes, and some only their nose. They don't bear arms, nor do they know them, for I showed them swords and they grabbed them by the blade, and cut themselves out of ignorance. They have no iron; their spears are like poles without metal points, some with a fish tooth on the end, and others with other things. They all are in general of good stature and size, and of good expression; well built; I saw some with signs of wounds on their bodies, and I asked them with gestures what they were, and they showed me how these people came from other nearby islands who wanted to take them, and they defended themselves; and I thought, and think, that here they come from firm land to take them captive. They should make good servants, and of a good nature, as I see that they quickly answer all that is said to them, and I believe that easily they

> could become Christians, as it seems they did not belong to any sect. I, God willing, will bring back to Your Highness from here at the time of my departure, six so that they learn to speak. I saw no animals of any kind on this island, except parrots." All these are the words of the Admiral.[10]

Before the quote in direct style that introduces the phrase "the words that follow are the formal words of the Admiral," and closes with the solemn formula "all these are the words of the Admiral," Las Casas compiles the happenings of that day in the habitual form: an account told in the epic preterite with quotations in indirect style:

> At two hours past midnight, land was sighted [...]. They worked the sails [...], waiting until daylight on Friday, when they arrived at an islet of the Lucayos, as it was called in the language of the Guanahaní Indians. Then they saw naked people, and the Admiral left for land in the armed boat, with Martín Alonso Pinzón and Vicente Anes, his brother, who was capitain of the Niña. The Admiral took out the royal flag [...]. Once on land they saw very green trees and much water and many kinds of fruit. The Admiral called to the two captains and the others to come onto land, and to Rodrigo Descovedo, clerk-recorder of the armada, and to Rodrigo Sánchez de Segovia, and told them to administer to him by faith and testimony, as he would take before them all, and as he in fact took, possession of the island for the King and Queen, his monarchs [...]. Then many people of the island gathered there.[11]

In his *Historia de las Indias* [*History of the New World*], Bartolomé de Las Casas proceeds in an almost identical manner as far as the direct quotes of the Admiral are concerned. At the end he adds anew the quasi-liturgical formula: "all these are the words of the Admiral." But in addition to the quote in direct style we find here an argumentative interpretation that picks up in an indirect style the same sentences of Hernando Colón, thus bringing to light Las Casas's intention: to show that the inhabitants of that island were those "beings" that Plinius, Ponponius Mela, Strabon, Virgil, Saint Isidore, Bœcius and other authors call "quite holy and happy" ("santísimos y felicísimos"). Here is the summary that, following that purpose, precedes the literal quotation in direct style:

> The Admiral, seeing them so good and simple, and
> that as much as they could were liberally hos-
> pitable, and as such were so pacific, gave them many
> glass beads and bells, and some colored caps and
> other things, with which they felt contented and
> enriched. (I, 204)[12]

Against the accusations of aggression Las Casas insists on the pacifism of these people who do not feel ashamed of their nakedness, so that according to Las Casas "it seemed that the state of innocence had not been lost or had been restored" ("parecía no haberse perdido o haberse restituido el estado de inocencia"). Against Sepúlveda who, on the basis of Aristotle's texts, considered the Indians to be inferior beings "without a soul," and thus were considered to be obliged to serve the Spaniards, Las Casas underscores their human qualities. In fact, it seems that the text seeks to prove that they are endowed with the three faculties that distinguish man from beast in Aristotelian-Thomist scholasticism: memory, understanding and will. He also highlights their favorable disposition to becoming Christians for they "did not belong to any sect." This last consideration is paramount because it deals with the prospects of "evangelizing" new people rather than destroying infidels. For Las Casas, the Spanish presence became legitimized as the fulfillment of the evangelizing mission conferred to the Spaniards by Rome. Sepúlveda, on the contrary, seemed not to have fully understood that if the Indians were not human beings, neither were they subjects apt to receive baptism. The title of property over those lands, which was based on the Spaniards' "evangelizing mission," thus disappeared for the sake of a greater liberty in order to submit its people to slavery (see Menéndez Pidal and Gómez-Moriana, "Entre la philologie"). Las Casas ultimately uses this text as an authoritative argument: he identifies it, defining the pragmatics of its enunciation at the same time that he seeks to distance himself from it, as Columbus's report directed to the King and Queen of Spain. This important fact regarding the internal receiver of Columbus's report is evident in the text itself:

> I, God willing, will bring back to Your Highness from
> here at the time of my departure, six so that they
> learn to speak....

However contrary to what happens in the *Diario*'s formula of presentation, which merely insists that it reproduces the "formal words of the Admiral," the formula of presentation of those words in the *Historia de las Indias* reads like this:

> Who [the Admiral], in this book of his first voyage, written for the Catholic Kings, says as follows...

> el cual [el Almirante], en el libro desta su primera navegación, que escribió para los Reyes Católicos, dice de aquesta manera (Las Casas 204).

The circumstances of its enunciation makes of the cited text a reliable document on which Las Casas can base his affirmations about the conditions of the Indians prior to their corruption at the hands of the Spaniards.

In his *Historia del almirante* ("History of the Admiral"), Hernando Colón interprets these texts practically in the same terms. In Chapter XXIII, entitled "How the Admiral Stepped on Land and Took Possession of It in the Name of the Catholic Kings" ("Cómo el Almirante salió a tierra y tomó posesión de aquélla en nombre de los Reyes Católicos"), Columbus's text about the condition of the Indians has been summarized as follows:

> This feast and gaiety was attended by many Indians, and when the Admiral saw that they were peaceful and tranquil people, and of great simplicity, he gave them some red caps and things of little value which were more highly regarded by them than if they had been high-priced stones.

> Asistieron a esta fiesta y alegría muchos indios, y viendo el Almirante que eran gente mansa, tranquila y de gran sencillez, les dió algunos bonetes rojos y cosas de poco valor, que fueron más estimadas por ellos que si fueran piedras de mucho precio. (112)

The transformation of the common phrase "precious stones" ("piedras preciosas") into "high-priced stones" ("piedras de mucho precio") demonstrates that in his reading Hernando Colón, contrary to Las Casas, has shifted the emphasis to the point of converting the idyllic scene, the old topic of the *locus amœnus* which dominates the whole scene surrounding the act of taking possession of the utopian island into a market scene of the exchange of goods.

Reading the text as economic discourse, as suggested by the reading given by Hernando Colón of his father's diary, what we see is a confirmation of that reality which has been pointed out by Beatriz Pastor from a different perspective.[13] Moreover, from the perspective of discourse analysis, I see that in the estimation of such goods, as expressed by the numerous adjectives in the text, there is a greater insistence on exchange value than on use value and the given is compared with the received using criteria of "profitability."

Let us begin with the syntactic organization of the narrative sequences in the words attributed with so much insistence to the Admiral by Father Bartolomé de Las Casas. The alternation of the verb tenses corresponding to what Harald Weinrich calls the "narrated world" with those corresponding to the "commented world" (in his book *Tempus. Besprochene und erzählte Welt*) permits us to see immediately that in the first part there is a predominance of verbs of action in the preterite, in the first person singular (Columbus) and the third person plural (the people of the island), while in the second sequence verbs in the imperfect or in the present predominate. Finally, in a third sequence we find modalizations such as "I believe" ("creo") or "should be" ("deben ser") as well as verbs in the conditional or the future tense.

The first sequence, with a predominance of verbs of action in the preterite, comprises a series of final sentences, some explicit ("in order to gain their friendship"), others implicit in copulatives that unite the action with the intentional result of the same ("I gave them... and they ended up being ours to an amazing extent"; "they brought us... and exchanged them"). The verbs corresponding to these final sentences are distributed in a way that could be summed up in an alternation between "give" ("dar") and "do" ("hacer") with its equivalents.

The structure of the sentences observed in this first sequence of the text corresponds precisely to the contractual formulas codified in Roman Law. They also correspond to our present division of commerce, depending on whether it deals with the exchange of goods, the exchange of services, or a mixed exchange:

I give	in order that	you give	(*do*	*ut*	*des*)
I give	in order that	you do	(*do*	*ut*	*facias*)
I do	in order that	you do	(*facio*	*ut*	*facias*)
I do	in order that	you give	(*facio*	*ut*	*des*)

In addition, as we have indicated, the adjectives that qualify the objects of that continuous exchange limit themselves to comparing what is given to what is received:

> I, to gain great friendship, [...] gave some of them colored caps and some glass beads [...] and other things of little value....

> [T]hey brought us parrots and balls of cotton thread and spears and many other things and exchanged them for other things which we would give them such as little glass beads and bells.

All of these comparisons lead to a double consequence: the first, which is implicit in the comparison itself in view of the unevenness that it establishes between the given and the received, is that of a "profitable" exchange; the second, which is explicit in the text and is included with some insistence, is that the final result of this commercial exchange consists of the possession of those people ("they ended up being ours to an amazing extent"). In addition, there is established an equivalence between friendship, self-surrender and conversion ("to gain great friendship, for I realized that they were people who could be freed and converted to our Sacred Faith better with love than by force").

The second sequence, dealing with the "nature and customs of those people," as Hernando Colón titles Chapter XXIV of his *Historia del almirante*, which refers concretely to the second sequence of Columbus's *Diario*, discussed herein, begins with a summary of the previous one in a consecutive manner ("Finally, they took everything we offered and gave of what they had willingly"). This is followed by the descriptive part, with frequent use of a rhetorical device common in the discourse of the Golden Age: the litotes ("they were all naked... I did not see any older than thirty [...]. They don't bear arms, nor do they know them [...]. They have no iron"). Finally, interconnected with the previous ones, this sequence closes with obsevations belonging to a European Renaissance man.

Those observing attest to the physical beauty ("They were well made, with very beautiful bodies and very beautiful faces. [...] They all are in general of good stature and size, and of good expression; well built"), and to the hair style and the colors with which they adorn themselves, but they also express surprise and astonishment toward female nudity. The conclusion of this second sequence, which also serves as a unifying nexus with the third and final one, seems to explain the functionality of all of these observations. Moreover, it connects with the first sequence, thus providing an overall textual coherence.

> They must be good servants and of a good disposition, for I see that they soon say everything that I told them, and I believe that they would easily become Christians, for it seemed to me that they did not belong to any sect.

Elsewhere, I have tried to show the impact that a discourse proper to an economic, bourgeois mentality can have on the discourse of official ideology, including the (neo)scholastic that informs the political and religious thought of Imperial Spain precisely at a time when there is an attempt to restore an already obsolete Medieval mentality. Not even Don Quijote, despite his unbridled idealism, can escape the contagion of his chivalric discourse by the discourse of economic calculation (ever more hegemonic, even if it does not as yet constitute an "official" discourse). It is possible that in the American adventure there was not the quixoticism that the Generation of 1898 tried to see in it by its (economic?) "reappraisal." Perhaps this diagnosis was simply due to the coincidence of the moment of their meditations after the independence of America (they called it "colonial disaster") with the fourth centenary of the publication of *Don Quijote* (Gómez-Moriana, "Discourse Pragmatics"). An adequate answer to this question would entail an analysis of many more texts from the period. For the time being I shall limit myself to a couple of documents dealing with the colonization of America (which appear in the Appendix of this volume). Like Colón's text, in his project of idealization of the "enterprise," these documents are not able to hide entirely that ever increasing presence of an economic discourse that corrodes the missionary discourse of those politicians concerned with "the health of the soul." As with the *Curriculum* of Miguel de Cervantes published in *Autobiography in Early Modern Spain* (Hispanic Issues Vol. 2), these documents come from the Archivo de Indias in Seville, and demonstrate that constant contagion of the "missionary spirit" by "economic discourse." They all deal with agreements or directives given to those who were sent to the West Indies (Columbus and Cortés in particular) by the Crown, and of the (missionary) interpretation of the "enterprise of the Indies." An analysis such as that which we are doing of Columbus's text demonstrates the same symptoms of contagiousness in the very (contractual) structure of these texts. To demonstrate that we are dealing with a constant, let us examine two more documents. The first of them, which is dated March 1485, refers to the struggle that Ferdinand and Isabella are preparing against the kingdom of Granada; the second, dated September 1632, refers to the evangelization of America. The first of these documents is the answer sent by Ferdinand V of Aragón to Pope Innocent VIII through his ambassadors in Rome, Antonio Graddino and Francisco Rojas, in reply to the Pope's desire to retain for the Apostolic See a third of the money obtained through the Crusade bull which he had just decreed in favor of the struggle against the Arabs in Granada (*do ut des*). After the King states that in that fight he sought neither power nor riches, the document goes on:

> But the desire we have to serve God and the zeal toward his holy Catholic faith, makes us postpone all interests and makes us forget the continuous toils and dangers that accrue to us for this cause. And while in a position of being able to safeguard not only our own treasures, but of having many more from the moors, who would voluntarily grant them to us for the sake of peace, we reject [the treasures] that are offered to us and we spill our own, hoping only for the advance of the holy Catholic faith and for the elimination of the peril which Christianity has here at its doors if these infidels from the kingdom of Granada are not extirpated and thrown out of Spain. (Góñiz Gaztambide 672)[14]

The second document that I transcribe was written by a commission named by King Philip IV to make a strong case to the Apostolic Nunciate in Madrid regarding the "right" of the Spanish Crown to maintain certain privileges (*regalías*) that Rome sought to abolish. In it, the ser-

vices rendered by the Spanish Crown to the Apostolic See
in the defense and propagation of the Faith are evoked.
Rome was expected to honor its commitments by maintaining such privileges (*facio ut facias*).

Point 38 of the document prepared by the above-mentioned commission says:

> Since this Crown spends its treasures and uses all of
> its powers in defense of the faith, and has propa-
> gated our holy religion through so many kingdoms
> and faraway provinces, bringing the Spanish nation
> other new worlds to the obedience of the Apostolic
> See. ("Parecer de la Junta sobre abusos en Roma y
> Nunciatura" in Aldea 143-354)[15]

It is in reality a historical constant that lasts until recent
times, plunging Spanish historiography in an ever-more
delirious interpretation of the past. For the delirium of the
"discursive interpenetration" grows to the same extent
that the economic mentality occupies an ever more hegemonic space in our Modernity. Let us end with an example, a (confessional?) text by Marcelino Menéndez y Pelayo,
taken from the second volume of his *Historia de los heterodoxos españoles:*

> *I* understand quite well that these things will cause a
> piteous smile in politicians and financial experts
> who, seeing us poor, down and humiliated at the end
> of the Seventeenth Century, do not find words con-
> temptuous enough for a nation that fought against
> half of conspiring Europe, and this [it was doing]
> neither to round out its territory nor to obtain war
> compensation, but for theological ideas... the most
> useless thing in the world. How much better would it
> have been to weave cloth and to allow Luther to
> come and go where he wished.... Never, from the
> time of Judas Maccabee, was there a people which
> for so many reasons could think of itself as a people
> chosen to be the sword and the arm of God; and they
> referred and subordinated everything, even their
> dreams of grandeur and universal monarquy to this
> supreme object: *fiat unum ovile et unus pastor* [Let
> there be one sheep pen and one shepherd]. (II, 328-
> 329)[16]

NOTES

[1] Assi que, después de repurgada la cristiana religion, por la cual somos amigos de Dios, o reconciliados con él; después de los enemigos de nuestra fe vencidos por guerra y fuerça de armas, de donde los nuestros recebían tantos daños y temían mucho maiores; después de la justicia y essecución de las leies que nos aiuntan y hazen bivir igualmente en esta gran compañía que llamamos reino y república de Castilla; no queda ia otra cosa sino que florezcan las artes de la paz. Entre las primeras, es aquélla que nos enseña la lengua.

[2] At the same time, it would be a mistake to explain the rise of the Spanish Nation-State simply within this frame, for its meaning seems to be precisely the opposite. Jean-Jacques Chevallier has summarized this process as follows in *L'Idée de Nation*:

"In spite of the survival of City-States, small in dimension but with appreciable commercial and political power, in spite of the desires for ephemeral achievements of unlimited Empires, what emerges irresistibly from the end of the Middle Ages to the beginning of the Modern Age (the Renaissance and the Reformation) are the great monarchical Nation-States: France, England, Spain. The notion of sovereignty, developed by Jean Bodin, would become their sturdy juridical-political armor. Sovereignty of the king, with or without Parliament, would be identified with sovereignty of the State."

"En dépit des survivances de Cités-Létats, aux dimensions petites mais à la puissance commerciale et politique appréciable, en dépit des velléités ou des réalisations éphémères d'Empires démesurés, on voit émerger irrésistiblement, de la fin du Moyen Age au début des Temps modernes (Renaissance et Reforme), les grands États-Nations de forme monarchique: France, Angleterre, Espagne. La notion de souveraineté, doctrinée par Jean Bodin, deviendra leur robuste armature juridico-politique. Souveraineté du roi, en Parlement ou non, et souveraineté de l'État tendront à l'indentification" (50).

[3] In his *Historia de la bula de la cruzada en España*, José Góñiz Gaztambide makes the terms "Reconquest" and "Crusade" synonymous within the context of the Spanish Middle Ages. In doing so, he points out the traditional use of the "Struggle against the infidel" in terms of the eight centuries of the Arabic presence in the Iberian Peninsula. Though, as he attempts to document the use of the word "crusade," he is content to affirm that "it already appears in the first half of the thirteenth century" (151). This comment, I believe, confirms my thesis that Pope Innocent III put forth this idea at the beginning of the thirteenth century.

[4] For more information on the titles of the Spanish Kings and their missionary activities, see Egaña and Rouco-Varela.

[5] Paraphrasing Ovid, Pedro Mártir de Anglería spoke of the Indians in the following terms in his *De orbe novo* (1530): "Without laws, without books, without judges, they naturally did right... content with nature's bounty... as is said of the Golden Age." ("Sine legibus, sine libris, sine iudicibus suapte natura rectum colunt... sylvestribus fructibus contentos... uti legitur de aurea aetate").

The words by Columbus that we will comment on in the pages that follow also echo similar (classical) texts as it describes the conditions of the Indians. Later, Sir Thomas More would locate his *Utopia* in America, and the Jesuits would achieve theirs in the settlements of converted Indians (*reducciones*) in Paraquay, for example. This myth, then, first guides a "reading" of "reality" and, later its "realization."

[6] Gonzalo Fernández de Oviedo transcribes and comments on the text of the *requerimiento* in Book 29, Chapter 7 of his *Historia general y natural de las Indias* (III, 227+). This (unlikely) anecdote is found in Picón Salas, 44.

[7] This polemical vision still predominates in our times. Not even Todorov could escape it in his *La Conquête de l'Amérique: La question de l'autre.*

[8] I cite from Columbus's *Diario*, compiled by Bartolomé de Las Casas, contained in Fernández de Navarrete's *Colección de los viajes y descubrimientos que hicieron por mar los españoles desde fines del siglo XV*, and currently available in *Obras de Don Martín Fernández de Navarrete* (I, 86+).

[9] Hernando Colón's text is found in *Crónicas de América*, I, ed. Luis Arranz. Columbus's text is echoed in the *Instructions* (*Instrucciones*) reproduced in the Apendix of the present volume and in his correspondence, especially in the "Letter to Luis Santángel, February 15-March 14, 1493" ("Carta a Luis de Santángel de 15 de febrero-14 de marzo de 1493"), in which we find a description of Indians using the terminology of the *Diary*. This letter can be found in Fernández de Navarrete (167+).

[10] Esto que sigue son palabras formales del Almirante, en su libro de su primera navegación y descubrimiento de estas Indias. "Yo [dice él], porque nos tuviesen mucha amistad, porque conoscí que era gente que mejor se libraría y convertiría a nuestra Santa Fe con amor que no por fuerza, les di a algunos de ellos unos bonetes colorados y unas cuentas de vidrios que se ponían al pezcuezo, y otras cosas muchas de poco valor con que hobieron mucho placer, y quedaron tanto nuestros que era maravilla. Los cuales después venían a las barcas de los navíos adonde nos estábamos, nadando, y nos traían papagayos y hilo de algodón en ovillos y azagayas, y otras cosas muchas y nos las trocaban por otras cosas que nos les dábamos, como cuentecillas de vidrio y cascabeles. En fin, todo tomaban y daban de aquello que tenían de buena voluntad. Mas

me pareció que era gente muy pobre de todo. Ellos andaban todos desnudos como su madre los parió, y también las mujeres, aunque no vide más de una farto moza y todos los que yo vi eran todos mancebos, que ninguno vide de edad de más de treinta años; muy bien hechos, de muy fermosos cuerpos, y muy buenas caras; los cabellos gruesos cuasi como sedas de cola de caballo, e cortos; los cabellos traen por encima de las cejas, salvo unos pocos detrás que traen largos, que jamás cortan; dellos se pintan de prieto, y ellos son de la color de los canarios, ni negros ni blancos, y dellos se pintan en blanco y dellos de colorado, y dellos de lo que fallan, y dellos se pintan las caras, y dellos todo el cuerpo, y dellos sólo los ojos, y dellos sólo el nariz. Ellos no traen armas ni las cognocen, porque les amostré espadas y las tomaban por el filo, y se cortaban con ignorancia. No tienen algún fierro; sus azagayas son unas varas sin fierro, y algunas de ellas tienen al cabo un diente de pece, y otras de otras cosas. Ellos todos a una mano son de buena estatura de grandeza, y buenos gestos, bien hechos; yo vide algunos que tenían señales de feridas en sus cuerpos, y les hice señas qué era aquello, y ellos me amostraron cómo allí venían gentes de otras islas que estaban acerca y les querían tomar, y se defendían; y yo creí, e creo, que aquí vienen de tierra firme a tomarlos por captivos. Ellos deben ser buenos servidores y de buen ingenio, que veo que muy presto dicen todo lo que les decía, y creo que ligeramente se harían cristianos, que me pareció que ninguna secta tenían. Yo, placiendo a nuestro Señor, levaré de aquí al tiempo de mi partida seis a V.A. para que desprendan fablar. Ninguna bestia de ninguna manera vide, salvo papagayos en esta isla." Todas son palabras del Almirante. (Fernández de Navarrete 95-96)

[11] A las dos horas después de medianoche pareció la tierra [...] Amañaron todas las velas [...] temporizando hasta el día viernes que llegaron a una isleta de los Lucayos, que se llamaba en lengua de indios Guanahaní. Luego vieron gente desnuda, y el Almirante salió a tierra en la barca armada, y Martín Alonso Pinzón y Vicente Anes, su hermano, que era capitán de la Niña. Sacó el Almirante la bandera real [...] Puestos en tierra vieron árboles muy verdes y aguas muchas y frutas de diversas maneras. El Almirante llamó a los dos capitanes y a los demás que saltaron en tierra, y a Rodrigo Descovedo, escribano de toda la armada, y a Rodrigo Sánchez de Segovia, y dijo que le diesen por fe y testimonio como él por ante todos tomaba, como de hecho tomó, posesión de la dicha isla por el Rey e por la Reina sus señores [...] Luego se ayuntó allí mucha gente de la isla. (Fernández de Navarrete 95-96)

[12] El Almirante, viéndolos tan buenos y simples, y que en cuanto podían eran tan liberalmente hospitales, y con esto en gran manera pacíficos, dióles a muchos cuentas de vidrio y cascabeles, y a algunos bonetes colorados y otras cosas, con que ellos quedaban muy contentos y ricos.

[13]In her *Discurso narrativo de la conquista de América*, Beatriz Pastor contrasts a "literary model" based primarily on Ailly, Aeneas Sylvio, Marco Polo, and Pliney and which guided Columbus's "fictionalization of reality" ("ficcionalización de la realidad") with another "process of

intense deformation" ("proceso de deformación profunda"). "The origin
of the latter," she states, "is not literary, but economic, and its
historical objective is the intent at first veiled and later increasingly
explicit, to exploit the reality of the New World for strictly
commercial purposes" ("El origen de este último no es literario sino
económico, y su finalidad histórica es la propuesta, velada primero y
luego cada vez más explícita, de instrumentalización de la realidad del
Nuevo Mundo con fines estrictamente comerciales") (82). Pastor
interprets Columbus's characterization of the Indians in his *Diary*
within this context: "The first three traits that characterize the
Indians according to Code 1—nudity, poverty and lack of weapons—
defined them as *savage* and *servile*. The fourth trait—generosity—
classified them as *beasts*, because of their incapacity to do business
according to the laws of exchange of the Western world" ("Los tres
primeros rasgos de caracterización de los indígenas según el código 1—
desnudez, pobreza y falta de armas—los definían com *salvajes* y *siervos*.
El cuarto rasgo—la generosidad—los califica como bestias, por su
incapacidad de comerciar de acuerdo con las leyes de intercambio del
mundo occidental") (96-97).

14 Pero el deseo que tenemos al servicio de Dios e celo a su santa fe
católica, nos face posponer todos los intereses y olvidar los trabajos e
peligros continuos que por esta causa se nos recrescen. Y podiendo, non
solamente guardar nuestros tesoros, mas aún haber otros muchos de los
moros mesmos, que muy voluntariamente nos los darían por la paz,
negamos los que se no ofrescen y derramamos los nuestros, solamente
esperando que la santa fe católica sea acrescentada y la Cristiandad se
quite de un tan continuo peligro como tiene aquí a las puertas, si estos
infieles del Reino de Granada no son arrancados y echados de España.

For other documents from this period, see *Tratados internacionales
de los Reyes Católicos con algunos textos complementarios ordenados y
traducidos por José López de Toro.*

15Pues esta Corona gasta sus tesoros y emplea todas sus fuerzas en
defensa de la fe, y ha dilatado nuestra sagrada Religión por tantos
reinos y provincias tan extendidas, trayendo la nación española a la
Sede Apostólica.

16Yo bien entiendo que estas cosas harán sonreir de lástima a los
políticos y hacendistas, que, viéndonos pobres, abatidos y humillados a
finales del Siglo XVII, no encuentran palabras de bastante menosprecio
para una nación que batallaba contra media Europa conjurada, y esto no
por redondear su territorio ni por obtener una indemnización de guerra,
sino por ideas de Teología...la cosa más inútil del mundo. Cuánto mejor
nos hubiera estado tejer lienzo y dejar que Lutero entrara y saliera donde
bien le pareciese!... Nunca, desde el tiempo de Judas Macabeo, hubo un
pueblo que con tanta razón pudiera creerse el pueblo escogido para ser la
espada y el brazo de dios; y todo, hasta sus sueños de engrandecimiento y
de monarquía universal, lo referían y subordinaban a este objeto
supremo: *fiat unum ovile et unus pastor.*

WORKS CITED

Aldea, Quintín. "Iglesia y Estado en España en la España del siglo XVII." *Miscelánea Comillas* 36 (1961): 143-354.

Bataillon, Marcel. *Erasme et l'Espagne*. Paris: Droz, 1937.

Casas, Bartolomé de Las. *Historia de las Indias*. 3 vols. Ed. Agustín Millares Carlo. México: Fondo de Cultura Económica, 1981.

Chevallier, Jean-Jacques. *L'Idée de Nation*. Paris: Presses Universitaires de France, 1969.

Colón, Hernando. *Historia del Almirante. Crónicas de América*. I. Ed. Luis Arranz. Madrid: Historia 16, 1984.

Columbus, Christopher. (Colón, Cristóbal). *Diario*. Fernández de Navarrete, Martín. *Obras de Don Martín Fernández de Navarrete*. Ed. Carlos Seco Serrano. Madrid: Atlas, 1954. Biblioteca de Autores Españoles, vols. 75-77.

Egaña, Antonio. *La teoría del regio vicariato español en Indias*. Rome, 1958.

Fernández Encisco, Martín. *Suma de Geografía*. Seville, 1519.

Fernández de Navarrete, Martín. *Obras de Don Martín Fernández de Navarrete*. Ed. Carlos Seco Serrano. Biblioteca de Autores Españoles, vols. 75-77. Madrid: Atlas, 1954.

Fernández de Oviedo, Gonzalo. *Historia general y natural de las Indias*. Ed. Juan Pérez de Tudelan Bueso. Biblioteca de Autores Españoles, vols. 117-121. Madrid: Atlas, 1959.

Gómez-Moriana, Antonio. "Discourse Pragmatics and Reciprocity of Perspectives: The Promises of Juan Haldudo (*Don Quixote* I, 4) and Don Juan." *Sociocriticism* 4 (1988): 87-109.

—. "Entre la philologie et la stylistique (Espagne)." *L'Enseignment de la littérature dans le monde*, special edition of *Études Français* 23.1-2 (1987).

Góñiz Gaztambide, José. *Historia de la bula de la cruzada en España*. Vitoria, 1958.

López de Gomara, Francisco. *Historia general de las Indias*. Bibioteca de Autores Españoles, vol. 22. Madrid: Atlas, 1946.

Machiavelli, Niccoló. *The Prince*. Trans. George Bull. New York: Penguin, 1979.

Menéndez y Pelayo, Marcelino. *Historia de los heterodoxos españoles*, II. Biblioteca de Autores Cristianos. Madrid: Editorial Católica, 1956.

Menéndez Pidal, Ramón. "Vitoria y Las Casas." *El Padre Las Casas y Vitoria con otros temas de los siglos XVI y XVII*. Madrid: Espasa-Calpe, 1958.

Nebrija, Antonio de. *Gramática Castellana*. 1492. Ed. R.C. Alston. Menston: The Scholar Press, 1969.

Pastor, Beatriz. *Discurso narrativo de la conquista de América*. Havana: Casa de las Américas, 1983.

Picón Salas, Mariano. *De la conquista a la independencia*. México: Fondo de Cultura Económica, 1969.

Rouco-Varela, Antonio. *Staat und Kirche im Spanien des 16. Jahrhunderts*. Munich: Max Hueber Verlag, 1965.

Tratados internacionlaes de los Reyes Católicos con algunos textos complementarios ordenados y traducidos por José López de Toro. Madrid: Imprenta Góngora, 1952. *Documentos inéditos para la historia de España*, vols. 7-8.

Todorov, Tzvetan. *La Conquête de l'Amérique. La question de l'autre*. Paris: Seuil, 1982.

Weinrich, Harald. *Tempus. Besprochene und erzählte Welt*. Stuttgart: Kohlhammer Verlag, 1971.

CHAPTER 3:
SILENCE AND WRITING:
THE HISTORY OF THE CONQUEST

Beatriz Pastor

(translated by Jason Wood)

It has been some time since the writing and reading of
history ceased to be considered as an innocent or natural
act, or as a task governed by a Ciceronian understanding of
the historian as an objective and impartial mirror of concrete reality.[1] Under the scrutiny of a criticism that has become increasingly concerned with the discursive practices
and the rhetorical techniques of historiography, and with
its multiple connections with narrative discourse and fictional practices traditionally associated with the literary,
the writing and reading of history have become ever more
problematic (see White, *Metahistory* and "Historical
Text").

Currently, a whole gamut of projects, conferences,
meetings and publications related to the quincentennial of
Columbus's discovery of America are in full swing.
"Celebration," "commemoration," "reexamination" and

"criticism" are some of the terms that, with different focuses and different ideological and epistemological implications, describe the objective of the various activities. Nevertheless, from the perspective of the almost five hundred years that separate us from the complex, turbulent and contradictory process of the discovery and conquest of America, I would like to propose that, if anything, 1992 should be the symbolic initiation of a project of radical criticism, one that should approach the process of discovery and conquest as part of a project of demystifying and reevaluating the way in which the encounter between two worlds took place, within its historical context and with its multiple economic, ideological, cultural and political implications as much for Europe as for America. Simultaneously, this critical inquiry should question the way in which this process found its place in the texts that shaped a history that represented and distorted this encounter, inventing and fictionalizing it for Western consumption within traditional European history. If anything, the symbolic date of 1992 should imply a radical deconstruction of the historiographical narrative that during almost five hundred years has elaborated the European version of the discovery and conquest, assimilating, misrepresenting and erasing many of the contradictions and complexities of that which the discovery and conquest really were: the tragic clash of Europe with America, of the West with the Other;[2] of imperial power with unexplored territory; the process of appropriation of one world by another; the creation of a society split between colonial masters and colonized servants.

In spite of the vast mirage created at times by traditional European historiography, the historical processes of conquest and domination cannot be narrated by one single voice. When this appears to be the case, it is only because all dialogue has been suppressed, alternate interlocutors silenced, all differences erased and every dissident eliminated. It is only because one voice has managed to assume for itself the monopoly of the word, emerging as the voice of authority and, in doing so, silencing all others.

Firmly anchored in the Eurocentric world view, formulated in accordance with European categories of

perception, analysis and exposition, the history of the discovery and conquest of America was, to a great extent,
built on silence, omission and absence. The critical
reevaluation of that history necessarily implies from the
beginning two inevitable objectives. It is, in the first place,
a question of realizing, verifying, and, insofar as it is
possible, correcting those omissions.[3] Secondly, it is necessary to go deeply into the analysis of the discursive
practices and the rhetorical mechanisms that shape, from
the texts of the conquerors to the historiographical
elaborations of the chroniclers, a historical discourse that,
more than revealing with precision the realities of the
process of discovery and conquest, shed light upon the European imaginary, the ideological structures of the Empire
and the economic, social and political aspirations of the
conquerors as well as of the chroniclers.[4]

In literary criticism, working with texts that relate the
discovery and conquest of America often implies the need
for a certain readjustment. At first glance, the displacement from the sphere of the fictional to that of the
historical appears to be a comforting admission into a real
and verifiable world. The infinite possibilities of the
imaginary seem to yield to the soundness of a concrete
world of provable facts. That illusory security, however, is
based upon a series of erroneous considerations fundamentally related with mistaken conceptions of objectivity
and truth. As one delves into the problem of the writing
of history, the opposition between history and literature
becomes less and less significant. The borders that seem to
delineate clearly the difference between historiographical
narrative and fictional narrative fade and begin to disappear. The *document* loses its talismanic character as a
repository of objective truths, its contours becoming more
and more porous and its content becoming problematized
as questions begin to multiply. What selective criteria
shape it? Who has a voice within its context and who does
not? Who represents, for what and for whom does it represent, and ultimately, how does it represent?

The issue of the definition of the observer and the interlocutor comes to light. It becomes necessary to break the
illusion of documental truth by inquiring into the relation

between the observer and the observed, questioning the constitution of the narrative "I" and the explicit or implicit definition of its interlocutors and its audience, revealing narrative strategies, rhetorical devices and modes of conceptualization that shape texts with characteristics similar to those of literary works. It is not a question, however, of revealing or of taking inventory of fictional modes within the historiographical discourse of the conquest of America. It is, rather, a question of examining in depth the elements that allow us to question documentary and historiographical discourse, examining in its epistemological and political implications, a model of historical representation that uses its own fictional techniques in order to legitimize, consolidate and perpetuate an undertaking of imperial aggression.

The ramifications of this issue are very broad and, therefore, I will here limit myself to three fundamental aspects. I would first like to point out a series of key moments in the process of defining the authoritative, univocal voice that establishes the European vision of the historical process of the conquest of America, transmuting it into an absolute category, the history of the Conquest. Secondly, I will attempt to suggest the extension of a silence, full of murmurs and dissent, perpetuated during that period through oppression, suppression and systematic violence. Finally, I will try to point out some of the profound implications of that process of apprehension, representation and silencing for the nature of the relation of discovery between Europe and America and for the constitution of Latin American colonial society.

II

Perhaps Columbus was, in part, a dreamer and perhaps that quality with which so many of his defenders actively identified themselves explains, in part, his trajectory as a discoverer of unknown places. Once in the New World, however, the problem would be whether the new reality were up to the level of his dreams and the degree to which his dreams would condition his knowledge of that reality.

From the first days that follow his arrival to the new continent, Columbus's texts convey a representation of the realities of the New World characterized fundamentally by the imposition of his own literary models and commercial expectations on a concrete reality, into the knowledge of which he does not delve deeply. The imaginary structures of the Admiral tie his perception to an entire European tradition of representation of unknown or different realities. Combined with his awareness of the royal audience to which his narration is directed, they shape an inexact perception that crystallizes in texts that oscillate between stereotyped description, distortion, wishful thinking and the wildest compensatory fantasy. This perception begins with the *Diario* of the first trip, in which he sketches a representation of America that reduces the inventory and characterization of concrete elements of the new reality to the conceptual categories and outlines of the literary sources of its project (see Morrison). Flora, fauna and territory, inhabitant and culture, are perceived in relation to the central elements that articulate the expectations expressed by the imaginary model in its double aspect: fabulous and mercantile. Spices not found in America, gold mines that never materialized, mythical places like Társis and Ofir reappear again and again in the texts of the Admiral, guarded by peaceful and primitive savages who do not even know the value of their own lands.

In the second voyage, the growing pressure from investors who were waiting for more tangible evidence of the success of the venture than the samples that Columbus brought with him from his first voyage is translated in the texts of Columbus as a growing stubbornness in the face of a reality that continues to challenge his expectations and promises. Only in this way can one explain the incident of the sworn statement Columbus extracted from his crew denying the insularity of Cuba and certifying that it was, in fact, *terra firma* of Asia.[5] Geographical descriptions, cultural and human evaluation and commercial inventory appear in the texts of the second voyage determined by an urgency to verify the impossible coincidence between the dicoverer's dreams and the discovered realities.

In the third voyage, the now more urgent necessity to confirm Columbus's perception and to legitimize his very project culminates in the fantastic transformation of Venezuela into the Garden of Eden. The very way in which Columbus argues this transformation reveals the importance of his imaginary model in the entire process of apprehension and comprehension of American reality. In fact, what this episode demonstrates is that it is easier for him to question the scientifically accepted vision of the sphericity of Earth in order to validate his perception of the New World than it is to modify the terms of the model in the face of its lack of correspondence with the new concrete realities of an unexplored continent.[6] That which is different becomes *deformed* in a perception that transforms hypothesis into unquestionable facts, revealing a total incapacity to modify its categories and approach. Even the misfortunes of the fourth voyage will not lead to a revision of deformed perception of the Admiral. In 1503, defeated by American nature, increasingly frustrated in his expectations of glory and wealth, Columbus would still cling in his exile on the island of Jamaica to a mistaken vision of the New World; he would still persist on a representation that situated Cathay in America, Terrestrial Paradise in Venezuela, the Golden Peninsula and the mines of King Solomon in Veragua.[7]

The writings of the Admiral charter the journey through his Indies, where he transforms Cuba into *terra firma* of China, Puerto Rico into Japan, Santo Domingo into the mythical kingdoms of Társis and Ofir, Panama into the Ciamba of Marco Polo where the mines of King Solomon where supposedly found and Venezuela into earthly paradise. Every mountain and every cove become signs that tie reality to the imaginary model. Every shrub turns into pepper, clove, aloe or nutmeg, thus confirming the existence of Asia for Columbus in middle of the Atlantic, and every positive identification of land with a model further distorts the reality of the New World. Revealing becomes hiding, representing becomes distorting, discovering becomes concealing as the Admiral, his mind too full of images for him to be able to perceive the world that surrounds him, strives in an ever increasing frenzy to convince the Crown and its investors that he is, indeed, the one chosen by God to carry forth the most profitable commercial venture of the century.

From the point of view of the writing of history, Columbus's narrative discourse immediately raises two fundamental problems. The first has to do with its accuracy. The modes of apprehension and the representation of reality sketched out above inevitably result in a very limited and subjective knowledge of the new reality. Given the processes of distortion and reduction that shape the articulation of his perception, the informative value of the texts in which this perception is materialized is, to say the least, questionable. As a result of these combined factors, the very concept of "discovery" as the representation of the encounter between Europe and America articulated by Columbus becomes problematic, as much in its cognitive as in its communicative aspects.

The second problem has to do with authority. Columbus was not alone in the New World. America was not a desert but a land populated with people who, unlike Columbus, knew this land and its nature through personal experience and collective history. They knew, for example, if there were gold and pearls, where spices could be found and what those spices were. They knew whether the land that they inhabited was island or mainland. They knew their respective customs, trading patterns and warfare styles. And, these people spoke, among themselves and also with Columbus and other Spaniards, though it was not true that they all spoke a common language, as Columbus asserted. The Admiral repeatedly questioned them concerning his objectives. He used them as guides and as informers. Nevertheless, the knowledge and information that these people possessed never made it to the pages of Columbus's texts; it was never inscribed in the "great book" of Western history.

Columbus inquires and the natives respond, but surprisingly enough, their answers always seem to coincide with the fantasies of the Admiral. They always confirm the validity of a perception that threatened to further distort the reality of the New World with each new "discovery." Bartolomé de Las Casas, who generally was a great supporter of the Admiral, comments with benevolent irony on the facility with which Columbus convinced himself that what he heard and what they told him was precisely what he wanted to hear: "He had already made up his mind. Thus, everything the Indians would say to him in sign language, being so distant as is the sky from the earth, he would twist the meaning and attribute it to what he desired" ("Habíase ya persuadido a lo mismo, así todo lo que por señas los indios le decían, siendo tan distante como lo es el cielo de la tierra lo enderezaba y atribuía a lo que deseaba" [Las Casas I:156]).

But Columbus was a methodical man and when we examine closely the systematic erasure of native voices in his dairies and letters and the fundamental implications of such an erasure for Europe and for America, it is difficult to share the benevolent tolerance of Las Casas. In the *Diario* of the first journey, Columbus still shows a certain caution in his transcription of the information supposedly given by the natives. "I felt that", "I recognized that", "I understood that he said to me," "according to what I was able to understand" ("Sentía que," "cognoscía que," "entendía que me decía," "según podía entender") are some of the expressions that fulfill the function of subordinating the accuracy of the recorded information to the capacity of the comprehension of the narrator. However, even though the validity of the information is somewhat relativized by these formulas, the conclusions that Columbus brought out were by no means relative. The lack of correspondence between the apparent subjectivization of facts and the objectivization of conclusions reveals that the true function of these rhetorical formulas does not fundamentally affect the nature of the message; above and beyond any lack of facts or communication barrier, Columbus knew exactly the reality about which he spoke. After the second voyage, however, even those formulas disappear as the Admiral sees, interprets, announces and affirms, basing himself on descriptions and words whose true meaning he does not know. Nothing indicates in his text his very ignorance of the verbal and non-verbal forms of communication of those natives that he quotes with such authority. "They say" ("Dicen") now introduces long lists of geographical, topographical and commercial data that recreate in detail the Admiral's promises to his investors upon returning from his second voyage. Columbus simultaneously appropriates and distorts their words in order to legitimize his own perception of the New World and to gain complete and exclusive control over its representation.

The process of usurpation of the right to the word that is developed in the texts of Columbus does not conclude here. Michele de Cuneo relates an incident that sheds light on the next stage:

> When we were approaching the great island he [Columbus] directed himself toward us with these words: 'Sirs, I have now taken you to the place from whence departed one of the three Magi who came to adore Christ. This place is called Saba'. When we disembarked on the island and asked its name they answered that it was called Sobo. The Admiral then told us that it was the same name *but that they did not know how to pronounce it correctly.*

> Cuando nos aproximábamos a la gran isla (Colón) se dirigió a nosotros con estas palabras: 'Señores os he conducido ahora al lugar del cual partió uno de los Reyes Magos que fueron a adorar a Cristo. Dicho lugar se llama Saba.' Cuando desembarcamos en la isla y preguntamos su nombre nos contestaron que se llamaba Sobo. Entonces el Almirante nos explicó que *era el mismo nombre pero que ellos no sabían pronunciarlo correctamente.* (95-107) [emphasis mine]

The word of Columbus becomes the undisputed authority as he grants himself the right to correct the natives' pronunciation of their own language, and he did not even know of the name of the island that they inhabited. The message of the natives, already blurred and distorted in the supposed transcriptions of the texts of the first voyage, is erased to the point of disappearance when Columbus discredits them as speakers of their own language. Only one more step remains toward the total elimination of the natives as speakers and interlocutors: the transformation of their inability to speak their own language correctly into a more general kind of linguistic incompetence. In his diary of the first voyage, Columbus refers to the convenience of bringing an indeterminate number of natives to Spain "so that they learn to speak" ("para que desprendan fablar"). In his letter to the Kings in January of 1494, within the context of his proposal for establishing a slave trade, Columbus declares the need for the indigenous people to go to the peninsula to learn "the language." Not Spanish, not our language, but rather *the* language, as if they had none.

The implications of Columbus's disqualification of the natives as speakers and interlocutors are considerable. First, by silencing them in his first voyage, Columbus grants himself the exclusive right to create and represent America in accordance with his own literary models. Secondly, his suppression of native speech implies the suppression of all forms of cultural plurality. In the same way that the language of Columbus becomes the Language in the context of the silence imposed by the narrator on the natives, culture becomes Culture within an implicit American cultural void. Columbus possesses Language, he represents Culture, and consequently, it is he who defines Language, Culture and Humanity.

The elimination of the word of the natives by Columbus is not an innocent slip. Nor should it be seen as a simple misunderstanding, more or less ridiculous, in the encounter between a man of ethnocentric vision and fixed ideas and the complicated realities of the New World. In fact this omission constitutes a symbolic act of brutal authority that historically marks the beginning of an unequal relationship of power between Europe and America, and, simultaneously, signals the beginning of a long philosophical, literary and historiographical tradition, characterized by the imposition of an exclusively European perspective and by the systematic elimination of the indigenous vision of reality.

Little by little, the word of the Tainos, then of the people of Paria and Veragua, became blurred, as Columbus further erased it. Finally, it disappeared from a history that would be built on the systematic elimination of all dissenting voices, a history that would be narrated by those who, like Columbus, would come to represent the voice of historical authority.

III

It is in the narrative voice of Christopher Columbus within the framework of the discovery and conquest of America that the authority of the European version of history is constituted for the first time. Although the authority of European historiography of the Conquest is maintained and prolonged beyond Columbus, not all of the inflections of this historiographical discourse take on the same characteristics as that of Columbus. The word, in service of the Empire, configures different narrative voices and shapes different types of narration. Warriors, monks, politicians, explorers and learned men all narrated the conquest in many different ways, shedding light upon the innumerable transformations of the imperial project. Yet, I want to limit myself here to two examples: those of Hernán Cortés and Alvar Núñez Cabeza de Vaca. Their juxtaposition is revealing of the range of possibilities, at times apparently antithetical or incompatible, offered by the writing of power in the framework of the historical process of the discovery of America.

According to Hegel, what distinguishes dreamers from great men is that dreamers do not hesitate to ignore reality, subordinating it to their personal fantasies, while great men think and act in correspondence and harmony with the concrete realities of their time.[8] This distinction, which coincides rather well with some of the obvious differences that separate the historical figure of Cortés from the figure of Columbus, does not tell us a great deal in terms of the specific differences that, within the same historical period and cultural tradition, shape historical modes of representation so different as those exemplified by these two figures.

What characterizes the version of the Conquest that Cortés narrates in his *Cartas de relación*, is its systematic quality. The narration of action appears to be articulated by a constant necessity to project its meaning beyond that of the facts and to integrate it into a rational superstructure that provides it with a totalizing coherence. It is not only a question of taking inventory or compiling data, but rather of organizing events in such a way that they allow the proposal of models and the formulation of general laws. This project is coherent with a vision that, during the Renaissance, increasingly identifies rational knowledge and scientific thought. Horkheimer refers to this fundamental development in his criticism of Machiavelli's theory of history:

> In the Renaissance the bases of contemporary natural science were placed. The objective of this science is to detect regularities in the course of nature with the help of systematically organized experiences in order to be able to dominate nature as much as possible. If the intellectual behavior of men during the Middle Ages was essentially oriented toward figuring out the meaning and the finality of the world and of life, for which the interpretation of the Revelation and that of the ecclesiastic and ancient authorities had just about completely exhausted, the men of the Renaissance began to ask themselves about interworldly causes, causes that must be established through sensible observation instead of interrogating themselves about the ultra-terrenial finality which was pretended to be understood by investigating tradition. (Horkheimer 18)

In this context, the observation of reality, the classification of elements and the categorization of facts became fundamental processes in a project that aims at an investigation of the laws that govern them and identifies knowledge with a process of analytical evaluation that will allow the formulation of rules and models of development and action that insure the control of that reality. The extraordinary importance of Machiavelli's thought resides precisely in his capacity to formulate a science of politics that lucidly and rigorously systematizes the political practices of the Renaissance and, to a large extent, its connections with Western traditions as a whole.

The similarities between Cortés and Machiavelli are numerous, and I have already addressed them elsewhere

(Pastor, *Discursos narrativos*, chapter 2, sections 2-3). Perhaps most important and what gives coherence to all of the other similarities is that which unmistakably joins them as representatives of the same mode of thought and the same use of reason. If it is certain that Machiavelli elaborates the bases of political science in Renaissance Europe, it is equally certain that the *Cartas de relación* can be read as a rigorous exposition of a scientific thought in three fundamental aspects: the exposition of the science of war, the elaboration of a science of domination and the formulation of a science of politics within the context of America and the formation of the Spanish Empire.

The characterization of territory, for example, presents two well-defined modes in the *Cartas*. The first one, chronologically, is articulated in relation to European models of representation of unexplored places, unknown civilizations and desirable objectives of imperial occupation. It is centered on aesthetic qualities—exoticism, refinement, etc.—and on material qualities—economy, commerce, commodities and riches. The initial descriptions of the market of Tenochtitlán or of the court and the houses of Moctezuma, for example, are part of the mode of characterization within this direction. The second is a military characterization which transforms each one of the topographical elements into strategic points and each one of the commercial and cultural centers into military objectives. Both modes of characterization do not exclude, but rather complement each other as different modes of rational understanding in the formulation of a scientific model of imperial conquest. The estimation of the value of the objective is followed by the formulation of a strategy of colonial aggression. The characterization of Cortés as a model connects the other two aspects of his scientific representation of the conquest. The often fictitious causality that links Cortés's military and political successes in his relation with the Aztecs and their subjects, showing any success as evidence of the validity of his methods of occupation, supports and illuminates Cortés's science of domination. The way in which that domination is systematized in the project of the creation of a model state sums up the political science of the conqueror.

The characterization of Cortés projects a figure whose control of reality acquires almost mythical proportions. But what is important from the point of view of the problem of the articulation of a scientific discourse is *what* this absolute control of Cortés in the *Cartas* is based on. If we closely examine the *Cartas* we see that in their context control results from the combination of tactics, strategy, foresight and clairvoyance. The first of these sends us to the area of the observed and simply implies a reaction before observed reality or immediate experience. The other three imply, together with a greater level of abstraction, the capacity to formulate principles, rules and laws that project the knowledge of concrete experiences into a more ample framework of comprehension and action that connects the present and the future. The importance of this will to abstract general principles for action and to formulate laws that assure the control of the new reality is precisely the trait that characterizes the narration of the *Cartas* as a discourse that, much like that of Machiavelli, links up with the scientific thought of the period. The fact that the fictional reelaboration, or the elimination of some of the most important episodes of the conquest, becomes subordinated to this necessity gives us an idea of the prime importance that this scientific conception of domination occupies in the consciousness and in the political project of Hernán Cortés.[9]

In the end, it is the will to systematize observation and experience, formulating upon this base the laws that guarantee the control of nature and history and articulate the representation of the conquest that Cortés carries out in his *Cartas*. The problem is that the formulation of these laws that insure the control of American reality by the European conqueror carries with it the understanding and classification of that reality in terms of European thought. The analytical characterization and rational presentation create an illusion of fictitious objectivity. Clarity and coherence are imposed without gaps in the history of the conquest of Mexico that Cortés narrates to us, but clarity and coherence are themselves defined in relation to logical categories and European stylistics. In fact, the very reason which is presented as a vehicle of objective knowledge functions in relation to America as yet another instrument of domination, one that categorizes according to alien terms the reality of the New World, reducing and instrumentalizing it. It is a domination that extends and complements, from the realm of writing, the other forms of domination of the conquest: military aggression, territorial occupation, political usurpation, cultural imposition and the subjugation of people.

In the writings of Cortés, reason is the privileged instrument of control of reality and, simultaneously, the instrument of legitimization of domination. In the *Cartas*, reason forms laws that are based upon the fictitious homologation of American cultural and political developments with European ones. That very reason validates imperial aggression and justifies violence as a means of establishing a superior social order (European social order). It legitimizes abuse, exploitation and cruelty as part of a political process whose only real superiority lies in the fact that it extends the political models of the European Renaissance. The laws that are formulated on the basis of that rational presentation are never concerned with the development of autochthonous socio-cultural processes or the full understanding of the new reality as primary objective. Their objective is simply the formulation of an optimum method for the control of that reality and, above all, its integration in the framework of a colonial relationship with the Spanish State.

The logical progression of Cortés's rational discourse creates an illusion of strict causality in which all action justifies itself as the necessary means for the creation of a superior order: the State of Cortés and Machiavelli. What its internal coherence tends to make us forget is that the narration is founded upon a double process of reduction and omission. The reduction of reality functions through the subordination of its presentation to the categories of a reason which proposes to formulate universal laws based upon a history, society and political model that are exclusively European. This implies the understanding and representation of America through the use of categories that are foreign to it—only from a totally Eurocentric perspective can these be considered universal—and consequently, the elimination, refusal or ignorance of the new reality to the extent that it obeys its own historical and socio-cultural processes. The omission, on the other hand, is quite obvious in the gaps that constitute the text of Cortés's *Cartas*. Of Moctezuma, for example, only the speech that becomes instrumental in Cortés's model of domination is extensively transcribed: the formulation of the myth of the return of Quetzalcoatl. Is this a coincidence or a deliberate strategy? It is definitely a strategy. Anything that is not functional within the rational scheme for the formulation of a scientific model of domination and the creation of a new state is eliminated.

In the version of history that Cortés elaborates in his *Cartas*, instrumentalized reason creates the illusion of a totalizing order that mutilates and profoundly discredits the reality of America and the meaning and implications of its conquest. Cloaked in the authority of scientific thought, the voice of Cortés, a voice that justifies with impeccable logic, the conquest, its cruelty and violence, exemplifies the violence of Logic itself in the context of the colonial encounter between Europe and America.

IV

Against the background of the distortions of the texts of Columbus and the instrumentalization of those of Cortés, Alvar Núñez Cabeza de Vaca appears to be, at first sight, innocence recaptured. The demystifying character of his *Naufragios* seems to break the limits of the discourse of domination, making way for a criticism of the conquest and a presentation of the American reality that characterizes it in its own terms. The merchant and the conqueror seem to yield to the ethnographer and the missionary.

The narrative structure of the *Naufragios* dramatizes the transformation of the character and traces the genesis of a different approach toward the American reality. This change of approach expresses itself in the substitution of a narrative discourse of domination by that of the ethnographer. The *Naufragios* give an account of narrator's journey from Santo Domingo to Florida where he becomes shipwrecked and of the ten years of pilgrimage through the south of the continent from Florida to Mexico, where he rejoins, once again, European civilization.

The narration presents a circular structure that begins with the symbolic disintegration of the model of conquest outlined by Cortés in his *Cartas*. Under the incompetent leadership of Pánfilo de Narváez, all illusion of control of action and environment disappears. The objective becomes blurred and the army disintegrates into a confused scattering that illuminates the impotence of Narváez and the failure of conquering action.[10] It is the first symbolic shipwreck of Alvar Núñez. Nature, its power, and the Spaniard's lack of understanding of the American environment take center stage, implicitly questioning the validity of the model of occupation of the *Cartas*. This questioning is clearly expressed in one of the most important and detailed episodes of the account. After several weeks of fruitless exploration, Narváez's army finds itself in a desperate situation. The land is so inhospitable that it seems that in staying there, "nothing but death could follow" ("no se podía seguir sino la muerte"). Being that the governor has left the ships behind, the first step to leave the land is the construction of boats, a thing that,

> to everyone, seemed impossible because we did not know how to do it, nor were there tools, nor iron, nor forge, nor tow, nor fish nor rigging, in sum, not a single thing out of so many that are necessary, nor is there anyone who knows anything to make all of this work and above all, nothing to eat while all this was being done.

> A todos parecía imposible, porque nosotros no lo sabíamos hacer, ni había herramientas, ni hierro, ni fragua, ni estopa, ni pez ni jarcias, finalmente ni cosa alguna de tantas como son menester, ni quien supiese nada para dar industria con ello, y sobre todo, no haber qué comer entretanto que se hiciesen. (Núñez Cabeza de Vaca 33)

The breakdown between reality and project is expressed here very clearly. There is no doubt that the expedition of Narváez was one of the largest and best equipped of the conquest. Nevertheless, after only a few weeks of exploration, its participants found themselves in a situation in the middle of nowhere, where everything they had became useless to them and where they lacked all the things needed to regain control and confront their desperate situation. The description of the boat's construction carries the questioning conquistador's action a step further. The nails and tools are made by melting down the armor, arms and riding harnesses of the conquerors. Their clothes are used for sails, their horses for nourishment and leather for the construction of bellows for the foundry and for hides for water transport. These transformations are, without a doubt, a practical way to resolve the problems to which Alvar Núñez refers in the previous quotation but simultaneously, they express the symbolic transformation of an imperialist and warlike order. In the context of the conquest and of the model of domination formulated by Cortés, imperial aggression appears represented by the figure of the conqueror with his attributes: armor, weapons and horse. It is this figure and all that it represents that Alvar Núñez symbolically liquidates in the episode of the boats. The weapons, useless in this context, are turned into objects that the new reality defines as necessary. Clothes, which, since Columbus, had symbolized Western civilization and its superiority over America are turned into sails in order to facilitate the retreat. Horses, objects of indigenous terror and for that very reason, symbols of the power and of the force of the invaders, are turned into food without which all action—not only that of the conquest—becomes impossible.

The liquidation of the model of the conquest becomes complete in the following phase of the personage's trajectory. The army disintegrates after Narváez's cry of "every man for himself"; Alvar Núñez and the other crew members of his ship are able to claim land. During the following days they apply themselves, with the help of the natives, to gathering provisions of fish, roots and water and, once well stocked, they decide to take to the sea in an attempt to recover the lost ships or to reach the coast of the nearest colony.

As we saw that we were stocked with fish, roots and
water and the other things that we asked for, we all
agreed to return aboard and to continue on our way
and we dug the ship out of the sand in which it was
stuck, and *it was necessary that we all stripped down
to nothing* and it was a huge job to set sail and then
all-aboard, with two shots from the cannon there
upon the sea, we were given such a blast of water
that all got drenched; and *being that we were all
naked and that it was extremely cold, we released
the oars from our hands,* the sea gave us another
blast of water, the boat completely changed direction, the supervisor and another two men *took hold of
it in order to escape but the opposite happened and
the boat pulled them under and there they drowned.*
As the coast is very treacherous, in one swoop the sea
spilled out the rest of the men and, all wrapped up in
waves and half drowned there on the coast of the
very island we were missing only the three that the
boat had pulled under. We escapees remaining,
*naked as we were born and everything we brought
with us lost,* and even though it was worth little, for
us it was worth much. As it was around November
and it was extremely cold, our bones could be counted,
we were exact replicas of death itself. (Núñez
Cabeza de Vaca 43) [emphasis mine] [11]

This is the last shipwreck of Alvar Núñez, and it
simultaneously represents the final point in the disintegration of the model of military conquest, the point zero of
the development of the critical consciousness of the narrator and the beginning of the new perception which crystallizes in the discourse of the *Naufragios*. At the point of
rupture related in the above-cited paragraph, the loss of
control—releasing the oars—is given as the result of the
cancelation of the model—the nudity. At the same time,
however, the attempt to cling to the residuals of the previous stage—the boat constructed with the weapons,
clothes and horses of the conquerors—leads to destruction.
The nudity metaphorically expresses the end of a process
of liquidation that has gradually stripped the narrator of
the attributes of the European conqueror, which amounts
to a symbolic death. But it also expresses the state of
primitive nudity from which this conqueror, now converted into mere man, will learn to see and know the new

reality with new eyes, obliged by a situation of vulnerability that excludes the use of force as an instrument of control, putting him at the mercy of nature and the inhabitants of the New World. The scene of the final shipwreck expresses, in the very continuity of *birth and death*, the symbolic birth of the perspective that Alvar Núñez will develop in opposition to the perspective of imperial conquest throughout all of the *Naufragios*.

From this point on, the narrator undergoes an apprenticeship of reality that leads to his increasing familiarization with the environment—the climate, the flora and the fauna—and its inhabitants. It is an apprenticeship in which Alvar Núñez, driven by the basic instinct of survival, will have to learn to distinguish among all the plants, those which will nourish him, among the entire fauna, the animals, mollusks and insects with which he will be able to satiate his hunger. Through the need for self-protection and through his contact with the different tribes with which he finds himself living, he learns to interpret and to better understand the customs of the natives and, little by little, we see him acquire a growing control of the American reality that will enable him to improve his situation. The successive metamorphoses of the narrator mark the different stages of the apprenticeship: from the state of limbo of the shipwreck to the insertion into the new reality in the capacity of slave; from slave to merchant; from merchant to miracle-working doctor; and finally, to son of the sun (*hijo del sol*).

With each new metamorphosis, the knowledge of reality grows and the level of control increases in direct proportion to that knowledge. Starting from the situation of ignorance and helplessness expressed in the nudity, hunger and cold of the last shipwreck, Alvar Núñez will first learn what is necessary to survive at the most basic level: to satisfy hunger and thirst and to protect himself from the cold. Later, the progressive knowledge of the commerce and customs of exchange among the natives will allow him to become a merchant and to recover the freedom that he had lost as a slave. The careful observation of the healing practices of the natives and the growing familiarization with their customs and beliefs will allow

him further on to play convincingly the role of a quack
doctor and to end up being worshipped with the prestige
of being *hijo del sol.*

The transformation of perception and consciousness
through the vicissitudes of action in the period of apprenticeship is expressed on the other hand in a central image:

> I've already told how we went walking naked
> through this land and not being at all accustomed to
> such a thing, like snakes we changed our skins twice
> a year.

> Ya he dicho cómo por esta tierra anduvimos
> desnudos; y como no estábamos acostumbrados a ello,
> a manera de serpientes mudábamos los cueros dos ve-
> ces al año. (Núñez Cabeza de Vaca)

Nudity, a sign of innocence, vulnerability and receptivity,
carries with it the progressive knowledge of the new environment, but also the transformation of consciousness
that the image of the shedding of skin connotes. The new
consciousness that is being gestated throughout the physical and psychic metamorphoses of the narrator is that
which will formulate in the text of *Naufragios* the criticism of the conquest and the proposal of an alternative
mode of relations between Spain and America. It is a proposal that echoes Las Casas in advocating a utopian model
of conquest based not on force, but rather, on the establishment of a pacific coexistence rooted in knowledge and
persuasion.

The difference that separates the conqueror of the beginning of the journey from the narrator that is progressively revealed to us in the pages of the text is dramatized
in a series of incidents and contrasts shortly after the return to Mexico. Specifically, the episode of Alcaraz is presented as a direct confrontation between what Alvar
Núñez was and the order that he personified at the beginning of his pilgrimage—represented here by Alcaraz
and by the realities of the colony—and the narrator of the
text who appears to be identified with the rejection of
colonial reality and with a project of pacific coexistence
with the natives that duplicates Las Casas's model. At

other times this difference is expressed in the form of an explicit contrast between two conceptions of the conquest:

> Rather, they spoke among themselves saying that the Christians lied, because we came from where the Sun came up and they came from where it set; and that we cured the sick and that they kill those who were healthy; and that we came naked and barefoot and they, dressed and upon horses and with lances; and that we did not have greed for anything, everything that was given to us we later returned and with nothing we remained, and the others did not have any motive other than that of stealing everything that they found, and they never gave anything to anybody; and in this way they related all of our things and they praised them contrary to the others.

> Antes, unos con otros platicaban entre sí diciendo que los cristianos mentían, porque nosotros veníamos de donde salía el Sol y ellos de donde se pone; y que nosotros sanábamos a los enfermos y ellos mataban los que estaban sanos; y que nosotros veníamos desnudos y descalzos y ellos vestidos, en caballos y con lanzas; y que nosotros no teníamos cobdicia de ninguna cosa, antes todo cuanto nos daban tornábamos luego a dar, y con nada nos quedábamos, y los otros no tenían otro fin sino robar todo cuanto hallaban, y nunca daban nada a nadie; y de esta manera relataban todas nuestras cosas y las encarescían por el contrario de los otros.
> (Núñez Cabeza de Vaca 99)

It would be an error, however, to assume that this transformation and the narrative discourse in which it is expressed implies a radical rejection of the colonial perspective and all of its forms of domination. The new perspective humanizes the representation of the New World but it does not resolve all of the internal contradictions of the narrator, nor does it cancel a project of colonial character. Both are evident in the text in passages that demonstrate the existence of a clear hierarchy that relegates inhabitants and cultures of the New World to an inferior place or that unequivocally marks the superiority of Europeans over natives. The characterization of the natives oscillates between the paternalism that underlies the proposal of pacific domination—"they are well-conditioned and resourceful people to follow any suitable thing" ("es gente bien acondicionada y aprovechada para *seguir* cualquier cosa bien aparejada") [Núñez Cabeza de Vaca 93]—and their disqualification as good savages in opposition to the Europeans, who continue to represent civilization:

> Throughout the whole land there are great and beautiful meadows of very good pasture for cattle; and it seems to me that *it would be very fructiferous if it were worked and inhabited by people of reason.*

> Por toda la tierra hay muy grandes y hermosa deshesas y de muy buenos pastos para ganados; y parésceme que *sería tierra muy fructífera si fuese labrada y habitada de gente de razón.* (Núñez Cabeza de Vaca 63) [emphasis mine]

Without a doubt, the text of *Naufragios* narrates a very different history from that of the texts of Columbus or Cortés. In the final balance, however, the journey and the metamorphosis of Alvar Núñez do not culminate in the recovery of innocence, but rather in the demonstration of its impossibility. This is not as true for Alvar Núñez, who does not seem to understand the significance or importance of his own internal contradictions, as it is for us, as readers of a very revealing text. Its historical context is the creation of the Spanish overseas Empire (*ultramar*) through a process of discovery and exploration whose final objective is the Spanish occupation of new lands and the creation of economic and political ties that subordinate the new Colonies to the Metropolis. This objective officially justifies itself with a rationale that oscillates between the supposed bestiality of the natives that turns them into natural slaves (as documented by Columbus) and a helplessness and ignorance that put them in need of religious, cultural, social and political guidance (as documented by Cortés).[12] In this context, where all personal or collective innocence becomes impossible, the relation of Alvar Núñez's ethnographical discourse with the very process of conquest that it denounces and apparently rejects, becomes very problematic.[13] In a way, the problems posed by Alvar Núñez's narrative are similar to those of Edward Said with respect to anthropology, when he indicates the problem created by the dissemination of anthropological studies on people and cultures of the third world beyond the area of intellectual and academic debate and the possible use of such studies by the machinery of power and its legitimizing mechanisms, especially through means of mass communication. Said asks:

> How does work on remote or primitive or 'other' cultures, societies, peoples in Central America, Africa, the Middle East, various parts of Asia, feed into, connect with, impede or enhance the active political processes of dependency, domination or hegemony?

Given the web of relations in which the ethnographic knowledge contained in the *Naufragios* is inserted, its use by Spanish colonial power was inevitable and its likely function would be that of adding new possibilities of domination and manipulation of America to the already existing range of mechanisms controlled by the Crown and its representatives. As Jean Franco has demonstrated in relation to the accounts of travelers of the nineteenth century, travel narratives—and *Naufragios* is precisely that— can, in an intentional way or not, be in direct service to colonial power (Franco 129-142).

The subordination of the ethnographic knowledge of Alvar Núñez to a project of colonial occupation is not limited in the *Naufragios* to the choice of its audience— the Crown and the colonial elite—nor to its insertion into the web of accounts already mentioned. After all, the account does not propose, in the end, a return to Europe nor the abandonment of discovered lands. Rather it formulates a program of peaceful conquest as the most efficient way to reach a wider and more profitable control of America and its riches.[14] On the other hand, it must not be forgotten that the writing of *Naufragios* also responds to a personal agenda. The point of departure of this writing is the failure of the expedition, and its central objective is, in the context of the personal aspirations of Alvar Núñez, the transformation of his failure as a conqueror into worthy service (see Pastor, *Discursos narrativos* chapter 3, section 2 and Pupo-Walker). This reveals another aspect of the meaning of his criticism of the model of military conquest. Criticism and alternatives serve to validate the trajectory of the shipwrecked traveler presenting it as a service as worthy of reward as all the achievements of any other conqueror with more luck and success than the narrator. The account of Alvar Núñez attempts to demonstrate that the trajectory of the narrator has allowed him, thanks to his exceptional personal qualities, intelligence and admirable determination, to acquire a knowledge of the new reality and to formulate a model of occupation whose possibilities of success are even greater than those of the military model.

Through his unfortunate experiences, the traveler becomes an expert, and the presentation of his knowledge ties in with a model of action whose result would be the colonization of America. This connection, rather explicit within the text, is prolonged beyond its limits. Because it should not be forgotten that it would be precisely on the basis of his unique skills as an explorer and of his expertise in the new continent that Alvar Núñez would request royal permission to go discover and populate Florida. When his request for nomination is denied, he does not become a Carmelite monk but rather continues with the vicissitudes of his career as conqueror in the Plata region.

The internal contradictions of the narrator, combined with the choice of the audience and with Alvar Núñez's personal aspirations, define the historiographical limits of the narrative voice of Alvar Núñez. Invested with the authority of the traveling ethnographer, this voice demystifies, without question, many of the previous representations of the reality of America and it harshly criticizes the process of military conquest. Nevertheless, the representation and knowledge of the new reality again appear instrumentalized insofar as they respond to the needs of the narrator's characterization and to the need to legitimize his trajectory and to demonstrate all the merits that make him worthy of coveted appointment. In its project of defining the narrative "I" and its need to legitimize both this definition and the narrator's history of the *Naufragios*, this narrative voice ties in with the picaresque novel.

In its instrumentalization, inescapable in text and context, of a knowledge with ulterior ends and applications, it belongs with the tales of travelers that, from the Middle Ages until the establishment of the great modern empires of the nineteenth century, helped pave the way for the imperial expansion of Europe and for the transformation of the vast unexplored territories of America, Africa, Asia and Oceania into colonial realms.

The authority of the traveling ethnographer that shapes the text of *Naufragios* does not reveal itself in this multiple context as the authority of a knowledge sought in real dialogue with the Other's "difference" and with its history, but rather as another facet of the imperial mask.

V

The authority of the European version of the history of the conquest does not lie in its accuracy nor in its objectivity, but rather results from complimentary processes. On one hand is the adoption of analytical and discursive forms that integrate those representations of the New World into European historical tradition. On the other hand is the distortion and systematic silencing of all voices that question hegemonic perception or representation. The violence of this silencing coupled with that of military aggression completes, in its entirety, the process of conquest. The silence created in the documents and chronicles that narrate the conquest of America by the erasure of any dissonance that might challenge, relativize or somehow question the official version of that conquest, implies the simultaneous appropriation of the present and the past, of the nature and history of America. Amilcar Cabral refers to the devastating importance of that parallel conquest when he says that the process of liberation of the colonized people should happen through "the recuperation of the historical personality of the colonized people, their return to history through the destruction of imperial domination to which they have been subjected" (*Unity and Struggle* qtd. Harlow 30). Mary Louise Pratt also alludes to that process of usurpation from a different perspective when she speaks of an underlying narrative strategy in the presentation of explorers and travelers from Columbus to Humboldt:

> It is the strategy to present America as a primitive world of nature; as another one that is not an enemy; as a space that contains plants and animals (some of which are human) not organized into societies and economies; a space whose only history is that which is just beginning. ("Humbolt and the Reinvention of America")

Eric Wolf points out that all European history should be rewritten to include "the peoples without history" (*Europe and People Without History* qtd. Harlow 4). In the case of Latin America, to rewrite the history of its conquest, to find the buried roots of its culture, implies retracing the lost steps, listening to other voices that could have related the history of a discovery rooted in dreams and lies, of a New World that, through the very process of its conquest, was lost forever.

But where, for example, can the voice of Malitzin be found? Her presence was a decisive factor in the spectacular successes of Cortés and in the final defeat of the Aztecs; her betrayal has obsessed Mexico to this very day. Nevertheless, none of the versions of this chapter in the history of the conquest supplies us with information or clues with respect to her vision of the world, of herself, of Cortés or of the events in which she played such a decisive role. The informants of Sahagún tell us how Moctezuma heard with dismay that "There is a woman, she is one of ours, and she speaks Náhuatl. Her name is Malitzin; her home Teticpac. They caught her down there, on the coast, when they first landed..." ("Una mujer, de nosotros los de aquí, los viene acompañando, viene hablando en lengua nahuatl. Su nombre Malitzin; su casa Teticpac. Allá en la costa primeramente la cogieron...") [Léon-Portilla 37]. The reference to her made by Cortés in his *Segunda Carta* is even less explicit. Referring to the series of incidents that lead to the massacre of Cholula, Cortés says that the first news of the supposed rebellion that the Cholutecas were planning came to him through "the tongue that I have, is an Indian woman from these lands whom I got in Potochán" ("la lengua que yo tengo, que es una india de esta tierra, que hube en Potochán") [Cortés 44]. Here Malitzin has neither identity nor name. She is only "an Indian," and it seems particularly ironic that, after reducing her to a total anonymity, after denying her a name, an identity and a voice, Cortés should refer to her precisely as "a tongue."[15] For, as in the case of Columbus's interlocutors, the reduction to the organ of speech does not carry with it the faculty of speech but only the function of assent and confirmation of the voice and the thoughts of the invader.

Bernal Díaz gives us a somewhat more detailed description of Doña Marina—the change of the name is, in itself, significant—but in his *Historia*, as in the rest of the texts of the period, the voice of Malitzin is hardly even heard. In all of them, the true identity of the woman who was one of the key figures of the conquest has been erased forever. In the voice of official history, Malitzin appears either reduced to the alienated role of treacherous go-between or turned into a symbol of duplicity and, in more romantic interpretations, of passionate love. But, what can "passionate love" mean for a woman who was given as a slave, along with other native women, to Cortés who "being that she was good-looking, assertive and self-assured" ("como era de buen parescer y entremetida y desenvuelta") [Díaz 82] gave her as a gift to Portocarrero and, upon his return to Spain, married her to another one of his men, Juan Jaramillo, while keeping her during all that time as his own mistress? It does not seem very far-fetched to imagine that her vision of the situation in which she found herself might not have coincided very well with the idyllic vision given to us by Bernal Díaz:

> God had been very gracious to her in freeing her from the worship of idols and making her a Christian, and giving her a son by her lord and master Cortés, also in marrying her to such a gentleman as her husband Juan Jaramillo. Even if they were to make her mistress of all the provinces of New Spain, she said, she would refuse the honor, for she would rather serve her her husband and Cortés than anything else in the world. (trans. Cohen 86)

Dios le había hecho mucha merced en quitarla de
adorar ídolos e ser agora cristiana, y tener un hijo de
su amo y señor Cortés, y ser casada con un caballero
como era su marido Juan Jaramillo; que aunque la
hicieran cacica de todas cuantas provincias había en
la Nueva España, no los sería, que en más tenía servir
a su marido e a Cortés que cuanto en el mundo hay.
(Díaz 84)

As for her characterization as a symbol of duplicity and
traitor of her people, to what people does this refer? To her
parents, Indians of Cempoal who sold her as a slave to
some Indians from Xicalango? To the Indians of Xicalango
who sold her to some Indians from Tabasco? To the Indians of Tabasco who gave her as a gift to Cortés? To the
Aztecs who ruled tyrannically over all the others? Is there
any connection between the literary creation handed down
to us by witnesses like Bernal Díaz, historians like López
de Gómara, writers like Paz, and the woman who in our
great book of history was only allowed to speak as her
master's tongue while she negotiated, made agreements,
interpreted and conquered with Cortés (for Cortés or
against all the others?) the richest empire of the New
World?

Where are the eyes that could show us the women's
side of the world of war and conquest, about which so
many famous historians have written so much? And
where are the words that could break the silence that covers the voices of all those women who, like Malitzin,
struggled in a world created and controlled by men, without even leaving a tiny scratch on the yellowing pages of
so many historical documents: words that could show us
what they were like as people, as women, as voices, as
eyes, as tongues?

VI

Against the backdrop of silence that covers, in the official accounts, every different, subordinate or dissonant
voice, the work of compiling and transcribing carried out
by the monks constitutes almost the only point of support

in an attempt to unveil the other side of the conquest. Thanks to them, we know something of the historical traditions and cultures of pre-Columbian America. Náhuatl poetry, for example, speaks to us of love, art and religion; their codices depict scenes of daily life before the conquest, telling us about arts, crafts and rituals. In the transcribed texts, we hear the Aztecs complain about the brevity of life, express their fear of death, their terrible anguish before the reality of a world governed by cruel, indifferent and arbitrary gods, their delight in the joys of spring and the beauty of a flower. All of this, however, is before the conquest, for afterwards, their voice changes dramatically before finally fading away. It is now in the graphic accounts of their experience of the conquest, of the pain, the loneliness and the desperation expressed in the Sad Songs (Cantos Tristes), where we hear the voices of the Indians of Tlateloco, of Chalco, of Texcoco and Tlaxcala for the last time.

These songs and narratives, however, do not mark the entrance of the Náhuatl world into Western history. They are only the swan songs of the Aztec nation. The monks allowed them to cry over the present and to remember the past, but once the conquest was finished, they would fall silent since there would not be a place in the new society for voices that the dominant order condemned to disappearance.

But, repression is never total, silence never absolute. And just as the voices of the marginalized, of the oppressed and the defeated seemed to be lost forever, we listen again to their echoes, in a different way and with a different sound. It is the sound of resistance, and it adopts all of the forms defined by the very vulnerability of the conquerors, while for more than a century, it shaped the discovery, defining objectives, tracing journeys, leading and misleading discoverers and conquerors anxious to materialize their dreams and personal utopias in the unexplored territories of the New World. I am speaking of the lying captives, the false guides and informants, the tireless weavers of fables, myths and lies that appear again and again in the Viceroyal courts and in the expeditions of exploration.

There were captives such as Andrés el Barbudo, servant to the Dean of the Island Española, who claimed that the fountain of eternal youth could be found in the islands of the Bahamas and that his very own father had been miraculously rejuvenated with its waters. Similarly, the captive Francisco de Chícora in 1523 persuaded Vázquez de Ayllón that in the land from which he came there were riches and pearls next to which the pearl of six carats that Gonzalo Fernández de Oviedo carried in the visit that he recounts in his *Historia* would seem insignificant by comparison. Finally, there was the case of the Indian Tejo de Nuño de Guzmán who created a fable according to which the coveted Seven Cities of Cibola—which, he claimed, he had repeatedly visited when, as a child, he accompanied his father to his markets where he exchanged feathers for gold—were to be found at the northern border of New Spain.

Between 1512, the year of the expedition of Ponce de León, and the failure of Narváez in 1526 and even later, many expeditions set out in search of the magical fountain, but they returned empty handed, having discovered nothing more than desolation, sickness and death.

In July of 1523, finally convinced by the tales spun by Francisco de Chícora, Lucas Vázquez de Ayllón directed an expedition which reached the Carolinas. Francisco took off and disappeared in the shady woods of his beloved native land as soon as they landed. The majority of the members of the expedition died in the months that followed of cold, hunger or sickness.

Between 1537 and 1540, the Viceroy Don Antonio de Mendoza organized two expeditions in search of the mythical cities promised by the Indian Tejo. The first of these, directed by Fray Marcos de Nizza, returned without getting any further than the town of Pueblos, where the expedition turned back after losing several crew members. The second, lead by Vázquez de Coronado, wandered aimlessly through the Great Plains for almost two years, and would probably have given up and returned prior to this had it not been for the incredible stories that another captive nicknamed Bigotes (Moustache) led Coronado to believe every time he decided that it was time to return. The expedition abandoned its search only after years of terrible hardships, and Coronado never recovered physically or politically from his failure.

Hernando de Soto had even less luck when in 1540 he organized an expedition in search of the magic fountain and the mythical cities with the secret hope of discovering a second Peru. De Soto died somewhere along the banks of the Mississippi after having rejected the tangible evidence of several hundred pounds of pearls offered by the Indian *cacica* Cutifachiqui and after having believed the promises of Perico, another captive who affirmed that in only a few day's journey, the mythical region of Coça which, according to him, harbored incalculable riches could be found.[16]

The list continues in the south of the continent where obliging natives continued to promise and confirm the existence of mythical objectives that combined elements of European legends and indigenous traditions, leading innumerable expeditions to their ruin in the interior of South America in search of the Sierra de la Plata, El Dorado or the Kingdom of the Omaguas.

Since the beginning of the discovery, the natives had gradually lost their world to people who did not care to grasp its complex realities. Their cultures had been destroyed, their languages ignored, their history distorted. From the writings of Columbus on, their words were turned into silence or into an echo of the voice of the invader. Gradually, however, they learned to transform word into weapon, and language became resistance. As they learned to use their growing understanding of the dreams of the conquerors to lead the natives into the trap from which they could not escape: nature, with its marshes, deserts, plains and jungles.[17]

Against the background of the conquerors' struggle with American nature, not finding and losing became simultaneous processes. The tale was a mask that concealed reality, a reality that was always lost and yet always triumphed in the process of looking for myths, reasserting itself in the very destruction of men and of their dreams.[18] In this process of reduction of the New World to European myths and personal dreams, the possibility of a true discovery of America was lost. But they lost more than that, for the

process of conquest would come to be for many a journey
without return that shattered their identity and forced
them to see with different eyes the reality they came from,
revealing contradictions, destroying illusions and shedding light upon their growing alienation with respect to
Europe and America.[19]

We will not be able to trace this process of growing
alienation and progressive awakening in the texts of the
official history of the conquest where there is little room
for error, criticism or failure. But we can see it unfold,
however, in some documents such as the letters of Lope
de Aguirre to Philip II and to the *Provincial* Montesinos,
where Aguirre characterizes the process of discovery as a
journey into despair, the conquerors as pilgrims full of
scars and as spirits of dead men, and finally, Philip himself
as a tyrant, crazed with an insatiable greed, thirsty for the
blood of his subjects. Should it be surprising then that
Aguirre died decapitated and quartered and that his contemporaries labeled him "the crazy man" ("el loco")?
Should it be surprising that his voice was silenced, his
memory erased and his writings lost until 1927?

In 1492, Columbus kept the word and confined the natives to silence. By 1531 (the year of the disaster of the
Marañones expedition and Aguirre's death), this silence
was no longer limited to the voices of the natives but extended to outsiders, subordinates and dissidents: natives,
slaves, women, critics and rebels. There was no place in
the official history of the conquest for any voice that
would express the obscure realization that a process of
conquest is, inevitably, a process of destruction; that the
chronicle of discovery had gradually turned into a chronicle of disillusionment, alienation and loss; that colonizing
and enslaving a people really implies the loss of any
possibility to understand the identity of the colonized and
simultaneously, the loss of ones own in the irreducible
challenge of the Other; that reducing the world to ones
needs and dreams destroys any possibility of truly discovering new worlds.

VII

Between 1569 and 1589 Alonso de Ercilla published the three parts of *La Araucana,* his lengthy poem on the wars between the Spaniards and the Araucano Indians that culminated in the conquest of the territory of Chile. Many of the fundamental elements that shape the complex problematic of the century of the conquest come together in *La Araucana.* The colonial character of the encounter between Europe and America is dramatized through action and characterization. The criticism of the process of colonial domination is slowly developed throughout the length of the poem to culminate in the implicit or explicit rejection that intermittently appears in each of its parts. The irreparable split in the consciousness of the well-intentioned colonizer is expressed in the oscillations of the characterization of the narrator.[20] The equivalence between discovery and loss and conquest and destruction within a colonial project is explored in the expedition to the south of Chile. And, finally, word and writing become problematized in the work in two ways. In the first place, the word is identified with the praise of the imperial ideology and criticism with silence. In the second place, a poetic project that aims directly at the writing of "another history" that implicitly corrects the omissions of the "general history"—American reality, its inhabitants, the corruption of the ideals of the conqueror, the destruction of the New World and the degradation of the colonial reality is defined.

The poetics of *La Araucana* coherently express Ercilla's project. Its particular structure, its modes of characterization and its transgression of the principles of composition of Renaissance epic express the very impossibility of a radical questioning of a colonial order from within that very same order (see Memmi). The poem proposes to narrate a history that rescues from oblivion that which the "general history" has not wanted to or has not been able to "recall."[21] But the very way in which this project of narrating a parallel history or re-writing history is carried out within *La Araucana* raises some fundamental questions. First of all, the recovery of the American identity toward which the project aims, is accomplished through the fictitious assimilation of the Araucanians to the ideology, literary models and cultural codes of European civilization. Secondly, the demystifying criticism of the real conquest is developed through a series of contradictions that limit its scope and seem to disavow at times, its purpose. Both the forced assimilation of the characterization and the contradictions in the critical presentation of the conquest reveal the impossibility of the very project within the context of the economic and military participation of Ercilla in a historical process of conquests which he morally condemns but whose imperial ideology he shares to some extent. The contradictions of the narrative "I" and its successive eclipses, confronted with an action that ties him to the very ideology which he attacks, express the narrator's unsuccessful attempt to reach a resolution of the conflicts that split him.

At the end of *One Hundred Years of Solitude*, the narrator tells us that the destruction of the Buendía family and their world is irrevocable because those condemned to one hundred years of solitude never have a second opportunity on earth. In *La Araucana*, the poet attempts to free himself from the process of destruction in which he sees himself participating by searching for a "second opportunity" through a utopian alternative—the discovery of another New World. This alternative is explored through the expedition to the south of Chile which opens a third hypothetical cycle where the Spaniards have, once more, the opportunity to create a new society based on radically different values from those that had shaped Europe as well as early American colonial societies. The terms of this proposal are formulated by the Indian chief and they include the substitution of greed for generosity, exploitation for brotherhood, repression for tolerance, cruelty for gentleness, violence for harmony, and the preservation of the integrity of the environment and the dignity of its inhabitants. But the radical transformation of the terms of the colonial encounter between Europe and America which this episode dramatizes, turns out to be as impossible as the preservation of the world of the Buendías. By their very internal dynamics, both are destined for destruction and in *La Araucana*, this destruction is prolonged *ad infinitum* when the Spaniards respond to the proposal of peace with the beginning of a new cycle of violence and destruction identical to that which had already given form to the conquest of America.

The failure of the utopic alternative fulfills a triple function. On one hand, it projects the denunciation of the true nature of the conquest of America beyond its actual history. On the other, it shows destruction as an inevitable result of any colonial encounter. And, finally, it creates a cycle of repetition that gives it a certain immutable character, absolving, in part, the narrator of individual responsibility for his participation in the conquest. If there is no escape and if the imperial expansion is an immutable and unstoppable cycle, then the participation does not imply a free choice between different alternatives, but rather, the fulfillment of fate. Only the isolation of the uninhabited islands where Ercilla writes his name, symbolically indicating the end of his pilgrimage, can preserve personal integrity. The "truth" that the poet discovers through his experience of the conquest is the realization of his own alienation and of the inevitable marginalization of a critical consciousness in the context of the Spanish conquest of the New World. It is also the realization that he cannot evade his own responsibility by adopting a critical attitude of moral superiority that is in contradiction with his own complicity with the project of colonial domination, and with his active participation in it through action and through writing (see Memmi 3-44).

Within the imperial context in which it is written and in relation to the problem of the writing of history, *La Araucana* expresses something similar to what the expedition to the south of Chile expressed vis-à-vis the conquest—an unattainable utopia. The project of inscribing "the American" ("lo americano") into Western tradition can only be accomplished by going through a process of fictitious assimilation that strips it of its own identity and history, transforming or eliminating everything that made it truly American. The very project of narrating another history leads only in that historical context, to weeping and silence. To tell the history of American reality, to inscribe its history and to recognize the identity of its people, reveals itself as an impossible undertaking as much in the historical scope as in the literary. The poet is as involved in the colonial machinery as the chronicler; his text, in spite of the growing lucidity of the author and his good intentions, carries out a different form of misrepresentation of the people and realities that it proposes to inscribe. The project of vindication of the difference and of inscription in history remains, from that perspective, a mere symbolic gesture. The irreconcilable oppositions and the unsolvable impossibilities accumulate in a poem that, far from rescuing a destroyed world from oblivion, becomes a chronicle of the growing awareness of a narrator split by the colonial situation and disillusioned by the impossibility of a true reinscription or recovery.

La Araucana begins as a song and ends as a lament. It opens with the word and closes with silence. It traces the awakening of the consciousness of the alienated "I" and reveals the "truth" of the experience of the conquest, which is to say, the comprehension that equates conquest with destruction, and personal history with error. But the development of this critical consciousness of colonial reality leads to silence, a silence that within the poem is shaped by the narrator's self-censorship and by the expression of his own alienation with respect to both worlds—the Spanish and the American. The Spanish world which he criticizes and, to a great extent, rejects, and the American world which he admires and symbolically vindicates but with which he does not succeed in deeply identifying himself.

The silence and omissions that characterized the writing of history during the conquest came thus to shape literary works as well. The censorship imposed on dissidents and natives is complemented here by the final silence of the poet "seeker of truths" who understands obscurely that, in the context of a process of colonial domination there is only one alternative—the adoption of the discourse of power or silence—the same silence that the discourse of power imposed and perpetuated in the writing of the history of the conquest, with its different inflections and modulations of the voice of authority.

And so the word of the Empire prevailed, used by kings and chroniclers, by Spaniards and by natives who came to realize that the word was power and that there could be no power without the word. It prevailed but never succeeded in completely obliterating all the murmurs of a silence made of difference, otherness and dissent.

Against the backdrop of this silence, against the loss of a new world, of reality and of self, History then became a monologue, spoken for centuries by the hegemonic voices of the West.

NOTES

[1] For a brief and informative review of the evolution of the concept of history from antiquity to our times, as well as of some of the aspects of the relationship between history and literature see Gossman.

[2] I use the term "Other" with caution to designate the reality of the New World. I want to emphasize, though it may seem unnecessary, that the term does not designate a reality defined in an immutable and univocal way confronted with the West by its difference with respect to it, but rather by a series of extremely complex and diverse realities whose otherness, difference, definition and categorization should be deliberately contextualized. As Edward W. Said lucidly points out, both terms—*other* and *difference*—are deeply conditioned by their specific historical context, and loosing this simple point of view can only lead to the fetishization of terms in detriment conceptual rigor and clarity of analysis (see his "Representing the Colonized").

[3] The recuperation and dissemination of other versions of the reality of America and of the process of its conquest is admirably exemplified by the work of specialists such as Miguel Léon Portilla and Angel M. Garibay. See also the attentive work of critical editions, such as Rolena Adorno's *Nueva Coronica* of Guamán Poma de Ayala.

[4] For an analysis of how those conqueror's narrative discourses best reveal European imaginary and ideological structures and concrete personal aspirations shed light upon the complex realities of the New World, see Pastor, *Discursos narrativos*. In his article "Historiografía oficial de Colón de Pedro Mártir a Oviedo y Gómara", Marcel Bataillon demonstrates to what point the historiography of the official chroniclers was conditioned by immediate political interests, in this case the legal battle between Columbus and the Crown for the control of lands

discovered by the Admiral. Roberto González Echevarría, on the other hand, approaches the linking between the rhetorical organization and articulation of the *Comentarios Reales* of the Inca Garcilaso de la Vega and a project of personal legitimization and integration in "The Law of the Letter".

5 Michele de Cuneo narrates the incident in his "Carta a Hyeronimo Annari" where he relates how, before the growing skepticism of the crew that was faced with the perception that Columbus had of the newly discovered lands, Columbus forces the crew members to sign a document that affirmed that Cuba was not an island but rather *terra firma* of Cathay and Mangi.

6 In his *Relación del Tercer Viaje* (*Account of the Third Voyage*), written to the Kings in August of 1498 Columbus states: "I've always read in the expertise and experiences of Ptolemy and all of the others that wrote of this place giving evidence and demonstrating it to be so, that the world, land and water was spherical, thus by eclipses of the moon and other demonstrations from the east to the west as the elevation of the North pole in the South wind. Now, *I saw so much deformity* as I've already said, and for this reason I put myself to contemplate the Earth and I found that it was not round in the way that they wrote but rather in the form of a pear that is very round itself except in the place where it has the stem which is taller, or as one who has a very round ball and upon it were placed the breast of a woman..." ("Yo siempre leí qu'el mundo, tierra e agua era espérico e(n) las auctoridades y esperiençias que Ptolomeo y todos los otros qu'escrivieron d'este sitio davan e amostraban para ello, así por ecclipses de la luna y otras demostraçiones que hacen de Oriente fasta Occidente como de la elevaçion del polo de Septentrión en Austro. Agora *vi tanta disformidad* como ya dixey por esto me puse a tener esto del mundo, y fallé que no era redondo en la forma qu'escriven, salvo que es de la forma de una pera que sea toda muy redonda, salvo allí donde tiene el peçcon que allí tiene más alto, o como quien tiene una pelota muy redonda y en lugar d'ella fuesse como una teta de muger allí puesta..." (see *Cristóbal Colón*) [emphasis mine].

7 In his *Relación del Tercer Viaje* (*Account of the Third Voyage*), written to the Kings from Jamaica in 1503, Columbus states: "To Solomon they brought sixty-six thousand, six hundred pounds of gold besides what the merchants and sailors brought besides what was paid in Arabia....If such was the case, I say that those mines of the Aureate are some and that they are controlled by these of Beragna...Solomon bought all of that, gold, stones and silver, and V.A. (Vuestra Alteza) Your Highness can order him to come forward if you summons him." ("A Salomón lle-varon de un camino seiscientos y sesenta y seis quintales de oro, allende lo que llevaron los mercaderes y marineros y alende lo que se pagó en Arabia....Si assi fuese digo que aquellas minas de la Aurea son unas y se contienen con estas de Beragna...Salomón compró todo aquello, oro,

piedras y plata, y V.A. le pueden mandar coger si le aplacen")
(*Cristóbal Colón* 302).

[8] Max Horkheimer points out the connections between Hegel's theory of
great men and Machiavelli's political theory and his psychological
concept of history (*Historia, metafísica y escepticismo* 34).

[9] The episode of the demolition of the idols in the main temple for example, one of the episodes of greater consequences in the entire conquest
of Mexico, is presented as being radically transformed in the version of
Cortés and his transformation obeys to the necessity of maintaining the
validity of the rational approach of Cortés as a model of a scientific
mode of domination that assures the success of the venture. The same
thing occurs in the incident of the liberation of Cuahuitlaua.

[10] Both are expressed in the text in a deplorable representation of the
exploration. The fabulous objectives that drove the expedition are substituted by "puppies" (*perrillos*), "mullets" (*lizas*) and "eggs" (*huevos*)
and other maintenances that rob the natives in order to satisfy hunger;
the impeccable solidarity and direction of the invading army of Cortés
yields to the "every man for himself" ("sálvese quien pueda") of the
final order of Narváez: "He responded to me that now was not the time
to order others; that each person do the best that he saw fit in order to
save his life" ("El me respondió que ya no era tiempo de mandar unos a
otros; que cada uno hiciese lo mejor que le paresciese que era para salvar
la vida") (Núñez Cabeza de Vaca 40).

[11] "Como nosotros víamos que estábamos proveídos de pescado y de raíces
y de agua y de las otras cosas que pedimos, acordamos de tornarnos a
embarcar y seguir nuestro camino, y desenterramos la barca de la arena
en que estaba metida, y *fue menester que nos desnudásemos* todos y
pasásemos gran trabajo para echarla al agua...y ansí embarcados, a dos
tiros de ballesta dentro del mar, nos dió tal golpe de agua que nos mojó a
todos; y *cómo íbamos desnudos y el frío que hacia era muy grande, solta-
mos los remos de las manos*, y a otro golpe que la mar nos dió, trastocó la
barca; el veedor y otros dos *se asieron de ella para escaparse; mas
sucedió muy al revés, que la barca los tomó debajo y se ahogaron*. Como
la costa es muy brava, el mar de un tumbo echó a todos los otros, envuel-
tos en las olas y medio ahogados, en la costa de la misma isla, sin que
faltase mas de los tres que la barca había tomado debajo. Los que
quedamos escapados, *desnudos como nacimos y perdido todo lo que
traíamos*, y aunque todo valía poco, para entonces valía mucho. Y como
entonces era por noviembre y el frío muy grande y nosotros tales que con
poca dificultad nos podían contar los uesos, *estábamos hechos propia
figura de la muerte.*"

[12] The polemic between Bartolomé de Las Casas and Ginés de Sepúlveda
picks up on aspects of these two extreme forms of characterization of the

natives. While the first is applied to dismantle the dominant perception that one has of America and its inhabitants (in the countryside and in the cities), the second is based upon elements of Aristotelian thought in order to justify a reality of exploitation and slavery as part of a project of legitimitized domination through the right of essential superiority given to the Spaniards. In relation to this polemic see Alejandro Lipschutz, *The Racial Problem in the Conquest of America.*

[13] The criticism of Albert Memmi of the Algerian Colonists in his book *The Colonizer and Colonized* is very revealing with respect to the possibility of innocence or lack of responsibility of the well-intentioned colonizer.

[14] It is interesting to see how, in the final chapters of *Naufragios*, the model of military conquest connects to the wasting or loss of riches and the peaceful alternative turns out to be much more profitable: "There are great signs and proof of gold and silver mines; the people of them are very well equipped; they serve the Christians (*those that are friends*) very willfully" ("Hay muestras grandes y señales de minas de oro y de plata; la gente de ella es muy bien acondicionada; sirven a los cristianos (*los que son amigos*) de muy buena voluntad." [100] [emphasis mine]).

[15] The term "tongue" (*lengua*) was used, beginning with Columbus, to designate the native interpreters used by the Spaniards to facilitate the exploration and the conquest.

[16] For a more detailed analysis of the process of the generation of mythical objectives during the period of the conquest see Gandía, and Pastor, *Discursos narrativos*, chapters 3-4.

[17] In the preface to her excellent book, *Resistance Literature*, Barbara Harlow makes reference to an account of the Nigerian writer Chinua Achebe—the one of the turtles and the birds—that marvelously illustrates the formation of a process of resistance of colonial domination.

[18] This is the same mechanism that several years later Cervantes would ironically explore in *Don Quijote de la Mancha.*

[19] It is impossible to not make reference here to the tale, "Camino de Santiago," where Alejo Carpentier explores with intelligent and magnificent humor, the fluctuations of consciousness to which the Spanish conqueror arrives, from pipe dream to pipe dream and from disappointmet to disappointment, as he buries himself in his own alienation.

[20] In relation to the theoretical distinction between colonizer and colonized and to the oscillations and real alternatives of the well intentioned colonizer in the context of a colonial society see Albert Memmi's,

The Colonizer and the Colonized. For a detailed study of the problematic of the split of consciousness of the narrator of *La Araucana* and of its implications, see Pastor, *Discursos narrativos,* chapter 5.

[21] Ercilla says in the Canto XII of *La Araucana*:

> I do not record its process in this history
> for [general] history will remember it.
> (No pongo su proceso en esta historia
> que dél la general hará memoria.)

In this way he implicitly formulates the criteria of selection that he proposes to continue in the composition of the entire poem.

WORKS CITED

Bataillon, Marcel. "Historiografía oficial de Colón de Pedro Mártir a Oviedo y Gómara." *Imago Mundi* 1.5 (1954): 23-39.

Casas, Bartolomé de las. *Historia de las Indias.* Biblioteca de Autores Españoles. Madrid: Atlas, 1958.

Columbus, Christopher. *Cristóbal Colón: Textos y documentos completos.* Ed. Consuelo Varela. Madrid: Alianza Universidad, 1982.

Cortés, Hernán. *Cartas de relación.* México: Porrúa, 1975.

Cuneo, Michele de. "Carta a Hyeromino Annari." *Raccolta Columbiana* III. 2: 95-107.

Díaz, Bernal. *The Conquest of New Spain.* Trans. J.M. Cohen. Middlesex, England: Penguin Classics, 1963.

—. *Historia verdadera de la conquista de México.* Madrid: Espasa-Calpe, 1975.

Ercilla, Alonso de. *La Araucana.* México: Porrúa, 1975.

Franco, Jean. "A Very Unromantic Trip: British Travelers Toward South America, 1818-1828." *Escritura* 7 (1979): 129-142.

Gandía, Enrique de. *Historia crítica de los mitos de la conquista de América.* Buenos Aires: Centro Difusor del Libro, 1946.

González Echevarría, Roberto. "The Law of the Letter: Garcilaso's Commentaries and the Origins of Latin American Narrative." *The Yale Journal of Criticism* 1.1 (1987): 107-131.

Gossman, Lionel. "History and Literature." *The Writing of History: Literary Form and Historical Understanding.* Ed. R.H. Canary. Madison: Univ. of Wisconsin Press, 1978. 3-39.

Harlow, Barbara. *Resistance Literature.* New York: Methuen, 1987.

Horkheimer, Max. *Historia, metafísica y escepticismo.* Madrid: Alianza, 1982.

León-Portilla, Miguel. *La visión de los vencidos.* México: UNAM, 1976.

Lipschutz, Alejandro. *The Racial Problem in the Conquest of America.* México: Siglo XXI Editores, 1963.

Memmi, Albert. *The Colonizer and Colonized.* Boston: Beacon Press, 1967.

Morrison, Samuel E. *Admiral of the Ocean Sea.* 2 vols. Boston, 1942.

Núñez Cabeza de Vaca, Alvar. *Naufragios.* Madrid: Espasa-Calpe, 1957.

Pastor, Beatriz. *Discursos narrativos de la conquista de América.* Hanover, NH: Ediciones del Norte, 1988.

Pratt, Mary Louise. "Humbolt and the Reinvention of America." *Nuevo Texto Crítico* 1.1 (1988).

Pupo-Walker, Enrique. "Pesquisas para una nueva lectura de los *Naufragios* de Alvar Núñez Cabeza de Vaca." *Revista Iberoamericana* 140 (1987).

Said, Edward W. "Representing the Colonized: Anthropology's Inter-locutors." School of Criticism and Theory, Dartmouth College, 1988.

White, Hayden. "Historical Text as Literary Artifact." *The Writing of History: Literary Form and Historical Understanding.* Ed. R.H. Canary. Madison: Univ. of Wisconsin Press, 1978. 41-62.

—. *Metahistory: The Historical Imagination in Nineteenth-Century Europe.* Baltimore: The Johns Hopkins Univ. Press, 1973.

CHAPTER 4:
THE APPREHENSION OF THE NEW
IN NATURE AND CULTURE:
FERNANDEZ DE OVIEDO'S *SUMARIO*

Stephanie Merrim

*Every man carries within him a world
which is composed of all that he has seen
and loves and to which he constantly returns even when he is traveling through,
and seems to be living in, some different
world.*

Chateaubriand
(Cited by Lévi-Strauss in
Tristes Tropiques)

As they explored and appropriated the New World, the early Spanish adventurers documented their findings with reports to the Crown, verbal explorations which grappled with the mysteries of the Indies. Inaugurated with these reports, the intellectual discovery and conquest of the New World by the Old (as J.H. Elliott has documented in *The Old World and the New*)[1] developed alongside the other conquest, but at a very different and rather secondary rhythm, functional matters being the primary concern. Indeed, the intellectual conquest would prove to be as arduous or complex as the physical, and to merit a history of its own. As one of its first proponents, Edmundo O'Gorman (*Invención*, Introduction), well knew, such a history would needs exceed the limits of history proper to embrace philosophical as well as ideological issues since the first obstacle for these explorers-turned-historians in appre-

hending the New World was to perceive and comprehend
it. The second act of apprehension then entailed catching
or fixing that reality in words. What means, wondered
Bernal Díaz del Castillo, could be adequate to represent
such marvels, "because there is so much to ponder in all
this that I don't know how to tell it: to have seen things
never heard of, nor seen before, nor even dreamt of, as did
we" (I, 311) ("porque hay que ponderar mucho en ello, que
no sé cómo lo cuente: ver cosas nunca oídas, ni vistas, ni
aun soñadas, como vimos"). As an historical process, both
types of apprehension proceeded unevenly, in fits and
starts. Therefore, the chronicles of different authors, or
even the work of a single author, would be variously successful in, as Alexander von Humboldt put it, making experience the subject of direct observation "and not of
vague presentiments, floating in varying forms before the
imagination" (601).

Much as they ultimately shed light on the Renaissance,
the dynamics of apprehension of the new are certainly not
limited to that period. The confrontation of explorers,
conquerors, soldiers or even anthropologists with
(an)'other' society provokes the questioning of self or
one's own society and often forms the eye of a philosophical debate. That is to say, encounter with the other incites
the definition or redefinition of self, throwing received
values into question. Montaigne, it is well known, par-
layed his knowledge of the 'barbarous' Brazilian culture
into a critique of the values of his own society, which he
exposed as barbarous in its own right ("So we may well call
these people barbarians, in respect to the rules of reason,
but not in respect to ourselves, who surpass them in every
kind of barbarity") (103). Conversely, as T. Walter Herbert's
Marquesan Encounters details, their experiences of
Polynesian society caused colonial North Americans to
formulate and assert their still nascent concept of civilization: the Polynesians became "mirrors" in which the
Americans could study their "own anxious selves"
(Beaver 452). As an anthropologist, Claude Lévi-Strauss
was able to contemplate the discovery of the New World
in similar terms. Approaching Brazil by ship, he mused
that the navigators of old "were less concerned with dis-

covering a new world than with verifying the past of the old" (74).

Did anyone, we might ask as has been asked before, see the New World for the first time? Or did they see only what their own world and its models of all sorts had prepared them to see and seek out? Such questions indicate that documents of the conquest such as Oviedo's should tell us equally as much, if not more, about the perceivers— their values, ideologies and culture—than the perceived, the New World,[2] which fact does not invalidate, but actually redeems their more absolute historical value. For, through their interplay of blindness and insight the chronicles provide an accurate portrait of a charged moment in Renaissance intellectual history, with its parting of the seas between faith and science, and charting of courses for historiography, the natural sciences and ethnography.

The full dimensions of this drama are present in the works of Gonzalo Fernández de Oviedo y Valdés (1478-1557), author of (perhaps) the first novel to be written in the New World (1519),[3] its first natural history (1526) and the first historical account (which he began to publish in 1535). A series of pointed contrasts in his life and works sets the stage for our study. Guardian of the old and purveyor of the new, Oviedo brought intact to the New World the cultural baggage of the Old, its social, political and moral values. Raised in the court, versed in Italian Renaissance culture, and a passionate devotee of all things aristocratic, Oviedo traveled early on to the New World (in 1513) to discharge the posts of General Scribe and Overseer of Gold. One can all too easily imagine how the spectacle of the recently settled tropics might have impressed Oviedo's aristocratic eye as barbaric and uncivilized, inciting him to formulate his notorious plan for an order of chivalry, the Order of Santiago, to be established in and rule Santa María. Yet Oviedo would make six trips to the Indies, spend most of his life there, and serve as Governor of Santa María, *regidor perpetuo* of Santo Domingo, and governor of its fortress, all the while remaining a staunch imperialist and, after 1524, an Erasmist. Vilified by the more charismatic Las Casas, he would go down in history as an incorrigible anti-Indianist.

At the same time, as he states in its prologue, Oviedo would consecrate the latter portion of his life to chronicling all the corners of this world to which he was so drawn, in the encyclopedic fifty volume *Historia general y natural de las Indias* ("General and Natural History of the Indies"):

> I will dedicate what life remains to me to acquitting to memory in this gentle and pleasing *General and Natural History of the Indies* all that I have seen and all that has and will come to my attention, from the very first discovery, with everything that I have seen and learned, for as long as I live (I,9).

> ocuparé lo que me queda de vivir en dejar por memoria esta dulce y agradable General y natural historia de las Indias, en todo aquello he visto, y en lo que a mi noticia ha venido e viniere, desde su primero descubrimiento, con lo que más pudiere ver y alcanzar dello, en tanto que la vida no se me acabare.

He dedicates the work to truth and, since he writes about the New World *from* the New World, to empiricism, promising a "true history divorced from all the fables which other writers, without having been here, have presumed to write, from Spain...in elegant and uncommon words, both Latin and Spanish..." (I,9) ("historia verdadera e desviada de todas las fábulas que en este caso otros escritores, sin verlo, desde España, a pie enjuto, han presumido escribir con elegantes y no comunes letras latinas e vulgares..."). Nonetheless, the Spaniard exclaims at his inability both to comprehend and (as did Bernal Díaz) to capture the new reality in words:

> What mortal wits could comprehend such diversity of languages, of habits, of customs, as that of the people of these Indies? Or such a variety of animals, both domestic, and savage and wild? Or such a multitude of trees, so overladen with diverse fruits, that they are impossible to describe [...] and since there is so much to be said about this most great and new empire, and the lessons to be learned from it are

> so admirable, let them redeem me before your Cae-
> sarean Majesty if I have not done full justice to the
> material...(I, 8-9)

> ¿Cual ingenio mortal sabrá comprehender tanta di-
> versidad de lenguas, de hábitos, de costumbres en los
> hombres destas Indias? ¿Tanta variedad de ani-
> males, así domésticos como salvajes y fieros? ¿Tanta
> multitud innarrable de árboles, copiosos de diversos
> géneros de frutas [...] y pues lo que deste grandísimo e
> nuevo imperio se podría escrebir es tanto, e tan ad-
> mirable la lección dello, ella misma me desculpe con
> Vuestra Cesárea Majestad, si tan copiosamente como
> la materia lo requiere no se dijere... .

Oviedo, repository of old values, herein sets forth the problematics facing the new historian.

These multiform paradoxes as well as Oviedo's own intentions, challenge us to examine the equally multiple premises, models and discursive strategies of the *Sumario de la natural historia de las Indias* ("Natural History of the West Indies"; citations in English are from this edition, with modifications where necessary. All other translations are mine). How, and to what ends, did Oviedo confront and resolve the problems of representing the newness of the New World?

Unevenly and variously, of course, in a process which begins, perhaps unwittingly, with a novel of chivalry. Curiously enough, Oviedo's first writings from the New World to see print are not historiographic, but rather consist of a somewhat irregular novel of chivalry, set in Europe, *Don Claribalte* (Valencia,1519). While *Claribalte* may qualify as the first novel written in the Indies, it contains not a single word pertaining to that reality. Rather, the novel abounds in descriptions of chivalric life, its protocol and trappings. Conventional novels of chivalry revolve around the marvellous; otherworldly obstacles overcome by awe-inspiring feats of courage. Oviedo, on the other hand, so caught up in the minutiae of his past life, largely purges *Claribalte* of supernatural elements. Instead, he nostalgically endows even the most prosaic features of the chivalric world with a marvellous cast, modifying this Old World genre by placing it in a familiar reality.

The fact that Oviedo launched his writings in the Indies with an evasion of the otherly heightens the drama of the change in his next work, a direct confrontation with the novelty of the New World. To satisfy the King's curiosity about his new holdings, and at his direct request, Oviedo wrote the *Sumario de la natural historia de las Indias* in Spain, from memory, reconstructing notes he had already taken for the *Historia general* (the *Sumario* reappears almost verbatim in the larger work). Though outwardly it follows what has been called a "biogeographical" path (Alvarez López, "Historia natural" 551) describing the phenomena of each country in the order that Oviedo visited them, and largely adheres to the taxonomy of Pliny's *Natural History*, at heart the *Sumario* remains a miscellanea, which resists structuring, of odd facts about the plants, animals, peoples and cultures of the Indies. To reveal the *novelty* of these subjects, Oviedo states in the preface, was his chief purpose and, quite clearly, the criterion according to which he selected his material: "I beg of Your Majesty to pardon any lack or order or arrangement that may be found in this book...But I also I should like you to observe *the new things in it, for this has been my chief purpose*" (9, italics mine) ("si no fuere tan ordenado lo que aquí está contenido...no mire vuestra Majestad en esto, sino en la *novedad de lo que quiero decir, que es el fin conque a esto me muevo...*" 49).

The *Sumario* is the turning point, a convocation of old and new sensibilities which together permit Oviedo to open himself to the new reality, sharpening his powers of observation. He perceives the similarities and, particularly, the differences from the Old World: "It is true from what one can see of the marvels of the world and the great differences among animals, that these differences are greater in some places than in others, according to the locality or the constellations under which these animals have been bred" (46) ("Verdad es que, según las maravillas del mundo y los extremos que las criaturas, más en unas partes que en otras, tienen, según las diversidades de las provincias y constelaciones donde se crían..."94). He emphasizes the raw newness of certain of the phenomena he presents from those described by the ancients: "The many animals that exist in the Indies that I describe here, or at least most of them, could not have been learned about from the ancients" (47) ("porque de muchos animales que hay en aquellas partes, y entre ellos aquestos que yo aquí pondré, o los más de ellos, ningún escritor supo de los antiguos" 95). Yet Oviedo has not abandoned the romance mode of *Claribalte*. In fact, his initial retreat into romance may well have been the decisive factor in making of Oviedo, according to O'Gorman, one of the first explorers capable of perceiving a new meaning in America:[4] a predilection for the novel of chivalry, based as the genre is on the miraculous and awesome, could easily have fostered the writer's propensity to seek out and acknowledge the new and marvellous. In other words, the mediation of the fictional world of romance prepared Oviedo to understand more comprehensively the Indies which he may have found more "novel" than new.

Though it undermines the work's structure, Oviedo's criterion of novelty determines his comprehension and representation of nature and culture—virtually polarizing them and turning the *Sumario* into something of a collage work, a meeting ground for two modes of representation. We shall consider, as a point of departure, Oviedo's portrait of the pineapple and the cactus in the *Sumario*:

> When the Indians and Christians plant pineapples, they put them in regular rows like vine stalks in a vineyard. This fruit smells better than peaches, and the whole house will be filled with this fragrance by one or two pineapples. In taste it is one of the best fruits in the world; it is also very handsome. In taste it is somewhat like peaches. The pineapple flesh is also like that of a peach, but it has very fine filaments like the thistle, which are harmful to the teeth if one regularly eats this fruit. The pineapple is very juicy, and in some places the Indians make some good wine of it. It is a healthful fruit and is given to sick people. For those who are surfeited and do not wish to eat, it is an excellent appetizer.

> There are some trees [cacti] in the Island Hispaniola that are very spiny, and I have never seen any plant or tree that is so wild, shapeless, and ugly. The branches are originally leaves, and as they grow

> longer and harder, other pulpy leaves grow from
> them. It would be very difficult to describe this plant
> with words; it would be much more satisfactory to
> make a sketch of it for through the eyes one might
> understand what cannot be described with words. The
> plant is good for one thing. The flesh and leaves are
> pounded to a pulp and spread on a piece of cloth. This
> is used to bind up a broken arm or leg. Even if the limb
> has been broken in many places, it knits and heals
> completely with a fortnight. (99-100)[5]

Truly this is an Adamic account, naming and founding an image of two, entirely new, phenomena. One cannot question the integrity of Oviedo's attempt to apprehend the object from all angles. Departing from comparisons with the known (vines, peaches) his words travel luxuriantly over and through the fruit, listing its properties according to two parameters, aesthetic and practical. Unlike other naturalists of the time, Oviedo lacked medical training, therefore no technical knowledge or language intrudes in the commonsensical cast of this "everyman's" narrative. Nor does Oviedo theorize about the origins or causes of these phenomena, remaining a describer of surfaces. Orderly and sustained, the description proceeds part by part along the sensuous surface in a fashion so thoroughly analytical that, in retrospect, it effectively 'makes strange' these now familiar objects. As is characteristic of Oviedo, he appeals one after another to the senses of sight, smell, taste and touch. The underlying authority of the writer's "I", which has experienced these wonders and can attest to their existence enhances the impact of these pre-Romantic depictions. But not, to Oviedo's mind, sufficiently: aware of the inadequacies of language, he would rather his pen were a paintbrush more satisfactorily to render the object for the reader.

The cornucopia of the New World offers up fruits and plants to which only superlatives can do justice (one of the best fruits; the wildest and ugliest tree). Manifold, almost miraculous, are not only the sensual but also the practical values of these novelties—such as the poultice which heals broken bones—and a tinge of awe akin to the *asombro* of novels of chivalry colors the narrative. "The secrets of this great world of our Indies will always teach us new things, both to us here now and to those who come in the future to this contemplation and beautiful reading of the works of God" ("Los secretos deste gran mundo de nuestras Indias siempre enseñarán cosas nuevas a los presentes e a los que después de nos han de venir a esta contemplación e hermosa letura de las obras de Dios"), declares Oviedo in the *Historia general* (I, 223-24). Such awe arises from nature, but, in accordance with the Renaissance belief in nature as a vehicle to God, ultimately constitutes a tribute to the Creator. The concept of nature as God's handiwork, which underlies the *Sumario*, adds an implicit devotional aspect to the bucolic, almost pagan, portrait: on the very first page of the *Historia general* Oviedo incites us to "investigate on land and sea the marvellous and innumerable works that God, Lord of all creation, shows us, so that we praise Him all the more..." ("inquirir en la tierra y en la mar las maravillosas e innumerables obras que el mismo Dios y Señor de todo nos enseña, para que más loores le demos..."). Oviedo, we recognize, was to (natural) history what Fray Luis de León was to poetry: a reader of the imprint of God in nature. All told, then, the natural world which Oviedo represents to his readers is a pastoral lightworld of over-abundance, better than the known world, only one step from its Maker.[6]

Yet all is not light in this world, which also contains dark negative elements such as hideous cacti and, elsewhere in the *Sumario*, venomous snakes and pestiferous insects. Unlike Columbus's unmitigated ecstasies over the nature of the New World in his first writings, the *Sumario* displays a fascination for the grotesque and even the macabre. As we can see here, Oviedo gravitates towards both extremes of the natural world. From sampling the pineapple's delights to gaping at the cactus, he accepts nature in all its diversity and appears to glory in its ambiguity, its double sign. Moreover, the chronicler displays an impressive ability to see beyond appearances to an unsuspected core. Symbolic of Oviedo's acceptance of nature's ambiguity are the many descriptions of elements like the cactus whose surface gives lie to their true (beneficial) nature. Under Oviedo's penetrating scrutiny, dark and light elements merge into light, for *all* of nature is God's hand-iwork and bears His message.[7] The greater nature's diversity, the greater God's accomplishment. In effect, then, Oviedo's religiously conditioned understanding of nature results in an early impartial and scientific account of the New World.

Much as Oviedo seems to be writing the New World in all its novelty, he is, to an important degree, rewriting it; the character and innovations of Oviedo's text derive not only from the reality of the New World and the theology through which Oviedo perceived it, but are a product as well of a dialogue between the *Sumario* and its principal intertext, Pliny's *Natural History* (which dates from the first century A.D.). Since Oviedo proclaims his debt to Pliny in the prologues of both the *Sumario* and the *Historia general*, the Spaniard's reliance on the *Natural History*'s scientific classifications of flora and fauna has been widely discussed (see, for example, Salas 143ff.). Yet the *Natural History*, which aspired to the condition of an encyclopedia of the natural world, appealed to Oviedo on other levels as well. An idiosyncratic and at times exuberant work, the *Natural History* exhibits a love for the marvellous and the novel. A kind of Book of World Records (I shall have more to say about this in the latter portion of this essay), it revels in the superlative and the curious with respect to both the human and natural worlds and gravitates to the extremes of these phenomena, often incurring incredulousness. Conversational and non-technical in tone, Pliny is so taken with his material that he often allows it to overflow the taxonomic structure of the work, all in service of revealing the powers and variety of nature:

> See how Nature is disposed to devise full wit-tily...pastimes to play with mankind, not only to make herself merry but to set us a-wondering at such strange miracles. And I assure you, she plays her part daily and hourly in such a manner that to recount every one of her efforts by themselves no one is able with all his wit and energy. Let it suffice therefore that we have set down these prodigious and strange

works of hers, shown in whole nations to testify and
declare her power (cited in Wethered 263).

Behind the associative and miscellaneous cast of Pliny's
work, then, lies a theory of nature as a divine energy operating in the world (Wethered 156), which is not dissimilar
to Oviedo's notion of God. Such a belief also leads Pliny to
emphasize the seemingly miraculous practical applications
of nature's bounty, which enterprise at times reduces his
Natural History to little more than a pharmaceutical guide
to the medicinal properties of natural phenomena.

Perhaps, as been noted by others, Oviedo set out to be
the Pliny of the New World[8] for, as the reader can judge
from our earlier descriptions of the Sumario, the points of
contact between the two works are multiple. The Natural
History furnished Oviedo with a formal model, and a theoretical justification for that model compatible with his
own thinking, which was both determining and liberating.
On the one hand, the Natural History spoke to Oviedo's
problems of writing the New World. In it Oviedo found a
means of ordering scientifically, seeing empirically, and
perhaps even writing, acceptable to both the imaginative
(romance) and the Erasmist (practical, religious) aspects of
his sensibility. Though Oviedo would surpass Pliny in the
exactness and directness of his descriptions, the Natural
History set the Spaniard on his course and would lend
authority and historical sanction to his findings. On the
other hand, the existence of such a model permitted
Oviedo to pursue what may well have been his own
inclinations towards novelty, the marvellous, miscellanea,
and fidelity to nature. The Sumario owes its lack of structure to the unconfining structure of the Natural History
(and to the concrete circumstances of its genesis in Spain),
and its "modernity" to this link with antiquity.

Besides freeing up and giving direction to new zones in
Oviedo's thinking, one might reasonably speculate that
the Natural History addressed his problems of representation on a rather more global scale. As depicted to Oviedo
by Pliny, the classical world placed enormous emphasis on
gold (its most important metal) and abounded in mirabilia
and extreme phenomena. As revived in general by the

Renaissance, the world of antiquity was seen as a pagan society, ruled by an Emperor, and was often portrayed as a utopia lost. Hence it is arguable that Oviedo—Overseer of Gold, and devoted subject of Emperor Charles V—finding himself in a pagan civilization fraught with curiosities and natural bounty, believed it to be an incarnation of the classical world. One striking support for this hypothesis is Oviedo's controversial claim,[9] put forth in Chapter Three, Book Two of the *Historia general*, that the Indies were actually the legendary Hesperides, to which legend Oviedo adds a Spanish corollary: "[I] take these Indies to be those famous islands, the Hesperides, thus named after the twelfth King of Spain, Hesperus" ("yo tengo estas Indias por aquellas famosas islas Hespérides, así llamadas del duodécimo rey de España, dicho Hespero"); "in my mind I have not doubt that they were formerly known to and possessed by the Sovereigns of Spain" (I, 17) ("e para mí no dudo haberse sabido e poseído antiguamente por los reyes de España"). Oviedo goes on to situate the Spanish rule of the Hesperides/Indies in the early classical era (the same period, interestingly enough, in which he situates *Claribalte*): "Beroso maintains that this King Hesperus succeeded the Egyptian Hercules in ruling Spain, one hundred and seventy one years before the founding of Rome, B.C.... (I, 17-18) ("Este rey Hespero quiere Beroso que comenzase a reinar en España, subcediendo a Hércules egipcio, antes que Troya fuese edificado, ciento e setenta e un años e antes que Roma fuese fundado, seiscientos e tres, que sería antes que nuestro Redemptor..."). Perhaps for this reason one scholar finds Oviedo's classical references to have a function beyond that of mere adornment: "Thus, in my opinion, Oviedo's constant allusions to the works of Pliny, Eusebius, Trogus, etc., are not a mere show of classical and humanist erudition...but represent his desire to find either relationship or parallels between the customs and things of America and those of the places to which the works he cites refers" (Ballesteros, "Etnólogo" 459-60) ("Así, pues, en mi opinión, la constante alusión de Oviedo a las obras de Plinio, Eusebio, Trogo, etc., no tiene un mero valor de erudición clásica y humanística...sino un deseo de hallar o parentesco o paralelo entre las costumbres y cosas americanas y las de los pueblos de los que hablan las obras que cita"). The classical world in its pagan splendor, and as represented by Pliny, was certainly a more apt model for Oviedo than Spain, and one that served to mitigate the otherness of the New World. Viewed in this light, the emphasis on novelty encountered in the description of the pineapple and the cactus—as well as the claim that Oviedo was one of the first to perceive a new meaning in America—acquires a particular shading. First, and naturally so, that like other Renaissance thinkers such as Pedro Mártir, Oviedo did not perceive the New World in a vacuum, but as over/against the classical world. And second, that if indeed Oviedo did understand the New World as new, it was to a degree because various mediating influences—the novel of chivalry, Renaissance theology, Pliny—conditioned and permitted him to do so.

The reader who approaches the *Sumario* knowing only that Juan Ginés de Sepúlveda drew upon Oviedo's work to argue against the Indians as rational beings (in his debate with Bartolomé de Las Casas in Valladolid) will be surprised to find Oviedo as appreciatively receptive to the novelty of certain aspects of indigenous culture as he was to New World natural phenomena.[10] Intermittently throughout the *Sumario*, Oviedo renders detailed discussions of certain practical aspects of Amerindian life such as food, food-gathering, and living arrangements. Such ethnographic depictions blend imperceptibly with those of natural phenomena for they share the same minutely analytic descriptive techniques and respond to the same criteria of sensuousness, empiricism, admiration and, particularly, of novelty. Unlike Columbus, whose formulaic characterizations reduce the Indians to a single paradigm, Oviedo displays a sensitivity to the diversity of Indian habits. Further, at several points he admiringly imparts their skill, ingenuity and resourcefulness—as swimmers, pearl gatherers, creators of foodstuffs and domestic goods. In recognizing the function of these practical aspects as characteristics of an organized society, Oviedo's ethnographic observations in the *Sumario* could, in fact, have fueled precisely the Aristotelian arguments used by

Las Casas in the *Apologética historia* to qualify the Indians as rational and thus not as 'natural slaves' by virtue of their being capable of forming a polity. As Manuel Ballesteros has noted, Oviedo acknowledged "the Indians to be human beings...capable of their own organization, creators of technical and alimentary solutions...which allowed them to establish societies, create ruling groups and to live off the land" ("a los indios como seres humanos....capaces de organizarse, inventores de soluciones técnicas y alimenticias...que les permitieron establecer sociedades, crear grupos directivos y sobrevivir sobre el terreno").[11]

While the criterion of novelty remains a constant, Oviedo's receptiveness to it as well as his appreciative equanimity fade into a mere gesture with his accounts of what emerge in the *Sumario* as the *inherent* characteristics of Amerindian culture. Although the early chapters of the work had interspersed natural history and brief ethnographic accounts, the long Chapter X is (the only one) explicitly dedicated to matters ethnographic. Thus, its title, "De los indios de Tierra Firme y *de sus costumbres y ritos y ceremonias*" (our emphasis) ("Indians of Tierra Firme, *Their Customs, Rites and Ceremonies*"), gives us a sense of what Oviedo considers to be the intrinsic or defining traits of the Indian world. And, as the following passage typifies, here Oviedo's apprehension of the new takes a turn towards the other meaning of the word, becoming one of fear, ill-will, and sensationalism—a reflection of the Spaniard's "anxious self":

> ...The differences over which the Indians quarrel and go to battle are concerning who shall have the most land and power. They kill those they can and sometimes they take captives whom they brand and keep as slaves. Each master has his own brand and some masters pull out one front tooth of their slaves as a mark of ownership. The bow-using Caribs, or the people of Cartagena, and most of those who live along that coast, eat human flesh. They do not take slaves, nor are they friendly to their enemies or foreigners. They eat all the men that they kill and use the women they capture, and the children that they bear—if any Carib should couple with them—are also eaten. [...]

To begin their battles or fights, and for many other
things that the Indians want to do, they have special
men whom they respect highly and whom they call
tequina. They call any man who excels in any art a
tequina, whether he is the best hunter or fisherman
or best maker of nets, bows, or other things. For
tequina means master. They also call *tequina* the one
who is master of communications and intelligence
with the devil. This *tequina* speaks with the devil
and receives replies from him. He then tells the Indians what they must do, and he predicts the future.
Since the devil is an old astrologer, he knows what
the weather will be, and he knows the outcome of
things and how nature rules them. And thus, by the
result that naturally is to be expected, he informs
them of the future and gives them to understand that
through his deity, or as lord of all and mover of everything that is and will be, he can foresee things of
the future and what will come to pass, and that he
causes the thunder, and makes the sun and rain, that
he rules the weather, and that he gives or deprives
them of food. The Indians, deceived by the *tequina*
since they have seen many of his prophecies come
true, believe everything he says, and fear and respect
him, and in certain places make sacrifices of blood
and human lives...(33-34)[12]

The shift in Oviedo's perspective, from a hyper-sensi-
tivity *vis-à-vis* the confounding nuances of nature to what
J.H. Elliott would call the closing of his "mental shutters"[13]
regarding those of humankind is reflected in the form of
argumentation apparent in this passage. Outwardly
Oviedo retains a factual stance and external perspective,
not overtly criticizing and interjecting his opinions only
indirectly ("deceived by him" ["engañados por él"]).
Nonetheless, as it mounts piece after piece of evidence to
build its case against the pagan Indians, his polemic takes
on the invective if flat legalistic cast which Oviedo might
have learned as Secretary of the Inquisition in Spain in
1506. A certain frenzy short-circuits the rigor of Oviedo's
arguments, which remain underdeveloped and associative
in their logic, and undefined in structure as they jump
from topic to topic. Unlike the lyrical and attractive docu-
menting of natural phenomena, absent from this writing

of fear and apprehension is the empirical force of the writer's "I" or an appeal to the senses. Instead, the argumentation applies to the intellect and emotions through the rhetorical techniques of persuasion—synthesis, overarching generalizations and anaphora—which effectively supplant the direct encounter with the object in all its particularity found in the descriptions of nature.

While the absence of an "I" gives the appearance of objectivity, more than anything else the selection of material bespeaks Oviedo's judgmental attitude towards the defining aspects of Indian culture. The indisputable novelty of the information would conceivably authorize the historian to discuss such damning curiosities as rape, cannibalism, devil worship and sacrifices—but not to dwell so obsessively on such topics. Nonetheless, the 'scandal sheet' criterion that we find here is almost mild compared to other parts of Chapter X and the *Sumario*, which treat the homosexuality, sodomy, polygamy, nudity, abortions, burial rituals, brutality, wife-swapping, and so on, of the Indians. The Indian women of the New World receive a particularly sensationalist treatment, represented by Oviedo as creatures of an unbridled sensuality who, for example, abort their babies because "they don't want to be occupied and give up their pleasures" (79) ("no quieren estar ocupadas para dejar sus placeres") and shore up their sagging breasts with bars of gold (92). At times, too, the language of the text curdles into epithets of summary condemnation, as in Chapter IX's description of the Indians of Urabá: "these Indians eat human flesh; they are filthy, cruel, and they are also sodomites" (26) ("y comen carne humana, y son abominables, sodimitas [sic] y crueles..."73).

Why does Oviedo so single-mindedly apply these criteria to the ethnographic material of the *Sumario*? Why does he craft this sensationalist and damning portrait of a world which Columbus (whom he admired) had already cast in the pastoral utopian mold of a civilization with no "sects" or idolatries? On the one hand, Oviedo's 'knee-jerk' negative reaction to threatening otherness is expectable, especially in view of the vaunting moralism so characteristic of all his writings and of his notion of the didactic role of history, both to a degree Erasmian traits. Here and elsewhere Oviedo styles himself as the bearer and conveyer of the Spanish moral code according to which he, at the same time, codifies the New World. For, under the guise of novelty, or with the justification of registering novelties, it is clear that Oviedo introduces those exotic aspects which go against the Spanish readers' expectations, and, moreover, contravene their moral code. Each point that Oviedo makes in the passage cited is a charged one, establishing how the Indians transgress yet another tenet of the Spanish code, be it of sexual prohibition, fraternity, or religious belief. To accentuate his implicit comparisons, the historian seeks out the sometimes grotesque Indian analogues of Spanish customs, particularly of aristocratic feudal practices: as here, where the masters pull out their slaves' teeth, or in numerous similar passages.

Indisputable as Oviedo's moralizing bent may be as an explanation of his choice of ethnographic criteria, it does not fully account for certain aspects of this crucial issue. The author's unabashed prurience, suspension of decorum (this is, after all, a *relación* addressed to the King), delight in telling transgressive tales, fascination with the sensational extremes of Indian culture, and so on, are unmatched in contemporaneous works from the New World and take us beyond sheer moralizing into the pre-history and 'universals' of ethnography. For example, in his *Histories* of the fifth century B.C., Herodotus of Halicarnassus, a founding precursor of ethnography, emphasized marriage customs, religious rites, burial practices, and food habits.[14] Analyzed in this light, Oviedo's categories prove quite similar, reducing down to the following topics: the physical characteristics of the Indians (ethnology); their religious, warring, and death customs; class divisions and practices; endogamy and exogamy (including sexual habits); food and shelter. As we can see, despite their sheen of the exotic, Oviedo's categories in fact respond to essential, time-worn ethnographic questions regarding how a society regulates itself internally and externally.

Even the sheen of the exotic, that is, the criterion of novelty, (as we began to suggest in examining Pliny's influence on Oviedo) takes its cue from two features of prior 'ethnographies', their marvel-ridden and popular nature. Following the extraordinarily influential line of Pliny, the pre-ethnographers of the Middle Ages and beyond eschewed Herodotus's direct inquiries to become what Margaret T. Hogden (Chapter 1) terms "epitomizers"—collectors rather than investigators of odd and unusual facts about little-known cultures. The "epitomizers," rather than creating new and more exacting categories for the study of culture and largely devoid of intellectual curiosity, credulously propagated tales of curiosities, marvels, magic, abnormalities, monsters, bizarre practices, and the like, all enhanced and rendered credible to the reader's mind by the remoteness of the places to which they referred. The result was a genre both popular (to the degree that it could be so in the pre-typographical world) in inception and in appeal. Hogden notes that "[o]f the twelve best sellers among incunabula in the 14th and 15th centuries, four.... dealt with marvels" (59). Now, in reconstructing Oviedo's extensive personal library from references in the Spaniard's works, Daymond Turner notes that, after Pliny, Saint Isidore of Spain figures as the author most frequently cited in the first part, or 1535 edition of the *Historia general y natural de las Indias* (168). According to Turner, Oviedo's library also included Pedro Mexía's *Silva de varia lección* and Caius Julius Solinus's *Polyhistor*. Each of these authors falls under the class of "epitomizers." The attraction that *this* type of ethnography, rather than Herodotus's, appears to hold for Oviedo, then, provides the missing link in our understanding of his ethnographic criteria. For the combination of a penchant for the bizarre and of a popular appeal characteristic of these works, albeit conflated with serious ethnographic parameters, would conceivably produce an ethnography such as Oviedo's *Sumario*, with its titillating 'scandal sheet' cast. In presenting his new material, Oviedo is still in a sense telling old tales.

Oviedo's, of course, was not the first ethnography of the New World. A work by a man of a much more limited formation, Fray Ramón Pané's *Relación acerca de las antigüedades de los indios* ("Relation of the 'Antiquities' of the Indians"),[15] preceded his by at least twenty-five years and provides a telling counterpoint to our history of what Rolena Adorno has called the "production of the exotic"(4). In this connection, unlike Oviedo, Pané had an explicit mandate to seek out the new: as the friar tells us, he was sent by Columbus to "learn and find out about the beliefs and idolatries of the Indians" ("aprender y saber de las creencias e idolatrías de los indios"), that is, of the Taínos of Hispaniola (21). Pané devotes a good portion of his book to transcribing the Indian myths which seemed to have escaped Oviedo's interest or attention—tales of transformations, tricksters, and sexual antics (which, as modern exegetes have been able to explain, encoded the regulating principles of Taíno society).[16] In those portions of the *Relación*, however, which reflect Pané's own sense of what constitute "beliefs and idolatries," we find that for both him and Oviedo the differences are the same. That is to say, both ethnographers focus on shamanic practices, consultations with the devil, sacrifices, death rituals, food, idol worship, and the like, often in similar terms. For example, as did Oviedo in the passage on the *tequinas* explicated above, Pané makes much of the *engaño* or trickery to which the *behiques* subjected their willing charges (see Chapter XV, "Of the observation of these *behiques*, and how they practice medicine, and teach the people and how, in their medical cures, they often trick them" ["De las observaciones de estos indios behiques, y cómo profesan la medicina, y enseñan a las gentes y en sus curas medicinales muchas veces se engañan"], and subsequent chapters on the same theme). The drunken lack of reason which for Oviedo typifies Indian ceremonial *areitos* (86), becomes the defining feature of the Taíno world for Pané, through the ever-present *cohoba* which "inebriates them in such a way that they don't know what they are doing; and thus say many senseless things, such as stating that they are speaking to the *cemis*" (35) ("les embriaga de tal modo que no saben lo que se hacen; y así dicen muchas cosas fuera de juicio, en las cuales afirman que hablan con los cemíes...").

The similarity of the 'difference' of Indian culture for both authors is all the more striking in view of the evident discrepancy in their backgrounds. We know little about the life of Pané apart from the fact that he was Catalonian by birth, became a "poor *ermitaño* of the Order of San Jerónimo" (21) ("pobre ermitaño de la Orden de San Jerónimo") and that Las Casas, who had met him (Arrom, *Relación* 3), calls Pané a "simple[-minded] man" ("hombre simple"), maintaining that he could teach only the rudiments of religion, and this in a "very defective and confused" way ("con harto defecto y confusamente").[17] The rest must be deduced from his text—whose lack of erudite references or comparisons, humanistic or otherwise, bespeaks a man of a very narrow cultural background and frame of reference. We might surmise that Pané, in contrast to the relatively erudite Oviedo or others,[18] *knew only one story*, that of his Spanish/Catholic world-view. His text, exceptional for its author's uncultivated unexceptionality, as we shall see gives us an 'everyman's' reading of New World Indian culture even more *vulgar* or common than that of the supposed founder of popular historiography in the New World, Bernal Díaz del Castillo (son of a town official, with at least some awareness of humanist culture).

If Oviedo is, relatively speaking, a *savant* whose models permit him to delight in telling transgressive tales, Pané inscribes himself in the tradition of the *idiotus* ("who lends his word the support of what his body has experienced and adds no 'interpretation'"; De Certeau 74), uncomprehending, repulsed and offended by the tales he is obliged to tell. The transgressive tales both of and by the Indians, of sacrilege, demonic practices, shameless adultery and unbridled sexuality, exceed Pané's narrow cultural frame of reference and deeply offend him ("these ignorante people hold this as a truth" ["y esto tiene por cosa ciertísima aquella gente ignorante"] 46). Encharged, as noted above, to tell these tales, he makes himself a passive vessel who assumes the attitude of a mere scribe, distances himself, and comments insistently on the production of his own text: (one example among several)

> And as they have neither a system of writing nor written documents, they don't know how to tell such stories well, nor can I write them down well. For this reason I believe that what I'm putting first should go last, and what should go last, I put first. But every-

> thing I write down I say just as they tell me, that's how I write it; I put things as I have heard them from the natives of the country (26).

> Y como no tienen letras ni escrituras, no saben contar bien tales fábulas, ni yo puedo escribirlas bien. Por lo cual creo que pongo primero lo que debiera ser último y lo último pongo primero. Pero todo lo que escribo así lo narran ellos, como lo escribo, y así lo pongo como lo he entendido de los del país (26).

With a popular saying, "Así como lo compré, lo vendo" (45) (roughly, "I'm selling it just as I bought it"), Pané sums up his encounter with the discourse and story of the other that he so unwillingly recounts. Yet, departing at the end of the text from his role as official and impartial *relator* (there is some evidence that Pané circulated this work as a book, which would explain the infringement of his official role),[19] this *lector mediano* (common reader) par excellence of the novelty of Indian culture concludes with another popular saying and deploys the knowledge he has presented as a justification for conversion by force:

> And truly the island has a great need for people who will punish the rulers when they deserve it [and] make known to these peoples the ways of the holy Catholic faith and indoctrinate them in it; because they cannot and will not resist. And I can say this in all truth because I have wearied myself to find it out, and I am sure that what has been said here will have made my message clear, for a good listener picks things up quickly (54-55).

> Y verdaderamente que la isla tiene gran necesidad de gente para castigar a los señores cuando son merecedores de ello [y] dar a conocer aquellos pueblos las cosas de la santa fe católica y adoctrinarlos en ella; porque no pueden y no saben oponerse. Y yo puedo decirlo con verdad, pues me he fatigado para saber todo esto, y estoy cierto de que se habrá comprendido por lo que hasta hasta ahora hemos dicho; y a buen entendedor, bastan pocas palabras.

Curiously enough, Pané ends as well by denying his experience and text any value: "This is what I have been able to find out and comprehend of the customs and rites of the Indians of Hispaniola, by my own diligence. I attach to this no spiritual or temporal worth" (56) ("Esto es lo que yo he podido saber y entender acerca de las costumbres y los ritos de los indios de la Española, por la diligencia que en ello he puesto. En lo cual no pretendo ninguna utilidad espiritual ni temporal"). Oviedo relishes his novelties, showcasing the exotic both positive and negative; Pané, having perforce produced the exotic, now suppresses it.

Returning now to the *Sumario* in its own right, it is only fair that we mention one final set of ramifications for his judging the new of Oviedo's familiarity with more than one story, in other words, of his sense of cultural relativism. As we have detailed, both the classical and the Spanish worlds shape Oviedo's thinking; the interplay between the two model worlds or *mundos-modelos* will add (not entirely redeeming) nuance to his representation of the Indians in the *Sumario* and the *Historia general*. Oviedo himself states in the former work that far from being unique to the Indians such practices as sacrifices, superstitions and devil worship were common to all pagans:[20]

> Returning to the subject of the Indian *tequina*, who speaks to the devil and through whose hand and advice those diabolical sacrifices, ceremonies and rites are performed, I say that neither the ancient Romans, nor the Greeks nor the Trojans, nor Alexander, nor Darius, since they were not Catholics, were free from these errors and superstitions (35).

> Tornando al propósito del tequina que los indios tienen, y está para hablar con el diablo, y por cuya mano y consejo se hacen aquellos diabólicos sacrificios y ritos y ceremonias de los indios, digo que los antiguos romanos, ni los griegos, ni los troyanos, ni Alejandro, ni Darío, ni otros príncipes antiguos, por no católicos estuvieron fuera de estos errores y supersticiones...(82).

We see here that second-hand familiarity with pagan practices, and the notion that such practices were a condition of paganism, tempered Oviedo's condemnation of the Indi-

ans, and, indeed, allowed him to perceive them as continuous with the human race: as his important statement
in the *Sumario* indicates ("Some men are black while in
other lands they are very white. *Still, they are all men*," 46
["los hombres, que en una parte son negros, en otras
provincias son blanquísimos, *y los unos y los otros son
hombres* " 94], italics mine), unlike other chroniclers, from
the first Oviedo did not doubt the humanity of the Indians.[21] Moreoever, in the light of Oviedo's Hesperides theory, the Indians would not only be human beings, but also,
given the Indies's condition as a former Spanish territory,
lapsed Spaniards. The Indians' apparent lack of reason,
then, is historical, not intrinsic (Vásquez 497) for they are a
fallen people in more than one sense. Culturally, the Indians' world represents a descent from the classical society
to which it once belonged.[22] Morally, the Indians are
deemed vastly more culpable than other pagans because, as
former Spaniards and Catholics, they possessed but then
abandoned the true faith. Hence the clash in attitudes between Bartolomé de Las Casas, who considered the Indians
perfect in their natural state, and Oviedo, who believed
that they could, or should be led (back) to a perfect state.
Since, for Oviedo, the Indians participate in the same nature as the Spaniards, they deserve to be judged, and
harshly, by Spanish standards.

The classical model may establish the Indians' humanity, but the standards against which they are ultimately
judged remain Spanish: the all-determining presence of
the Devil in the New World makes the Indian civilization
something more than a distorted mirror image of Spanish
society. As would most of his contemporaries, Oviedo
states outright that the Indians are ruled by the Devil, a
Devil in whose existence we can see that the Spaniard of
course believes ("since the Devil is an old astrologer"
["como el diablo sea tan antiguo astrólogo"]). Not doubt-
ing, either, that the reader shared his convictions, Oviedo
states that since hurricanes are the work of the Devil,
"everywhere Holy Communion has been celebrated, these
hurricanes and terrific storms have not occurred in large
numbers" (37) ("todas las partes donde el Santo Sacramento se ha puesto, nunca ha habido los dichos huracanes

y tempestades grandes" 85). The Devil, as Oviedo's moralizing tendencies already intimated, stands at the heart of
Oviedo's portrayal of the Indies as a savage and infernal
world, not only of transgression of all standards of decency
but indeed of total licentiousness. Anything can happen in
this upside-down world, stripped of reason, and populated
by a people fallen from grace. Concrete proof of the moral
climate is a phenomenon first described by Oviedo and
later termed the "tropicalization of the white man,"
according to which certain Europeans, supposedly corrupted by the Indies, cast aside their consciences and fear of
either divine of human law to behave like savages themselves: "some have gone to the New World who, having
cast aside their consciences and fear of either divine or
human law, have done things characteristic not of Christians but of dragons and infidels" (34) ("porque han pasado
a aquellas partes personas que, pospuestas sus conciencias y
el temor de la justicia divina y humana, han hecho cosas,
no de hombres, sino de dragones y de infieles" 81)."[23] Believing himself to be in the Devil's realm, Oviedo lends
credence to and propagates without verifying them the
sordid tales of castration, anthropaphagy and consultations
with the Devil found in the excerpt quoted above and at
other moments in the *Sumario*. At heart, then, the Indian
culture of the New World stands as a darkworld, worse
than our own, where standards of the moral or the possible lose their sway.

Split into a darkworld of human curiosities and a
lightworld of natural *mirabilia* each providing some kind
of moral lesson, the *Sumario* seems to resemble a medieval bestiary more than a (modern) objective history. Yet
despite appearances, Oviedo's work incarnates progress in
science and historiography. Oviedo comes down to us as a
forerunner in the fields of natural science and ethnography which in the Renaissance were beginning to emerge as
independent scientific disciplines. As we saw in Oviedo's
correcting of the ancients, the discovery of the Americas,
with their as-yet-uncharted flora and fauna, challenged
botanists and zoologists to detach themselves from the
study of classical notions and to assume a more empirical
course (see Alvarez López,"Plantas" 225-26). Similarly, the

old "ruling class" histories of the nobility, their politics and wars, could not satisfy the enormous curiosity about the peoples and cultures of the New World.[24] The two acts of apprehension that Oviedo brought to bear on New World nature and culture—one of comprehension, the other of fear—indicate something of a pattern in these fields. For example, in the *Sumario* (regardless of the role of religion) we see natural science assuming its place as a science, with all that the modern sense of that word implies. Ethnography, on the other hand, born under the sign of didacticism and dogma, would remain harnessed to religion: there is some sense to the fact that cultural history would come to be called "moral" history, as in Father Joseph de Acosta's *Historia natural y moral de las Indias* (*Natural and Moral History of the Indies* [1590]).

Viewed in such a perspective, both nature and culture serve as testing grounds of sorts for the writing of novelty. But what of the two poles together, of the total effect the *Sumario* was intended to produce in its own time? We return on a different level to the notion that the key lies more in the perceiver than in the perceived, for we must remember Oviedo's post as Overseer or *Veedor*—one who sees officially. This is not, as the emphasis on the practical attests, a totally disinterested narrative, but rather like so many others in part a "compromised" report cognizant of the interests of the Crown. Therefore, making a display of his knowledge on mines and spices in the final three chapters, Oviedo directly addresses (albeit for the first time in the *Sumario*) the Crown's material concerns. With a fanfare of superlatives he impresses upon the King the existence of "innumerable riches" (120) ("innumerables riquezas" 177) in spices, "innumerable treasures" ("innumerables tesoros" 177) of pearls, and ends with the peroration: "certainly no Prince could claim such a quantity of gold coin as in your Majesty's kingdom, nor could there be such a quantity, of millions and millions in gold, as is yours. All this wealth comes from the Indies, which I have briefly described above " (120) ("de ningún príncipe del mundo no se hallaría más cantidad de oro en moneda, ni que pudiese ser tanta, con grandísima cantidad de millones y millones de oro como la de vuestra majestad. De todo esto es la causa las dichas Indias, de quien brevemente he dicho lo que me acuerdo"178). The very criterion of novelty, in effect, serves the double interests of God and King, for each new element yielded by the conquest comprises another tribute to God as creator of a varied world and King as possessor of these riches. The diverse natural phenomena of the New World, with their sensual pleasures and practical applications, will enhance the Crown once their potential has been understood. The idolatry and savagery of the Indians present an evangelical challenge, as well as justifying their pacification. In sum, this world at once better and worse than their own is there for the apprehending—to be appropriated, domesticated and naturalized.

Its final thrust notwithstanding, we would argue in conclusion that at least for Oviedo the real currency of the *Sumario* lies in a less material commodity. We mentioned above that only at the end of his work, in fact almost as an afterthought, does its author directly address the economic advantages of the new territories; surprisingly absent from the *Sumario* are the allusions to gold with which other writers of the times hoped to seduce the Crown. Instead, in the "Dedication" ("Dedicatoria") and echoed throughout, Oviedo attributes the merit of his work to his own qualifications as an historian with firsthand experience of his subject and possessor of a certain erudition.[25] Oviedo goes on in the "Dedicatoria" to create a special platform for himself as a writer, *authorizing himself* , in both senses of the word. He showcases himself *as a writer*, of a "natural inclination" (4) ("natural inclinación" 48), and as the author of the encyclopedic *Historia general* who for many years has been engaged in chronicling the Spanish world. Now, for his contemporaries such as Columbus and Cortés, action is *servicio*, writing ancillary. Undoubtedly aware that he has not played a determining role in the events of the New World, Oviedo represents as a service to his Sovereign the imparting of information: "which service is one of the greatest that any subject ever performed for his Prince, and it is as useful to the realm as it is famous"(4) ("el cual servicio hasta hoy es uno de los mayores que ningún vasallo pudo hacer a su príncipe, y tan útil a sus reinos como es notorio" 49) a subject which he again underscores in the last paragraph of the work.

With the *Sumario*, we see that Oviedo makes one further contribution to the intellectual conquest of America as he becomes the first writer about and from the New World to define himself primarily as such. In so doing, he makes heightened claims for both himself and his facts, they being "without comparison so strange and unusual that I consider well employed all my night study, as well as the time and labor it has cost me to see and observe these things" (Conclusion,121) ("tan apartadas y diferentes de todas las otras historias de esta calidad, que por ser sin comparación esta materia, y tan peregrina, tengo por muy bien empleadas mis vigilias, y el tiempo y trabajos que me ha costado ver y notar estas cosas" 178), which conceivably provides the ultimate justification for the criterion of novelty with respect both to nature and culture. Exalting himself through the exaltation of his material, Oviedo makes knowledge his commodity, his stepping stone to power and *fama* (fame). This may explain the final two chapters' atypical conjunction of (a show of) *knowledge* about lucrative enterprises and *pragmatics* (promising riches to the Crown). The "interested" and self-interested writer has effectively turned knowledge into a valuable unit of exchange in the conquest of America. Oviedo, who according to Alberto Salas may well have considered himself "in a small way master and author of the Caribbean" (96) ("un poco dueño y un poco autor del Caribe"), thus leaves his mark on the early writings of America as the first to constitute the conquest of the New World first and foremost as an intellectual enterprise.

NOTES

[1] In Chapter One of this work, "The Uncertain Impact," Elliott lists four processes involved in the incorporation of the New World within Europe's intellectual horizon, similar to mine of apprehension: observation, description, dissemination, comprehension (18).

2 In this connection, on p. 6 of *The Old World and the New*, Elliott states: "The evidence of the texts can tell us...something of interest about European society—about the ideas, attitudes and preconceptions which made up the mental baggage of Early Modern Europeans on their travels throughout the world. What did they see or fail to see? Why did they react as they did?"

3 There has been much discussion on the subject of whether *Don Claribalte* was written in the New World. On p. 344 of my article on this novel (1982), I argue from textual and biographical evidence that Oviedo wrote at least the longest section, the first, during his first trip to the Indies. The reader is referred to this article for further discussion of this and the other points raised here regarding *Don Claribalte*.

4 In discussing the *Sumario* on p. xv of his "Prólogo" to *Sucesos y diálogo de la Nueva España*, for example, O'Gorman maintains: "It is clear to me that only because he was capable of perceiving a new meaning in America could Oviedo consider the subject a novelty" ("Me parece evidente que sólo porque Oviedo fué capaz de percibir en América un nuevo significado, pudo considerar el tema americano como novedoso.")

5 ...y estas piñas ponen los indios y los cristianos cuando las siembran, a carreras y en orden como cepas de viñas, y huele esta fruta mejor que melocotones, y toda la casa huele por una o dos de ellas, y es tan suave fruta, que creo que es una de las mejores del mundo, y de más lindo y suave sabor y vista, y parecen en el gusto como melocotones, que mucho sabor tengan de duraznos, y es carnosa como el durazno, salvo que tiene briznas como el cardo, pero muy sutiles, mas es dañosa cuando se continúa a comer para los dientes y es muy zumosa, y en algunas partes los indios hacen vino de ellas, y es bueno; y son tan sanas, que se dan a dolientes, y les abre mucho el apetito a los que tienen hastío y perdida la gana de comer.

Unos árboles hay en la isla Española espinosos, que al parecer ningún árbol ni planta se podría ver de más salvajes ni tan feo, y según la manera de ellos, yo no me sabría determinar ni decir si son árboles o plantas; hacen unas ramas llenas de unas pencas anchas y disformes, o de muy mal parecer, las cuales ramas primero fue cada una una penca como las otras, y de aquellas, endureciéndose y alongándose, salen las otras pencas; finalmente, es de manera que es dificultoso de escribir su forma, y para darse a entender sería necesario pintarse, para que por medio de la vista se comprendiese lo que la lengua falta en esta parte. Para lo que es bueno este árbol o planta es, que majando las dichas pencas mucho, y tendido aquello a manera de emplasto en un paño, y ligando una pierna o brazo con ello aunque esté quebrada en muchos pedazos, en espacio de quince días lo suelda y junta como si nunca se quebrara... (153-54).

[6] The reader will recognize in the categories of "lightworld" (and, later, "darkworld") those of Northrop Frye from his book on romance, *The Secular Scripture*. As the reader will recall, according to Frye, to fulfill his quest the romance hero descends from a lightworld, or world of reason, into the adventure darkworld of non-reason. On pp. 114-117 of my article on the *Historia general y natural de las Indias* (1984) I suggest the influence of the structuring situation of romance on Oviedo's longer work, intimations of which may be found in the polarization of nature and culture in the *Sumario*.

[7] Hence, even the vile insects "that nature produces as a pest to man" ("que para molestia de los hombres produce la natura") serve to "make man realize that even worthless and petty things can disturb his peace of mind" ("darles a entender cuán pequeñas y viles cosas son bastantes para los ofender y inquietar") and that "he should not forget the chief end of man, which is to know his Creator and seek the salvation of his soul" (103) ("no se descuiden del oficio principal para que el hombre fue formado que es conocer a su Hacedor y procurar cómo se salve" 158). Though Oviedo stresses the sensual properties of nature, he does draw one or two explicit moral lessons from it.

[8] Gerbi (*Nature in the New World* 386-87) notes various points of contact between Oviedo and Pliny, including the fact that Pliny, too, was an insatiable gatherer of information; an official and later administrator of imperial revenues; that Pliny dedicates his work, as an absolute scientific novelty, to the emperor (Titus). Gerbi observes that "Pliny could also easily have been the source, or at least the supporting authority, for certain aspects of Oviedo's 'philosophy'," among them, "his aversion for the magic arts combined with a belief in prodigies, the idea of nature as a multiple revelation of the single God..." and so on (387).

[9] Controversial because, as his heirs well understood, it detracted from the momentousness of Columbus's discovery; Oviedo's Hesperides theory was seen by some as a ploy to curry favor with the Crown by adducing its age-old rights to the Indies.

[10] I am grateful to Ana Cecilia Rosado for her comments on the *Sumario*, in a recent graduate seminar at Brown, which led me to this point.

[11] Ballesteros 1986, 39. The reader can also consult his "Fernández de Oviedo, etnólogo," for further discussion of this point in Oviedo, and Chapter 6 of Pagden's *The Fall of Natural Man* , which examines the Aristotelian premises of Las Casas's argument in the *Apologética*.

[12] ...Las diferencias sobre que los indios riñen y vienen a batalla son sobre cuál tendrá más tierra y señorío, y a los que pueden matar matan, y algunas veces prenden y los hierran, y se sirven de ellos por esclavos, y cada señor tiene su hierro conocido; y así, hierran a los dichos esclavos,

y algunos señores sacan un diente de los delanteros al que toman por esclavo, y aquello es su señal. Los caribes flecheros, que son los de Cartagena y la mayor parte de aquella costa, comen carne humana, y no toman esclavos ni quieren a vida ninguno de sus contrarios o extraños, y todos los que matan se los comen, y las mujeres que toman sírvense de ellas, y los hijos que paren (si por caso algún caribe se echa con las tales) cómenselos despues; [...]

Para comenzar sus batallas, o para pelear, y para otras cosas muchas que los indios quieren hacer, tienen unos hombres señalados, que ellos mucho acatan, y al que es de estos tales llámanle tequina; no obstante que a cualquiera que es señalado en cualquier arte, así como en ser mejor montero o pescador, o hacer mejor una red o un arco o otra cosa, le llaman tequina; y quiere decir tequina tanto como maestro. Así que el que es maestro de sus responsiones y inteligencias con el diablo, llámanle tequina; y este tequina habla con el diablo y ha de él sus respuestas, y les dice lo que han de hacer, y lo que será mañana o desde a muchos días; porque como el diablo sea tan antiguo astrólogo, conoce el tiempo y mira adónde van las cosas encaminadas, y las guía la natura; y así, por el efecto que naturalmente se espera, les da noticia de lo que será adelante, y les da a entender que por su deidad, o que como señor de todos y movedor de todo lo que es y será, sabe las cosas por venir y que están por pasar; y que él atruena, y hace sol, y llueve,y guía los tiempos, y les quita o les da los mantenimientos: los cuales dichos indios, engañados por él de haber visto que en efecto les ha dicho muchas cosas que estaban por pasar y salir ciertas, créenle en todo lo demás, y témenle y acátanle, y hácenle sacrificos en muchas partes de sangre y vidas humanas...(80-81).

[11] Referring to the surprisingly limited interest of Europeans in America, Elliott (14) eloquently remarks, "It is as if, at a certain point, the mental shutters come down; as if, with so much to see and absorb and understand, the effort suddenly becomes too much for them, and Europeans retreat to the half-light of their traditional mental world."

For a brief analysis of the different treatment Oviedo accords nature and culture in the *Historia general*, the subject of this section of my study, see Salas, 85-87.

[14] My understanding of the pre-history of ethnography draws heavily upon Hogden, and, to a lesser degree, Olschki.

[15] I have, of course, used Arrom's excellent 1974 edition of Pané's work. In its Introduction, Arrom places the completion of the *Relación* around 1498.

[16] For interpretations of the myths that Pané recounts, see Alegría; Arrom 1975; and, particularly, López-Baralt.

[17] Arrom's edition includes the texts of Las Casas and Pedro Mártir which mention Pané and his *Relación*. This quote is to be found on p. 105 of Arrom's edition and is taken from Chapter CXX of the *Apologética*.

[18] Mártir's and Las Casas's reactions to the myths that Pané transcribes demonstrate the enormous difference that a broader cultural framework made in their reception of the discourse of the other. Mártir, *Décadas* (p. 99 in Arrom's edition), expectably, compares the Taíno legends to classical myths. Las Casas, *Apologética* (p. 114 in Arrom's edition), attempts (if unsuccessfully and judgmentally) to discern the deeper meaning of these myths: "These behiques presented them with a variety of other fictions and hoaxes, which, if they weren't intended by them, *as by the ancient poets*, as allegories or parables, were inventions of the Devil or great nonsense" (our emphasis) ("Otras ficciones muchas y patrañas les hacían entender aquellos behiques, que si no pretendían significar alguna alegoría o moralidad, *como los antiguos poetas*, eran invenciones del demonio o grandes desvaríos").

[19] Alegría (41) states, "Pedro Martir's allusion to the fact that Fray Ramón 'was the author of a little book' suggests the possiblity that Panés *Relation* was actually published, now figuring among the lost unpublished works of Spain. [...] This possibility is reinforced by the fact that rather than being written as a report to Columbus, the Relation is written as if it were to be an independent publication...The work isn't addressed to Columbus, but rather seems to appeal to a a general audience" ("La alusión de Pedro Mártir en el sentido de que Fray Ramón 'fue autor de un librito' nos hace pensar en la posibilidad de que la *Relación* de Pané hubiese sido impresa y contarse en el número de los incunables españoles perdidos. [...] Refuerza esta posibilidad el hecho de que redacta su texto, no como un informe a Colón, sino como si hubiera de ser una publicación independiente...La obra tampoco va dirigida a Colón, sino que parece dedicada al público general").

[20] In this connection, on p. 123, Salas writes, "The customs of the native Americans, in a word, didn't shock a learned man like Oviedo, who seems already to be familiar with them from other sources" ("Las costumbres de los indígenas americanos, en una palabra, no asombraron a un hombre culto como Oviedo, que parece conocerlas ya de antemano por referencias bibliográficas").

[21] Salas, in the chapter on Oviedo from his *Tres cronistas de Indias*, and Josefina Zoraida Vásquez, effectively argue this point.

[22] In this connection, Ballesteros ("Fernández de Oviedo, etnólogo") comments on p. 460 that all of Oviedo's pejorative judgments "are directed against the present state of the Indian, who lives in a complex of low culture which Oviedo judges in qualitative terms; this doesn't take

away from the fact that there are Indians, languages, customs and orga-
nizations, etc., that deserve to be studied for their correspondence to
forms of human life which, according to the (for Oviedo, unimpugnable)
testimony of classical authors, already existed in other places," ("van
en contra el estado actual del indio, que vive en un complejo de baja cultura, que Oviedo aprecia cualitativamente, pero no por ello dejan de
existir los indios, sus lenguas, costumbres, organizaciones, etc., que mere-
cen ser estudiados porque corresponden a formas humanas de vidas, que
ya fueron en otros sitios, según el testimonio, para él indudable, de los
autores clásicos").

[23] Oviedo has been credited with providing the first documentation of
the "moral reversal" or "tropicalization" of the conquerors. See Gerbi,
The Dispute of the New World, particularly pp. 40 and 571.

[24] Fueter (320), contends, "The discoveries and conquests in America
posed an entirely new problem for historiography. Such events afforded
subjects to which the techniques of previous classical histories were
unequal. Readers would hardly have been satisfied were the discovery
of the New World to have been treated in the old manner of the annals.
What interested them was not so much the details of the conquest as the
marvellous peoples and countries the Europeans had discovered. They
wanted to know how these people, making their first appearance on the
European horizon, lived..." ("Los descubrimientos y las conquistas en
América plantearon a la historiografía un problema enteramente nuevo.
Tales acontecimientos ofrecían una materia a la que no bastaban los
procedimientos de la historia clasicista anterior. Los lectores se
hubieran sentido poco satisfechos de ver tratar el descubrimiento del
Nuevo Mundo de acuerdo con el plan de los anales. Lo que les interesaba
no eran tanto los detalles de la conquista como los pueblos y los países
maravillosos descubiertos por los europeos. Querían saber cómo vivían
esos hombres que aparecían por primera vez en el horizonte de Europa").

[25] Oviedo's defense of firsthand experience takes up much of the first
page of the "Dedicatoria" and is thus too long to reproduce here. Instead, on the need for the apt historian to combine experience and
learning, I quote from p. 94: "All these things, and many others that
could be said in this connection, can easily be proved, and should be believed when they have been related by men *who have read widely or
who have traveled about the world*" (italics mine,46) ("Todas estas
cosas , y otras muchas que se podrían decir a este propósito, son fáciles de
probar y muy dignas de creer de todos aquellos *que han leído o andado
por el mundo* , a quien la propia vista habrá enseñado la experiencia de
lo que es dicho"). Oviedo refers to the lesson of the world's diversity
and, clearly, to himself as an historian.

WORKS CITED

Adorno, Rolena. "Literary Production and Suppression: Reading and Writing about the Amerindians in Colonial Spanish America." *Dispositio* XI, 28-29 (1986): 1-25.

Alegría, Ricardo E. *Apuntes en torno a la mitología de los indios taínos de las Antillas Mayores y sus orígenes suramericanos.* Barcelona: Centro de Estudios Avanzados de Puerto Rico y el Caribe, 1978.

Alvarez López, Enrique. Introduction to his edition of the *Sumario de la natural historia de las Indias.* Madrid: Editorial Summa, 1942.

—. "La historia natural en Fernández de Oviedo." *Revista de Indias* XVII, 69-70 (1957): 541-601.

—. "Las plantas de América en la botánica europea del siglo XVI." *Revista de Indias* VI, 20 (1945): 221-89.

Arrom, José Juan. Edition and Introduction, Fray Ramón Pané, *Relación acerca de las antigüedades de los indios.* México: Siglo XXI, 1974.

—. *Mitología y artes prehispánicas de las Antillas.* México: Siglo XXI, 1975.

Ballesteros. "Fernández de Oviedo, etnólogo." *Revista de Indias* XVII, 69-70 (1957): 445-467.

—. Introduction to his edition of *Sumario de la natural historia de las Indias.* Madrid: *Historia* 16, 1986.

Beaver, Harold. Review of *Marquesan Encounters. "Times Literary Supplement,"* April 24, 1981:452.

Certeau, Michel de. "'Montaigne's 'Of Cannibals': The Savage 'I'". *In Heterologies: Discourse on the Other.* Trans. Brian Massumi. Minneapolis: Univ. of Minnesota Press, 1986.

Díaz del Castillo, Bernal. *Historia verdadera de la conquista de Nueva España.* Ed. Miguel León Portilla. Madrid: *Historia* 16, 1984.

Elliott, J. H. *The Old World and the New.* Cambridge: Cambridge Univ. Press, 1970.

Fueter, Edward. *Historia de la historiografía moderna*. Trans. Ana María Ripullone. Buenos Aires: Editorial Nova, 1953.

Frye, Northrop. *The Secular Scripture*. Cambridge, Mass.: Harvard Univ. Press, 1976.

Gerbi, Antonello. *The Dispute of the New World*. Trans. Jeremy Moyle. Pittsburgh: Univ. of Pittsburgh Press, 1973.

—. *Nature in the New World: From Christopher Columbus to Gonzalo Fernández de Oviedo*. Trans. Jeremy Moyle. Pittsburgh: Univ. of Pittsburgh Press, 1985.

Herbert, T. Walter. *Marquesan Encounters*. Cambridge, Mass.: Harvard Univ. Press, 1980.

Hogden, Margaret T. *Early Anthropology in the Sixteenth and Seventeenth Centuries*. Philadelphia: Univ. of Pennsylvania Press, 1964.

Humboldt, Alexander von. *Cosmos: A Sketch of a Physical Description of the Universe*. London: Henry G. Bohn, 1849.

Lévi-Strauss, Claude. *Tristes Tropiques*. Trans. John and Doreen Weightman. New York: Atheneum, 1974.

López-Baralt, Mercedes. *El mito taíno: Raíz y proyecciones en la amazonia continental*. Puerto Rico: Ediciones Huracán, 1976.

Merrim, Stephanie. "The Castle of Discourse: Fernández de Oviedo's *Don Claribalte* (1519)."*Modern Language Notes* 97 (1982): 329-346.

—. "*Un mare magno e oculto*: Anatomy of Fernández de Oviedo's *Historia general y natural de las Indias*." *Revista de estudios hispánicos* (1984): 101-120.

Montaigne. *Essays and Selected Writings*. Ed. Donald M. Frame. New York: St. Martin's Press, 1963.

O'Gorman, Edmundo. *La invención de América. El universalismo de la cultura del Occidente*. México: Fondo de Cultura Económica, 1958.

—. Prologue to Fernández de Oviedo, *Sucesos y diálogo de la Nueva España*. México: UNAM, 1946.

Olschki, Leonardo. *Marco Polo's Precursors*. Baltimore: Johns Hopkins Univ. Press, 1943.

Oviedo y Valdés, Gonzalo Fernández de. *Historia natural y general de las Indias*. Ed. Juan Pérez de Tudela Bueso. Madrid: Biblioteca de Autores Españoles, 1959.

—. *Natural History of the West Indies*. Trans. Sterling A. Stoudemire. Chapel Hill: Univ. of North Carolina Press, 1959.

—. *Sumario de la natural historia de las Indias*. Ed. Manuel Ballesteros. Madrid: Historia 16, 1986.

Pagden, Anthony. *The Fall of Natural Man: The American Indian and the Origins of Comparative Ethnology*. Cambridge: Cambridge Univ. Press, 1982.

Pané, Fray Ramón. *Relación acerca de las antigüedades de los indios*. México: Siglo XXI, 1974.

Salas, Alberto M. *Tres cronistas de Indias*. México: Fondo de Cultura Económica, 1959.

Turner, Daymond. "Biblioteca Ovetense: A Speculative Reconstruction of the Library of the First Chronicler of the Indies." *The Papers of the Bibliographical Society of America*. 57 (1963): 157-183.

Vásquez, Josefina Zoraida, "El indio americano y su circunstancia en la obra de Oviedo," *Revista de Indias* XVII, 69-70 (1957):433-519.

Wethered, H. N. *The Mind of the Ancient World: A Consideration of Pliny's* Natural History . London: Longman's Green and Co. Ltd., 1937.

CHAPTER 5:
ARMS, LETTERS AND THE NATIVE
HISTORIAN IN EARLY COLONIAL
MEXICO

Rolena Adorno

In Chapters 37 and 38 of the First Part of Cervantes's *Don Quijote*, the Knight of the Sad Countenance, (as Don Quijote called himself), got up to declaim to the party assembled his views on the relative virtues of arms and letters (Cervantes, *El ingenioso hidalgo* 3: 320-321). In his estimation, arms were superior, for they required the employment of the intellect and prudent judgment as well as strength, the exercise of the spirit as well as the body. What is curious is that, after he began to speak, no one took him for the fool: "Don Quijote pursued his discourse in such a way and in such well-chosen language that none of his hearers could possibly take him for a madman just then. On the contrary, as most of them were gentlemen connected with the profession of Arms, they listened with great pleasure" (Cervantes, *Adventures* 341). All seemed quite willing to grant that it was gun powder and the invention of artillery that "allowed a base and cowardly hand to take the life of a brave knight" (344). (Even the famous dictionary of the time, Covarrubias's *Tesoro de la lengua castellana* (139) called the harquebus an invention of the devil forged in hell.)

I would like to interrupt Don Quijote's supper speech to highlight two points of particular interest: the effect of Don Quijote's words on his audience with respect to how they viewed him, and the ideas he expressed on the conduct of war itself. With regard to the cultural other in sixteenth-century postconquest Mexico, both issues illuminate the position of the writing colonial subject. The locus of this other, the Náhuatl-speaking Christianized *ladino*, is a complex intersection of various and seemingly contradictory subject positions. I would like to explore the complexity of this subject's position in light of some of de Certeau's insightful notions regarding the 'cultural other.'

Two important formulations on this problem are Tzvetan Todorov's *The Conquest of America: The Question of the Other* and de Certeau's *Heterologies: Discourses on the Other*. They are very different inquiries, and I think it will be useful to contrast them with regard to their respective treatments of the other. Two significant differences between them should be noted at the outset: First, Todorov interprets texts and seeks to persuade us of his interpretation for our own salvation; in this way his work is a sort of "sermon."[1] De Certeau, scrupulous in the study of sources, exercises erudition as "a field of play rather than a substantiation of fact," as Conley remarked (Conley xv). That is, de Certeau opens rather than closes the possibilities of interpretation by suggesting the complexity of factors that would need to be taken into account in order to arrive at the facts. Second, in *The Conquest of America*, Todorov attributes a particular character to discourse and textuality; in *Heterologies*, de Certeau explores them. In my view, each of these contrasts contributes to the explanation of why and how de Certeau in particular facilitates our ability to hear and therefore to listen to the discourse not *on* but *of* the other. Whereas Todorov invites us to contemplate the power of the written word to crush the other (creating a dominant discourse in which the other as subject would not recognize oneself), de Certeau's work invites us to consider the other as a colonial subject who is not only the observed but also the observer.[2]

I would like to examine the first contrast by beginning with the statements which are, in Benveniste's system, discursive, consisting of the exchange between the grammatical persons "you" and "I." Todorov writes an "Epilogue" to his book; de Certeau offers a "Conclusion." Let us compare them.

Todorov states, with reference to the dedication with which he began his book ("I dedicate this book to the memory of a Mayan woman devoured by dogs"): "I am writing this book to prevent this story and a thousand others like it from being forgotten...My hope is...that we remember what can happen if we do not succeed in discovering the other. For the other remains to be discovered" (247). If this is the conclusion of the story that began by the author stating that his subject was to be "the discovery *self* makes of the *other*," then he has shown us that Europeans in the sixteenth century, specifically the Spaniards, failed the task assigned them.

Since Todorov begins his book by declaring that he is more interested in the present than the past, his explanation of his use of the historical case is of interest. He states that he chose "the problematics of the exterior and remote other... somewhat arbitrarily and because one cannot speak of everything all at once" (3). On the last page (254), he seeks to persuade the reader that, even though the "conquest of America" does not represent a faithful image of *our* relation to the other, "their history can be exemplary for us because it permits us to reflect upon ourselves, to discover resemblances as well as differences: once again self-knowledge develops through knowledge of the Other." (The other, in this case, are the Genovese and Spanish observers of the sixteenth century).

If the study of the historically remote case cannot provide answers to our own contemporary dilemmas—and Todorov acknowledges that it cannot—can it clarify for us our own questions? This is an arguable and important issue and I would like to take it up from the viewpoint of what I consider Todorov's contemporary concern to be. His own question, I would argue, is not about sixteenth-century European conquests abroad but rather about twentieth-century violations of state sovereignty and human and civil rights. That is, his agenda is to tell the story not of struggle against foreign invasion or even accommodation as a result of defeat (the other does not speak in his work, except to corroborate information given in European accounts [78, 135]), but rather to evoke the twentieth-century story of oppression.[3]

I posit this shift from defeat to oppression on the basis of the reading of a leitmotif, barely discernible but persistent throughout *The Conquest of America* and fully realized in the "Epilogue." This is the concern for totalitarian regimes with implicit reference to the Soviet state. Todorov makes parenthetical comparisons between the Christian conquest of the sixteenth century and the communist takeovers of the twentieth; here the unstated referent is Eastern Europe (69, 87, 177, 179). Also, he makes occasional references to state violence, the army or police, and state secrets (144, 176, 181), all of which have little to do with the historical tale he is telling.

His preoccupation is revealed best when he speaks of the present age: "The discovery the 'I' makes of the 'others' inhabiting it is accompanied by the more alarming assertion of the disappearance of the 'I' into the 'we' characteristic of all totalitarian regimes" (251). The chilling and deadly mask of this 'we' hides behind it the integration of "massacre-societies" and "sacrifice-societies," the distinguishing characteristics by which Todorov had identified the Spanish and the Aztecs respectively (143-145). In relation to these, he contemplates a modern hybrid, the "*massacrifice* society." Deadly serious but nestled in the humor of G.B. Shaw's retort to Isadora Duncan, "What if our child had your brains and my looks?", this horrific image is not an "aside." It is instead the focal point of the

"Epilogue," which leads us back to a chapter in the body of the book. There, Todorov had described the two models of sacrifice and massacre societies and ended—now, reread, the more tellingly—with this reflection: "But what if we do not want to have to choose between a civilization of sacrifice and a civilization of massacre?" (145).

Todorov's book has a peculiar power when seen in this light. His articulation of the desire to have "equality without its compelling us to accept identity; but also difference without its degenerating into superiority/inferiority" (249) could not be more eloquent. But the question and my criticism remain: Was he able to teach us this by narrating what he called "the conquest of America"? In the penultimate pages of his book, he cites the examples of Fray Diego Durán and Fray Bernardino de Sahagún for affirming the exteriority of alterity while recognizing the other as subject (250). He suggests that this was not only a new way of experiencing alterity, but a characteristic feature of our own time, as the French philosopher and Talmudic scholar Emmanuel Levinas proposed: "Our period...is action for a world to come, transcendence of its period— transcendence of self which calls for the epiphany of the Other" (cited in Todorov 250).

Todorov asks if his book illustrates this new attitude toward the other, through his relation with the authors and figures of the sixteenth century. He acknowledges rightfully that he can only testify to his intentions, not the effect they produce (250). Yet, in my view and in the end, it is the moral self-absorption of the subject in power that reigns in Todorov's book. It is an ethical discussion of conduct of the self vis-à-vis the other in which, in the sixteenth-century case study, the other as subject is absent. It emerges, in reflections on the twentieth, as the self being objectified or 'othered' by the state, particularly the totalitarian regime. Where we might have expected to hear from the sixteenth-century Amerindian others, these potential subjects slip immediately from sight only to emerge, at the end of the book, as ourselves. Through conquest or under totalitarianism, the speech of the dominated subject is silenced.

Whereas Todorov's 'other' is ultimately the 'us' persecuted by the totalitarian 'we,' de Certeau's 'other' tends to
be associated more with the 'other' that we find at the explicit level in Todorov, namely, non-European peoples,
and not in their remote historical but rather contemporary
and recent lived experience. Let us see how he treats it.

Michel de Certeau's work on the other, although profoundly serious, has a lighter touch than that of Todorov.
He avoids creating the effects of outrage (at the expense of
a particular nation or culture) or pathos (at the expense of
those already victimized once). We are not to be persuaded
to accept a particular interpretation of historical actions
nor a causal explanation for them (such as Todorov's argument about the absence of an Aztec writing system). Instead, we are invited to contemplate alterity, and therefore
identity, from a variety of perspectives. Nevertheless, de
Certeau's *Heterologies* has a "Conclusion," which for the
purposes of this comparison I shall consider as a
counterpart to Todorov's "Epilogue."

In "The Politics of Silence: The Long March of the Indians" de Certeau examines native and peasant activism organized in the mid-1970s and invites his readers to participate in information sharing and active support work. He
closes *Heterologies* with the final remarks of the essay
originally published in 1976, in these words: "Readers, you
and I stand invited to assist in this work, which is inspired
by concern for the other, and is meant to rise to the same
beat as the Indian awakening" (de Certeau, *Heterologies*
233). The phrase "Indian awakening" is taken from a
speech by Justino Quispe Balboa before the first Indian
Congress of South America, October 13, 1974: "Today, at
the hour of our awakening, we must be our own historians" (227, 261). The "awakening" in Quispe Balboa's
speech refers to political activism; to "become their own
historians" is not to invent historical memory, for this, as
de Certeau had noted (227), had been preserved over four
and a half centuries in contrast to European
"forgetfulness." To become their own historians means to
"determine the course of their own history" in the future
(226). By these means, de Certeau invites the reader to go
beyond the reading of the text to take action. Like Todorov,

de Certeau concludes with a call to ethical action. Moreover, at the conclusion of de Certeau's discussion of 'discourse on the other,' the voice of the other—the contemporary South American native—is heard. However small, this is yet a qualitative difference between *The Conquest of America* and *Heterologies* and an invitation to also ponder the importance to de Certeau of Levinas's thought.[4] To hear a little better the voice of the other—to at least pick up its recuperable resonances—are the directions in which de Certeau's *Discourses on the Other* leads us.

THE NATURE OF DISCOURSE AND TEXTUALITY

It seems to me that different theoretical positions on discourse and textuality separate de Certeau and Todorov on the issue of the other. Briefly, in *The Conquest of America* Todorov seems to invest in those who control the text, whereas de Certeau seems to confide in the potential of textuality itself. Todorov gives us a huge mosaic of texts—observations and arguments—which we are to read as an "exemplary history." De Certeau puts those observations and arguments—and the character of written history—into question. Todorov does not interrogate the texts he uses as his sources but treats each statement as though it were straightforward and not part of its own larger rhetorical scheme. He claims that he has allowed his sources to speak for themselves: "I question, I transpose, I interpret these texts; but also I let them speak (whence so many quotations) and defend themselves" (250).

De Certeau takes the opposite view, "But the written discourse which cites the speech of the other is not, cannot be, the discourse of the other. On the contrary, this discourse, in writing the Fable that authorizes it, alters it" (*Heterologies* 78).[5] Furthermore, de Certeau refrains from telling us how to interpret particular texts and instead explores how those texts produce the meanings we are likely to infer. In his essays on Léry and Montaigne, for example, de Certeau's discussions of ethnographic writing reveal the potential of textuality when the topic is cross- or multicultural. He testifies to the power of the text to compose and distribute places, to determine the boundaries limiting cultural fields. This is an important point, for it defines or describes the entire tradition of ethnological or ethnographic writing. The space of culture is "here," the space of non-culture (barbarity, savagism) is "over there." In de Certeau's essay on Montaigne, Montaigne's writing redistributes cultural space but not in the expected manner. Savagism is inverted and barbarism comes "over here" (*Heterologies* 73). From this viewpoint, the text can change socio- or ethno-cultural boundaries. This principle of textuality that de Certeau elucidates becomes extremely important in the writings of those who know that they are perceived as other by their intended audiences. I shall return to such examples later.

In *The Conquest of America*, Todorov assumes rather than explores the nature of discourse and textuality, insofar as he describes a discursive system in its capacity to crush the individual or small-group effort and diminish the agential dimension of human action. In contrast, de Certeau explores these very terrains, thanks to his psychoanalytic notion of event.[6] By emphasizing the role of conflicting imaginations rather than power relations, de Certeau moves outside the contemplation of the exclusionary effect of 'officialized' versions of history to contemplate not power but consciousness. In a theoretical terrain in which places are assigned by virtue of the exercise of power, the consideration of voices raised but not heard, openly resistant but publicly suppressed, has no place. De Certeau, however, contemplates human agency and is concerned for "the impulses, the enabling conditions, for living in relation to these hegemonic forces" (Godzich xiii). De Certeau's attention, furthermore, to "practices and discourses ...that are either on the wane or in the making or that even do not quite manage to constitute themselves" (Godzich xiv) are truly the 'enabling conditions' that allow us to take seriously the writing colonial subjects of the early period of European overseas expansion.

THE *MESTIZO* HISTORIAN

The position of the other as subject is of course a complex one, and it becomes more so in the case of the colonial subject. Colonialism, I think, makes special demands on the subject even when that subject is the colonizer. My favorite example comes from the 1611 *Historia eclesiástica de nuestros tiempos* written by the Dominican priest Alonso Fernández. Here he describes Bartolomé de las Casas: "When the emperor came from Germany, Las Casas presented his cause with much erudition and prudence, speaking like a saint, informing like a jurist, giving judgments like a theologian, and testifying as an eye witness" (Fernández 30).[7] Producing a discourse that could combine so many virtues was even a greater challenge to the colonized colonial subject. I would like to take the example, in this regard, of Don Fernando de Alva Ixtlilxochitl, descendant of the lords of Texcoco (one of the three ruling houses of the Aztec Triple Alliance). Don Fernando authored many works on the precolumbian and colonial history of the Central Valley of Mexico from the perspective of the Acolhua-Texcocan peoples.

As to the multiple subject positions of this individual, he was descended from the Texcocan dynasty which had lived in uneasy coexistence with the Mexica (Aztecs) and had often engaged in internal power struggles against them within the Triple Alliance of the Aztec federation. As was common within imperial circles, Don Fernando also had blood of the rival Aztecs in his veins.[8] His political legacy was complicated in the postconquest period in which he lived, for his ancestors had been allies of Cortés in the conquest of Mexico and his own political agenda consisted in presenting his case to the new, distant Spanish overlord and his local representatives in a way that would be persuasive to them and yet not alienate the native colleagues whose support he needed.[9]

Born around 1578 and deceased in 1650, Don Fernando's life seems to have been typical of the colonial Aztec aristocracy. Studying for several years with the Franciscans at the Colegio de Santa Cruz de Santiago Tlatelolco, he spent much of his adult life in short-term occupations of local colonial government. He lived during that early colonial period when the intrusion of non-hereditary *gobernadores* and the diminished position of *caciques* and *principales* induced the native aristocracy to take up Hispanic ways and to "Hispanize themselves as actively as circumstances allowed" (Gibson, "Aztec Aristocracy" 180-181).[10] The evidence we have regarding Don Fernando's life and writings corroborate this tendency.

I would like to concentrate on two aspects which reveal the ways in which de Certeau's views on the nature of discourse and his insights into the "discourse *on* the other" are helpful in examining the "discourse *of* the other." First, de Certeau posits, as noted earlier, the text's power of composing and distributing spaces and its ability to determine boundaries limiting cultural fields (*Heterologies* 68).[11] Second, de Certeau's concept of discourse recovers an agential dimension insofar as it recognizes discursive activity as a form of social activity (Godzich xxi).[12]

It seems to me that the writing subjects that best reveal the process of the textual distribution and redistribution of cultural space are those from the perceived 'non-culture.' In the first place, these subjects had to persuade their skeptical readers that their own space, dismissed as non-culture or inferior culture, is the very site of culture. Their goals were not only to be true but also to persuade their readers of the truthfulness of their accounts. Secondly, they had to 'earn their right', so to speak, to raise their voices and be heard before a European audience that, as Todorov has shown, tended to deny their role as subjects. Actually, de Certeau put it most eloquently with reference to Montaigne's writing about his encounter with the other: "The project was to redistribute cultural space and affirm a locus of utterance" (*Heterologies* 68).[13]

In the case of writing subjects like Fernando de Alva Ixtlilxochitl, taking pen to paper and asserting adherence to the Christian faith and loyalty to the Spanish crown served simultaneously to reorganize cultural space and affirm a place of utterance. Don Fernando made two moves: first, to pull Christian warrior culture over to his side, and secondly, to fill that reorganized space with heroic actions and actors that were entirely missing from Spanish accounts of the same episodes of the war of the Mexican conquest (1: 468, 514). At the same time, he had to reduce to an absence the image of Mexican sacrificial society as 'non-culture.' His historical research was based on sources, including the ancient paintings and oral traditions of his people, whose election and precise details have yet to be determined. He declared proudly in his *Historia chichimeca*: "All that which I have written and in future I will write is according to the narrative accounts (*relaciones*) and paintings that the natural lords, who found themselves in the events which occurred then, wrote shortly after the territory was taken over" (2: 235).[14]

To reorganize and redistribute cultural space, Don Fernando partly emptied the Spanish cultural space of the histories such as those of López de Gómara and made their contents his own. He had read those works and he cited explicitly López de Gómara, Antonio de Herrera, and Toribio de Benavente (Motolinía). Bravery and prudence were continually attributed to Cortés by his historians, notably Gómara, Cervantes de Salazar, and Juan Ginés de Sepúlveda. Alva Ixtlilxochitl recreated the bellicose character and battle portrait of his ancestor, the prince Ixtlilxochitl, as an important ally of Cortés, according to his own traditions and sources. Nevertheless, the dominant discourse already had determined the boundaries limiting cultural fields and the colonial subject had to appropriate that field in order to reorganize the spatial divisions that defined the dominant culture (see de Certeau, *Heterologies* 68).

As the text's reworking of space simultaneously produces the space of the text, Ixtlilxochitl's elaboration of conquest history affirmed his own locus of utterance, as he identified himself as an historian (1: 287). In this regard, even as he criticized Gómara, he nevertheless empathized with him as a fellow historian, continually in search of reliable sources. Yet while he saw the historian's art as one, he nevertheless contemplated the fact that there were many histories. It is just this consciousness that makes vivid de Certeau's concern for the conflicting imaginations that produce history. Don Fernando saw his own work as a different version of conquest history—that which told the Texcocan version of the story—and suggested that his readers look at Gómara, Herrera, Torquemada, and the letters of Cortés himself if they wished to learn about the deeds of "our Spaniards" (2: 235). For Cortés's biography, Alva Ixtlilxochitl invited his readers to peruse the same sources. His declaration in the *Compendio histórico del reino de Texcoco* reveals his consciousness about the fragmentation of history: "Here I have not treated of conquistadors, as they say, for they are not of my history, besides there are many historians who have occupied themselves with them, which they have not done for Ixtlilxochitl and his vassals" (1: 514).

Condemning Cortés's failure, in his own writings, to mention the prince Ixtlilxochitl and the thousands of warriors he commanded, Don Fernando registered his awareness of being made invisible, of being erased from history, that is, from the partial history of the powerful, altogether.[15] Furthermore, although Alva Ixtlilxochitl created a Cortés of impressive evangelical accomplishments in the same conventional and glowing terms that the Spanish historians had used in decades past, he parted company with the humanist historians when he described the war as "the most difficult conquest that the world had ever seen" (2: 194). Alva Ixtlilxochitl may have been very pleased with the accounts of mass Christianization and postconquest abandonment of "cruel practices" which he read in Gómara, but it is clear that he did not accept Gómara's view of a swift and easy conquest. The European historian had not understood the character of the war (which had been in reality a question of "so many against so many," rather than "so few against so many" as the marvelling Spanish historians had written) nor had he appreciated the qualities of the Mexican allies of Cortés and their warriors.

The main thrust of the portion of Alva Ixtlilxochitl's history devoted to the Spanish conquest was to expound on the enormous contributions that his ancestral namesake and the Texcocan leadership had made to Cortés's war effort. His goal was to put forward the military values that characterized his own culture (including the quintessential traits of prudence and valor) but which had been exclusively associated with the European war hero (Alva Ixtlilxochitl 2: 259). In this regard, the polemical character of the colonial writing subject's history affirms de Certeau's view of discursive activity as social practice. For the native Mexican historians of the postconquest, 'fighting words' were words about fighting. The debates about how the wars of conquest were waged and won was yet another early colonial battleground from the viewpoint of the vanquished.

THE NATIVE WAR COMMUNITY

Among the native Mexican chroniclers, as with the Spanish writers, conduct in war was the hallmark of the society. Bravery, diplomacy, and prudence were the keys to assessing the worth of the culture. Alva Ixtlilxochitl's denial of the familiar stereotype of native cowardice and inertia, and his assertion of loyal service to Cortés, gave twofold significance to his claim that the war in Mexico was "the most difficult conquest the world had ever known." In this manner, Don Fernando staked a claim to the dominant values of Christian militancy. His efforts point out the fact that the concept of *la milicia cristiana* itself had no place—thanks to its Eurocentrism—for the hero who was not European. Cortés, as Alva Ixtlilxochitl had pointedly remarked, as well as European humanist historiography had given short shrift to the critical role that the Mexican allies of the conquerors had played in the wars of conquest; Spanish historians always cited the large numbers of enemies vanquished—not the multitude of allies mobilized—in order to emphasize the extraordinary nature of the Spanish victory.

Alva Ixtlilxochitl's emphasis on the collective effort of the native war community was realized, nevertheless, through the construction of individual leadership and heroism. Thus, while he carefully documented the thousands of troops who intervened on behalf of the Spanish, he took special pains to foreground the role of his forebearers' leadership, wisdom and bravery. In this respect,

Alva Ixtlilxochitl was typical of those native American chroniclers who responded to a European oversight.[16] In most of the accounts of Spanish authorship, "process gave way to frozen image," as Conley (xv) put it. That is, the figure of the incarcerated lord Moctezuma became the proof of European cultural superiority and the site of Christian mercy. In the end, the response of writers like Don Fernando to the view that deprecated the native populations for being so easily conquered was to inscribe that collaboration as the evidence of the values—*prudencia, ingenio,* and *valor*—of which they were accused to be lacking. Their agenda to build the historical reputation of their peoples in the postconquest era depended on expressing their values in terms understood and appreciated by the European audience to whom those claims were directed.[17]

Clearly, historians such as Alva Ixtlilxochitl countered such views of their own peoples as the defeated collective enemy by emphasizing their wartime conduct in ways that expressed their adherence to the values of a military culture. Yet the values the colonial subject celebrated were Mexican, not European. For the Aztecs, militarism was fundamental to their way of life. The close relation of trading and warfare and the association of military prowess and nobility were regular features of imperial life (Ingham 380-382). Noble status generally required legitimation through feats of bravery in battle, and since armed trading caravans often acted as spies, armed reprisals against them afforded the Aztecs further pretext for war and imperial expansion (382). Correcting earlier characterizations of Aztec warfare as primarily ritual in nature, recent studies (Isaac 128) emphasize ethnographic sources which reveal that Aztec "ordinary wars" had the typical features of state-level warfare elsewhere: heavy slaughter of combatants, calculated slaughter of non-combatants, seizure of lands, burning of elite structures, and the incorporation of the vanquished as tributaries. Valor on the battlefield was an important means for the ordinary soldier to receive honors and even advance in social status. From the point of view of the Aztec administration, war was the means to meet the ever-increasing food tribute demands of the Aztec state (ibid.). This meant that a primary objective was the outright conquest of other groups, not the taking of captives as in the ritualistic "Wars of the Flowers."

Military values were indeed the highest in the society that Alva Ixtlilxochtil (2: 179) described: those worthy of serving their lords were those who had proven themselves in military feats. In electing a successor to the deceased Nezahualpiltizintli, the ability to govern and proof of valor in war were taken by our author to be the principle criteria for selection (2: 190).

Nowhere in Alva Ixtlilxochitl's narrative is this bellicose character of Mexican culture more aggressively realized than in his account of the early life of the prince Ixtlilxochitl: Killing his nurse when he was but three for her crime of fornication with a palace guard, forming armies and squadrons with his friends at age seven, executing, with the help of his military arts teachers, two royal advisers who sought his life when he was but ten or twelve, he persuaded his father that his deeds exemplified the values most highly esteemed in his kingdom. By the age of sixteen, he had earned the insignia of a great captain (2: 175-176). In that same year, the prince Ixtlilxochitl opposed his uncle Moctezuma's selection of Cacama as successor to Nezahualpilzintli and the prince Ixtlilxochitl over-powered and captured in hand-to-hand combat the Mexican captain Xochitl. The prince had him burned alive, declares our chronicler, so that his enemies would show him greater fear and respect (2: 192). Don Fernando continues his narration by noting that three years later, in 1519, the prince Ixtlilxochitl met and allied himself with Cortés. He captured Cacama and turned him over to Cortés for punishment. Don Fernando assured his readers that Cortés was delighted to have as his friend this prince, "the most feared and respected person in all the kingdom" (2: 223-223). In the *Historia chichimeca*, the prince Ixtlilxochitl and his armies played a large role in fighting off the Mexica and bringing other groups around, as well as supplying the provisions that made possible the siege of Tenochtitlán (2: 250-254, 258-259).

In spite of the fact that Alva Ixtlilxochitl celebrated the military values shared by the peoples of the Central Valley of Mexico, it would be misleading, as Richard Terdiman has warned, to overstate his independence of expression from that of the conqueror. Alva Ixtlilxochitl's subject position is not that of the pure indigenous prehispanic past, but that of a colonial subject, as Georges Baudot has observed, whose conscious attempts to accommodate himself to new doctrinal and discursive norms bespeak an ethnic ambition and a search for identity. That identity is bound up with an over-bearing emphasis on the House of Texcoco from which he descends, and the effort, as we have seen, to place Texcoco centrally with regard to Spanish welfare at the time of the conquest. In this way, the Mexican values of prehispanic origin are compromised by Alva Ixtlilxochitl who renders them in the language of the conqueror and sets them in the context of European fortunes. To acknowledge this complicity is not to deny the legitimacy of the position of the colonial subject, but rather to outline its features. In my view, it is wrong to deny the authenticity of this complex and compromised subject position because it fails to fit the neat model of binary opposition. In this respect, the acknowledgment of a third or intermediate type of alterity is probably closer to historical reality than a more abstract model of alterity which in itself is likely to be a feature of a crushing dominant discourse.

THE CULTURAL CONSTRUCTION OF THE OTHER

There is no question that European cultural concepts of warfare played a decisive role in the European humanistic "construction of the other." It is borne out by the discursive practices of the colonial subject who simultaneously dismantled and reconstructed the discourse on war in order to take an effective adversarial position on the battle lines drawn by Spanish imperial history and colonial law. Due to the fact that one of the mainstays of the discourse on the Indies was the European exploration of Amerindian ritual and religious practices, ("witchcraft" and "superstition" as they were commonly called), the autochthonous Amerindian versions of the history of the conquest played a virile and "defeminizing" role.

Here we need only recall the key elements in Juan Ginés de Sepúlveda's interpretation of Amerindian behavior on the battlefield, of how in precolumbian times the Mexicans fought endless and ferocious wars but how, during the Spanish conquest, they "fled like women."[18] Indigenous American historians writing about the wars of conquest cast aside that feminizing construction of alterity on two counts: first by denying the characterization of historical behavior as ferocity and feminine cowardice (both being signs of the surrender to appetite and passion), and secondly, by inscribing their lived experience in the discourse of dynastic history rather than that of "false beliefs." Rejecting the representation of traditional native experience as rituals and customs or "folklore," the Alva Ixtlilxochitls reinstated native history, which was denied in foreign accounts, by constructing diachronic sequences intelligible to Europeans and based on the serialization of dynasties and the narration of wars. The devotion to letters was a retrospective devotion to arms. Thus, the discourse on war was a chief means by which not only the invading Europeans but also the colonial (and precolumbian) Mexica, Acolhuas, and other groups took the measure of their own civilization and that of others.

Even as the seventeenth-century historian Alva Ixtlilxochitl immortalized his own society's military values in such a way that the European would find familiar resonance in them, he had to deterritorialize the society of Mexican sacrifice. Suppressing such ritual practices in general, he acknowledged them briefly, summarily noting that prisoners of war had been sacrificed to "false gods".[19] The importance of prowess in war rings clear, however, in his account of the origins of his people; Tlotzin, great lord, led his people to be cultivators of fertile lands, hunters of wild beasts, husbands strictly monogamous; they constituted a nation, in short, "the most bellicose that there ever was and has been in this new world, for which reason they ruled over all others."[20]

Ixtlilxochitl's autochthonous model of civilization was an empire established by military conquest. Heir to a dynasty since vanished, some of whose features he carefully suppressed, he nevertheless celebrated the virtues of the Texcocan war community as central to the formation of historical institutions and relations which would exist, after the turn of the seventeenth century, only retrospectively.

War and military culture as vehicles of self-definition and, concomitantly, of the positing of otherness, are revealing sites—paradoxically—for getting at notions of civilization. In the European/American encounter, the figure of the warrior stands as the reigning symbol of civilized culture. Ironically, this warrior figure was an archaic one, in both its European and native American manifestations. The conquistador of the 1520s and 1530s was far removed from the chivalric Castilian *caballero* of the Reconquest; by 1600, the native American elites and their warrior classes had already been processed into undifferentiated masses as "Indians." The war community, central as it was to both Europeans and Amerindians in conceptualizing civilization, was, in each case, a community imagined and formed in discourse which lingered long after the plenitude of its existence.

To return to Todorov, it seems clear that concepts of war were central to discussions of notions of the civilized order and that this discussion, overall, is relevant to reconstructing the ways that Europeans and Americans strove to comprehend each other in the Spanish settlement of the Indies. There is, however, much more than meets the eye in Todorov's account. Meanwhile, de Certeau's contemplations of text and discourse break the bonds of European propriety pertaining to written culture, first, by positing a textuality that can be inhabited as well by the other as by the self, and, secondly, by remembering that behind the label of 'otherness' stand real people in their lived experience.

I would like to close now by returning to Don Quijote's suspended speech: The narrator of *Don Quijote* tells us that after our wandering knight began his discourse, his speech obliged his audience to listen to him seriously, and not to take him for a madman. At the end, all agreed with his arguments, yet felt renewed pity for this man who was so sane and wise in all he discussed, except when he brought up his confounded devotion to his own chivalric actions (*Adventures* 345).

For those moments when Don Quijote expressed the values that his company shared, he ceased to be the other in their eyes. Cervantes's astute observation suggests to us how, in an analogous fashion, the speech of the Alva Ixtlilxochitls could erase, for a moment and from their locus of utterance, the spectacle of otherness itself.

NOTES

[1] Todorov begins his narration with the declaration: "...my main interest is less a historian's than a moralist's; the present is more important to me than the past" (4).

[2] I am indebted to Josaphat B. Kubayanda for this definition of the colonial subject and for bringing to my attention the importance of the work of Franz Fanon in this context. Sartre's preface to Fanon's *The Wretched of the Earth* made it explicit: The colonizing discourse of the colonizer was turned on its head ("talking of Man while you murder men") and the consciousness of the colonized achieved recognition. With Fanon's work, terminated by his premature death, the colonized no longer would be defined by others; they defined themselves.

[3] Although Todorov does not feature Aztec accounts of the conquest of Mexico in this work, he edited a collection of them, translated into French, with Georges Baudot (*Récits*).

[4] As Godzich observed (xvi), the work of Emmanuel Levinas has been important to Todorov (*Conquest* 250). Levinas's notion of finding truth in the lived experience of the other, and thereby constituting the self as an ethical being (see Godzich), is implicit in de Certeau's "Conclusion" to *Discourses on the Other*.

[5] De Certeau's notion about what happens when one utilizes the speech of another has much in common with the views of Bakhtin and Volosinov on 'double voicing' and reported speech.

[6] As Conley (xv) put it, "The author uses a psychoanalytic notion of the event (or *venement*) to remind us that every 'fact' that has been

recorded and is today assumed to be historically valid is shaped from conflicting imaginations, at once past and present" (see de Certeau, *Writing* 6-11, 327-328).

[7] "Cuando vino [el Emperador] de Alemania, [Las Casas] le propuso su causa con mucha erudición y prudencia, hablando como santo, informando como Iurista, decidiendo como Teólogo, y testificando como testigo de vista."

[8] His mother, from whom he took his last name, was the great-granddaughter of Ixtlilxochitl, the last lord of Texcoco, and Beatriz Papantzin, daughter of Cuitlahuac, the penultimate lord of Mexico. His father, Juan de Navas Pérez de Peraleda, was Spanish (Martínez 139).

[9] In November of 1608, Don Fernando presented his *Compendio histórico del reino de Texcoco* and other documents to the native authorities of Otumba and San Salvador Cuatlazinco. His goal was to obtain their approval and ratification of his accounts of Toltec and Chichimec history, the eighty laws and ordinances of Nezahualcoyotzin, and the kind and quantity of tribute paid by the provinces of New Spain to the Spanish monarchy. All were approved and ordered to be translated from Náhuatl to Spanish by the interpreter Francisco Rodríguez (O'Gorman 1: 23, 521).

[10] Don Fernando's own testimony (1: 287) on the problem of non-hereditary *gobernadores* indicated that it was common to select an individual who was "*muy ladino*," that is, well versed in European ways and language, and raised by clerics, even though he might be of low birth.

[11] In this regard, it is of interest to note de Certeau's reference to the work of the Soviet semiotician Juri Lotman on spatial conceptions of cultural typology.

[12] De Certeau recovers, as Godzich (xiv) noted, the "mode of interaction that constitutes the lived experience" of the people.

[13] As de Certeau observed (*Heterologies* 68), "these two aspects are only formally distinguishable, because it is in fact the text's reworking of space that simultaneously produces the space of the text."

[14] He makes such statements in his commentary on sources in his *Sumaria relación de las cosas de Nueva España* (1: 285-288), his *Historia chichimeca* (2: 215, 235), and in his "Dedicatoria" to the *Sumaria relación de la historia de Nueva España* (1: 525-528).

[15] Here Alva Ixtlilxochitl (1: 468) performs his own slight of hand, because no one was more aware than he that there were conflicting native versions of the history of the conquest or of the credit that one or an-

other group received: "No one remembers about the Acolhuas-Texcocans and their lords and captains, although it is all the same house, but rather the Tlascaltecas, who, according to all the historians, say that most often they came to rob and plunder rather than help...."

[16] Although I have not considered epic poems of the conquest here, their content echoes that of the histories. In the published epic poems on the conquest of Mexico, the importance of native allies is minimized and individual heroic figures are seldom created. The Cacique de Tabasco in Gabriel Lobo Lasso de la Vega's *Mexicana* [1594] and the personage of Guatemozin in Antonio Saavedra Guzmán's *El peregrino indiano* [1599] are notable exceptions (Van Horne 360). The most striking exception to the general practice is, of course, Ercilla's *La Araucana* [1569-1581]. Ercilla responded to anticipated criticism that he had emphasized Araucanian affairs and their bravery more extensively than was warranted for "barbarians" by defending his choices in the prologue to his work (see Alonso de Ercilla y Zúñiga 1: 121-122).

[17] To put this treatment of the Amerindians as opponents in war in relief, it is interesting to note that, during the reign of Charles V, enemies in war closest to the Spanish in culture and ideology were lauded for their battlefield comportment while those farthest removed (Moors and Turks) were condemned. If chivalry, courage, liberality, and perseverance characterized the French (as Christian and Catholic enemies), the Turks and Moors (as infidels and "enemies of Christ") were cited contemptuously for cowardice, treachery, and inertia.

As Moorish fortunes declined in Spain, the general attitude expressed in literature was "religious hatred and contempt for a foe no longer able to struggle with Spain on something like equal terms" (Van Horne 349). The literary evidence of appreciation of courage on the part of individual Moors was one vestige of the respect no longer held for Moorish power in general (see Van Horne 341-361). Thus, the *morisco* romance of the fifteenth and sixteenth centuries indirectly exalted Castilian heroism by elevating the prestige of the conquered Moorish enemy, hopefully stimulating in the Spanish audience the desire to emulate military virtues (Carrasco Urgoiti 48). In this way, we find that the figure of the Moorish warrior and courtier shared certain values of the Christian warrior. What this multiplication of Moorish images represented was the exaltation of the distant Moorish enemy vis-à-vis the disparagement of the internal and domestic *morisco* enemy at home (54).

[18] Sepúlveda (*Demócrates* 35). We might also recall his specific modification of that feminized view ("se trataba no de hombres con espíritu femenino, sino de gente fuerte") in the *De Orbe Novo* (442).

[19] Alva Ixtlilxochitl (2: 163): "In the year 1494, Tlacahuepantzin, one of the legitimate sons of Axayacatzin, was taken prisoner in a battle by

those of Atlixco and was sacrificed to their false gods....In the year of 1496 the armies of the three heads of the empire went against those of the province of Tequantópec, in which they were again defeated and suffered loss of face and reputation and God punished them for the many sacrifices they had made, and it did not stop there but God sent them further punishments, as will be seen later." My translation.

[20] Alva Ixtlilxochitl (2: 27): "Y finalmente fue y ha sido la nación más belicosa que ha habido en este nuevo mundo, por cuya causa se seáorearon de todas las demás."

WORKS CITED

Adorno, Rolena. "On Pictorial Language and the Typology of Culture in a New World Chronicle." *Semiotica* 36.1-2 (1981): 51-106.

Alva Ixtlilxochitl, Fernando de. *Obras históricas*. Ed. Edmundo O'Gorman. Serie de historiadores y cronistas de Indias 4. 2 vols. México: UNAM, 1985.

Bakhtin, Mikhail. "Discourse Typology in Prose." *Readings in Russian Poetics*. Ed. Ladislav Matejka and Krystyna Pomorska. Ann Arbor: Univ. of Michigan Press, 1978. 176-196.

Baudot, Georges, and Tzvetan Todorov, ed. and trans. *Récits aztéques de la conquête*. Paris: Seuil, 1983.

Benveniste, Emile. *Problems in General Linguistics*. Trans. Mary Elizabeth Meek. Coral Gables, Florida: Univ. of Miami Press, 1971.

Carrasco Urgoiti, María Soledad. *El moro de Granada en la literatura del siglo XV al XX*. Madrid: Revista del Occidente, 1956.

Certeau, Michel de. *Heterologies: Discourses on the Other*. Trans. Brian Massumi. Foreword Wlad Godzich. Theory and History of Literature 17. Minneapolis: Univ. of Minnesota Press, 1986.

—. *The Writing of History*. Trans. Tom Conley. New York: Columbia Univ. Press, 1988.

Cervantes de Salazar, Francisco. "Epístola al muy illustre señor don Hernando Cortés, marqués del Valle." *Obras*. Alcalá de Henares: Juan de Brocar, 1546.

Cervantes Saavedra, Miguel de. *El ingenioso hidalgo Don Quijote de la Mancha.* Ed. Francisco Rodríguez Marín. Clásicos castellanos 8. 7th ed. 10 vols. Madrid: Espasa-Calpe, 1962.

—. *The Adventures of Don Quijote.* Trans. J.M. Cohen. Middlesex, England: Penguin Books, 1950.

Conley, Tom. "Translator's Introduction: For a Literary Historiography." *The Writing of History* by de Certeau. Trans. Tom Conley. New York: Columbia Univ. Press, 1988. vii-xxiv.

Covarrubias, Sebastián. *Tesoro de la lengua castellana o española.* Ed. Martín de Riquer. Barcelona: Horta, 1943.

Ercilla y Zúñiga, Alonso de. *La araucana.* Ed. Marcos A. Moríñigo y Isaías Lerner. Madrid: Castalia, 1983.

Fanon, Frantz. *The Wretched of the Earth.* Preface Jean-Paul Sartre. Trans. Constance Farrington. New York: Grove Press, 1961.

Fernández, Alonso. *Historia eclesiástica de nuestros tiempos.* Toledo: Pedro Rodríguez, 1611.

Gibson, Charles. "The Aztec Aristocracy in Colonial Mexico." *Comparative Studies in Society and History* 2 (1959-60): 169-196.

—. *The Aztecs under Spanish Rule: A History of the Indians of the Valley of Mexico, 1519-1810.* Stanford: Stanford Univ. Press, 1964.

Godzich, Wlad. Foreword. *Heterologies: Discourses on the Other.* By de Certeau. Trans. Brian Massumi. Minneapolis: Univ. of Minnesota Press, 1986. vii-xxi.

Ingham, John M. "Human Sacrifice at Tenochtitlan." *Comparative Studies in Society and History* 26.3 (1984): 379-400.

Isaac, Barry. "Aztec Warfare: Goals and Battlefield Comportment." *Ethnology* 22 (April 1983): 121-131.

López de Gómara, Francisco. *Historia general de las Indias.* Ed. Jorge Gurria Lacroix. 2 vols. Caracas: Biblioteca Ayacucho, 1979.

Lotman, Juri M. "On the Metalanguage of a Typological Description of Culture." *Semiotica* 14.2 (1975): 97-123.

Martínez, José Luis. *Nezahualcóyotl: vida y obra.* Serie Literatura indígena: pensamiento y acción. México: Fondo de Cultura Económica, 1972.

O'Gorman, Edmundo. "Estudio introductorio." *Obras históricas*, I. By Alva Ixtlilxochitl. Ed. Edmundo O'Gorman. México: UNAM, 1985. 1-257.

Sahagún, Bernardino. *The War of Conquest: How it Was Waged here in Mexico*. Trans. Arthur J.O. Anderson and Charles E. Dibble. Salt Lake City: Univ. of Utah Press, 1978.

Sartre, Jean-Paul. Preface. *The Wretched of the Earth*. By Fanon. Trans. Constance Farrington. New York: Grove Press, 1961. 7-31.

Sepúlveda, Juan Ginés de. *Demócrates segundo o de las justas causas de la guerra contra los indios*. Ed. Angel Losada. Madrid: Consejo Superior de Investigaciones Científicas, 1951.

—. *Hechos de los españoles en el Nuevo Mundo y México. Juan Ginés de Sepúlveda y su crónica indiana*. Valladolid: Seminario Americanista de la Universidad de Valladolid y Excmo. Ayuntamiento de Pozoblanco, 1973. 185-494.

Todorov, Tzvetan. *The Conquest of America: The Question of the Other*. Trans. Richard Howard. New York: Harper and Row, 1984.

Van Horne, John. "The Attitude Toward the Enemy in Sixteenth-Century Spanish Narrative Poetry." *Romanic Review* 16 (1925): 341-361.

Volosinov, V. N. "Reported Speech." *Readings in Russian Poetics*. Ed. Ladislav Matejka and Krystyna Pomorska. Ann Arbor: Univ. of Michigan Press, 1978. 149-175.

CHAPTER 6:
MONTAIGNE AND THE INDIES:
CARTOGRAPHIES OF THE
NEW WORLD IN THE *ESSAIS*, 1580-88

TOM CONLEY

> Let's fall back to our coaches. In their place
> and that of any other transport, [a king]
> was carried thus by men and on their shoul-
> ders. That last king of Peru, the day he was
> taken, was carried thus on golden stretch-
> ers, and seated in a golden chair, in the
> middle of his battle. No sooner than these
> porters were killed to make him fall down
> (for they wanted to take him alive) did
> others eagerly take the place of the dead,
> such that he could not be knocked down,
> however these people were murdered, until
> a horse-man dashed to grab him by his
> body and bashed him into the earth.[1]

Notes on the Spanish conquests are not often dropped
in the *Essais*, but when they do, they fall with a thud. By
1580, when Montaigne published the first two volumes of
his autobiography, Spain was ready was ready to celebrate
its centenary anniversary of the Iberian takeover of the
New World. Accounts of Columbus, Cortés, Pizarro and
others had already flourished in Zaragoza, Venice, the
Netherlands, and France. Montaigne's readings were apparently limited to translations of Benzoni and López de
Gómara along with the travels of the French cosmographers Jean de Léry and André Thevet. Yet the *légende
noire* is so marked in "Des coches" (*Essais*, III, vi, cited
above) that readers might wonder if Montaigne had been
aware of the debates over the invasions that had been
heard in Valladolid in 1550-51, when Fray Bartolomé de
las Casas disputed Juan Ginés de Sepúlveda about the hu-

man rights of Indians. Most scholarship associates Montaigne with a "clairvoyant skepticism" that favors the early development of ethnography.[2] So general are the humanistic strains of the *Essais* that immediate historical relation between the writer and the recent debates cannot be located. Montaigne's passing reflections on the Iberian heritage in the New World amount to a late testimony, if not a Frenchman's footnote, simply remarking that his time was in toss and stir.

Were Montaigne's allusions to Spain sign of a European's marvel about the curiosities of the New World? A wish to be seen accounting for history taking place? A desire to tell tales of the Indies and to recall his sight of naked Indians being paraded through Rouen? Or do they indicate something about early modern geography, in which the world was seen at once expanding and shrinking or running out of time? In their latency, do they contain elements of specific policy, or do they merely betray evidence of a general humanism? Questions of this type can be approached through Montaigne's relations with the Spanish accounts that informed his observations about the world recently discovered.

"Montaigne has to be situated in his person, who also knew Benzoni and Gómara but was unaware of Las Casas" ("Il faudrait placer Montaigne en personne, qui a connu lui aussi Gómara et Benzoni, mais ignoré Las Casas")[3] : In his studies of the impact of Las Casas on modern Europe, Marcel Bataillon has argued that the Spanish humanist never exercised any direct influence on Montaigne. Broader work, he underscores, is needed to follow the influence of Benzoni and Las Casas as forces disseminating news of the Black Legend. Since the *Essais* are of their own protean, evasive, and grotesque character, any transcription or deduction of the New World from one account to another would have to be seen altered in the more complex graphic movements of their style. For defensive and esthetic reasons, original materials are cribbed but fashioned into collages; historical reports are rewritten by virtue of the context that distorts them. The essayist reminds his public that it must read his words diligently, with eyes distracted, applied and divided. They must

glimpse where his vocables steal away, translate themselves, and where they at once evanesce and fall into form.
Foreign sources figure in his idiolect, or what elsewhere he
calls his "dictionnaire," in blatantly allusive ways. Here his
Iberian material must be scanned with a geometer's com-
pass and then mapped and plumbed according to the elliptical logic of Montaigne's arcane textual geographies.

The whole of the *Essais* forms a world of dynamic but
self-containing order. Whatever occupies a place in his
work does so relationally. By 1588, upon publication of the
third volume, the allegorical plan of the *Essais* was firmly
rooted: each of the three books was likened to a spoke of a
verbal wheel—of Nature or Fortune—or the contour of a
projection with its axis, circumference, and a curvilinear
plan. Two sets of identical numbers of essays abutted a
central hub that figured as a vanishing point marking an
absence or a confusion of oppositions. These in turn determined the spot where the coordinates of his project
converged but receded and pushed themselves out of
view. The area concretized worlds known and others unknown, as both visible and invisible points at the limits of
the autobiographical self and the indigenous, universal
other of its unconscious.[4] The evasive center of the first
volume, located between two even units of twenty-eight
chapters each (1-28 and 30-57), forms a cartouche in which
the memory of his dead friend and political activist, Etienne de la Boëtie, is encrypted. The chapter holds twenty-
nine sonnets that match its number (xxix) to herald an
emblem of autobiographical, architectural, and pictorial
design. The hub of the second volume, "Of the Liberty of
Conscience" (xix) ("De la liberté de conscience") takes the
liberty (and conscience) of assuming a pose of Janus by re-
counting the divided life of Julian the Apostate. Like the
two-faced god of antiquity, but cognizant of the Wars of
Religion that promise no easy future, Montaigne protec-
tively looks forward to one time, world, and religion—one
law, one faith, one king (*une loy, une foy, un roy*)—just as
he looks back to others. The essay changes its aspect
according to the posterity of historical change. The tiny
chapter of the third book, "Of the Incommodity of Greatness" ("De l'incommodité de la grandeur") (vii) is a vir-

tual vanishing point toward and away from which are oriented his fugal meditations on love, travel, decrepitude and experience.[5]

Almost uncannily, however, his remarks on the Spanish New World are inserted immediately adjacent to each of the three axes. In volume one, "Of Cannibals" ("Des cannibales") is a near-perfect mirror to "Of Friendship" ("De l'amitié") which rests along the frame that is drawn by the place held for La Boëtie's sonnets. Allusion in volume two to Mexican sacrifice in "Of Giving the Lie" ("Du desmentir" [II, xviii]) adjoins "De la liberté de conscience," an essay whose theme of moderation resembles the way that "Of Moderation" ("De la moderation" [I, xxx]) is juxtaposed to the Amerindians of the "Cannibales" (I, xxxi). And in the third, "Of Coaches" ("Des coches" [III, vi]), with its lower edge bearing reports of the murder of the king of Peru, forms a unit with the speculations on kingship in the following chapter, "De l'incommodité de la grandeur" (III, vii), once again the vanishing point of the third volume. A textual cartography is ordered; its allegorical bearings weigh heavily on contemporary representations of the New World. The Western hemisphere offsets the binarity of past and present by impugning the classical tradition that compares the ancients to the moderns on Mediterranean shores; it adds an ocular, even anamorphic element to the design of the *Essais*. At the same time the allusions to the Spanish Indies figure in political agendas that interpret international strife, commerce, and Franco-Spanish relations.

Montaigne's compositional tactics, that are discussed slyly in "Of Vanity" ("De la vanité" [III, ix]),[6] possess cardinal and geographical virtue that bear on policy. The relation of history and allegory is no doubt grounded in a practice that shares much with Jean Bodin's world-view of man and his climates taken up in the fifth book *Of the Republic* (*De la république* [Paris, 1577]). In that world-mirror Bodin theorizes a realm of space and history in order, it appears, to cope with the effects wrought by the Columbian discoveries and the recent Religious Wars on French soil since 1562. He maps the world by superimposing the four humors over the four cardinal directions:

Northerners are phlegmatic, heavy, dull, and of fair complexion while Southerners are constant, grave, and of darker tint that betrays a melancholic bent. Those to the East tend to be nimble and courteous, and of yellow—Chinese—skin signalling choleric origins, while Brazilians, to the West, are sanguine as the wood of their name: strong, cruel and savage. Bodin apportions the two hemispheres into three units of thirty degrees each from the Equator to the North Pole, and likewise, to the South. "The difference of manners and dispositions of people, is much more notorious betwixt the North and the South, than betwixt the East and West."7 Northern and Southern nations "can never concur together for the contrarietie of manners and humors" (552) between them.

Projecting an immortal dynamic order beyond history, his cosmography appears to emerge from the recent events it schematizes. Populations of the median regions (France and Italy, located between the thirtieth and sixtieth parallels) enjoy a moderation of opposites. Gallic souls have more temperate ways than their German or Iberian neighbors, and for that reason are given to democratic rule. Northerners govern themselves "by force of arms," while Southerners elect to follow the laws of religion. The Germans find their patron in *Reiters*, whose might makes right; the French abound in reason and judgment; the Spanish "in craft and subtilitie, like unto foxes; or unto Religion: for eloquent discourses agree not with the grosse wits of the Northern people" (559). Most crucially, "It is not mervail then if the people of the south are better governed by religion, than by force or reason, the which is a point verie considerable to draw the people, when as neither force nor reason can prevaile: as we reade in the historie of the Indies, that *Christopher Columbus* when he could not draw the people of the West Indies into humanitie by any flatterie or fair meanes, he showed them the Moone the which they did worship, giving them to understand that she should soone lose her light: "three days after seeing the Moone eclipsed, they were so amazed, as they did what he commanded them" (560).

The feats of Columbus are put forth to show that a mild dose of constancy of religion might eventually cure a

France sickened by its civil wars. Yet, France serves as a corrective to the bloodly events that the Spanish precipitated in the New World: following Aristotle's observations, Bodin remarks that Southerners are prone to lust and lechery, like hares by virtue of "spondious melancholie" (557). Moderate peoples cannot see or hear of Northern or Southern cruelties. He implies that a likeness attracts the Spanish to South America, where Brazilians "are not contented to eat the flesh of their enemies, but will bathe their children in their blood" (559), in punishments no less horrifying than those the ancient Egyptians were wont to practice in former times. The model appears to be used, on the one hand, to account for and react to the Treaty of Câteau-Cambresis (1559), by which Spain craftily acquired Savoie which Francis I had gained in his Milanese campaigns earlier in the century; on the other it argues for a course of reason or calmer "interior heat" that should be followed to avoid repeating what took place in the West Indies. In Bodin's scheme, moderation of extremes through analogy puts events into movement that can allow for their perpetual revision. By superimposing the four humors over the Ptolemaic map, Bodin manages to combine a ruse of analogy with the forces of history. The contingency of battles between Charles V and Francis I colors his world-view, but its aura of timelessness owes much to its quasi-Aristotelian form taken from the *Politics*. In one way, the book is supple; it can move with current history of the Indies, while in another, the book is clad in its own allegorical chain mail. Bodin offers a prototypical semiotic grid for the sake of a French cause, but all the while the coordinates of human and geographical space tend to distance the views of the writer from identifying with his synthetic design.

Montaigne, who may have contemplated the same analogy about religion, leadership, and fear in his discussion of Mexican religion concluding "Des coches," no doubt shared with the jurist a critical view of Franco-Iberian relations as they had developed over the course of the sixteenth century. Nonetheless, writing against overly schematic logic, he remarks, "We must not nail ourselves so forthrightly here to our humors and complexions," ("Il ne faut pas se cloüer ci-fort à ses humeurs et complexions" the opening sentence of "De trois commerces" (III, iii) set under the third chapter of the third volume, appears to criticize the rigidity of designs that combine geometry and the elements of humors.[8] The *Essais* share the same principles evident in Bodin's *République*—in their view of Spanish history and in their dynamic form—but embody far more serpentine movement. Their common term is *moderation* in its inflections of meteorology, mood, space, and political conduct. The political groundplan of the essays is drawn to yield a dynamic moderation that will assure a future climate of bodily and international equilibrium. Following an ideology of apparent political conservatism that wills to guide the national vessel through its time of turbulence, the allegory indicates that moderation results from a constant balancing of multifarious forces at play in the cosmos. In the same way, examples are incised into the marquetry of the *Essais*. Like the shifting shores of the Dordogne described in "Des cannibales" (201), recent news from the Indies moves over time and betrays a more urgent consternation about the efficacy of the universalizing heritage of history.[9] Cartography avers to be more reliable than naturalistic versions of history, and thus the Western hemisphere of the *Essais*, like the perplexities of the New World, accrues increasing structural importance between 1580 of the first two volumes and 1588 of the third. "Des cannibales," Montaigne's showcase chapter of the first edition, corresponds to "Des coches" of the third. Each is situated next to center of their respective volumes; each takes up a specific historical issue and then digests it into smaller units (sentences, syntagms, words, letters and marks) that describe a circle in which moderating forces are put to play. "Des coches," it will be seen, completes a graphic vision begun in the earlier essay.

As in the most carefully crafted chapters, "Des cannibales" (I, xxxi) begins not below its title, but in the last lines of the essay that precedes it. In that essay, "De la moderation" (I, xxx), the author takes up what Bodin and other political thinkers had wished their French compatriots would heed. "I like median and temperate natures" (195) ("J'ayme les natures temperées et moyennes"), he writes, as if to show how extremities, whether in virtue, philosophy, marriage, theology, or even books can harm the world's order: an archer who overshoots a bull's eye is no less immoderate than one who can't reach the target. Discourse leads to accounts from the New World that abound with massacre and homicide, two extremes, alas, "universally embraced by all religions" (199). There living idols drink human blood. Young subjects are burned alive, half roasted and withdrawn from pyres only to have their heart and entrails ripped out and be collectively consumed. For other gods women are skinned alive, their hides used to clothe and mask tribal fetishes. The display of extreme religious practice is taken directly from the French translation of López de Gómara's *Histoire generalle des Indes* (II, 4) but appears, however, to have a spatial role in prefacing another passage taken from an Italian translation of the same author's *Istoria di don Fernando Cortes* (Venice, 1576), in which the Spaniards' Tlaxcalan enemy, having been defeated at the hands of Cortés, Montaigne reports, offers the conqueror a choice of gifts:

> I will still relate this account. After being beaten, some of these peoples sent envoys to acknowledge him and seek friendship; the messengers offered him three kinds of presents, in this manner: 'Lord, here are five slaves; if you are a fierce god who lives on flesh and blood, eat them, and we shall bring you more; if you are a worldly god, then take our perfume and feathers; if you are a man, please accept the birds and fruits we offer you.'

> Je diray encore ce compte. Aucuns de ces peuples, ayant esté batuz par luy, envoyerent le recognoistre et rechercher d'amitié; les messagers luy presenterent trois sortes de presents, en ceste manière: 'Seigneur, voylà cinq esclaves; si tu es un dieu fier, qui te paisses de chair et de sang, mange les, et nous t'en amerrons d'avantage; si tu es un Dieu debonnaire, voylà de l'encens et des plumes; si tu es homme, prens les oiseaux et les fruicts que voyci.' (199-200)

Thus ends the essay, without resolve, turning Gómara's description into a riddle and suspending it above "Des cannibales," in the shape of an emblematic superscription to the essay that follows. The question prompts readers to ponder the choice that the account refuses to resolve: What kind of man did he turn out to be? What did Cortés do? Or, from the perspective of its placement at the lower extremity of one essay and at the beginning of another, how does it bind moderation to cannibals?

In Montaigne's textual geography the Spanish account is turned against itself. In Gómara's original Cortés tells the Mexicans that he is mortal, like themselves, but that he is truthful, as opposed to their penchant to lie; he is friendly, but forced to engage in battles they had begun. The envoys are dismissed; the Indians attack and are again beaten. On a second mission the Mexicans return with gifts but, the historian notes, with the intent to spy. Cortés learns of (or conceives) the stratagem and in consequence has the hands of each of the fifty envoys dismembered before he sends them back to their people.[10] The abridged sequel is juxtaposed to the exemplum of Pyrrhus in the sentences directly below that inaugurate "Des cannibales." Pyrrhus too is an awesome leader but, unlike Cortés, he realizes that his Roman enemies are hardly so savage as popular Greek belief had taught him. Across the sides of each essay Cortés is opposed to Pyrrhus and, likewise, so are the tenets of "De la moderation" to "Des cannibales." Given the friendly motives that the Tlaxcalans personify, "Moderation" has thematic strands leading back to "De l'amitié." At its end, the Mexicans are seen seeking the bond of friendship that had been at the center of the former chapter. Montaigne thus *rewrites* Gómara's account of Cortés by leaving aside the details of the Spaniard's pillage and by adding, in a clause that does not figure in the original account that is otherwise transcribed verbatim from the biography, "[ils] *envoyerent le recognoistre et rechercher d'amitié*" (199). Gómara does not portray the Indians in search of friendship. *Amitié*, the trait unmarked in the Spanish chronicler's history, is situated precisely at the other cardinal end of the chapter on moderation. In its quest of a median demeanor in human action, the text puts the Spanish conqueror at the *extremity*, the southern, or, following Bodin's map, barbarous end of the composition. The more familiar and temperate end of the chapter is contained in the essay in homage to Etienne de la Boëtie. The essay "moderates" a course between cultural and geographical extremities by staging the scene of civility that his forthcoming cannibals will personify in ways no less compelling than those of the Mexican Indians.

The design appears to draw its course from two vectors that are part of the reigning plan of the *Essais*. One traces the axial schema of center and circumference that shapes the allegory of Destiny or ambivalence at the hub of each volume. The first and last chapters are at the periphery of the axis, located between chapters 28 and 29, which demarcates the world into two halves, or "moitiés" (akin to two friends or, in the logic of an archaic political organization, two groups that share an identity through the nominal differences they impose upon each other[11]):

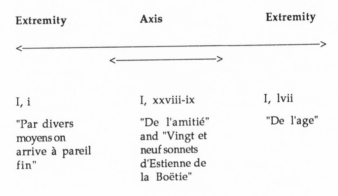

Extremity	Axis	Extremity
I, i	I, xxviii-ix	I, lvii
"Par divers moyens on arrive à pareil fin"	"De l'amitié" and "Vingt et neuf sonnets d'Estienne de la Boëtie"	"De l'age"

On another level, as these chapters are placed at the center of the first book of *Essais*, a similar division bisects the axis itself. The 29 sonnets, congruent with the 29th chapter, are set between friendship and moderation, two virtues that will color the picture of the cannibals adjacent to (or just to the East of) the immediate center:

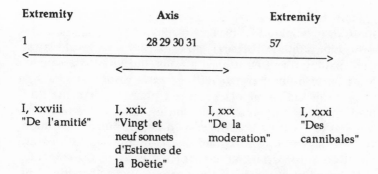

Extremity	Axis	Extremity
1	28 29 30 31	57

I, xxviii	I, xxix	I, xxx	I, xxxi
"De l'amitié"	"Vingt et neuf sonnets d'Estienne de la Boëtie"	"De la moderation"	"Des cannibales"

"Age" is the end of the meander announced in "By Diverse Means We Arrive at the Same End" ("Par divers moyens on arrive à pareil fin") (I, i) while the median ground, the double center (or ellipsis) of the friendship of two different souls, Montaigne and La Boëtie, concretizes the bond that holds the essayist to the cultural "other", that is, his dead companion and the Indians of "Moderation" and "Cannibales". Each unit tends to temper the other and to move, as in astronomical drawings of the Renaissance describing the play of micro-and macrocosm, back and forth from an unconscious humanity of Indians, recently born into history, to the essayist and his readers.

Hence chapter 31 acquires a historical specificity immediately manifest in spatial and graphic terms.[12] The praise of Amerindians virtually counters Gómara's orthodox view of conquest. The essay appears to develop from a series of visible inversions contained in words, in the representation of Spanish and French accounts, and in the focal properties of point of view. One of the favored terms is *barbarie*, a word recurring at several nodal points, that reveals how the expansionist and self-centering policies of European culture exceed all report of barbarity in the New World. The aphorism that crowns the first half of the chapter, "We call barbarity whatever is not of our custom" (203) ("Chacun appelle barbarie ce qui n'est pas de nostre usage"), foreshadows the more direct allusion to the Black Legend when it is used again, five pages below, to impugn European reason. The Indians are barbarous, but in no way are they so loathsome as their conquerors: "We can therefore surely call them barbarous in respect to the rules of reason, but not in respect to ourselves, we who exceed them in every kind of barbarity" (208) ("Nous les pouvons donq bien appeler barbares, eu esgard aux regles de la raison, mais non pas eu esgard à nous, qui les surpassons en toute sorte de barbarie"). With *barbarie* valorized as a sign of culture, the cannibals become ciphers or, like the doubled shape of the word itself, shifters that locate how and where the West surpasses its own geographical dominion. *We* are slaves to an expanding economy, while *they* are not. The anti-Iberian moment of the early essay coincides with an oblique praise of the homeostatic, self-moderating order of pre-Columbian Americas:

> *They are not debating the conquest of new lands*, for they still enjoy this natural fecundity that provides them without travail or difficulty with all necessities, in such abundance that *they do not have to expand their limits*. They are still at this happy point of only desiring as much as their natural needs provide; for them everything beyond that is superfluous.[13]

Debat underscores the recent fortunes of Spanish policy—perhaps by alluding to the Valladolid debates of 1550-51, while the praise of self-containment does not come as residue of edenic myths or utopian belief. Rather, the cultural model of their symbolic ecosystem is aimed against European nations (including France, as "Des coches" will emphasize below) and their policies of economic expansion.

For most of the sixteenth century the French had directed their principal commerce toward the Mediterranean. Trade went West for dyes taken from Brazilwood in the South and for fish in the North. The nation did not stand to profit through massive colonial programs that the Southern neighbors had conceived. A byproduct of economic history and the counterpart to the *légende noire*, the myth of the French *génie colonial* depended on exchange only with riverain and coastal cultures but not, as Spain and the bitter experience of Villegagnon had shown, a motive to settle or to convert indigenous populations.

Possibly for these reasons the text immediately qualifies its initially serene view of a steady-state culture in heeding how they are like any culture insofar as they engage in war. But their battles are matters of equilibration, that is, of balancing or, like the text itself, of *essaying*, rather than of expansion. When the cannibals do transgress their borders, they cross only natural limits (*montaignes*, a toponym that through its rapport with the author's name indicates an unswerving and self-containing locus moving back to the printed page) which separate one culture from another:

> If their neighbors cross over the mountains to attack them, and if they win over them, the victor's spoil is glory and the advantage of being supreme in value and virtue; for otherwise they can live without the booty of the vanquished, and then return to their homeland where they lack none of life's necessities nor, what is more important, knowing how to take pleasure in their condition and be happy with it.[14]

These "extreme" conditions nonetheless attest to policies that accord glory not to goods or lands gained but to symbolic abstractions. Physical waste of prisoners or dead bodies are not worth being managed. Subsequent description about how captives "neutralize" their enemies by offering themselves to be eaten, "a stratagem hardly smacking of barbarity" (211) ("invention qui ne sent aucunement la *barbarie*"), folds an only apparent horror of anthropophagia into a dynamic balance of physical and cultural economy. The cannibals prove how a "triumphal loss" where valor and skill supersede the untimely results of battle took place when Ischolas fought against the Arcadians. In topographical terms that ratify the order of "cannibales" adjacent to "moderation," Ischolas "opted for a middle choice between these extremes" (210) ("print entre ces deux extremitez un moyen parti"). His enemy won, but only, like the Spaniards who lurk in the margins of the exemplum, at the price of being seen as butchers who put their victims to a senseless demise.

Wherever it falls in the essay, *barbarie* becomes associated with cultural moderation. Another visible inversion in the text, each of Montaigne's intermediaries, also figures in dialogue with Spanish reports of the New World. His first interpreter is a simpleton, a prototypical topographer, unlike many a recent historian, who does not "incline or mask" his matter "according to the countenance that they had" of the Indians (202). His information is truer than "what cosmographers say of them" (203). The words are ostensibly aimed against his source, André Thevet's *Singularitez de la France antarctique* (1557), that drew much from Gómara's *Historia general de las Indias* (first Spanish edition printed in Zaragoza, 1552). The description of the cannibals comes not from the go-between's mouth of experience, which could use the ocular evidence of having "seen" the Indians in their true habitat, but from the mediation of the woodcuts that illustrated Thevet's *Singularitez*. The 1580 material depicting the cannibals' wars and weapons, the decapitated head of their enemies placed over the entrances to their homes, the ways they placed prisoners in bondage, and the dietary fashion of eating the enemy communally (207) are taken from six

FIGURES 1&2. From André Thevet's *Les singularitez de la France antarctique* (Anvers, 1557).

woodcuts that are set in Thevet's middle chapters on South America.[15] The personified intermediary whom Montaigne evokes happens also to be the ensemble of images that grounds these descriptions. The Indians that were sought to be found without mediation of others, the text reveals, are already filtered through pictures. The Indians happen to be as much a familiar product of Fontainebleau style as of reported alterity; they are represented only through the combination of text and image which conspires to produce an effect of authentic immediacy. Here the descriptions make their fiction of veracity the ground of truth.

The principal "horrors" of the Indians—nudity, cannibalism, and idolatry—were already conventions that Italian artists in France had been depicting in their renditions of classical myths.[16] Their drawings of masses of contorted bodies function according the laws of vanishing points that organize the mythologies they depict. Montaigne's description flattens the pictorial aberrations of the models and in turn reduces the accompanying rhetorical amplifi-

FIGURE 2. The Cannibals.

cation of the written sources. The text mediates the images and hence incorporates its concept of "experience" through its own visual patterning of expression. The style is far more optical than the French translation of Gómara's Spanish, a narrative written in a moralizing tenor, and it is less inclined to supply commentary than the original. In the folds of his own words, but not in direct experience, Montaigne engages what Thevet had announced at the conclusion of the *Singularitez*: "It is difficult, indeed (*voire*) impossible, to be able (*pouvoir*) to represent correctly the remarkable sites and places, their situations and distance without having seen them with the naked eye: which is the most certain of all knowledge, as everyone can judge and well understand" (f. 161v.) ("Il est malaisé, voire impossible, de pouvoir justment representer les lieux et les places notables, leurs situations et distance, senz les avoir veuës à l'oeil: qui est la plus certaine cognoissance entre toutes, comme un chacun peut juger et bien entendre"). The essay conflates the imaginary and objective sides of Thevet's report along the very crease of the highly visible writing that divides them. In its distance his secondary account appears more real, more balanced, and far more veracious than either Thevet or Gómara.[17]

Nonetheless the experience of recent history, Montaigne implies, is better founded than Aristotle. The Greek authority is mentioned in "Des cannibales," it appears, in order to be dismissed. "Aristotle's story is not in accord with our new lands" (202) ("Cette narration d'Aristote [on explorations dating to Carthage] n'a non plus d'accord avec nos terres neuves"), Montaigne concludes, effectively rejecting the same authority that papal authorities had marshalled to adduce the cultural inferiority of the Amerindians. Montaigne opts for an intermediate form of *experience*, that is, a combination of observation, analogy, writing and language, to move toward a mapped view of the New World that is inseparable from the textual coordinates of the *Essais*. The effect of concomitance of world and essay prompts the voice to move back and forth, from one world to the other over and again.[18]

Here a third axis of inversion is manifest, one that focalizes Montaigne and the Amerindians at the center of a mystical projection. Two shapes of alterity, Montaigne and his subject, are combined into a single viewpoint, but like two points of an ellipse, they remain independent of each other.[19] The process duplicates the movement toward and away from center and circumference in the overall plan of the *Essais*, but now the effect approaches the subject along the axis (or sightline) of the very alterity it describes. In this light Montaigne does not merely observe the "noble savage," nor does the chapter mark a step on a path toward an enlightenment that would move from marvel to deeper understanding of the foreign world. The other, the cannibal with whom Montaigne identifies, is both himself and other.[20]

The end of the essay stages the same inversion. Using his unreliable memory as a lens through which he can discern their fate, Montaigne recalls that recently three Indians met King Charles IX (in fact, in 1562 when the adolescent monarch ruled under the regency of Catherine de Medici) in Rouen. The French asked them what they found most admirable about the nation. "They answered three things, but I've lost the third and am quite ashamed; but I still recall two of them" (212) ("Ils respondirent trois choses, d'où j'ay perdu la troisiesme, et en suis bien marry; mais j'en ay encore deux en memoire"). Failure of memory authenticates the encounter; it also demonstrates a play of doubling in which his distance from them affords an uncannily common proximity. Montaigne enables his words to speak *through* the Indians and to gain a perspective on the state of his nation from at once within and without its borders.[21] The text reports that he met three of the natives, and that they could not understand how grown and strong men—"perhaps the Swiss guard," Montaigne qualifies in a protective measure—submitted themselves to a child. In a move that cannot fail to be read as calling into question the sorry state of the national budget of the post-1550 years, it tells how, for all its wealth and pomp, the nation insulated the elite from a mass of homeless subjects. "Secondly (they have a way of language such that they name men half the one and the other), that they noticed how among us there were men stuffed and filled with all kinds of fine things, and that their other halves, shrivelled by hunger and poverty, were begging at their doors" (212-13) ("Secondement [ils ont une façon de leur langage telle, qu'ils nomment les hommes moitié les uns des autres] qu'ilz avoyent aperçeu qu'il y avoit parmy nous des hommes pleins et gorgez de toutes sortes de commoditez, et que leurs moitiez estoient mendians à leurs portes, décharnez de faim et de pauvreté").

Critique of French economic policies is done through the other, who amounts to the "half," which contains the self (*moy*-tié), but doubles it in a way that calls into memory the friendship with La Boëtie, when it was "a rather great miracle to be doubled" (190) ("un assez grand miracle de se doubler"), and where "we were entirely halved" (192) ("nous estions à moitié de tout"). Through the filter of uncommon amity Montaigne reports that "I spoke to one of them for a long time, "but in a way that the syntax makes *one* of them *two* ("je parlay à l'*un* [1] *d'eux* [2] fort long temps,") (213), or a double of himself and his position. Two points of view are held within the narrational perspective.[22]

Clearly the three modes of inversion (the focal or vanishing term, *barbarie*; the presence of intermediary images, reports or reporters; and the elliptical axis of self and Indian) utterly change the status of the historical sources that inform the writing. The immediate political views that argue for self-contained and self-regulating domestic and international policies and a more even redistribution of wealth bring forth elements unknown to Gómara or Thevet. Further, the essay dismantles the authority of Aristotle that had been used to favor policies encouraging conquest of the New World. To test further the strength of these views, attention can be directed to "Des coches" (III, vi), an essay placed next to the axis of the third volume, that itself forms a point of a double axis with "Des cannibales."

"Des coches" (III, vi) projects the optical structure of "Des cannibales" into a mirrored duplication *en abyme* or a self-reflective daedalus. The ostensive topic about regal coaches, signs of munificence in the European aristocracy, apposes that of litters on which Indians display their monarchs. The title, *Des coches*, equivocates with the second person singular of the verb *descocher* ("descoches") that tells its interlocutor or viewer to "release," "let an arrow fly," or "fire!" The verb is laden with amorous connotations developed in poetry of the Pléiade, but here it is imbued military history in the discussion that compares harquebuses to long bows (879), and that leads to consideration of guns on mobile wagons and their effects on cavalry and infantry (the Hungarians beat the Turks when "they released their fire on them to their squadrons to break them open and clear a way" ("les *descochoient* dans leurs escadrons pour les rompre et y faire jour"). Like the entire essay, the word forms its own abyss. At its center is the letter O, a sign of the axis and circumference of the *Essais*; of the wheel that is the metaphor of metaphor or of representation in general; the origin of mechanical printing; the figure of European weapons aimed at those looking directly at armed European conquerors readying to kill them; the circle of Time and Saturn.[23] Discursively, the O of the wagon wheels of chariots evokes the open mouth of subjects aghast at the view of extravagant public display or at the impact of a projectile as it splatters into their bodies. The figure ramifies to reflections on economy, by which the O signifies the shape of golden coins, Spanish plunder, mercantilism, and deficit spending. The letter at the center of the title

d-e-s-c—O—c-h-e-s

specifies the *abyme* where all the topics converge and finally into which they fall. It is the nexus of a geography that marks the intersections of the Old and New Worlds; North and South; antiquity and present time; France at its center and its periphery.

Gómara's accounts of Mexico and Peru play a crucial role in the overall design. The Spanish Indies offset the Old World by opening a space where contemporary France can be studied from without and within. At the fulcrum of the essay the text turns about-face to the New World in order to develop the convention of Europe beginning its decline upon contact with the Indies; it underscores how the static condition of lavish wealth has equalled whatever

Europe has displayed to its populace. The descriptions are lifted almost verbatim from Fumée's translation of *La Historia general de las Indias* that appeared in Paris in 1569. No doubt it was sold in France to make a public take note of the accounts of the fourth book, the translator notes, that "discourses amply on the civil wars, that came about among the Spaniards for the domination of the Peruvian king," and offers comparative examples that might help give perspective to "such calamitous times" of French civil strife. "It was fitting for the turbulent times in which we were living" ("Il convenoit au temps turbulent, auquel pour lors nous estions"). Fumée adds that Thevet's *Singularitez*, one of the principal French sources for depictions of The New World, is "filled with lies, not only forged by the author but also the sailors who told them to him so that he could pass them on." "You will see exaggerated accounts of the Amazons, errors in the designation of places, and abuses in the interpretation of many things" (f. ix) ("Vous y verrez de beaux comptes des Amazones, des faultes en la situation des lieux, et des abuz en l'interpretation de beaucoup de choses"). Cosmographers, historians, warriors, and philosophers, he adds, stand to gain from Gómara. The *Histoire* will correct French perceptions of the New World, and its example will buffer the horrors of the Wars of Religion that resemble what recently occurred in Peru. Montaigne's motives for using the source are not distant from Fumée's; yet with it he elaborates a different textual geography and a cultural critique arching back to the first volume. An icon of a world past and another freshly discovered, the coach figures in Gómara's relation. The Peruvians, Gómara notes, were a population led by the rich. "These lords were not equal on their thrones, nor in other honors because some came ahead of others, while others were carried on litters, and others by porters, while still others went on foot. Others were seated on high and great seats, others being not so high, while others walked on the ground" ("Ces seigneurs n'estoient pas egaux à s'asseoir, ny és autres honneurs, parce qu'aucuns procedoient les autres, autres se faisoient porter en lictière, autres en portoires, autres alloient à pied. Autres se seoient sur des sieges hauts et grands, autres sur des sieges plus bas, autres à terre").[24] Gómara offers a discursive emblem to the title of "Des coches." And like the images used to produce descriptions in "Des cannibales," the text clearly sets forth what contemporary illustrations had used to figure the New World—supine Indians in hammocks, long houses, human members roasted on skewers over fires, nude maidens, in sum the paraphernalia that had illustrated the *Singularitez*, was part of Oviedo and Benzoni, and that would soon be recast in Théodore de Brye's *Grands Voyages: Americae tertia pars, Navigatio in Brasiliam Americae* (Frankfurt, 1592).[25] The observer of 1588 appears to have obtained more information in the eight intervening years since "Des cannibales," or as if information about the Black Legend, combined with the excess found in Gómara's descriptions, were already impetus enough to argue further against colonial development.

Opposed once again to European barbarity are the Indians. Attabalipa signifies one mode of courage, and the King of Mexico another. When comparing Mexican cosmology to that of Christianity, the text draws on Gómara, verbatim again, to describe the five ages and five consecutive suns of human time. The first perishes when all humans and animals are drowned in diluvian waters; the second comes with the fall of the sky; the third by a fire which burned and consumed everything; the fourth, "through a commotion of air and wind that razed everything as far as several mountains; men were not killed but changed into *magots*" (a species of monkey). After fifteen years of darkness, a man and a woman are created to refashion the human species. The chapter follows Gómara quite closely except with a slight—but crucial—change in wording. Fumée reports,

> As for the third sun, they say that this was consumed by fire, the earth burning for many years, and during which the whole human race and all animals were immolated: and that the fourth came to an end through air, the wind being so strong and violent that all buildings, lairs and rocks fell to the ground: but that men no longer died, and that they were only transformed into monkeys.

> Quant au tiers soleil, ils disent icelui avoir esté con-
> sumé par le feu, ce monde bruslant par longues années,
> et durant lesquelles tout le genre humain, et tous les
> animaux furent enflambez: et que le quatriesme print
> fin par l'air, estant le vent si fort, et si violent, que
> tous les edifices, antres et rochers tomberent par terre:
> mais que les hommes ne moururent point, et qu'il
> furent seulement convertis en singes.[26]

Montaigne appears merely to abbreviate his model, tight-
ening the description of the third and fourth cataclysm:

> the third, by fire which burned and consumed every-
> thing; the fourth, through a commotion of air and
> wind which razed as far as several mountains; men no
> longer died, but they were turned into *magots* (from
> what impressions suffers the cowardice of human be-
> lief!)[27]

Two changes sally forth. First, Montaigne replaces the *quatriesme print feu par l'air* by *une émotion d'air*; then, "les
hommes ne moururent poinct..., ils furent seulement
convertis en singes," is altered quite extensively into "ils
ne moururent poinct, mais ilz furent changés en *magots*"
prior to the interjection in parenthesis. *Magots* replaces
singes, while an appositive sigh about the risible condition
of humanity infuses Gómara's model with the presence of
the essayist's sardonic irony. *Lácheté* is printed, it appears,
to reflect on the motif of chairs (*la cheze, la chaise*, suggested by *lácheté*, along with release, as *lascher* is triggered
from the synonym of *descocher*). The spatial and allegorical frame of the context might explain why *magots* replaces
singes. A synonym of *singe* (or a monkey without a tail, of
the "mazacques" family), *magot* appears to duplicate the
cardinal design of the chapter, since it also refers to
sacoche, or a pouch that contains money. According to Lit-
tré, "the *magot* must have been a money-bag; it would
have to be written *magaut*, and hence confused and
assimilated as *magot*, or monkey." The philologist traces it
back to provincial usage in which *magaut* also means "old
coins found in the ground." The word is hence a corruption of the old Latin *imago*. Not only does it mean a
genre of monkey, a "sum of round money usually hidden

in a secret place," but also an image or a visual figure. As such in "Des coches" the term is thus self-perpetuating in its play between its referent and its own visible form. Allusion to a simian confirms Montaigne's avowedly mimetic tendency, his "monkey-like and imitative condition" ("condition singeresse et imitatrice") (853), and all the more in respect to Gómara's text that he apes. In contemporary iconography the monkey was an animal that signified the sin of copying (among others, Bruegel's engraving of the prodigal son pillaged by apes) and parodied the curious souls who looked vainly for worth in secret places.

But *Magot* also ramifies into nominal and theological issues. As an allegorical landscape, the essay is striated by a line of demarcating worlds old and new; by apposed cosmologies that explain in different languages the beginnings and endings of man; by the sight of one world in decline and another in rebirth. The essay writes at its center, foretelling the end of Europe and the growth of the West, "The universe will fall into paralysis; one member will be withered, the other in vigor" ("L'univers tombera en paralisie; l'un membre sera perclus, l'autre en vigueur") (887). It cannot fail to be inflected by at least two theories of apocalypse that had attempted to explain the origins of "man" that news of Columbian discoveries had unearthed. They are related to the beginning of "Des cannibales" (200-02). On the one hand, an argument for polygenesis superseded the belief that the Indians were born of the sons of Noah. According to the teaching of the Apostolic church, the discovery of a New Jerusalem would usher in a new world to replace that of the old. In this millenarian view which was current at the end of the sixteenth century,[28] the Books of Genesis and Apocalypse figured prominently in the interpretations of the origins of the Indian. The *magot* would certainly point allusively to Gog and *Magog*, the two characters in the terror of a second coming who embody the millenarian moment that Gómara draws out of Mexican cosmology. *Magot/Magog* would refer, to be sure, to the *Book of Ezechiel* (38-39), in which God tells his son to warn Gog, King of Magog, that all creatures will quake in his presence, and that mountains will be levelled. Biblical wrath is aimed against the avatars of Gog's peoples, but in ways that identify Montaigne with a hidden, common god of his own letter. In Persian, *Gog* signified a mountain, such that Magog meant a "great gog," high mountains, a high plateau or, following a common gloss, it would result that Gog and Magog were a collective name for Barbarians coming to conquer inhabited lands. In the eyes of the natives the Spaniards would be a sign of what was revealed in their cosmology. In the concomitantly political dimension of "Des coches," where Montaigne's critique of munificence and endorsement of thrift is invested in the density of his words, *magot* becomes a substantive, like the letter O, or the title, through which pass all the themes of the chapter. It becomes a miniature exemplum, a word-coin struck with poetic thrift countering the *lâcheté* of the Spanish legend and its official historians.

In this light, Montaigne's rewriting of Fumée's Gómara changes a descriptive account into a specular machinery that conflates time, legend, and figure according to coordinates located at once at the cardinal extremities of the essay and in the analogical configuration of words and letters that mark and mirror those same points. Such is *magot*, in the aparté, "(quelles impressions ne souffre la lâcheté de l'humaine creance!)," where the opening of the parenthesis is akin to that of a textual body farting an "émotion d'air et de vent qui abbatit jusques à plusieurs montaignes" (993). Montaigne replaces Gómara's image of land levelled ("rochers tomberent par terre") with the toponym of his signature in the common plural, thus inserting in his own writing the signs of a second coming. But now, in the overall geography, it remains to be seen how the "emotion of air and wind" reflects the initial figure, placed at the beginning of the essay, that asks why we bless those who sneeze. Aristotle is invoked for his clever reasoning that can adduce specious origins to be the cause of common effects. Sly rationale allows truth to be bent for the end or elegance of those who fashion their arguments as they do.

> Do you ask me whence originates this custom of blessing those who sneeze? We produce three kinds of

wind: what goes out the bottom is too dirty; what
goes out the mouth carries some reproach of gluttony;
the third is sneezing; and, because it comes from the
head and is blameless, we accord it this honest
reception. Don't laugh at this subtlety; it belongs
(they say) to Aristotle.[29]

The implicit geography of the body and its orifices is remi-
niscent of Bodin's map of the humors and climates, a
moderate body conceivably balancing its extremes of expulsion according to cardinal virtues. But the origins or
maistresse cause (876) given to bless the sneezer come
from without or a space *off* that remains undesignated except by passing reference to Aristotle. Whence comes not
only the custom of blessing but its very agency? Who has
the right to *benire*? In the portmanteau style of the *Essais*
Montaigne cannot but refer, in the figure of those who
bless, to dominant powers of religious authority.[30] But
those who sneeze (*estrenuent*) can also allude to those
who traffic naked beings (*estres nues*), that is, in the context of the greater part of "Des coches," to Iberian slavers.
Those who bless could only be the authorities, from Aristotle to Pope Alexander VI, who give Spain reason enough
to conquer the Indies.[31] Further, the conquistadors are
those who "sneeze" or, in the associational webbing of the
chapter, popes and armed soldiers who fire (*descocher*)
figuratively or literally on the Amerindians. They sneeze
"at" the very beings they plunder, incarcerate, torture, buy
and sell. At the same time, when the text ironically compares the empyrean regions of the head to goodness, it also
inflects the standard picture of the political body with nag-
gingly historical innuendo. The head is not just a source of
abstraction, for it is attached to what it seeks *in its own
name*, since *teste* refers to golden kind in circulation (from
teston, a very common piece of money stamped by Francis
I that held value throughout the sixteenth century).

   Now it stands to reason how and why the figure of
wind establishes the cardinal configuration of the essay.
The sneeze at the beginning rhymes spatially with what
Montaigne visibly alters from Gómara's original description of the Mexican ages of man. The "émotion d'air" in
the cosmology described at the end of the essay responds to

this passage on the other side of its textual line of demarcation. The Mexicans have as much right, as long as their economy is not expansionist in policy, to believe in an age when man is swept away (as far as some *montaignes*) in an *émotion d'air*. The sneeze on one side of the chapter gives political and economic cause to the effect of windy cataclysm on the other. It wipes out everything, including a number of *montaignes*.

If Montaigne had exclaimed parenthetically about why men were turned into monkeys and from what impressions suffers the cowardice of human belief, he does not refer solely to Mexican Indians. *Impression* implies the effect of printing, an agency of power that divides and conquers the indigenous tribes no less efficiently than gunpowder.[32] And what suffers (*souffre*) is homonymically what "sulphers" from the effect of harquebus fire in the same connections "We were exclaiming about the miracle of the invention of our artillery and of our printing" ("Nous nous escriïons du miracle de 'invention de nostre artillerie, de nostre impression," 886). The *lâcheté* of human belief happens to weigh upon its "coachness," or its will to accept authority because authority, like a pope or a king, gains its effect of power while sitting on a throne, in a coach, or on a palanquin. The pun had already marked his choice of Alcibiades' tale of Socrates's courage next to *Lachez* (877, taken from the *Symposium*), which equivocates on cowardice (*lâcheté*) and chairs (i.e., *la chaise*). Here it recurs in the network of figures denoting authorities as well as those of release, as the verb *descocher* had implied. It associates whomever "releases" a bull, that is, the popes aligned with Spanish foreign policy, with those who are cowards. Both conquistadors and the Roman Church bless those who sneeze or shoot and those who pillage the Americas.

The essay is so arcanely drawn that its allusions encircle the effect of its discourse into its verbal (visual, syntactic, graphic) causes. When seen juxtaposed to its Spanish sources, its apparent "difficulty," a convention of the official critical canon of Montaigne studies, becomes clear and resonant. Montaigne crafts a dense, parsimonious style whose worth contrasts the inflated value of gold flooding the European market; the words display a firm resolution to counter strife-ridden France of the Wars of Religion with its own image of itself—the monkey business of its (i)*magot*—in its discourse. It continues to argue obliquely against colonial development and insists that European nations would do well to curtail deficit spending, arrest plunder of the New World, and regain a balanced economy that distributes wealth more evenly among its subjects. The example of what the text prescribes is found in the scriptural economy of the essay itself, and its homeostasis, its ecological relation with its sources and its own discourse. From another standpoint, the text also shows exactly where and how far Montaigne's views of the colonial ventures had come in the eight years passed since "Des cannibales."

The 1588 essay writes guardedly,[33] amidst civil war, and happens to be congruent with Bartolomé de Las Casas's view of the New World in the wake of his debates in Valladolid with Ginés de Sepúlveda. It turns the sources of Spain's official history against itself for the sake of advancing positions against intervention and expansion. Still, the issue of Montaigne and Las Casas needs further elucidation. In its spatial and discursive areas the *Essais* appear to respond to the debates. Sepúlveda, following Oviedo's biased accounts of the Indies, adduced the inferiority of the Indians by way of Aristotle and Saint Augustine. The Greek authority had stated that indigenous groups function effectively in mechanical, but not in rational, ways: they have no apparent form of governance, and they need order imposed upon them from without. Las Casas argued that the Indians had the right to their lands and that the Spaniards had no business in taking them over.[34] Las Casas's work had been known since mid-century and had reached France by the time Montaigne was rewriting his essays.[35] In strictly historical terms he may have neither read Las Casas's reports from the New World, nor had much inkling of the events of Valladolid.

But in more pervasive and unconscious ways the relation may have been far more intimate. At the end of "De la vanité," in one of his typically Freudian gestures,[36] Montaigne states how his first, living impressions of

Rome (captured during his voyage on November 30, 1580, first related in the *Journal de voyage en Italie*, 1203-25, especially 1212-13) were more immediate in his childhood than in the experience of later life. In the essay he writes,

> We are advised to take care for the dead. Now, I have been nourished by them since my infancy; I have known of the affairs of Rome for a long time before those of my own house: I knew the Capitol and its map before I knew of the Louvre, and I knew the Tiber before the Seine. (975)[37]

The scene recounts how a stronger bonding is gained through the passage of death and life—that is, the experience of writing—than the contingencies of history which are ostensibly more secondary in their impact. In the moving, mystical element of writing which creates a present past of living relations through its own means, "De la moderation," "Des cannibales" and "Des coches" appear to bond an unconscious rapport with Las Casas through an absolute identity of viewpoint. Montaigne and Las Casas meld in their study of slavery and excess. Textually, both challenge the currency of Aristotle in modern times, and both reject political appropriations of his work in modern times. The intimacy they gain across these issues makes their rapport, like the concept and practice of friendship in "De l'amitié," all the more compelling in both human and political spheres. Where Las Casas's appeal to human rights is based on observation, Montaigne fashions his experience of the Indian other through the productive alterity of his textual means. The essays refuse to arrogate the figure or the rights of the other into its own discourse. Montaigne's Hispanic issues, therefore, develop an anthropology through their own verbal and visual form, in a style not of a detached observer of man, nor of a figure who acquires his political views after coming to terms with himself. The political effectiveness of Montaigne's relation to New Spain is immediate and clear. Developed through its complex relations with its sources, its cartographies establish a focal distance in respect both to the Western hemisphere and its own discourse, and they comment now, with uncanny force, on the program of geocide in which we are engaging against our planet.

NOTES

[1] Retombons à nos coches. En leur place, et de toute autre voiture, ils se faisoient porter par les hommes et sur leurs espaules. Ce dernier roy du Peru, le jour qu'il fut pris, estoit ainsi porté sur des brancars d'or, et assis dans une cheze d'or, au milieu de sa bataille. Autant qu'on tuoit de ces porteurs pour le faire cheoir à bas (car on le vouloit prendre vif), autant d'autres, et à l'envy, prenoient la place des morts, de façon qu'on ne le peut oncques abbatre, quelque meurtre qu'on fit de ces gens là, jusques à ce qu'un homme de cheval l'alla saisir au corps, et l'avalla par terre.

[2] Among others, Hugo Friedrich, in *Montaigne*, trans. R. Rovini Paris: Gallimard, 1968: 219.

[3] Preface to *Etudes sur Bartolomé de Las Casas*, Paris: Centre de Recherches de l'Institut d'Etudes Hispaniques, 1965: xxxvii. Bataillon develops the argument through an extensive thematic comparison of Gómara and "Des coches" in "Montaigne et les conquérants de l'or," *Studi francesi* 9 (1959): 353-67. It will be shown, however, that Montaigne does *not* attempt to "adopter le point de vue de son *semblable*" (353), the Indian. The essays argue for decolonialization but do not pretend to assimilate the alterity of the native.

[4] In *Les eléments de l'interprétation*, Paris: Gallimard, 1985, Guy Rosolato develops a productive analogy between the figure known to classical painting and the quest for knowledge in the world of psychoanalysis. It appears uncommonly productive for early modern literature and will be taken up in the paragraphs below.

[5] Michel Butor has written of the spatial allegories of center and edge in his *Essais sur les 'essais'*, Paris: Gallimard, 1968, but he does not extend the relation it holds with common Mannerist practices of framing inspired by Italian artists brought to Fontainebleau under the patronage of Francis I. Mary McKinley, in *Words in a Corner*, Lexington: French Forum Monographs, 1982: 46ff., studies some of the ramifications of Montaigne's relation with the destabilizing practices that Italian masters had developed during their residence at the king's castle.

[6] C'est l'indiligent lecteur qui pert mon subject, non pas moy; il s'en trouvera tousjours en un coing quelque mot qui ne laisse pas d'estre

bastant, quoy qu'il soit serré" (It is the intelligent reader who loses my subject, and not I; somewhere he or she will always find in it a corner of a word that does not suffice enough, although it is tightly embedded), in the *Oeuvres complètes*, Paris: Gallimard-Pléiade, 1962: 973. All other references to the *Essais* and *Journal de voyage en Italie* will be taken from this edition and cited between parentheses above.

[7]*The Six Books of a Commonweale* (Facsimile reprint of the English translation of 1606), ed. Kenneth Douglas McRae Cambridge: Harvard Univ. Press, 1962: 562.

[8]The implication of order and play are developed in my "*De capsula totæ*: lecture de 'Trois commerces,'" *L'Esprit créateur* 28.2 (Spring 1988): 5-12.

[9]Claude-Gilbert Dubois explains the temporal and spatial coordinates of this type of history in *La conception de l'histoire en France au XVIe siècle*, Paris: Nizet, 1977: 159ff.

[10]Francisco López de Gómara, *Historia de la conquista de México*, t. 1 Mexico: Pedro Robredo, 1943: ch. 47 and 48 (164-69). In English: *Cortez: The Life of the Conqueror*, trans. and ed. Lesley Byrd Simpson, Berkeley: Univ. of California Press, 1964: ch. 47-48 (105-07). Montaigne's source is an Italian translation (Venice, 1576) by Cravalix.

[11]Claude Lévi-Strauss, "Les organisations dualistes existent-elles," *Anthropologie structurale*, Paris: Plan, 1958: 147-80, touches on the dual structures among some of the cannibals (the Bororo) that Montaigne takes up by way of André Thevet, and that he will embody in his writing of friendship.

[12]In the opening lines of his study of "Des cannibales" Michel de Certeau notes that the topography of the essay "places into question both the text's power of composing and distributing places, its ability to be a narrative of space, and the necessity for it to define its relation to what it treats, in other words, to construct a place of its own," "Montaigne's 'Of Cannibals:' The Savage 'I,'" in *Heterologies*, trans. Brian Massumi Minneapolis: Univ. of Minnesota Press, 1986: 67. One area will be the space Montaigne "opens for the other," while another will be the alterity it ascribes for the surface of the printed page and emblematic design of the *Essais*.

[13]*Ils ne sont pas en debat de la conquest de nouvelles terres*, car ils jouyssent encore de cette uberté naturelle qui les fournit sans travail et sans peine de toutes choses necessaires, en telle abondance qu'*ils n'ont*

que de faire d'agrandir leur limites. Ils sont encore en cet heureux point, de ne desirer qu'autant que leurs necessitez naturelles leur ordonnent; tout ce qui est au delà est superflu pour eux. (208, italics mine)

[14]Si leurs voisins passent *les montaignes* pour les venir assaillir, et qu'ils emportent la victoire sur eux, l'acquest du victorieux, c'est la gloire, et l'avantage d'estre demeuré maistre en valeur et vertu; car autrement ils n'ont que faire des biens des vaincus, et s'en retournent à leur pays, où ils n'ont faute de aucune chose necessaire, ny faute encore de cette grande partie, de sçavoir heureusement jouyr de leur condition et s'en contenter (208-09, italics mine).

[15]*Les Singularitez de la France antarctique*, Anvers, 1557: f. 69-74.

[16]See Henri Zerner, *The School of Fontainebleau: Etchings and Drawings*, New York: H. N. Abrams, 1969. Connections between the Fontainebleau style and Thevet's illustrations are suggested in *La Renaissance et le nouveau monde*, Québec: Bibliothèque nationale du Québec, 1984: 67-82 and 257ff.

[17]Here the encounter with a theme of Spanish historiography is also put in view. Gómara and Thevet establish hyperboles of objectivity that tend to give credence to ocularity or the truth of their "science". "Francisco López de Gómara se adhiere, en su 'Historia General de las Indias' (1552), remarks Victor Frankl, "enfáticamente a la tesis de que la experiencia constituye la única fuente de la verdad en historia, a pesar de que él mismo escribió su Historia sin haber estado en Hispano-américa," in *El 'Antijovio' de Gonzalo Jiménez de Quesada y la concepciones de realidad y verdad en la época de la contrerreforma y del manierismo*, Madrid: Ediciones Cultura Hispánica, 1963: 87-88. He and Thevet are secondary eye-witnesses who ground their truth in the contradiction of the immediacy of their written sources. In other words, the printed page and its illustrations of text and image produce the effect of untrammelled marvel. By contrast, in his avowedly tertiary contact Montaigne comes closer to his origin as he takes an increased distance from it.

[18]Michel de Certeau remarks that Montaigne's voice "circulates in the space of cannibalistic orality" (*Heterologies*, 77) and constantly must return from one world and go back and forth to the other.

[19]The remark is similar to what Claude-Gilbert Dubois calls *enstasis*, where Montaigne is at a double center, a blind point, around which the autobiography turns. See *L'imaginaire de la Renaissance*, Paris: PUF, 1985: 223-25.

[20]A similar paradox results from Gisèle Mathieu-Castellani's reading of "D'un enfan monstrueux" (II, xxx), an essay in the second book that corresponds to "moderation" and "cannibales" both numerologically and thematically. See *Montaigne: l'écriture de l'essai*, Paris: PUF, 1988: 222-24.

[21]The last sentences of "Cannibals" thus ground the structure of a tradition of social criticism and fable that Montesquieu will use for his *Lettres persanes*, and that has since been used frequently in political fables. No doubt *Gulliver's Travels* shares much with the tactic used here.

[22]Simûltaneity of the two points of view that are Montaigne's and the Indians' would tend to negate the sense of *delay* inscribed in Jean Starobinski's reading of this passage, in which he shows how political action is only gained by a movement that goes from the self to the other. "Adhérer étroitement à la vie sensible, *puis*, par sympathie, *étendre* cette adhésion au-delà des limites de la vie personnelle, c'est vivre dans la non-violence, où, du moins dans la moindre violence" [To stick closely to sensible life, then, through friendliness, stretch this adhesion beyond the limits of personal life is to live in non-violence or at best in the least violence], he notes in *Montaigne et le mouvement*, Paris: Gallimard, 1982: 301 (italics mine). Delay allows his reading to bind social criticism with what appears to be the *Essais*'s thematically conservative view of political institutions. The optical facets of the text and the self-contained structure of the chapter do not allow such thematic "movement" to emerge from the writing.

[23]Some of the network has been elaborated in R. A. Sayce, *The Essays of Montaigne. A Critical Exploration*, London: Northwestern Univ. Press, 1972 and in our "Cataparalysis," *Diacritics*, 8.3 (Fall 1978): 41-59. John O'Neill has reviewed the principal literature on "Des coches" in *Essaying Montaigne: A Study of the Renaissance Institution of Writing and Reading*, London: Routledge and Kegan Paul, 1988: 188-209.

[24]*Histoire generalle des Indes occidentalles & Terres neuves, qui iusques à present ont esté descouvertes, traduite en françois par M. Fumée Sieur Marly le Chastel*, Paris, 1569: f. 140a.

[25]One thinks especially of engraving 37, "Cérémonies pour la venue de la future reine," ill. in *La Renaissance et le nouveau monde* (96). Frank Lestringant is helpful on de Brye's use of Las Casas' *Brevísima relación de la destrucción de las Indias* to illustrate the horrors of anthropophagia (207).

[26]*Histoire generalle des Indes descouvertes, augmentée en ceste cinquiesme edition de la description de la nouvelle Espagne, & de la grande ville de Mexicque, autrement nommee Tenuctilan: composee en espagnol par François Lopez de Gomara, traduite en françois par le S. de Genillé Mart.* Fumée, Paris: M. Sonnius, 1587: f. 158b. The Mexican religion is also taken up in chapter 72 of Thevet's *Singularitez*. Roger Schlesinger and Arthur P. Stabler furnish bibliography (C. A. Burland, *The Bases of Religion in Aztec Mexico;* B. C. Brundage, *The Fifth Sun;* and David Carrasco, *Quetzalcoatl and the Irony of Empire*) in their *André Thevet's North America: A Sixteenth Century View,* Kingston and Montréal: McGill-Queen's Univ. Press, 1976: 170-71.

[27]Le troisiesme, par feu qui embrasa et consuma tout; le quatriesme, par *une émotion d'air* et de vent qui abbatit jusques à plusieurs montaignes; les hommes n'en moururent poinct, mais *ilz furent changés en magots* (quelles impressions ne souffre la lácheté de l'humaine creance!). (893, italics mine)

[27]See Frank Lestringant, "Les Indiens antérieurs (1575-1615): du Plessis-Mornay, Lescarbot, De Laet, Claude d'Abbeville," in Gilles Thérien, ed., *Les figures de l'indien,* Montréal: Cahiers de l'Université de Montréal, 1988: 51-85; "Calvinistes et cannibales," *Bulletin de la Société du Protestantisme français,* 126 (1980): 9-26; "Millénarisme et l'age d'or," in *Réformes, enracinement socio-culturel,* Paris: Guy Trédaniel, 1985: 25-42. See also Anthony Pagden, *The Fall of Natural Man: The American Indian and the Origins of Comparative Ethnography,* Cambridge: Cambridge Univ. Press, 1982.

[29]Me demandez-vous d'où vient cette coustume de benire ceux qui *estrenuent?* Nous produisons trois sortes de vent: celuy qui sort par embas est trop sale; celuy qui sort par la bouche porte quelque reproche de gourmandise; le troisiesme est l'*estrenuement;* et parce qu'il vient de la teste et est sans blasme, nous luy faisons cet honneste recueil. Ne vous moquez pas de cette subtilité; elle est (dict-on) d'Aristote. (876, italics mine)

[30]That is, a multiple layered set of verbal affinities that circulate within or through words, and by which their forms and shapes acquire the archaic function of motivating various analogies. The style is as old as what Cratylus puts forward in Plato's dialogue of his name, and is invoked with no less conviction in Claude Lévi-Strauss, *La potière jalouse,* Paris: Plon, 1985, where he notes, referring to the *Essais,* how "popular thought claims to be founded on experience but also puts to work all kinds of symbolic identities based on the plan of metaphor"

(11) ("la pensée populaire prétend se fonder sur l'exprérience mais met aussi en oeuvre toutes sortes d'équivalences symboliques sur le plan de la métaphore").

[31]Bataillon reviews them in *Las Casas et la défense des indiens*, Paris: Julliard, 1971: 58. From the *Inter Caetera* of 1493, papal bulls, he recalls, were political instruments that the Spanish monarchy invoked to give cause to its conquest of the New World. See also André Vincent, *Las Casas, apôtre des indiens*, Paris: Editions de la Nouvelle Aurore, 1975: 111-99.

[32]See Michel de Certeau, *L'écriture de l'histoire*, Paris: Gallimard, 1975: 224.

[33]Patrick Henry has taken up Montaigne's defensive stance in view of papal censure in *Montaigne in Dialogue*, Stanford French and Italian Studies 57, Stanford, California: Anma Libri, 1987: 3-23.

[34]See Olive Dickason, *The Myth of the Savage in the New World*, Alberta: Univ. of Alberta Press, 1986: 56-57. On torture, notably absent from the first-hand accounts (but present in Montaigne's), Dickason recalls that Europeans used it to punish offenders in the growing centralized monarchy, whereas Amerindians were seen using it against enemies in order to consolidate a tribe's position in respect to the outside world. The most telling accounts in English of Aristotle's use and abuse are Lewis Hanke, *Aristotle and the American Indians: A Study in Race Prejudice in the Modern World* (Bloomington: Indiana Univ. Press, 1959), and his *All Mankind is One: A Study of the Disputation between Bartolomé de Las Casas and Juan Ginés de Sepúlveda in 1550 on the Intellectual and Religious Capacities of the Indians*, DeKalb: Northern Illinois Univ. Press, 1974.

[35]In his *Nouveaux horizons de la Renaissance*, Paris: Droz, 1935, Geoffroy Atkinson lists two French translations: Las Casas' *Tyrannies et cruautés des espagnoles*, Anvers, 1579; Paris, 1582 and his *Histoires des insolences et cruautés....*, Paris, n.d. De Brye's illustrations (1598) confirm what had been visibly obvious since the early years of the century. They are inspired by the first Latin edition (Frankfurt, 1594) of Las Casas's *Brevísima relación de la destrucción de las Indias* and accompany Benzoni's *Historia del nuevo mundo* (1550). Citing Pierre Chaunu, Marianne Mahn-Lot remarks that Dutch editions of the *Brevísima relación* became the weapons of psychological warfare aimed against Spain, in *Las Casas et le droit des Indiens*, Paris: Payot, 1982: 252-53.

[36]The affinities of Freud and Montaigne are well known. "Freud has more in common with Proust and Montaigne," notes Harold Bloom, "than with biological scientists, because his interpretations of life and death are mediated always by texts, first by the literary texts of others, and then by his own earlier texts, until at least the Sublime mediation of otherness begins to be performed by his text-in-process," from "Freud and the Sublime," quoted in Malcom Bowie, in *Freud, Proust and Lacan: Theory and Fiction,* Cambridge: Cambridge Univ. Press, 1987: 8. Bloom notes that certain writers read and assimilate each other without needing to have any empirical relation with each other; nor does an antecedent text necessarily form a pre-given source for a later one: often a later work will reread and effectively complicate matters that had been undetected in earlier ones. The argument shows where a "map of misreading" can change the picture of both literary history and historiography in general. The hypotheses repeat what Michel de Certeau determines through a psychoanalytical reading of Freud and history in *L'écriture de l'histoire,* 312-58.

[37]Le soing des morts nous est en recommendation. Or j'ay esté nourry dès mon enfance avec ceux-ci; j'ay eu connoissance des affaires de Romme, long temps avant que je l'aye eue de ceux de ma maison: je sçavois le Capitole et son plant avant que je sceusse le Louvre, et le Tibre avant la Seine. (976)

WORKS CITED

Atkinson, Geoffroy. *Les nouveaux horizons de la Renaissance française.* Paris: Droz, 1935.

Bataillon, Marcel. *Etudes sur Bartolomé de Las Casas.* Paris: Centre de Recherches de l'Institut d'Etudes Hispaniques, 1965.

—. "Montaigne et les conquérants de l'or." *Studi francesi* 9 (1959): 353-67.

—. *Las Casas et la défense des indiens.* Paris: Julliard, 1971.

Bodin, Jean. *The Six Books of a Commonweale.* Facsimile Reprints of the English Translation of 1606. Ed. Kenneth Douglas McRae. Cambridge: Harvard Univ. Press, 1962.

Bowie, Malcolm. *Freud, Proust, and Lacan: Theory and Fiction.* Cambridge: Cambridge Univ. Press, 1987.

Butor, Michel. *Essais sur les 'Essais'*. Paris: Gallimard, 1968.

Certeau, Michel de. *L'écriture de l'histoire*. Paris: Gallimard, 1975.

—. *Heterologies*. Minneapolis: Univ. of Minnesota Press, 1986.

Conley, Tom. "*De capsula totœ*: lecture de 'Trois commerces,'" *L'Esprit créateur* 28.2 (Spring 1988): 5-12.

—. "Cataparalysis," *Diacritics* 8.3 (Fall 1978). 41-59.

Dickason, Olive. *The Myth of the Savage in the New World*. Alberta: Univ. of Alberta Press, 1984.

Dubois, Claude-Gilbert. *La conception de l'histoire en France au XVIe siècle*. Paris: Nizet, 1977.

—. *L'imaginaire de la Renaissance*. Paris: PUF, 1985.

Frankl, Victor. *El 'Antijovio' de Gonzalo Jiménez de Quesada y las concepciones de realidad y verdad en la época de la contrarreforma y del manierismo*. Madrid: Ediciones Cultura Hispánica, 1963.

Friedrich, Hugo. *Montaigne*. Tr. R. Rovini. Paris: Gallimard, 1968.

Hanke, Lewis. *Aristotle and the American Indians: A Study in Race Prejudice in the Modern World*. Bloomington: Indiana Univ. Press, 1959.

—. *All Mankind is One: A Study of the Disputation Between Bartolomé de Las Casas and Juan Ginés de Sepúlveda in 1550 on the Intellectual and Religious Capacity of the American Indians*. DeKalb: Northern Illinois Univ. Press, 1974.

Henry, Patrick. *Montaigne in Dialogue*. Stanford: Anma Libri, 1987.

López de Gómara, Francisco. *Historia de la conquista de México*. 2 v. México: Pedro Robredo, 1943.

—. *Histoire generalle des Indes occidentalles & Terres neuves, qui iusques à present ont esté descouvertes, traduite en françois par M. Fumée Sieur Marly le Chastel*. Paris: B. Turrisan, 1569.

—. *Histoire generalle des Indes...descouvertes, augmentee en ceste cinquiesme edition de la description de la nouvelle Espagne, & de la grande ville de Mexicque, autrement nommee Tenuctilan: composee en espagnol par François Lopez de Gomara, & traduite en françois par le S. de Genillé Mart. Fumée*. Paris: M. Sonnius, 1587.

Lestringant, Frank. "Les Indiens antérieurs (1575-1615): du Plessis-Mornay, Lescarbot, De Laet, Claude d'Abbeville." Gilles Thérien, ed. *Les figures de l'indien*. Montréal: Cahiers de l'Université de Montréal, 1988. 51-85.

—. "Calvinistes et cannibales." *Bulletin de la Société du Protestantisme français*. 126 (1980): 9-26.

—. "Jean Bodin, cosmographe." *Actes du Colloque interdisciplinaire d'Angers* (24-27 May 1984). Angers: Presses Universitaires d'Angers, 1985). 133-45.

—. "Millénarisme et l'age d'or." *Réformes, enracinement socio-culturel*. Paris: Guy Trédaniel, 1985. 25-42.

Lévi-Strauss, Claude. *Anthropologie structurale*. Paris: Plon, 1958.

—. *La potière jalouse*. Paris: Plon, 1985.

Mahn-Lot, Marianne. *Bartolomé de Las Casas et le droit des Indiens*. Paris: Payot, 1982.

Mathieu-Castellani, Gisèle. *Montaigne: l'écriture de l'essai*. Paris: PUF, 1988.

McKinley, Mary. *Words in a Corner*. Lexington, KY: French Forum, 1981.

Montaigne, Michel de. *Oeuvres complètes*. Paris: Gallimard, 1962.

Pagden, Anthony. *The Fall of Natural Man: The American Indian and the Origins of Comparative Ethnography*. Cambridge: Cambridge Univ. Press, 1982.

—. *La Renaissance et le nouveau monde*. Quebec: Bibliothèque nationale, 1984.

Rosolato, Guy. *Les éléments de l'interprétation*. Paris: Gallimard, 1985.

Sayce, Richard A. *The Essays of Montaigne: A Critical Exploration*. London: Northwestern Univ. Press, 1972.

Schlesinger, Roger and Arthur P. Stabler. *André Thevet's North America*. Kingston and Montreal: McGill-Queen's Univ. Press, 1986.

Starobinski, Jean. *Montaigne et le mouvement*. Paris: Gallimard, 1982.

Thevet, André. *Les singularitez de la France antarctique*. Anvers, 1557.

Vincent, André. *Las Casas, apôtre des indiens.* Paris: Nouvelle Aurore, 1975.

Zerner, Henri. *The School of Fontainebleau: Etchings and Drawings.* New York: H. N. Abrams, 1969.

CHAPTER 7:
UTOPIAN ETHNOLOGY IN
LAS CASAS'S *APOLOGÉTICA*

José Rabasa

Padre Bartolomé, gracias por este
regalo de la cruda medianoche,
gracias porque tu hilo fue invencible...

—Pablo Neruda, *Canto general*

Las Casas has been considered a precursor of divergent
and often contradictory understandings of human rights,
modern parliamentarism, and development, among other
forms of modern political culture.[1] His debates at Valladolid with Juan Ginés de Sepúlveda (1550-1551) over the
inferiority of the Amerindians, and his affinities with the
principles of international law developed by the so-called
School of Salamanca have been cited as examples of
Spain's unique sense of justice and civilizing mission in
the history of modern colonialism.[2] These views of Las
Casas entail two contradictory, nevertheless, complementary approaches to history that I believe are equally
misleading. On the one hand, the first judgements find in
Las Casas anticipations and early manifestations of later
anthropological and political concepts; on the other hand,
the appraisal of Spain's utopian sense of justice presumes

continuous, common beliefs and sensibilities with the past. This Janus-like pattern recurs in numerous important studies that have specifically addressed Las Casas's contributions to anthropology and utopian political thought.[3] Since neither utopia nor anthropology were significant forms of discourse in the sixteenth century, traditional scholarship tends to write about Las Casas's contributions to these cultural forms, as I have already implied above, from either the fallacy of "presentism," assuming that a model or concept had a parallel meaning in the past, or that of "finalism," finding prefigurations of today's dominant categories in the past.[4]

As I write these methodological specifications, I ask myself how does my project avoid falling prey to the same fallacies I am challenging? Isn't it generally acknowledged in contemporary historical studies that one is always bound to project the present into the past?[5] Or, even more forcibly, isn't the projection of the present a desirable predicament that should be fully exploited, as Jameson would seem to argue in *The Political Unconscious* when he states that "our readings of the past are vitally dependent on our experience of the present"? (quoted by Simpson 738, Jameson 11). I believe there is a difference between finding present meanings in the past (presentism) or tracing in the past the kernel of the present (finalism) and sustaining a mutually enlightening dialogue that rather than using the past to reinforce existing beliefs retains historical differences and opens the future to new possibilities. Though the questions I am asking about Las Casas build on recent critiques of anthropology,[6] the present study does not take a series of established truths as its point of departure; on the contrary, it seeks to contribute to the ongoing radical examination of anthropology's dominant categories and claims to knowledge while providing an alternative reading of Las Casas.

In this essay I will approach Las Casas's *Apologética historia sumaria* (1559) not as a moment in the historical development of the social sciences but as a prophetic dissolution of anthropology as the disciplinary formation where the West studies the "rest" of the world. First, I will point out shortcomings in studies that ascribe to Las Casas concepts and motifs drawn from modern anthropology or from contemporary understandings of utopia as an ideal (more-or-less realizable/desirable) social order. In their place I will outline a reading of Las Casas's ethnology as cultural critique and a textual form of utopian practice. Secondly, following these alternative approaches to anthropology and utopia in Las Casas I will examine the function of the *noble savage* and a paradisiacal *natural garden* in the *Apologética*. The analysis of these two figures should ultimately render the semantic field from which the "West" defines the "rest" and posits itself as a universal cultural model. Thirdly, in the light of these theoretical revisions we will see how the *Apologética* dismantles the grounds for historico-evolutionary schemas. Thus Las Casas and contemporary critiques of anthropology would seem to share a common concern, but the point would be less to posit a similar intent or sensibility than to underscore historical distances that would explain the different rhetorical functions and values of such a figure as the *noble savage*. Let us then begin with a brief description of the *Apologética* and its critique of the concept of barbarism.

The *Apologética* is divided into three books and an epilogue. Book One is dedicated to the climate of the island of Española, and gives a geographic foundation for demonstrating the Amerindian's physical fitness in Book Two, which in turn serves to argue in favor of the New World cultures in Book Three. While Book Three contains a series of ethnographies originally compiled by several authors in different areas of the Americas, the organization and interpretation of the ethnographic materials follow a chain of causality initiated in the first two books: climate produces bodies which affect culture. The descriptions of geography, physiology and culture are determined by the initial demonstration of a temperate climate. The Epilogue develops a semantic critique of four possible meanings of the term barbarism.[7] Las Casas discusses the applicability of the following definitions to the Amerindians:

1) in a broad (and equivocal) sense barbarism refers to a temporal loss of reason, as when a person blinded by pas-

sion becomes cruel and commits crimes worse than those of a wild beast;

2) in a more restricted sense those who lack letters and a learned language such as Latin are barbarians *secundum quid* that is, they lack some cultural aspect but otherwise are polished and wise. It also includes those who speak a different language;

3) in its proper sense, *simpliciter*, the term refers to peoples who have strange customs, lack laws, settlements, cities, have no marriage rules, and live scattered in the woods fleeing contact with other humans;

4) in the cultural sense of lacking the true religion barbarism comprises all infidels however wise and civil they might be.

The first two meanings of the term can be applied to any culture since cruel individuals exist in all nations and on linguistic grounds the Spaniards would be barbarians with respect to the Amerindians. The third definition is the most relevant, and the one the *Apologética* sets out to disprove, since it comprises whole peoples and the possible reduction of all Amerindians to barbarians. As for the fourth meaning referring to all infidels, Las Casas makes a distinction between those who have turned against Christianity and those whose infidelity is pure negativity since they have never heard the Gospel. Amerindians are obviously infidels in the second sense and under no reason whatsoever could war be legitimately waged against them.

The fourth category also entails an important distinction in the *Apologética* between European nations before and after Christianity which establishes a comparative ground with Amerindian cultures. Comparisons, however, are not based on a historical evolutionary scale but simply in terms of Augustin's teleology of history which posits the incorporation of all peoples into the Church as the end of history. In this respect one can speak of Las Casas's position as medieval (as one could also speak of More's *Utopia* as embracing medieval values). But Las Casas not only emphasizes incorporation but opposes definitions of barbarism that prevent other cultures from being considered ready for civilization[8] thus a straight-forward reduction of Las Casas to a medieval mentality is problematic.[9] Las Casas wants to argue that even if the ideals of Christianity define the end of history, that does not mean that one Christian nation, such as Spain, necessarily fulfills the ideals of the Church nor that it can use Christianity to define itself as superior to an infidel nation. There are, furthermore, aspects of culture that do not fall within the province of religion and where infidels, such as the Greeks and the Romans, but also the Amerindians, have surpassed Spain. Whereas the *Apologética* demonstrates how the third definition of "barbarism" (referring to people who have customs that are foreign to those seen as pertaining to civilized life) has no corresponding referent, the figure of the *noble savage* subverts differentiations of Christians and infidels on the basis of the former's inherent superiority.

This monumental work was not published in its entirety until the nineteenth century; parts of it, however, were used against Juan Ginés de Sepúlveda in the 1550-1551 Valladolid debates over the inferiority of the American Indian and the legitimacy of their conquest. Although Las Casas mentions 1527 as the date when he started writing the *Apologética*, the bulk of the text as we know it was written between 1556 and 1559.[10] The debates defined the political context that led Las Casas to develop an ethnology. However, in approaching anthropology in Las Casas one must avoid defining his brand of ethnology with modern concepts that all too often betray contemporary prejudices.

Take for instance Anthony Pagden's *The Fall of Natural Man*, which traces a "programme for comparative ethnology" in the works of Las Casas. Pagden, repeating a commonplace, attributes to Las Casas the following beliefs: "Just as the child is taught by his elders to understand the physical and moral world in which he is to live, so too entire races of men may be taught by those who have reached a higher level of civility than they" (143). Even if Las Casas held such an opinion, there is nothing worth praising in a comparison of cultural Others to children. Moreover, placing Amerindians in "an historical scale which is the same for all people" (ibid) presupposes that Las Casas had a secular as well as a naturalized un-

derstanding of time.[11] For the record let us recall that even
when the Jesuit José de Acosta in the *Historia natural y
moral de las Indias* (1590) explicitly postulates what resembles a secular evolutionary scale, he does so by defining the Asiatic origins of the Amerindians as peoples who
had degenerated from the civilized stages represented by
Noah in the process of migrating to the New World (54-56
and passim).[12] So even in Acosta the evolutionary model
is far from some sort of naturalized time that would be
neutral, that is, separate from events meaningful to a history of mankind. On the other hand, Las Casas's examples
to explain the origin of society, drawn in the main from
Cicero, are stories of hypothetical states of savagery and
legendary heroes that convey their civilizing mission in
the span of one generation—its an all-or-nothing paradigm with no intermediate stages.

Pagden's notion of educable "races" of men (that is, not-
self-sufficient peoples) amounts to placing Las Casas as an
ideologue, if not of conquest, of colonialism (in precisely
very close grounds to Juan Ginés de Sepúlveda's apology
of Spanish rule in the Americas)—indeed, at the origins,
to borrow Johannes Fabian's phraseology, of one of anthropology's most embarrassing uses of Time to make the
Other. If it is true that the "children" metaphor and the
notion of Amerindians lacking self-sufficiency are com-
monplaces in sixteenth-century Spanish New World historiography—not only among the Conquistadors and *Encomenderos* but also among the Franciscan missionaries
and such defenders of the Indians as Vasco de Quiroga—
they are not, however, defining categories in Las Casas's
discourse.[13] It is my contention that Las Casas seemingly
adopts these devices in order to contradict their use by
apologists of the conquest. Moreover, the substitution
(apparently more progressive) of a "redeemable humanity" for the supposedly Aristotelian notion of "natural
man" introduces a racial specification in Pagden's
"narrative" not necessarily manifest in Aristotle's concept
of natural slavery which is primarily defined in opposition to legal slavery and only incidentally as "part of the
art of war, or of the art of hunting" (Aristotle 18). What
amounted to a few sentences in Aristotle, with no refer-

ence to specific ethnic groups, expanded during the Middle Ages and Renaissance into a theory of legal slavery with racial undertones in St. Thomas's commentary of the *Politics* (c. 1259) and with specifically racist categories in Sepúlveda's *Democrates secundus* (1543-1550).[14] The historical record, it seems to me, does not suggest an overcoming of racism but the formation of a discourse on race. Padgen's narrative of the "fall of man," of the end of natural slavery as a dominant political concept, could very well turn out to be a chapter in the history of modern racism. The supposedly more advanced anthropological categories that Pagden attributes to Las Casas would suggest the beginnings in modern colonialism of imperialistic policies with a civilizing mission for their ideology.

As I pointed out above "presentism" and "finalism" are fallacies that emerge when we study the past in terms of the present. We certainly find in the sixteenth century elaborate ethico-juridical treatises on the legitimacy of war and ethnographic descriptions used as instruments for conversion. These treatises could be read as early forms of modern anthropology. But I can further redefine the project—in this case, utopian ethnology in Las Casas—by not taking for granted the "truths" of modern anthropology and consequently not projecting them into the past. A more fruitful alternative is to carry a dialogue with the past where a critique of the present explores a utopian forward vision in Ernst Bloch's sense of the *Not-Yet-Conscious*, or anticipatory forms of consciousness (I:114). Johannes Fabian has diagnosed an eventual dissolution of anthropology's colonial legacy that I believe sums up well a critical position that Las Casas had already envisioned at the beginning of Modernity:

> Little more than technology and sheer economic exploitation seem to be left over for the purpose of "explaining" Western superiority. It has become foreseeable that even those prerogatives may either disappear or no longer be claimed. There remains "only" the all-pervading denial of coevalness which ultimately is expressive of a cosmological myth of frightening magnitude and persistency. It takes imagination and courage to picture what would happen to the West (and to anthropology) if its temporal

fortress were suddenly invaded by the Time of its
Other. (35)

Fabian here calls into question all the supposed attributes that enable the West to claim superiority over the
"rest" of the world, and projects a utopian scenario where
the Time of the Other invades the West; one recognizes
these topics in Las Casas's rebuttals of the political and
economic lack of self-sufficiency attributed to Amerindian
cultures. By juxtaposing Fabian and Las Casas we may define a historical narrative where from the start of European expansionism in the sixteenth century there was an
eminent collapse of the myth that placed universal pri-
ority in the West's historico-temporal patterns.

To compile and disclose knowledge about all the
Amerindian cultures are Las Casas's reasons for writing
the *Apologética*. But Las Casas names two objectives of the
book that imply an ethnology beyond an encyclopedia of
New World ethnographies: the first seeks to undo the
slanderous assertion that Amerindians were not rational,
"that they were not rational people able to govern themselves, lacking human polity and orderly republics..."
("que no eran gentes de buena razón para gobernarse,
carecientes de humana policía y ordenadas repúblicas...")
(I: 3); the second, to compare their cultures with ancient as
well as other contemporary nations to the advantage of
the former: "This superiority and excess, with everything
said so far, will will be evident when, God willing, we
compare one with the others" ("Esta ventaja y exceso, con
todo lo que dicho queda, parecerá muy a la clara cuando, si
a Dios pluguiere, las unas con las otras se cotejaren") (I: 4).

The *Apologética* opens with a theologico-religious argument against the notion of a monstrous nation, of a
state of barbarism encompassing more than isolated individuals: "as if Divine Providence had been negligent in
the creation of such innumerable peoples..." ("como si la
Divina Providencia en la creación de tan inumerable
número de ánimas racionales se hobiera descuidado...") (I:
3). But instead of pursuing an argument on Biblical or
theological grounds, which would demonstrate why Divine Providence could not err, Las Casas goes on to ex-

plain how the natural milieu contributed to the production of accomplished New World cultures. It is not until the Epilogue that Las Casas develops a sustained, systematic critique of the concept of barbarism.

According to Las Casas, the Amerindians suggest a stage of innocence and natural virtue in which physiology becomes a mirror of the soul:

> Consequently, since all the inhabitants of this Indies, for the most part, and especially the boys and girls have a good semblance and concordance, of beautiful faces and proportioned limbs and bodies, and this since birth, as the philosopher said, it demonstrates, it follows that God and nature gave and endowed and granted them with noble souls, and therefore to be very reasonable and of good understandings.

> Así que, pues como todos los moradores destas Indias, por la mayor parte, y especial en los niños y niñas y adolescentes, sean de buenos aspectos y acatamientos, de hermosas caras y proporcionados miembros y cuerpos, y esto desde su nacimiento, como el filósofo dijo, se muestra, síguese haberles Dios y la naturaleza dado y dotado y concedido nobles ánimas naturalmente, y así ser bien razonables y de buenos entendimientos. (I:179)

Aristotle's theory of the determination of the soul's potentialities by body structures is here implied and marks the transition from physiology to noble souls (*nobles ánimas*) This enthymeme (an imperfect syllogism lacking the middle term) thus allows Las Casas to integrate the metaphor "noble" into his characterization of an ideal primitivism: the Amerindians do not merely have rational souls, but "natural nobility" as well. Ultimately the chain of causation falls back, obviously to God, but also to nature, to paradisiacal imagery that informs his depiction of Española's natural milieu:

> It is all painted with grass, the most beautiful that can be spoken, and fragrant, very different from the one in Spain. Charming creeks that transverse it paint it from league to league, each one of them car-

ries on both borders of its banks a strip or eyebrow or
line of trees always green, and so well placed and ordered as if they had been placed by hand, and which
do not occupy more than fifteen or twenty steps on
each side. And as this fertile lowland and the whole
island always are as the fields and trees in Spain on
the month of April and May....Who would not con-
cede that the happiness, joy and consolation and
jubilation of one who may see it, would be inestimable and beyond compare.

Está toda pintada de yerba, la más hermosa que
puede decirse, y odorífera, muy diferente de la de
España. Píntanla de legua a legua, o de dos a dos
leguas, arroyos graciosísimos que la atraviesan, cada
uno de los cuales lleva por las rengleras de sus ambas
a dos riberas su lista o ceja o raya de árboles siempre
verdes, tan bien puestos y ordenados como si fueran
puestos a mano, y que no ocupan poco más de quince o
veinte pasos en cada parte. Y como siempre esté esta
Vega y toda la isla como están los campos y árboles
en España por el mes de abril y mayo.... ¿Quién no
concederá ser el alegría gozo y consuelo y regocijo del
que lo viere, inestimable y no comparable?
(Apologética I: 49)

The Apologética, indeed, represents the Indies as a
paradisiacal landscape populated with naturally virtuous
people. Once Las Casas demonstrates the temperate climate, he can deduce the corresponding human condition.
Las Casas first describes the beauty of the Amerindians and
then goes on to argue that the soul's potentialities are determined by body structures. His examples are the inhabitants of the Caribbean, in particular the Lucayos as
Columbus referred to the first people he encountered, and
draws a generalization that encompasses all other cultural
areas in the Americas:

The people from the island of the Lucayos, the first
discovered by the admiral...all of them, men and
women, had angelical features....And it is necessary
that it should be so over the most part of this Indies,
because, as we have said it, the semblance and figure
of the sky and the virtue of the stars...favor the gra-
cious and beautiful disposition of these peoples.

Las gentes de las islas de los Lucayos, que el almirante descubrió las primeras...todas a una mano, hombres y mujeres, eran de aspectos angélicos.... Y es necesario que así sea en todas por la mayor parte destas Indias, porque, como habemos dicho, el aspecto y figura del cielo y la virtud de las estrellas...esta graciosa y hermosa dispusición destas gentes favorecen. (I:178-79)

For Las Casas, their angelical physiognomy, their beautiful faces and proportionate bodies prove that they have by nature received noble souls (*nobles ánimas*). In describing their facial expression, walk, laughter, posture, and especially their talk, Las Casas wants us to picture their behavior as if they had been raised under "the rule of good friars" ("regla de muy buenos religiosos"). All these attributes, ranging from angelical facial features to spiritual traits comparable to the instruction of friars, create the image of the Amerindians as *noble savage*, in the sense of being naturally virtuous. The figure of the *noble savage* has a parallel function to the exemplary landscape and climate of Española in Book One. Particular cultures in the Americas can be explained as variations of the Lucayos. Thus the Lucayos function as a common denominator for understanding specific cultural forms such as the perforation of noses and cheeks to acquire warlike, ferocious appearances, or the urban sophistication of Tenochtitlan and Cuzco. This primal cultural form, as embodied in the simplicity and natural virtuosity of the Lucayos, cancels all possible grounds for judging cultural differences in the light of an evolutionary model. This counter-discursive move against the apologists of conquest becomes evident once we understand that the semblance of the Lucayos is a powerful fiction and not just one particular empirical example of Amerindian culture.

It's a commonplace in discussions of utopia in Las Casas to correlate anthropological statements about the Amerindian's ideal primitivism with the viability of establishing an ideal Christian society (Cro, "La utopía cristiano-social" 106-116, Maravall 114 and passim). We certainly find Las Casas drafting alternative projects of colonization in a series of *Memoriales* written between 1516 and 1518, and even involved in their realization in Cumana, in present day Venezuela (1520-1521). Moreover, the usage of the term *familias* to define the socio-economic units comprising a Spanish family and five Indians in the *Memorial de catorce remedios* (1516) has suggested to readers an adoption of Thomas More's ideal society as described in *Utopia*. And yet arguments about whether this project was utopian or not adopt disparate if not contradictory meanings of the term utopia, and incur in endless discussions over the possibility of its realization. Similar conflictive interpretations recur when discussing *Del único modo de atraer a todos los pueblos a la verdadera religión* and the peaceful evangelization of Vera Paz, Guatemala (1537-50).[15] Here we shall not pass judgement on whether these documents and "social experiments," as Lewis Hanke calls them, can be considered legitimate utopias, nor on whether they were realizable (*The Spanish Struggle* 39). Moreover, the *Apologética*, which postdates these events, defines a theoretical and political transition to a later Las Casas that condemns outright the Spanish colonization of the New World and calls for a full restitution of Indian sovereignty.[16]

Although the primitivism of the Amerindians certainly suggests potential ideal Christian subjects, the figures of the *noble savage* and a paradisiacal *natural garden* in the *Apologética* are not defined in terms of a new Spanish social order. The *noble savage* and the *natural garden* are discursive and rhetorical fictions that dismantle the possibility itself of predicating the need of imposing a new order on the Americas. Instead of evaluating the feasibility of political projects in Las Casas, let us, then, redefine the utopian dimension of these fictions in the *Apologética* with the following observations on "utopic practice" in Louis Marin's *Utopics: Spatial Play*:

> When talking about the Perfect Island, the Lunar States, or the Austral Continent, utopia talks less about itself or the discourse it has on the island, moon, or lost continent than about the very possibility of uttering such a discourse, of the status and contents of its enunciating position and the formal and

material rules allowing it to produce some particular
expression. (10)

We may thus add to Marin's list of utopian *topoi* the
noble savage and a paradisiacal *natural garden;* their inherent contradiction of terms (nature and culture coexist)
encloses on their figural surface (thus concealing and revealing at once) the rules of the code that produce them.
These figures do not convey a synthesis of a nature-culture
opposition but a neutral term that manifests the semantic
field from which the opposition emerged in the first place.
Indeed, the *noble savage* figure reveals the ideological
underpinnings of a binary opposition.[17] If "noble" encompasses Christian and civilized ideals, which is certainly the
meaning Las Casas gives to the term when he attributes it
to the Amerindians, who in turn are reduced to "savages"
or "barbarians" in apologetics of conquest, the *noble savage* figure cancels the opposition while prompting a
fetishistic reification. Such a reification becomes evident if
we consider that "noble" in sixteenth-century Spanish
refers to *cristianos viejos* (non-savage, i.e., not recently
converted) in opposition to *conversos* (non-noble, i.e., not
old Christian); so, in this respect, the reference to
Amerindians as *noble savages* would retain the same values of the opposition it sets out to critique in the first
place—the "savages" because of their recent conversion
are by definition non-noble. At its face value, the *noble
savage* figure is a contradiction of terms and works against
itself.[18] The figure, obviously, can also work in the other
direction with its assumption that "savages" might truly
incarnate the ideals of Christianity vis-à-vis nominal
Christians. This last possible semantic shift, however, only
lends itself to endless squabbles over proper meaning.
Though the constitution of the antinomy and, consequently, of infinite polemics[19] is already an accomplishment since it undoes authoritative univocal meanings, we
must note that the *noble savage* figure manifests, beyond
itself, the "conditions of possibility" of anthropological
discourse in general.

Las Casas, then, according to our reading is not so much
attempting to substitute the description of a "barbarian"

with that of an empirical "ideal primitive" that would exist in some unproblematic way in the Americas, than to convey how the term "barbarian" does not have a corresponding referent and yet it certainly constitutes a powerful device that produces juridico-anthropological statements which define the Other in terms of political, economic, linguistic, and cultural deficiencies.[20] Thus the *noble savage* is not an opposite to the barbarian but a neutral term that manifests the semantic mechanisms that give rise to the latter. It marks the passage from a concept of civilization to barbarism by including in a double negation "non-civilization" and "non-barbarism." In the neutral one can read simultaneously the concurrence of two negations and an assumed distance with regard to this conjunction: "As if the neutral were an 'other' place (neither one nor the other) but also the other of place (non-place, utopia)" (13). For Marin, the neutral is, indeed, what "would substantialize a process, a movement from the same to the other" (14). This otherness of place, this non-place ("no longer the one and not yet the other" [14]), would have as an equivalent in the *Apologética* the notion of infidels as *pura negatividad* that Las Casas retakes from Saint Thomas (II: 647). Pure negativity—although defined in the *Apologética* as a form of barbarism, does not convey attributes opposite to civilization—is merely an absence of faith in Christ, which cannot be condemned in itself. If read as an empirical description of a culture, as I have already pointed out, the noble savage suggests a fetishistic reification. As a utopian, hence fictive construct, the figure of the *noble savage* perfectly embodies the neutral as a "no longer and not yet".

These indications, drawn from Marin, define the utopian character of the *Apologética* as a type of book and discourse, and not with respect to a political and social project to which it might be connected. By this I am not suggesting that the debates with Sepúlveda and, in general, the overall concrete political situation of the *Apologética* are not relevant. I do wish to insist, however, that the *Apologética* is first of all a book, and as such a utopian instrument.

Several narrative and descriptive devices point to the fictive nature of the *garden* and the *noble savage*. From the beginning of Book One, Las Casas draws our attention to the textual production of the island of Española by framing the description in terms of four circular surveys, or *vueltas* as he refers to them. These *vueltas* move from the exterior to the interior, from the coastline to the inner fertile lowlands that Las Casas, following Columbus, calls "La Vega Real." The *vueltas* also provide a historical narrative as they chart and describe Española. Accordingly, Las Casas traces the coastline closely following the itinerary of Columbus's first voyage, and persistently documents how Spaniards abandoned settlements after the extermination of the Indians. Thus each of the *vueltas* traces partial totalizations of Española that incorporate a narrative of destruction into the geographic description. For instance, Las Casas begins describing the first province by reminding us, within a parenthesis, that its name used to be Bainoa "when it was full of its native settlers and now is depopulated of humans and full of beasts..." ("cuando estaba llena de sus naturales pobladores y agora es despoblada de hombres y llena de bestias...") (I: 15). He concludes the survey of Bainoa, by recalling that Columbus, due to its fertility, had named its principal haven "puerto del Paraíso." The whole province, adds Las Casas, resembles a terrestrial paradise. Las Casas, repeatedly introduces himself as an eye-witness, "I have traveled and very well seen" ("he andado y muy bien visto"), to further corroborate Columbus's paradisiacal landscape. By including first hand experience and historical information in geographical descriptions, Las Casas calls our attention to the Spaniards's destruction of a utopian horizon in a paradisiacal land. The juxtaposition of an ideal landscape and a wasteland augments the sordid behavior of the Spaniards. Thus the fictive landscape of Española conveys not only the sliding of the term utopia (no place) into utopia (place of happiness), but also brings the term distopia as a figure for European intrusion.

A *natural garden* and the figure of the *noble savage* thus define a utopian character in Las Casas's ethnology as they entail a critique of the present. These primal figures that undo nature-culture oppositions do not imply positing the New World in a distant historical past. Moreover, utopian ethnology in the *Apologética* implies a neutralization of evolutionary schema that would place the Amerindians in some kind of imperfect or underdeveloped state with respect to Europe:

> because they equalled in government, polity, and customs many and diverse nations, of the highly praised and lofty that there were and are today in the world, and the most prudent of them as were the Greeks and Romans, in following the rules of natural reason they surpassed by no small margin.

> porque a muchas y diversas naciones que hobo y hay hoy en el mundo, de las muy loadas y encumbradas, en gobernación, política y en las costumbres, se igualaron, y a las muy prudentes de todo él, como eran los griegos y romanos, en seguir las reglas de la natural razón con no chico exceso sobrepujaron." (I: 4)

It is evident from this quotation that Las Casas includes both past and present in the *hobo y hay* (there were and are). Las Casas's comparative ethnology does not seek to use ethnographic materials to illustrate and explain the origins of European culture as Lafitau would prescribe it in the eighteenth century, but to assert the coevalness of cultural Others in cross-cultural juxtapositions. Las Casas wants to define the terms of future encounters of Europeans and Amerindians as well as to restore Indian sovereignty by underscoring, chapter after chapter, culture after culture, the self-sufficiency of the cultures of the New World. Although by the 1550's, information about Mexico and Peru could challenge the climactic and anthropological exemplariness of Española, Las Casas refuses to elaborate an evolutionary scale for measuring the accomplishments of different cultural forms in the Americas. This is one of Las Casas's unique contributions to ethnology; especially evident when compared with the evolving historical stages in the already mentioned Acosta's *Historia natural y moral de las Indias* (1590), or in Garcilaso de la Vega's *Comentarios reales* of the Incas (1609) (Cf. Pagden 143). Las Casas's appeal to a Golden Age, then, does not intend so much to suggest the image of a first people, but, paradoxically, to create a powerful fiction that condemns any justification of conquest based on the Amerindian's imputed savagery or primitiveness.

Book Three specifically addresses the concept of savagery (and consequently evolving patterns in history) when Las Casas discusses scattered villages in the mountains of Guatemala. Las Casas offers two explanations for their dispersed settlements: first, he gives the ruggedness of the terrain as not being propitious for building several houses together; secondly, he considers their poverty an impediment to urban development. With respect to the latter, Las Casas underscores the idea that they were poor by choice, and quotes the Gospel against cupidity. Las Casas needs a description of an original state of mankind at the beginning of Book Three before he examines the plurality of Indian cultures in the New World. The description and speculation on barbarism establishes a precedent Las Casas can take for granted and presume as an absent middle term mediating statements and conclusions. Las Casas's allusions to a first man would ultimately echo Augustine's use of hypothetical "savages," in *The City of God*, to deny their historicity and value for understanding the origins of society: "It is better, then, to believe that such a man or semi-man never existed, and that this, in common with many other fancies of the poets, is a mere fiction" (XIX.12). This position underlies the impossibility, according to Las Casas, "that one whole nation be so unable or of such poor and very barbarian judgement and of a low and limited reason that it would not know how to govern itself..." ("que una nación toda sea inhábil o tan de poco y barbarísimo juicio y de baja y apocada razón que no se sepa gobernar...") (*Apologética*, I: 260). Las Casas closes this discussion by leaving open the possibility that some absolute savages might exist in Florida. These antithetical statements that juxtapose the necessity that all nations know how to govern themselves and a hypothetical absolute savage in Florida open cultural forms to endless varieties, while reducing the term barbarism to a limited technical sense without referent in the Americas. In the end these apparently contradictory moves reinforce cultural pluralism.

Whatever state of barbarism the Spaniards, among them Alvar Núñez (Cabeza de Vaca) attributed to the nomadic peoples of Florida, Las Casas in Book III, chapters CCVI-CCVII insists on their full rationality. If chapter CCVI opens its discussion of nomadic peoples with a denial of civility, in the course of the chapter Las Casas draws ethnographic descriptions from Cabeza de Vaca that contradict the initial stripping of culture and reduction to absolute savagery. Las Casas resumes in chapters CCVII the discussion of Cicero that he had left behind in chapter XLVIII. Here, again, the model of a civilizing hero and a hypothetical original barbarian state is less important than Cicero's praise of eloquence and its power to teach, which ultimately is what *De inventione* and *De legibus* are all about. In the "Prologue" to his *Historia de las Indias*, which provides his most elaborate ideas on historiography, Las Casas highlights the importance of eloquence and the peaceful conversion policies advanced in *Del único modo;* indeed, the preachers of the Gospel have an advantage over the eloquence of Cicero's hero because the conversion of souls bears a greater efficacy, "since it is a gift from above, than whatever human industry and diligence" ("como es don concedido de arriba, que cualquier industria y diligencia humana" (*Historia de las Indias,* [I: 16]). In these contexts and others Las Casas cites the inherent potential of all men to develop their rationality and to receive the Gospel. But a distinction of peoples in terms of intellectual and religious capacities in potency or in act does not entail a model of historical stages. Rather, the figure of the *noble savage* encompasses the notion of a people who are both "primitive" and able to learn. Las Casas does not subscribe to the validity of the concept of savagery as representing peoples not yet ready for civilization or Christianity, a concept which is fully operative in Acosta's judgement that savages must be taught "first how to be men and then Christians" ("primero a ser hombres, y después a ser cristianos") (320).

At this point it is worthwhile recalling that Las Casas points out how the Amerindians surpassed Ancient cul-

tures including the Greek and Roman, "en seguir las re-
glas de la natural razón." In the *Apologética* Las Casas
draws civilizing heroes from Western myth in order to
place them on a par with the founding narratives from the
Americas. Thus Las Casas introduces the account of the
Inca's origins with a parallelism to Antiquity:

> In telling the origin of the Inca kings, I want first to
> relate a fable the Indians tell, that perhaps only
> partially contains fable and the origin could have
> been history, as it is very common among ancient
> peoples to make this mixture. (II: 572)

> Para dar noticia del origen de los reyes inca, primero
> quiero referir una fábula que cuentan los indios, que
> parte puede contener de fábula y el fundamento pudo
> ser historia, como harto de esta mezcla hobo entre las
> gentes antiguas.

In the course of narrating the Incas' founding heroes'
ascent to the heavens, Las Casas compares their account to
Roman history: "the way the Romans held Romulus was
the same, and there was among them persons of great authority that confirmed having seen, with their own eyes,
under oath, how he ascended" ("la manera que los romanos tuvieron que de Rómulo fue lo mismo, y hobo en-
trellos persona de grande autoridad que afirmó haberle
visto él por sus ojos subir, con juramento...") (II: 574). Romans and Incas are comparable not only in terms of the
content of their myth but also in terms of the function
hearsay and the role of the authorities in the conflation of
history and fable. The mixture of fiction and fact, obviously, does not devoid these narratives of all wisdom as it
is evident in Las Casas's praise of Amaro Inga's (sic)
speech: "in which he conveys things, certainly, much
more elevated than those to be found in the Politics of
Plato nor of Aristotle, nor in any other studied philosopher, since they pertain to the natural light which in him
was very clear..." ("en el cual dio a entender cosas, cierto,
harto más altas que había en la Política de Platón ni
Aristóteles, ni otro filósofo estudiado, sino lo que la lumbre natural que en él estaba bien clara...") (II: 616). As for
"natural reason," Las Casas implies here, the Incas had lit-

tle to learn from Aristotle or any other Ancient philosopher.

Although Las Casas takes Aristotle's (Aristotle 299 and passim) three orders of prudence (monastic, economic and political) and the six classes required in an ideal state (farmers, craftsmen, warriors, rich men, priests, judges and rulers) to organize Book Three, it does not necessarily follow that he adopts the Aristotelian contents as universal standards to evaluate Amerindian cultures. Las Casas underscores the self-sufficiency of Amerindian cultures, even though some of the Aristotelian requirements might be absent.

Las Casas intimates that Europeans have something to learn from the cultures of the New World:

> Let us now leave behind all these kingdoms, within which if we were perceptive enough we would see more things in their polity and such order that we would be better off learning from them how to perfect our own than insulting theirs.

> Dejemos agora todos estos reinos, dentro de los cuales si penetrásemos veríamos que en más cosas en sus policías y tal orden que pudiésemos más con razón aprender dellos para perficionar las nuestras que improperárselas. (*Apologética*, I: 339)

Statements such as the above illustrate well Las Casas's comparativism and the intent of the *Apologética* to go beyond a mere collection of individual ethnographies in order to clear the ground for a fuller understanding of Amerindian cultures.

Despite the fictive character of the *natural garden* and the *noble savage*, these figures cannot be dismissed as mere idealizations of reality or as imaginary entities since they gain an autonomous position within the text's interweaving of historical fact and geographic description. But by the same token, fiction in the *Apologética* keeps the veracity of the historico-geographical references from being disproved by a straightforward comparison with some kind of permanent New World reality.

Las Casas's *natural garden* and *noble savage* have similarities with the Golden Age of antiquity, and they may have a function, or may even anticipate that of the "primitive" in modern political philosophy from Hobbes to Rousseau. As fictions of a state of nature these figures enable abstract reflections on society and the State. The difference resides in that for Las Casas the *noble savage* serves the purpose of reinserting coevalness in ethnographic representations, while for modern political theorists, the myth of the *noble savage* confined cultural Others within a time prior to the Constitution of the historical State.

If Las Casas's purpose is to assert the present one may ask why he makes constant reference to classical antiquity. One can think of two main reasons. The first has to do with the importance of Antiquity as an "Other." For the Renaissance that "Other" referred to Ancient Greece and Rome whose cultures were deemed to be worthy of emulation. Indeed, classical studies not only unearthed pictures of the world as Ptolomey's, but also provided models of language, thought and culture, and while developing dictionaries and grammars they shaped the ethnographic tools of modern Europe. References to Antiquity inevitably mediated the representation of otherness in the so-called voyages of discovery. Let us also recall that the the myth of "barbarism" and that of the Golden Age are *topoi* derived from ancient sources.[21] But Las Casas also sought to have his contemporaries question themselves and learn about the Amerindians in the same fashion that they learned from the Ancients; but beyond drawing comparisons between the two cultural Others we find the *Apologética* engaging in what anthropologists call today cross-cultural defamiliarization (Marcus and Fischer 137+). In very simple terms, defamiliarization in the *Apologética* amounts to stating that the Other worthy of emulation (i.e., Antiquity) is inferior to the New World Other that is being viciously destroyed.

Many positions of Las Casas might strike us today as idealistic or plainly ideological. To begin with, we distrust the figure of the *noble savage*, while perhaps still retaining the image of a paradisiacal landscape, of a Golden Age within our wish-horizon: the ideal correspondence of base and superstructure, as Ernst Bloch fancies, Columbus's merging of Eldorado and Eden (*The Principle of Hope*, II: 746 and passim). Las Casas's adoption of the *noble savage* figure to critique the denial of coevalness in representations of cultural Others is a powerful example of Louis Marin's thesis ("Utopia is an ideological critique of ideology"). But whether we see utopias as anticipations of the social sciences, or as powerful ideological critiques, it should not keep us from appreciating the richness of utopian practices, nor from engaging in utopian play.

NOTES

[1] See the studies dedicated to the contemporaneity of Las Casas in Friede and Keen. Take as an example the following statement by Angel Losada: "Las Casas posed the problem, so relevant today, of the attitude of 'cultured' or 'developed' people and masterfully defined the philosophy of aid to underdeveloped peoples, as follows. A condition of intervention by a developed people in the affairs of an underdeveloped nation, whether with the aim of material assistance or of imposing a new religion or ideology, must be absolute respect for the beliefs of the latter, until that people, of its own will, peacefully decides to accept the proffered aid or intended change" (296-297). To say the least it is arguable that Las Casas's position can be expressed in terms of "developed" and "underdeveloped" nations.

[2] Notably by Hanke, *The Spanish Struggle for Justice in the Conquest of America* and *Aristotle and the American Indians*.

[3] For studies of anthropology in Las Casas, see, for instance, Mahn-Lot; Todorov; Pagden, "A Programme for Comparative Ethnology (1) Bartolomé de Las Casas"; Hanke, "Bartolomé de las Casas: El antropólogo." On utopia in Las Casas, see Cro, *Realidad y utopia*, and "La utopía"; José Antonio Maravall.

[4] Anthropology as a social science obviously did not exist, and Thomas More's title of the book *Utopia*—though elements from More's "ideal society" are adopted by Vasco de Quiroga for the *hospitales-pueblo*—had not given place to the concept of utopia as a distinct political mode of thought. For a study of Vasco de Quiroga's adoption of passages from Thomas More, see Zavala, *La utopía de Tomás Moro*. I am drawing the

definitions of "presentism" and "finalism" from Dreyfus and Rabinow 118-119.

[5] For a recent assessment of contemporary theory and its positions towards history, see Simpson, "Literary Criticism."

[6] I am especially relating my reading of Las Casas's critical anthropology to Fabian, and Marcus and Fischer.

[7] For a study of the political implications and theories of barbarism that Las Casas writes against, see Mechoulan.

[8] This is what Johannes Fabian refers to as *denial* of *coevalness* that is, "*a persistent and systematic tendency to place the referent(s) of anthropology in a Time other than the present of the producer of anthropological discourse.*" (Fabian 31, emphasis in original).

[9] For an interpretation of Las Casas medieval mentality vis-à-vis a modern mentality in Sepúlveda, see Phelan; O'Gorman also opposes Sepúlveda and Las Casas in these terms (lxxii-lxxv esp.).

[10] For bibliographical data of the *Apologética* and the *Apología* (in Latin and Spanish) that Las Casas read at Valladolid during five straight days, see Zavala, "Aspectos formales de la controversia"; Lozada, "Observaciones sobre 'La Apología'"; Pérez Fernández.

[11] For a brief history of secular and natural Time, see Fabian 7-35.

[12] See the historical trajectory and long range implications of Acosta's concept of cultural degeneration in Blanckaert. Cf. Pagden, chapter 7 "A Programme for comparative ethnology (2) José de Acosta" (194-197 esp.).

[13] See Zavala "La utopia"; Baudot, especially chapter 2 "La découverte spirituelle du Méxique par les frères Mineurs" (71-118).

[14] See Bataillon, "Las Casas face à la pensée d'Aristote sur l'esclavage." Also of interest is Delacampagne (233-250). O'Gorman and Phellan have underscored the modern character of Sepúlveda's theory of Empire. However, since Las Casas is confronting a modern concept of colonialism he cannot simply be reduced to some sort of medieval mentality as both O'Gorman and Phellan argue.

[15] For a study of the the texts and experiments as well as the conflictive interpretations of Cumana and Vera Paz, see Bataillon (137-243 esp.).

The most complete study to date of Cumana continues to be Giménez Fernández.

[16]   See, for instance, "Carta al Maestro Fray Bartolomé Carranza de Miranda," in *Obras escogidas.*

[17] For a reading of Marin, see Jameson, "On Islands and Trenches".

[18]   Cf. White, "The Noble Savage Theme" 183.

[19] On antinomies and infinite polemics in utopian practices, see Marin 3-28.

[20] For the categories of primitive and savage as conceptual devices, see Fabian 32.

[21] For an analysis of how the Renaissance archaeological enterprise is the matrix of modern cultural anthropology, see Michel Beaujour (220-221), and the seminal study by Rowe. Also of interest are the observations on the "Ancients" and the "Moderns" in Struever (95 and passim).

WORKS CITED

Acosta, Joseph de. *Historia natural y moral de las Indias.* Ed. Edmundo O'Gorman. Mexico: FCE, 1979.

Aristotle. *Politics.* Ed. and trans. Ernst Barker. New York: Oxford Univ. Press, 1979.

Bataillon, Marcel. *Estudios sobre Bartolomé de las Casas.* Trans. J. Coderch and J.A. Martínez Schrem. Barcelona: Península, 1976.

—. "Las Casas face à la pensée d'Aristote sur l'esclavage." *Platon et Aristote. XVIe Colloque International de Tours.* Paris: J. Vrin, 1976. 403-429.

Baudot, George. "La découverte spirituelle du Méxique par les frères Mineurs." *Utopie et histoire au Méxique.* Toulouse: Privat, 1976. 71-118.

Beaujour, Michel. *Miroirs d'encre.* Paris: Seuil, 1980.

Blanckaert, Claude. "Unité et Alterité. La parole confisquée." *Naissance de l'ethnologie?* Paris: Cerf, 1985. 11-22.

Bloch, Ernst. *The Principle of Hope*, 3 vols. Trans. Neville Plaice, Stephen Plaice, and Paul Knight. Cambridge: MIT Press, 1986.

Casas, Bartolomé de las. *Apologética historia sumaria*. Ed. Edmundo O'Gorman. Mexico: UNAM, 1967.

—. *Historia de las Indias*, 3 vols. Ed. Agustin Millares Carlo. Mexico: FCE, 1965.

—. "Carta al Maestro Fray Bartolomé Carranza de Miranda." *Obras escogidas de Bartrolomé de Las Casas. Opúsculos, cartas y memoriales*. Ed. Juan Pérez de Tudela. Madrid: BAE, vol. 110, 1958.

Cro, Stelio. *Realidad y utopía en el descubrimiento y conquista de la América hispánica*. Troy: International Book, 1983).

—. "La utopía cristiano-social en el Nuevo Mundo." *Anales de Literatura Hispanoamericana* VI:7 (1978): 87-129.

Delacampagne, Christian. *L' Invention du racisme*. Paris: Fayard, 1983.

Dreyfus, Huberet L., and Paul Rabinow. *Michel Foucault: Beyond Structuralism and Hermeneutics*. Chicago: Univ. of Chicago Press, 1982.

Fabian, Johannes. *Time and the Other: How Anthropology Makes its Object*. New York: Columbia Univ. Press, 1983.

Friede, Juan, and Benjamin Keen, eds. *Bartolomé de las Casas in History: Toward an Understanding of the Man and His Work*. De Kalb: Northern Illinois Univ. Press, 1971.

Giménez Fernández, Manuel. *Bartolomé de las Casas*, 2 vols. Sevilla: Escuela de Estudios Hispano-Americanos de Sevilla, 1953, 1960.

Hanke, Lewis. *The Spanish Struggle for Justice in the Conquest of America*. Philadelphia: Univ. of Pennsylvania Press, 1949.

—. *Aristotle and the American Indians: A Study in Race Prejudice in the Modern World*. Bloomington: Indiana Univ. Press, 1975.

—. "Bartolomé de las Casas: El antropólogo." *Bartolomé de las Casas. Pensador político, historiador, antropólogo*. Trans. Antonio Hernández Travieso. La Habana: Sociedad Económica de Amigos del País, 1949. 69-101.

Jameson, Frederic. *The Political Unconscious: Narrative as a Socially Symbolic Act.* Ithaca: Cornell Univ. Press, 1981.

—. "On Islands and Trenches: Naturalization and the Production of Utopian Discourse." *Diacritics* 7 (June 1977): 2-21.

Lozada, Angel. "Observaciones sobre la 'Apología' de Fray Bartolomé de Las Casas (respuesta a una consulta)." *Cuadernos americanos* CCXII:3 (Mayo-Junio 1977): 152-162.

—. "The Controversy between Sepúlveda and Las Casas in the Junta of Valladolid." In Friede, and Keen, eds. *Bartolomé de las Casas in History: Toward an Understanding of the Man and His Work.* 279-307.

Mahn-Lot, Marianne. "Les precurseurs de l'anthropologie Bartolomé de las Casas et les Indiens d'Amérique." *L'Ethnographie* LXXVII:85 (1981): 169-172.

Maravall, José Antonio. "Utopía y primitivismo en el pensamiento de Las Casas." *Utopía y reformismo en la España de los Austrias.* Madrid: Siglo XXI, 1982. 111-206.

Marcus, George E., and Michael M.J. Fischer. *Anthropology as Cultural Critique: An Experimental Moment in the Human Sciences.* Chicago: Univ. of Chicago Press, 1986.

Marin, Louis. *Utopics: Spatial Play.* Trans. Robert A. Vollrath. New Jersey: Humanities, 1984.

Mechoulan, Henry. "La notion de barbare chez Las Casas." *Moreana* 45 (February 1975): 39-48.

O'Gorman, Edmundo. "La Apologética historia, su génesis y elaboración su estructura y su sentido." Introductory study to Las Casas, *Apologética historia sumaria.*

Pagden, Anthony. "A Programme for Comparative Ethnology (1) Bartolomé de Las Casas". *The Fall of Natural Man.* 119-145.

—. "A Programme for Comparative Ethnology (2) José de Acosta." *The Fall of Natural Man.* 146-200.

—. *The Fall of Natural Man: The American Indian and the Origins of Comparative Ethnology.* Cambridge: Cambridge Univ. Press, 1982.

Pérez Fernández, Isacio. "Dos apologías de Las Casas contra Sepúlveda: la 'Apología en romance' y la 'Apología en latín'." *Studium* XVII:1 (1977): 137-160.

Phelan, John Leddy. "El imperio cristiano de Las Casas, el imperio español de Sepúlveda, y el imperio milenario de Mendieta." *Revista de Occidente* 141 (1974): 292-310.

Rowe, John Howland. "The Renaissance Foundations of Anthropology." *American Anthropologist* 67:1 (1965): 1-21.

Simpson, David. "Literary Criticism and the Return to 'History'." *Critical Inquiry* 14:4 (Summer 1988): 721-747.

Struever, Nancy. *The Language of History in the Renaissance.* Princeton: Princeton Univ. Press, 1970.

Todorov, Tzvetan. *The Conquest of America: The Question of the Other.* Trans. Richard Howard. New York: Harper & Row, 1984.

White, Hayden. "Getting out of History: Jameson's Redemption of Narrative." *The Form of Content: Narrative Discourse and Historical Representation.* Baltimore: Johns Hopkins Univ. Press, 1987. 142-168.

—. "The Noble Savage Theme as Fetish." *Tropics of Discourse: Essays in Cultural Criticism.* Baltimore: Johns Hopkins Univ. Press, 1978. 183-196.

Zavala, Silvio. "Aspectos formales de la controversia entre Sepúlveda y Las Casas en Valladolid, a mediados del siglo XVI," *Cuadernos americanos* CCXII:3 (Mayo-Junio 1977): 138-151.

—. *La utopía de Tomás Moro en la Nueva España. Recuerdo de Vasco de Quiroga.* Mexico: Porrúa, 1965.

CHAPTER 8:
THE EARLY STAGES OF LATIN
AMERICAN HISTORIOGRAPHY

Beatriz González Stephan

(*translated by Gwendolyn Barnes
and Néstor E. López*)

On a certain occasion, Mario Benedetti singled out as an increasingly significant task the necessity of recovering our system of values from a situation of dependence that had been perpetuated by dominant cultural practices throughout Latin American history.[1]

> Together with our poets and writers, we must also create our own critical approach, our own methods of research, our own unique values, born from our conditions, from our necessities....I do not propose to do so without European opinions or contribution....But this apprenticeship—no matter how important it is—should not substitute for the direction of our own convictions, our own scale of values, our own sense of orientation. (Benedetti 52-53)

> Junto a nuestros poetas y narradores, debemos crear también nuestro propio enfoque crítico, nuestros pro-

pios modos de investigación, nuestra valoración con
signo particular, salidos de nuestras condiciones, de
nuestras necesidades....No estoy proponiendo que,
para nuestras valoraciones, prescindamos del juicio o
el aporte europeos....Pero tal aprendizaje por impor-
tante que sea, no debe sustituir nuestra ruta de
convicciones, nuestra propia escala de valores, nuestro sentido de orientación.

In this way, an approach frequently categorized within the
field of literary studies as "Eurocentric" has considered
pertinent problems related not only to literary production
but also to literary critique and history by basing its
premises and patterns upon those established for other realities—basically Western Europe's realities. As a corollary, this type of evaluation in some cases resulted in a
distortion of our cultural practices; in other cases, unfor-
tunately, it also resulted in the silencing of certain elements that defined the distinctive character of the Latin
American process. We refer to the fact that at times we face
a gap in or a lack of cultural production because of un-
justifiable carelessness.

As far as Latin American literary history and historiography are concerned, we observe the following phenomenon: just as our literary historiography has been
conceived in the terms of the European process, the history of our literary studies has usually been characterized
as short-lived and devoid of any tradition of criticism.
This has inevitably led to familiar accusations, such as the
lack of a critical tradition in our literary studies or of a tradition of literary history or historiography. In other words,
if we adopt the point of view of the "other", we shall
obviously not find in the American continent renowned
masters of modern literary history like Winckleman,
Herder, Schlegel, Gervinus, De Sanctis, Brunetiére, Taine,
Dilthey, Lanson, just to mention those names that are
frequently heard when speaking about the history of
literature—names canonized by the institutions of Eurocentric criticism.

Although the above-mentioned literary historians influenced the Latin Americans of their time, it is necessary
to reestablish the contributions made by the Latin Ameri-

can tradition. Until recently, the focus of Latin American studies has neither centered on the recovery and elaboration of the history of literary criticism nor on the history of the history of literature. At present there are insufficient systematic studies on the reflections of our intellectuals concerning literary phenomena. For that reason we understand the new achievements in the field of historical-literary studies and the review of the traditional histories of Latin American literature to be interrelated tasks. Obviously, the work in these areas could result in a Latin American history of literature which, besides creating a discourse essential to overcoming the limitations of literary histories, would also make an important contribution to the history of Latin American ideas, another field that has been neglected.

For instance, it is commonplace to talk about literary historiography and to trace its origins to the nineteenth century. This century was the century of history. Moreover, it was the century of national literary histories, which appeared both in Europe and Latin America, fomented by the seething atmosphere of the configuration of political nationalisms. The emergence of such nationalisms brought about a new historical awareness (historicism) which shook all the fields of human knowledge and made the absolute and universal concepts that prevailed in the previous century relative. As a consequence, there developed a remarkable comprehension of phenomena according to the epoch, the environment and the historical moment in which they occurred. In addition, there arose a new interest in the formulation of laws that would explain the causes of evolution and progress of all aspects of society.

Thus the nineteenth century is the century *par excellence* for historical consciousness-raising—an undeniable fact—and, therefore, it is also the century of literary history. Yet there are a number of implicit questions to be considered. For instance, when establishing a concomitant relationship between the rise of historical awareness and its discursive objectivization in literary histories, the fact that the nineteenth century developed a type of historical awareness and knowledge—and of historical-literary awareness—that did not necessarily imply that other types of historical perception which had developed previously had been obviated. In fact, during the colonial period there were in Latin America other discursive forms that preceded the nineteenth century literary histories but which carried out similar functions. Foremost among these was the compilation and classification of vast groups of literary works, sometimes from a historicist perspective and others times, from an Americanist one, so as to reaffirm the New Continent's potential vis-à-vis the Old World. The existence of these discursive forms allows us to trace the origins of the process of the formation of our literary history back to the colonial period, to the seventeenth and eighteenth centuries.

Nevertheless, we must consider that such origins are not, strictly speaking, literary histories. The concerns of Latin American men of letters and intellectuals were inscribed in discourses that, because of their functions, served as literary histories. In many chronicles, general and natural histories, poetic compositions, catalogues, anthologies (*parnasos*), dictionaries and bibliothecae, we find pioneering attempts to compile a corpus of works and provide it with a certain organicity. In 1629 the first monumental American history by Antonio de León Pinelo appeared, prolifically entitled: *Epitome of an Oriental and Occidental Nautical and Geographical Library, etc., which Contains Writers of the West Indies, especially from Peru, New Spain, Florida, El Dorado, Terra Firme, Paraguay and Brazil, and Voyages to Them, and the Authors of Navigation and their Materials and Appendices.*[2] In 1672, Nicolás Antonio made public a similar work entitled: *Bibliotheca hispana sive hispanorum.*

Let us compare publication of these works with what was occurring in a European context. The first attempt at a historical-literary history is written in France by the Benedictines of Saint Maur around 1733. It is a catalogue containing only French authors. In contrast, the *Epitome* and the *Bibliotheca*, in addition to being earlier works, constitute the first continent-wide projects in this field. Thus, it is impossible to say that Latin America showed up late at the feast of the origins of this branch of literary studies.

By using these examples, we do not intend to deny the fact that literary histories known as such were not written until the nineteenth century. Yet, the circumstances surrounding the development of the dominant Spanish culture as well as the expressions of a marginal culture—whether of erudite Spanish origin or *mestizo* origin, in Spanish or an indigenous language in Latin America—lead us to assume tensions among the cultivated and privileged elites, who rapidly rose to defend what they considered their literary heritage in the new lands. These tensions could be the reason for the compiling, listing and recording of materials, sometimes with the mere coherence of alphabetical or geographical order, and at other times in a more complex chronological arrangement. The absence of literary histories as such should not lead us to think that other ways of recording the literary past or of organizing literary production were impossible. These other discursive forms never constituted a science of literary history, but nonetheless, they were a condition for its subsequent development.[3]

Thus far, we can trace the origin of the formation of the history of Latin American literature to the colonial period as a response to an emergent Creole culture and consciousness. Catalogues, bibliothecae, epitomes were not only recording devices, but were also social practices that constructed a discourse which, modestly and rudimentarily, met the requirements of a history of literature.

These founding works of Latin American literary histories operated on implicit notions about what was literary and, by extension, about literary collections. Thus, the early compilers were led to document materials with a certain degree of historical awareness regarding written production. This awareness served as a strong reply to the positions of those who mercilessly disparaged any social and cultural expression produced in the New World. In short, these works carried out the primitive practical function of offering knowledge about a given subject and meeting the subsequent demands. First, they outlined a historically accepted concept of "literature" that allowed the establishment of a relatively homogeneous corpus composed of written works and authors, which canonized the cultivated enlightened tradition. Secondly, they tried to order that corpus according to coordinates that implied a twofold effort: 1) the categorization of the works according to a geographical space of enormous dimensions (especially in the seventeenth century) or according to more limited areas (particularly in the eighteenth century when the borders of the present nations started to be determined) and 2) their logical classification (whether according to historical, geographical, thematic, or alphabetical determinates).

Furthermore, in the nineteenth century, literary histories, as one of the discursive practices of the liberal project, played a leading role in the ideological construct of a national literature, which would serve the dominant groups in fixing and codifying symbols needed to project the image of the national political unit. In this way, "literature"—according to the liberal conception—had the capacity to operate upon material conditions in order to effect social progress. And, literary histories would represent the institutionalized language of the interests of those classes to whose members would be attributed the formation of the national states.

Consequently, the knowledge of the literary is historically perfectible, and that is precisely the subject of this essay. However, it may be worthwhile to define some methodological parameters to avoid any confusion regarding *literary production*, the *history of literature*, and *literary historiography*. We can distinguish three levels which have distinctly different discursive natures, tasks, and objectives.

1. The first of these levels is composed of the empirical corpus of literary production. In other words, it consists of all the written and oral social imaginary. This is the most immediate level, and it constitutes the foundation of the discipline's work. It is a non-systematized reality whose determination as a corpus already depends, most of the time, on an ideologized, theoretical operation. It constitutes a type of social practice and as such is substantially historical. Evidently, the concept of *literature* will vary in

different time periods according to the collective consensus and to the patterns established by academic groups.

2. Those discourses whose target is the study and analysis of literary production comprise the second level. Such discourses organize this production around a temporal axis, thus understanding production as a process. This level corresponds to the *histories of literature* and represents an attempt to abstract and construct a model for interpreting empirical production critically. At this level, questions to be confronted include: the way of systematizing the corpus and the type of periodization that will be implemented to design the historical outline of a literature. Both the systematization and configuration of literary periods are the consequence of a theoretical *construct* that always responds to certain social and historic perspectives. In addition, the construct must be adjusted to the project that the dominant groups need to build from their cultural past. This level includes the above-mentioned epitomes and catalogues of the colonial period as antecedents of the national literary histories of the nineteenth century.

3. *Literary historiography*, although closely linked with theoretical and methodological aspects of the history of literature, constitutes a type of metadiscourse devoted to the critical study of historical-literary knowledge and the quality of this analysis. Literary history and historiography are not terms that can be easily interchanged. Yet, it is not superfluous to point out that historiography does not operate directly upon literary production and its evolution, but upon the way literature has been historically organized: the history of literature also has a history. Historiography studies the reflections on the problems of literary history, the ways in which periodization and literary systematization have been carried out and the ideological conceptions eventually controlling such practices. To avoid any ambiguity, it is worthwhile to highlight that, although historiography has a sphere of competence and uses a rigorous methodology, it is not a science in itself. It belongs to the field of the literary studies (theory and criticism) and can receive valuable contributions from the sci-

ence of history. In this way, literary historiography will be able to provide a systematic understanding of the process of the formation of the history of our literature. In turn, it will form part of Latin American cultural history and will make a major contribution to our literary studies.

Although the history of literature, as such, begins as a kind of discursive form specifically connected to the consolidation of the national states in the second half of the nineteenth century, other historical-literary forms came into existence in the colonial period. These early forms provide the history of literary history with a greater continuity in its process of development.

The first attempts to understand our continent's reality were made at the beginning of the colonial period, when conquistadors, missionaries and, later, intellectuals initiated the European reflection on America by inscribing it within various forms of discourse. First, they tried to explain the world they were conquering, and, later, they attempted to consolidate their dominion over the conquered peoples through military and ideological impositions. In their writings—integrated into that complex corpus called "chronicles of the Indies"—they not only described natural, physical conditions of the New World, but they also recorded an image of the social and cultural life led by the peoples inhabiting those new territories.

The fact that the conditions imposed upon the indigenous people ensured the development and consolidation of a culture bearing the sign of the socially dominant and historically victorious group did not, however, impede either the emergence of a "counterculture" shared by the defeated groups and or the appearance of hybrid forms within institutionalized structures. But, it was the cultivated and Hispanic tradition which left references and critical-bibliographical works about the culture of the colonial period for posterity. Likewise, we assume that there could have been similar attempts on the part of authors of mixed parentage (mestizos) who, aware of the marginalization suffered by their culture, felt the need to leave evidence about their poets in some type of discourse.

Although the first bibliographical works and other references about the literary and cultural expressions of Latin

America carry the mark of the values of the dominant groups, they are not lacking in merit if we consider the shackled conditions under which the culture of the conquistadors itself had to survive. The internal clashes among Spanish-speaking producers of culture made this literary system less than homogeneous. On one hand, there was intense censorship governing the patterns of cultural consumption and, on the other, there were constant legal subterfuges employed by the elites in order to supply their libraries with prohibited books.

Certainly, the conditions under which colonial culture was to "flourish" were not easy. The Inquisition, through the Council of the Indies, regulated and controlled not only the production of books but also their import and circulation. Vicente Quesada summarized Law 1, Title 24, Book 1 of the *Recopilación de las Indias* ("Compilation of Indies"), dated September 21, 1560, in the following terms:

> In the West Indies...judges were ordered not to approve of or permit the printing of any book concerning any subject related to the Indies without prior license granted by the Council; likewise they were ordered to collect as soon as possible any book found and to forbid dealers to sell or print them....It also was prohibited to ship books "about the Indies" that had been printed in Spain or abroad "without the same prior review andapproval by the Council." (Quesada 48-49, 56)[4]

Such provisions not only restricted the book trade—both the import/export and publishing industries—but even led to a ruling prohibiting Americans and Spaniards "dwelling in America from studying, observing or writing about subjects related to the Colonies" ("avecinados en América estudiasen, observasen y escribiesen sobre materias relativas a las colonias") (Quesada 49).

Notwithstanding these decrees jeopardizing cultural activities, in practice, such laws and instructions ended up being notoriously useless. Today it has been demonstrated fully that America was an excellent bibliographical market, although for a long time the opposite opinion prevailed. For example, in the eighteenth century the Peruvian, José

Eusebio de Llano Zapata, who was the first to propose the usefulness of a written history of Spanish America, noted:

> Its libraries are Lima's greatest treasures. The public libraries that I have seen in Seville—the Cardinal of Molina's library at the Colegio San Acacio, the Cardinal of Belluga's library at the Colegio Santa María de Jesús, and the St. Peter Library at the Convent of the Dominican Order—are diminutive in comparison with Lima's private ones. This will not astonish those who realize that just as all the riches of gold and silver from our Indies have been buried in Mongolia (according to the most truthful travellers and judicious politicians), the most singular books venerated in the Republic of Letters have been collected in American libraries. There is not a second-hand shop, used-clothes shop, or junk shop in America, especially in Lima, that does not have editions...that can barely be found in Europe. (qtd. Cornejo Polar 92) [5]

Without the support of all the bibliographic material accumulated since the sixteenth century, neither the existence of catalogues and epitomes nor the possibility of thinking about a literary history in the mid-eighteenth century would have been possible. Despite the void that many critics feel characterizes the colonial period, there was an entire discourse (formalized in various ways) that started to develop in order to affirm literary products, whether those referring to the threatened indigenous cultures or to the new Hispanic culture that began to emerge. References about Indian poems and chants, about Spanish works and writers who came to America as well as about Creole writers are available in chronicles, natural and moral histories, miscellanies, anthologies (*parnasos*), fiction works, catalogues, bibliothecae and epitomes. In other words, the critical-bibliographical work—a prerequisite *sine qua non* for the history of literature— did not have a specific discourse of its own during the sixteenth and seventeenth centuries that would allow us to establish demarcations. The evaluation of literature and the reference to men of letters from certain regions or cities were in most cases, mixed in with other kinds of discourse. The dividing line between natural and literary histories was not clear, nor was the distinction between a list of authors and the subject of a poetic text.

For instance, Pedro Cieza de León in his *Crónica del Perú* (1552) referred to the existence of an Inca theater and to the richness and tenderness of the idiomatic inflections of Quechuan poetry. Likewise in 1575, Cristóbal de Molina, called "El Cuzqueño", made public his *Relación de las fábulas y ritos de los Incas*. Previously, in 1532, Father Andrés de Olmos had published in Spanish *Cantares Mexicanos*. In addition, several important works were published by missionaries, among them the well-known *Historia general de las cosas de Nueva España* (1580) by Fray Bernardino de Sahagún, which was first written in the Mexican language and then translated into Spanish, the *Historia natural y moral de las Indias* (1590) by Father José de Acosta, and in the eighteenth century, the *Storia antica del Messico* (1780-81) by Francisco Xavier Clavijero. Even without these last works, there are sufficient examples that demonstrate how general histories constitute a vast source of references about the indigenous cultures. Moreover, in the case of the history by Sahagún (250 years before Voltaire and Herder), we see the existence of a "powerful intuition of what later would be called the '"history of culture'" (Picón Salas 90).

As far as poetry is concerned, a female writer from Lima who preferred to remain anonymous, took pride in her erudition in 812 hendecasyllabic verses entitled "Discurso en loor de la poesía". In these verses she mentions, alongside classical authors a few Spaniards and a host of Mestizo poets—Pedro de Oña, Diego de Ojedas, Gaspar Villarroel, Diego Avalos, Cristobal de Arriaga, Pedro Carvajal—from the Academia Antártica in Lima. According to Antonio Cornejo Polar, that constituted the starting point of "what we could call the 'history' of Peruvian literature" (22). And among European writers, Cervantes himself, in *Viaje del Parnaso* and in the sixth book of his novel *La Galatea* (1585) entitled "Canto a Calíope", listed the geniuses of the "Antarctic Region", citing names which, nowadays, are barely known. Lope de Vega's epic poems *La Filomena*

(1621) and *El Laurel de Apolo* (1630) also constitute a parade of American writers.

The criteria ruling the praise of the Antarctic poets and American writers seemed to be based upon friendship or contemporaneity, and not on aesthetic principles. Nonetheless, all authors quoted somehow moved within the framework of the Italian Renaissance and the spirit of the exquisiteness of the court, and all of them—some more, some less—admired classical culture. It is important to stress that, unlike in the afore-mentioned chronicles (where, when referring to indigenous society, more attention is paid to *culture* in general terms), in these texts, the discursive practice is inserted into a certain poetics and rhetoric and generates the axioms of an elitist Renaissance ideological conception. In other words, the scholarly man of letters is privileged in the field of culture and the "author of *belles lettres*" is honored.

The critical-bibliographical discourse of the New World was combined with other types of discourse. Yet, it was not until the seventeenth century that there began to be a separation between historical and fictional discourse and a bibliographic type of discourse based on references to authors and works. Evidence of this separation can be found in catalogues—Andreas Schott's *Hispaniae ilustrae seu rerum urbium. Hispaniae, Lusitaniae, Aethiopie, et Indiae, scriptores varii* (1608), Leon Pinelo's *Epítome* (1629), or Nicolás Antonio's *Bibliotheca hispana* (1672)—as well as in perhaps the first work based on the more specific notion of literature—Gil González Dávila's *Teatro eclesiástico de la primitiva iglesia de las Indias Occidentales, vidas de sus arzobispos* (1649). The distance between historical and fictional discourse, on one hand, and bibliographic discourse, on the other, would grow wider in the eighteenth and nineteenth century with the appearance of literary histories. In these later centuries, we can speak of dictionaries, bibliothecae, anthologies, and literary histories in terms of their specific discursive functions.

Those who left written testimony about the culture of the West Indies, the New World, or of Spanish or Hispanic America either from a perspective reflecting a degree of Americanism or from one closely associated with European values, were, first of all, Spaniards (conquerors and missionaries). Later, they included Jesuits and American or Creole Spaniards; in some cases, people of mixed parentage (*mestizos*, like Cristóbal de Molina); and finally, in the eighteenth century, European travelers (for example, the Italian Lorenzo Boturini Benaduci). This situation reveals the extent to which the reflection on and evaluation and compilation of all the literary and cultural material produced in America and other overseas regions came from a sector that was socially linked with religious institutions, the power of the Crown, the economic power of the Creole elite and the academic world. (Nevertheless, it would be dangerous to understand this relationship as a necessary prerequisite for such critical-bibliographic work.) In several cases, the sensibility and the historical-social awareness of various historians led them to study the ancient native cultures in an attempt to preserve through their accounts a world that was burying their grandeur. Nevertheless, their approach was based on a Eurocentric system of values, or at least, on the Spanish point of view which was, if not the dominant culture at that moment, the one officially recognized. Therefore, any selection of the corpus to be arranged hierarchically (including popular indigenous songs and dances [*areítos*], sonnets, chronicles, treatises, catechisms, grammars, Aztec rituals, or works by the court poets in the viceroyal cities of Lima or Mexico) was made according to the values of Spanish culture, which conditioned the nature of such critical work.

But our understanding of such catalogues, bibliothecae and other records as discursive practices in defense of colonial culture can only be correctly assessed if they are integrated into the framework of the discussions and polemics generated from the beginning of the Discovery. The main voices in these polemics, which took place in Europe, were Buffon and De Pauw. Their theories about the uninhabitability and deformation of the American geography and about the immaturity and incompetence of the American people unleashed aggressively polarized discourses, some for and others against the human, social and historical character of the New World (see Gerbi, *La disputa* and *Viejas polémicas*).

Such arguments were grounded in an implicit postulate that questioned and even denied the possibility that Latin America constituted an ideal space for a flowering of *belles lettres* and a development of European society, on one hand, and, on the other hand, that cultural manifestations could have existed among the native peoples. There was a tendency to discredit the indigenous heritage under the assumption that the native people both possessed a different capacity of reason and were unable to create an alphabetic writing system. At the same time, the work that was being carried out by the European and American Spaniards in the Indies also discredited indigenous cultures under the pretext of the ominous influence exerted by the climate, the flora and the fauna. These attitudes served as key incentives in the creation of a cultural and bibliographical framework for a discourse transmitted and received by those critical of the American enterprise.

A clear example of this phenomenon motivated Don Juan José Eguiara y Eguren to write the *Bibliotheca Mexicana* (1755). In the first of his "Anteloquias" (chapters of the extensive foreword), he explains:

> We were very far from thinking about this project because we were busy ... when ... the twelve *Epistolas* by the dean of the Church of Alicante Don Manuel Martí fell into our hands .... We started to thoroughly steep ourselves in the work ... although many attacks ... aimed at discrediting Spaniards vis-à-vis the cultivation of the literary disciplines caused us great pain.(...) All the author's efforts were centered on persuading his adolescent friend Antonio Carrillo not to undertake a journey to the New World and on advising him (...) to settle down in Rome and to stay as far away as possible from the Mexican shores. "But, let's get down to business" he says, "Who will you turn to in the midst of such a horrible solitude like the one you will find among the Indians as far as letters are concerned? Will you find, by chance, if not teachers to lecture you, at least people to talk to, not because they already know something, but because they wish to learn something? Or—to be clearer—people who do not regard cultivation of the *belles lettres* with aversion? What books will you consult? What libraries will you frequent? ... Looking for such

> things there would be like trying to shear a donkey
> or milk a billy goat." ... Despite the extension of the
> West Indies ... he dared to point to Mexico as the
> most barbarian site in the whole world, as a country
> enveloped by the thickest darkness of ignorance ...
> Thus, it occurred to us then to endeavor to compose a
> *Bibliotheca Mexicana*, in which we could vindicate
> such a tremendously atrocious insult to our country
> and people and demonstrate that his defamatory
> letter was ... a product of the most supine ignorance.
> (55-213)[6]

In this way, Eguiara y Eguren attempted to demonstrate
in his *Bibliotheca*—which was the first attempt at a Mexican literary history—not only the "culture of our Indians,
by referring to their codices and libraries" but also the
literary process initiated by the Spanish Conquest. He understood that natives

> did not know how to use alphabetic characters,
> which cultivated European nations utilized to com-
> mit the memories of their events to posterity ...
> notwithstanding, they were not to be described as
> brutish and uncultured, ignorant of all sciences and
> unfamiliar with books and libraries.

> desconocieron el uso de caracteres alfabéticos, de que
> las naciones europeas y cultas se sirven para comu-
> nicar a la posteridad la memoria de sus hechos ...
> más no por eso ha de tachárselos de brutos e incultos,
> ignorantes de todas las ciencias y desconocedores de
> libros y bibliotecas. (*Bibliotheca Mexicana* 55-213)

Within this state of affairs, we will see how the various
bibliographical works and historical interpretations of
culture in Hispanic America (according to the type of
literature that they selected and the versions of the past
they reconstructed) represented ideological variables that
simultaneously corresponded to the different political and
social projects of the historically dominant elites. Bearing
in mind the defamatory positions that underlie any
response to the evaluation of culture in these lands, some
possibilities emerge. One of these—which is circumscribed
within a Eurocentric approach—defended the flourishing

European and/or Spanish culture as a reproduction of the values of the mother country. Ideologically, this position signaled the absolute legitimacy of such values in addition to refutating the argument limiting European culture to the European continent.

For this reason, bibliographical compilation and cataloguing as discursive practice seemed to be closely related to an ideological perspective that, by listing the cultural and literary wealth of the New World transferred to the realm of cultural production what has been called the American "horn of plenty." In other words, catalogues and epitomes—especially in the seventeenth century when they begin to appear—were discursive forms that, besides accomplishing their specific function, produced an ideological effect parallel to that of the entire rhetoric that supported the grandeur and magnificence of the Spanish Empire. Moreover as ideological practices, they compensated for the imminent decadence of the Spanish supremacy, which was starting to disrupt both overseas trade and Spain's social and economic control of the American continent.

In the "Discurso Apologético" at the beginning of León Pinelo's *Epitome*, an implicit correlation is established between an unmeasurable geographic space in the Indies and the number of books existing within that territory.

> Not only did he collect names of writers for this bibliotheca, he also saw and read with careful attention what the Histories, Navigational Guidebooks, Voyages, Letters, and Historical Accounts, in forty languages and by more than a thousand authors, that comprise this Epitome contain...from the Province of Santa Cruz in Brazil to the Kingdoms of Malacca and the Archipelago of the Molucca Islands; westward from where the Prime Meridian forms a line of demarcation [separating east and west] in the Atlantic Ocean; embracing this part of the world, the Fourth and Greatest, divided into the two famous duplicate continents, Northern and Southern America or Iberia....

> No sólo juntó nombres de Escritores para esta Biblioteca, sino que vió, i leió con atento cuidado lo que contienen las Historias, Derroteros, Viages, Cartas, i

Relaciones, que en quarenta Lenguas, i mas de mil authores forman parte de este Epítome...comprendidos desdo la Provincia de Santa Cruz del Brasil, hasta los Reinos de Malaca, i Archipiélagos del Moluco: I Occidental, desde donde demarca el verdadero Meridiano la misma sección, hasta salir por el Occidente a nuestro Oceano Atlántico; abarcando esta parte, la Quarta, i maior de le Mundo, el los dos famosos continentes de la duplicada América ó Iberica Septentrional, i Meridional....[7]

It is noteworthy that these first bibliothecae—by Andreas Schott, León Pinelo, Nicolás Antonio, González Dávila and possibly others we do not mention here—contained literary manifestations in Spanish and Latin and excluded any reference to the indigenous cultures. In doing so, they implicitly reinforced the hegemony of a purely Hispanic culture that in its supremacy projected over the *belles lettres* a sensation of "stability" in colonial society. In short, that literary supremacy served to effectively offset a situation of increasing instability.

There was a new wave of awareness among these sectors which led them to perceive that the accumulation of knowledge, books, libraries, like the accumulation of goods, was as legitimate and necessary as the investment in gold and silver. León Pinelo regarded this activity in the following terms:

The desire to know is the glory of power; cherishing the *belles lettres* insures success; an inclination toward wisdom makes one's character superior....It is as if the number of Soldiers on the Battle fields were as much a measure of power as the number of Books in Libraries. These times are to be praised for we see Nobles occupied in worthy pursuits, and the chambers of the highest Princes are not only embellished with Paintings, but also adorned with Books....Because in the Indies [people] long only for Silver and Gold, their Writers are long forgotten and their Histories rarely read.

La gloria del reinar, es el deseo de saber: acariciar letras, es asegurar aciertos: la inclinación sabia, hace la naturaleza superior....Como si fueran índices del poder, tanto los muchos Soldados, en los Campos,

> como los numerosos Libros, en las Bibliotecas. Ala-
> bança es de esta edad, ver la Nobleça bien ocupada, i
> los maiores Principes con Camarines, no sólo vestidos
> de Pinturas, sino adornados de Libros....Como de las
> Indias solo se apetece Plata, i Oro, estan sus Es-
> critores tan olvidados, como sus historias poco vistas.

Perhaps it is worthwhile to highlight one detail at this point. In the seventeenth century, a breach began to separate the "Creoles," who held economic power, and the group that exercised political power. The loss of the former's ability to intervene in the direction of commercial affairs led them to emphasize knowledge and erudition as a patrimony equal to the ownership of material goods. We could venture to say that, in a certain way, such a store of books and authors, accumulated by the same criteria used for stockpiling goods, acquired its full momentum with the appearance of the mercantile and bourgeois view of social relations.

Consequently, these works, except for León Pinelo's *Epitome*, were written in Latin, thereby insuring limited access to them. The use of Latin was not only consonant with the traditional use of this language to deal with academic or "cultivated" matters; it also signaled the elimination of the indigenous cultures and past, excluded oral culture and other forms of written codification, and consecrated the printed book as a sign of cultural prestige and historical transcendence.

Another position defended not only the culture in the New World but also the American people. It attempted to reconstruct and find value in the indigenous past as the ancient cultural base upon which the Spanish civilization in America was founded. This task of restoring the indigenous past was carried out during the sixteenth, seventeenth and eighteenth centuries in valuable chronicles, historical accounts (*relaciones*), and histories. Yet, it was the new critical and methodological orientation of Eguiara y Eguren's *Bibliotheca mexicana* and Lorenzo Boturini Benaduci's *Idea de una nueva historia general de la América septentrional. Fundada sobre material copioso de figuras, símbolos, caracteres, y geroglíficos, cantares y manuscritos de autores indios, últimamente descubiertos* (1746), that gave coherency to this historical-literary task.

Also, in the eighteenth century, a new historical awareness under the influence of the scientific spirit of the Enlightenment promoted intellectual activities by orienting them toward a more "positive" study of the American reality. As a matter of fact, the strengthening of the economic power of the Creole oligarchy paved the way for an increasingly clear development of a social consciousness that, among the so-called "American Spaniards" or "white Creoles", manifested itself in their aspiration to consider themselves legitimate owners of a world they still did not rule politically.

The formation of this libertarian consciousness among the dominant classes appealed, in the process of the authentication of their interests, to an ideological operation that allowed them to ensure their power. Therefore, their historical perspective led them to redesign their concept of the past and to plant their roots in the pre-Colombian antiquity. Thus, the cultural originality of these groups was indebted to a past that had been excluded from the catalogues and bibliothecae written in the previous century.[8]

In effect, the interest in learning about documents, codices, and indigenous painting revealed not only a mere nostalgia for an exotic past to serve as the basis for an American idiosyncrasy, but also demonstrated that the incipient social project was to be supported by a reality with historical underpinnings. In other words, the New World was one in which little was new. Indeed, its existence was not due to Europeans; on the contrary, it was a world with a different culture, society, and history, despite the ahistorical character attributed to it by many.

Eguiara y Eguren, admiring the ancient Mexicans, ponders their rich and complex culture in the following lines:

> In addition to poetry, the Mexicans cultivated rhetoric, oratory, arithmetic, astronomy, and other disciplines that have left us with illustrious monuments and testimonies worthy of great merit....Among that nation's five most important books were the *Ruedas* (Wheels), painted with exquisite art. Each one of them covered the space of a

> century, with a perfect distinction between years,
> months, weeks, and days....Carlos Sigüenza y Gón-
> gora investigated the origins of the Mexicans from
> the most remote times, and through the study of solar
> and lunar eclipses and other strange phenom-
> ena...made manifest the history and events of the
> Mexican Empire...Regarding libraries, it is no wonder
> that the Indians had so many of them....One charac-
> teristic that increased the value of these Mexican
> books was that, through symbolic representations,
> they preserved for posterity the chronology and ex-
> act succession of their centuries of history.
> (*Bibliotheca Mexicana* 55-213)[9]

Neither the recovery of the indigenous world nor the attention devoted to the scientific study of the natural, social and historical realities of America were groundless. Aggressive movements of masses of Indians and *mestizos* shook the continent between 1749 and 1782. Although they were neither pro-independence nor revolutionary, they pursued better economic and social conditions. The expulsion of the Jesuits in 1767 resulted in a broader defense of the American World, seen in the study of the indigenous societies, the dissemination of social reformism (based on a broad policy of *mestizaje* or mixed parentage), and the spread of theories of progress as the antithesis of the dissatisfaction felt by that religious order with respect to the caste system. Moreover, it facilitated the circulation of the idea—so typical of the eighteenth century—of a universal culture that would transcend the differences among nations and would situate the concept of Humanity within the field of history. Likewise, travelers and scientists—like Humboldt, La Condamine and Boturini—helped to disprove fallacies and refute absurdities through their works, which were saturated with the new rationalistic spirit of Encyclopedists.

All this disturbed the stability and rocked the foundations of life in the Colonies. It allowed the emergence of a historical consciousness, sustained primarily by the white Creoles, that permitted a systematic comprehension of their reality. For the first time ever, cultural reality was thought of as a process. Its stages were designed carefully and each one was considered historically necessary and meaningful.

In the critical-bibliographical works of the previous century, the criteria used to order material—either by subject or by alphabetical order of the authors' names—created a discursive space that was ahistorical and that paralleled the immovability that the colonial regime tried to project into its rigidly stratified societies. The dominant groups' preservation of the social and political order was formalized as a discourse in the early catalogues, which lacked a dynamic, historical perception for epistemological reasons. Regarding historical activities in the mid-seventeenth century, Michel Foucault points out that historians reproduced the signs they saw. This resulted in a duplication in written discourse of the immobile social order.

> Until the mid-seventeenth century the historian's task was to establish the great compilation of documents and signs - of everything, throughout the world, that might form a mark.... His existence was defined not so much by what he saw as by what he retold, by a secondary speech which pronounced afresh so many words that had been muffled. The Classical age gives history a quite different meaning: that of under-taking a meticulous examination of things themselves for the first time, and then of transcribing what it has gathered in smooth, neutralized, and faithful words. It is understandable that the first form of history constituted in this period of 'purification' should have been the history of nature.... The documents of this new history are not other words, texts or records, but unencumbered spaces in which things are juxtaposed: herbariums, collections, gardens; the locus of this history is a non-temporal rectangle....
> The ever more complete preservation of what was written, the establishment of archives, then of filing systems for them, the reorganization of libraries, the drawing up of catalogues, indexes, and inventories, all these things represent, at the end of the Classical age, not so much a new sensitivity to time, to its past, to the density of history, as a way of introducing into the language already imprinted on things, and into the traces it has left, an order of the same type as that which was being established between living creatures. (Foucault 130-132)

Nevertheless in the eighteenth century, the Creole oligarchy became a class that believed it had the power to carry out its historical project. This new class began to think about its future and also about the need to have a past in which to anchor its roots. For obvious reasons, the white Creole oligarchy could not explicitly identify with the Conquest since it needed to distinguish itself from the Spanish Crown. Thus, the indigenous past served as historical leverage to establish a suitable distance from the Spaniards. What made the white Creole oligarchy affirm its origin in indigenous culture was not a humanitarian concept, but a political one. It recognized the strength of the popular and indigenous sectors of society on the eve of the independence movement. Moreover, by incorporating these sectors into their historical project through an ideological operation, the white Creole oligarchy could successfully neutralize social tensions. This type of historiography still had a Hispanic perspective. Yet, for historical-political reasons, it incorporated indigenous literature and cultures as finished past, a stage completed prior to the Conquest. However, it resulted in an improvement over the catalogues in use.

At this point, it is important to emphasize the emergence of a viewpoint that saw the world in terms of changing realities. Even though the intention to consider American culture as distinct and separate from Spanish culture was not always clear, the desirability of ordering indigenous culture historically to provide it with the necessary organicity and rationality was apparent. Evidence of this is "La carta persuasiva al señor don Ignacio de Escandón sobre Assunto de Escribir la Historia literaria de la América Meridional" (Cádiz, 1768) by José Eusebio de Llano Zapata.[10] Llano Zapata, concerned that the "distinguished men of letters who honor our country" not be forgotten, wanted to encourage Escandón, "to devote his time to writing a work which America needed and Europe desired. It is the *History of Our Writers*, who have been forgotten, in detriment to the Sciences and an affront to our Literature". Llano Zapata reminded Escandón of the urgency of such a task as it was the Spaniards themselves who voiced the necessity of knowing about overseas writers. In the letter he quoted a long excerpt from "La Historia Literaria de España" by Fray Raphael Rodríguez Mohedano:

> In regard to America, of course we will include it in the scheme of our Literary History. Despite its distance [from the Iberian Peninsula], we cannot fail to appreciate the great progress of its Literature, which has enriched a Region no less abundant in Talent than in Mines, or look upon them as Foreigners....In order to carry out this task with all possible accuracy, and with the glory that corresponds to the merits of such a Literary Nation, we effectively implore Our American Experts who have special instruction or interest in the literary history of the Indies to assist us.

> (P)or lo que toca a la América, desde luego la incluimos en el Plan de Nuestra Historia Literaria, en atención, a que, no obstante su distancia, no podemos mirar, como extraños, ni dexar de apreciar, como grandes los progresos de la Literatura, conque no hé enriquecido una Región, no menos fecunda en Ingenios, que en Minas....Para desempeñar este assunto con la exactitud possible, y con la gloria que corresponde a los méritos de una Nación tan Literata, implorámos eficazmente el socorro de Nuestros Sabios Americanos...que tengan especial instrucción, ó interés en la Historia-Literaria de Indias.

These ideas reinforced Llano Zapata's request for the Americans to hurry and write their own history because "distance leads them to believe we are asleep, when in fact we may be fully awake." In addition, he understood that memories and archives "protect the literary corpuses," and that they were a "wealthy treasure" for such an undertaking. He advised the use of a criterion that "does not serve the evil slavery of flattery, interest, party or faction." Escaping from the subjectivity and the biographical critiques that characterized nineteenth century criticism, he pointed out that it was not necessary to include "genealogical matters" in literary history,

> it being sufficient to say: *a native of Lima, Cuzco, Quito, and Originally from this or that part of the*

World. If this information is not available, it does not matter, nor will it be missed in texts of this type. It is impertinent to waste time in digging up lineages....The proofs that count in the Tribunal of Literature are the demonstration of the Author's talents, genius, wisdom, spirit, and judgement, which can be examined. (Letter from Llano Zapata to "Dr. D. Gregorio Mayáns y Siscar")

bastando decir: *Natural de Lima, Cuzco, Quito, Oc.* y *Originario de esta, o de la otra parte del Mundo*. Si esto último no se encuentra, nada importa, ni se echará de menos en escritos de esta naturaleza. Es grande impertinencia, en estos casos, gastar el tiempo en remover alcuñas....Las pruebas que más califican en el Tribunal de la Literatura, son la demostración de los talentos, del ingenio, del juicio, de espíritu, y sinderesis del Autor que se examina.

Although there is no evidence in this document of Llano Zapata's wish to incorporate the indigenous cultures into his intended project of an American literary history, he does not leave this flank uncovered. He considers it to be important for such a history:

In the same way I have studied the Indian annals called *quipus* [knotted cords used as record-keeping devices by the Incas]. Despite ignorance and despise, even now one can find relics in ruined temples, palaces, and other moments of American antiquity. Truly, *quipus* must be the most precious treasure of our Indies. They will illuminate History with that light that today is barely visible in such a great darkness and confusion of information and [that we need] if we wish to ascertain that origins of that vast monarchy.

Igualmente he estudiado los *quipus* ó anales de que, aún a pesar del desprecio y la ignorancia, hasta hoy se encuentran algunas reliquias de ellos en templos arruinados, palacios destruídos y otros monumentos de la antigüedad. Los *quipus* verdaderamente se hubieran tenido como el más precioso tesoro de nuestras Indias, y servirán á la Historia de aquella luz que apenas hoy podemos demostrar en tan grande oscuridad y confusión de noticias si queremos averiguar los orígenes de aquella vasta monarquía. (547-587)

Llano Zapata's historiographical observations represented the beginning of a historical awareness which would be realized fully in the works by Eguiara y Eguren and Lorenzo Boturini. The historical-literary dimension is made manifest in that both Eguiara y Eguren and Boturini were able to establish two major eras in the cultural and literary history of Mexico and South America. They distinguished a pre-Columbian phase and another one initiated by the conquest and the colonization of the New World. These are not necessarily "periods" (a concept that was perfected by Hegel and that was used in the histories of the nineteenth century), but qualitatively different temporal stages that assume both a "before" and an "after". This was not a simple division if we consider the one-dimensional manner of organizing literary material in vogue at that time.

Furthermore, Boturini's *Ideas de una Nueva Historia General...* applied the principles of Giambattista Vico's *Scienza nuova* (1725, 1730) to heathen peoples. In line with European contributions to the science of history, Boturini organized the time line of indigenous cultures according to a series of laws. This organization imparted both to the discipline and the subject matter a systematization and rigor never before attained. The structure of Vico's *Scienza nuova* allowed Boturini to consider the indigenous historical process as one in which history is seen as the development of human societies and institutions. Boturini's particular interest in exploring in depth the remote, dark periods and in establishing a regularity in the temporal succession led him to apply the three ages institutionalized by Vico: the Age of Gods, the Age of Heroes, and the Age of Men. In this sense, Boturini's work, through the appropriation of Vico's contributions, introduced into the historical-cultural or historical-literary discourse a rigor which make it shift from a mere narration or record of facts to an interpretative discourse on the basis of a method. Likewise, he introduced the idea of the cyclical nature of human societies and the notion that the course of each culture could be different according to the conditions of each social group.

Consequently, Boturini's work remains clearly within the movement to defend the culture and history of "heathendom." In order to do so, he undertook, with a genuine scientific spirit, the compilation of all types of sources: testimonies, maps, codices, rare books, and manuscripts by Indian and Spanish authors. Thus, he created one of the richest collections of documents about ancient Mexican, Chichimec, Tecpanec, Tlaxcaltec, Tlatelolc, cultures from Michoacán, Maltlaltzinco, Huexotzinco, and Guadalupe. Furthermore, he grounded his study in a theoretical basis that enabled him to build, within the framework of Vico's work, a historical discourse that began to acquire the legitimacy of a science.

Regardless of our current understanding of scientific rigor in the social sciences, Vico's principles provided the framework for the methodic periodization of civilizations. This framework permitted an understanding of their evolution within a series of laws based on a secularized concept of history, far removed from the Medieval and Renaissance views of history in which history was made by kings. Yet, it would not be until the nineteenth century when the victorious historicism made possible a division of periods, according to the political and social history of each country. Vico's "course and resource" model was still inscribed within an overly abstract conception characteristic of the universalism of the Enlightenment.

As can be perceived in the catalogues and epitomes of the seventeenth century, temporal order was absent. There were attempts at periodization in the bibliothecae and histories of the eighteenth century, but the notion of the space or area that should be covered by the compilation of "literary" materials varied widely. Although there had always existed histories of regional demarcation, (chronicles about Peru, New Granada, New Spain, South and North America) side-by-side with a more continental view (seen in histories of the West Indies, Hispanic America and the New World) compilations by León Pinelo, Andreas Schott, and Nicolás Antonio included not only products and authors from the Indies (the Mainland, Brazil, and Florida) and Spain, but also from the New World understood in a broader sense, including even Ethiopia (at least in the case of Schott). León Pinelo's *Epitome* differentiates the general histories of Indies from the partial histories of Florida, New Mexico, New Spain, the Philippines, the Molucca Islands, the River Plate, Marañón, El Dorado and Santa Cruz of Brazil.

In contrast, the eighteenth-century bibliothecae, as in the case of Eguiara y Eguren, geographical space was more limited. He dealt only with Mexico. At the same time, he used a very lax notion of what was "Mexican" for it permitted the incorporation of Colombian, Venezuelan, Guatemalan, Honduran, Cuban, Peruvian and Puerto Rican authors, provided they had studied or lived in New Spain.

An emphasis on a regional approach was evident in the eighteenth century, especially in historical-literary or critical-bibliographic works. Perhaps it was a response to a greater meticulousness in the study of the realities that began to be defined as "countries" (*patrias*) or, possibly, the volume of materials was such that it demanded the specialization afforded by regions. In any case, the appearance of a *Bibliotheca Mexicana* in 1755 which spoke of "our Indians" and "our country" with a historical sense of the processed material was the semantic sign of a social group that felt able to lead and represent the destiny of a region's ethnic group.

As a consequence, we can conclude that the incipient geopolitical conditions that would serve as bases for later national cultures already existed during the colonial period. The continental and regional approaches seemed to coexist even in the nineteenth century, when the perspective that exalted national values to the detriment of a political and cultural Americanism began to prevail.

The bibliographical work carried out during the colonial period laid the foundations for *one* literary tradition. Yet, its existence does not preclude that of *another* tradition. Bibliographical work shaped a corpus based on a privileged concept of what should be literary (derived from certain printed books; the literary precepts of the European Renaissance; and the aura of the Christian, Spanish-speaking man of letters). Subsequent literary history has legitimized this corpus.

But, despite this heritage, we must recognize, as José Antonio Portuondo once said, that "Latin American literary historiography was born from the intent to strengthen the cultural personality of our lands, denied by some critics from the other side of the Atlantic Ocean" ("la historiografía literaria hispanoamericana nació del propósito de afirmar la personalidad cultural de nuestras tierras negada por ciertos críticos del otro lado del atlántico") (231). It is our duty to recover and systematize all the traditions of our America, precisely because they are ours.

NOTES

[1] With another slightly modified title, this essay in Spanish is one chapter of the prize-winning book entitled *La historiografía literaria del liberalismo hispanoamericano del siglo XIX.*

[2] In Spanish, *Epítome de una Biblioteca Oriental y Occidental náutica y geográfica, etc., en que se contienen los escritores de las Indias Occidentales especialmente del Perú, Nueva España, La Florida, el Dorado, Tierra Firme, Paraguay y Brasil, y el viaje a ellas, y los autores de navegación y sus materiales y apéndices.*

[3] For this essay, it has been very useful to apply the distinction made by Pierre Vilar between the *knowledge* of a subject and the *subject* of that knowledge. We understand by *subject* that which deserves to be known, that which is studied; and by *knowledge* of the same, the different ways to acquire wisdom about said subject. Thus, we will have different conceptions about what is historical, according to the apprehension of the subject, and thus, different ways to "historically" formalize that wisdom (see Vilar 17-47).

[4] "En las Indias Occidentales...se mandó que los jueces no consintieran ni permitieran que se imprimiese libro alguno que tratara materias de Indias, sin especial y previa licencia del Consejo de las mismas, ordenándoles que mandasen a recoger, con la mayor brevedad posible, todos los libros que se encontraran y prohibiéndose que librero algunos los vendiese ni imprimiese....Estaba prohibido mandar a las Indias libros

impresos en España o en el extranjero «que pertenezcan a materia de Indias, o traten de ellas, sin ser vistos y aprobados» por el Consejo."

[5] "Son sus bibliotecas los mejores tesoros que guarda Lima. Las públicas que yo he visto en Sevilla, que son las del señor Cardenal de Molina en el colegio San Acacio, la del señor Cardenal de Belluga en el Colegio Santa María de Jesús, y la de San Pablo en el Convento de la Orden de Predicadores, son muy diminutas en comparación con las de aquellos particulares. Esto no causará admiración al que contemplare que, así como (según los viajeros más verídicos y políticos más juiciosos) se han sepultado en el Mongol todas las riquezas de oro y plata de nuestras Indias, del mismo modo se han juntado en ellas (las bibliotecas americanas) los más singulares libros que venera la república de las Letras. Las ediciones...que hoy apenas se encuentran en Europa, no hay baratillo, ropavejería o tendejón en nuestra América, principalmente en Lima, donde no se encuentren."

[6] "muy lejos estábamos de pensar en este proyecto por hallarnos ocupados...cuando...vinieron a caer en nuestras manos las doce *Epístolas* del deán de la iglesia de Alicante don Manuel Martí....Comenzamos a penetrarnos de ellos...aunque nos dolíamos de ciertos ataques...encaminados al desprestigio de los españoles en los que toca al cultivo de las disciplinas literarias....Todo el empeño de su autor se cifra en disuadir al adolescente amigo Antonio Carrillo de su propósito de trasladarse a este Nuevo Mundo, y en aconsejarle...que fijase su residencia en Roma y se apartase lo más posible de las costas mexicanas. «Pero vamos a cuentas» —le dice—. «¿A dónde volverás los ojos en medio de tan horrenda soledad como la que en punto a las letras reina entre los indios? ¿Encontrarás, por ventura, no diré maestros que te instruyan, pero ni tratar con alguien, no ya que sepa alguna cosa, sino que se muestre deseoso de saberlas, o —para expresarme con mayor claridad— que no mire con aversión el cultivo de las letras? ¿Qué libros consultarás? ¿Qué bibliotecas tendrás posibilidad de frecuentar? Buscar allá tales cosas, tanto valdría como quere trasquilar a un asno u ordeñar a un macho cabrío.»...Es decir, que aún siendo las Indias Occidentales de tan grande extensión...se atrevió a señalar a México como el sitio de mayor barbarie del mundo entero, como país envuelto en las más espesas tinieblas de la ignorancia....Ocurriósenos la idea de consagrar nuestro esfuerzo a la composición de una *Biblioteca Mexicana*, en que nos fuese dado vindicar de injuria tan tremenda y atroz a nuestra patria y a nuestro pueblo, y demostrar que la infamante nota es...hija tan sólo de la ignorancia más supina."

[7] The original edition of this work was published in 189 pages, and more than 90 of them are devoted to the foreward and indexes. The edition

after 1737 by Francisco Martinez Abad was consulted for this essay. Facsimile edition by Carlos Sanz López (Madrid: 1973).

[8] In no case is the image of the historical process that is projected neutral. As Enrique Florescano states: "Because the reconstruction of the past is an operation performed in the present, the interests of those who decide and rule that present participate in the recovery of the past .... Thus in any time and place, the recovery of the past has primarily been political rather than scientific." ("En tanto que la reconstrucción del pasado es un operación que se hace a partir del presente, los intereses de los hombres que deciden y gobiernan ese presente intervienen en la recuperación del pasado....Así, en todo tiempo y lugar la recuperación del pasado antes que científica, ha sido primordialmente política.") In this way, the sixteenth century missionaries preferred to record the vile events of the pre-Hispanic style of living in order to expedite its fragmentation. The revolting Creoles in the early nineteenth century aired the dirty linens of the colonial times in public by exhibiting the greedy origins of the colonization; and the liberal historians, demanding a clean slate, established the vital origin of the nation in the Republic. ("De la memoria del poder a la historia como explicación" 93).

[9] "Los mexicanos cultivaron además la poesía, la retórica, la oratoria, la aritmética, la astronomía y otras disciplinas, de las que nos quedan los monumentos insignes y testimonios degnos de entero crédito .... Entre los cinco libros más importantes de la nación se contaban las 'Ruedas' pintadas con arte primoroso. Cada una de ellas abarcaba el espacio de un siglo, con perfecta distinción de años, meses, semanas y dias....Carlos Sigüenza y Góngora investigó los origenes mexicanos desde los tiempos más remotos, y mediante el examen de ls eclipses solares y lunares y otros raros fenómenos...puso de manifiesto la historia y acontecimientos del Imperio mexicano....En lo que a librerías se refiere no es extraño que los indios tuvieran cantidad de ellas....Una circunstancia que acrecía el mérito de estos libros mexicanos, era haber perpetuado, mediante representaciones figuradas, la cronología y exacta sucesión de los siglos de su historia.'

[10] I was able to consult this document thanks to the Brown University microfilm collection (Microfilm # HA-M214-21). The original document is available at the Biblioteca Nacional de Santiago de Chile, Collectio Medinensis, Biblioteca Americana "José Toribio Medina."

WORKS CITED

Benedetti, Mario. "La palabra, esa nueva cartuja." *El escritor lati-noamericano y la revolución posible*. Buenos Aires: Latinoamericana de Ediciones, 1977.

Cornejo, Polar. "*Discurso en loor de la poesía. Estudio y edición.*" *Letras* (Separata) 68-69 (1964).

Eguiara y Eguren, Juan José. *Biblioteca Mexicana*. Latin edition 1755. Span. trans. Agustín Millares Carlos. México: Fondo de Cultura Económica, 1944.

Florescano, Enrique. "De la memoria del poder a la historia como explicación." *Historia, ¿para qué?* México: Siglo XXI, 1980.

Foucault, Michel. *The Order of Things: An Archaeology of the Human Sciences*. New York: Vintage, 1973.

Gerbi, Antonello. *La disputa del Nuevo Mundo*. México: Fondo de cultura Económica, 1982.

González Stephan, Beatriz. *La historiografía literaria del liberalismo hispanoamericano el siglo XIX*. La Habana: Casa de las Américas, 1987.

León Pinelo, Antonio de. *Epítome de una Biblioteca Oriental y Occidental náutica y geografica, etc., en que se contienen los escritores de las Indias Occidentales especialmente del Perú, Nueva España, La Florida, el Dorado, Tierra Firme, Paraguay y Brasil, y el viaje a ellas, y los autores de navegación y sus materiales y apéndices*. 1629 Ed. Francisco Martínez Abad. 1737.

Llano Zapata, Juan Eusebio de. "La carta persuasiva al Señor Don Ignacio de Escandón sobre Assunto de Escribir la Historia-Literaria de la América Meridional." 1768. Lima: Oficina de los Niños Huérfanos 1769.

—. Letter to "Dr. Don Gregorio Mayáns y Siscar, Catedrático del Código de Justiniano en la Real Universidad de Valencia," Cádiz, 21 May 1758. Rpt. *Memorias Histórico-Físicas-Apologéticas de la America Meridional*. Lima: Imprenta y Librería de San Pedro, 1904.

Picón Salas, Mariano. *De la conquista a la independencia*. 1944. México: Fondo de Cultura Económica, 1978.

Quesada, Vicente G. *La vida intelectual en la América española durante los siglos XVI, XVII y XVIII.* Buenos Aires: Cultura Argentina, 1917.

Vilar, Pierre, *Iniciación al vocabulario del análisis histórico.* Barcelona: Grijalbo, 1980.

CHAPTER 9:
REPRESENTING THE COLONIAL SUBJECT

Iris M. Zavala

> A name is a word taken at
> pleasure to serve for a mark.
> —Hobbes

Before the end of the eighteenth century, as Foucault points out, language was primordially "representational." This quality was not questioned, and humankind's situation in nature and its limitations were part of an all-encompassing systematic, tabular-like ordering of knowledge. Knowledge was the sum of observations classified and categorized through language, a system of referential signs connected by logical operations suited to represent external reality. Furthermore, as Foucault adds, in the *episteme* of the sixteenth century, signification consisted of three components: the "marked" object (the signified), the "marker" (the signifier), and a presumed resemblance between the two. "Resemblance" was essential; knowledge could not be verified without some "real" link between signified and signifier.

Language was thus conceived as purely representational—a conception which lasted through the seventeenth and eighteenth centuries; the notion of resemblance was basic. This denoting structure was presented as a taxonomical compilation of conventional symbols operated by the mechanisms of a logic whose aim was to represent directly the reality perceived by the senses. The denoting, taxonomical conception of language was linked to natural history (see Adanson, Turgot and later Buffon). According to Foucault, naturalists, economists and grammarians employed the same rules to define the objects proper to their study. These were scientific "representations," or products dispersed throughout the natural history, economics, and philosophy of the classical period (see *The Order of Things*).

This general system is closely connected to the problem of the subject: in our specific line of questioning, the representation of the colonial subject from the sixteenth through the eighteenth century. My primary referent is the negative cultural identity expressed in a recognizably negative symbolic language of differences, organized as political constructions of enslavement and control as the dominant values of the field of objectivity of such discursive formation. I am fully aware that the concept of identity in a colonial society is rather ambiguous; therefore I am specifically addressing the question of how Americans (Indians) and the children of miscegenation experienced their own image as negative in contrast to that of the colonizers, using primarily Mexican sources. However, the reader could rightly conclude that throughout the Spanish Empire, the Indians, Creoles, and mulattoes generally felt that they possessed distinct identities, particularly because derogatory markers were widely used. In addressing the question of the constitution of the colonial subject as a formative part of the discourse of imperialism, I hope to avoid the pluralistic homogenization of "Third World" quite frequent in the work of many contemporary theorists.[1]

The problem of the representation of the colonial subject is directly linked to the distinction between the same and the "other." As André Thevet, a royal cosmographer in France and popular story teller in the sixteenth century wrote in his invented picturesque stories about North America, "It is not possible for any man to see all things in his lifetime [...] but God has given us a way to be able to represent them" (see *André Thevet's North America*). These marvels assigned the "exotic object" strange categories and fantastic constructs in accordance with the fabulous animals and beings which haunted the imagination of the conquerors in the New World, familiar with romances of chivalry, travel literature, medieval bestiaries, and classical mythology. America became the great oniric horizon just as the Orient had been the great reservoir for the Medieval Occident. Strange combinations of images were used to unravel the world of the "other" and its disquieting phantoms. Through the powers of contagion, the New World was perceived as populated by "fantastic" entities—fauna, flora, landscape, space, human beings—which were denoted according to "phantasmatic" taxonomies which had already been proved effective within the Medieval system. For example, Locke was exuberant in his description of the evolution and detailed scale of nature—fishes that had wings, birds which inhabited the water, animals so near to birds and beasts that they were between them both, brutes that seemed to have reason and knowledge, saying "we shall find everywhere that the several species are linked together, and differ but in almost insensible degrees" (qtd. Lovejoy 184). Travelers' narratives described fabulous beings, and the scientific preoccupation with the question of man's relationship with the anthropoids provoked "philosophical" interest in "savage races": the Hottentots or "stupid natives of Nova Zembla." In treating the scale of creatures some believed that in humankind itself there were several species and that "the Negroes who live about the Cape of Good Hope [are] the most beastlike of the sorts of men with whom our travelers are well acquainted," as Sir William Petty wrote in 1677 (qtd. Lovejoy 363). European supremacy was based on a cognitive function of contrast with the "other," and, in particular, on the qualitative difference between the "savage mind" and the negative representations of it.[2]

In what concerns the New World, the fabulations and exuberant descriptions specifically refer not only to the realm of imagination, but to what I call a *social imaginary* of mythical utopias (Thomas More's appeared in 1516), of an Eden before the Fall, which, in Lévi-Strauss's words, offered a Golden Age to anyone. Such was the *imperial gaze*. The simple formula was to translate a "libidinal economy" to the objective "real" denoted as an economic prospect; the New World was first a producer of precious metals while later, it supplied luxury and consumer products. Cultural referents and codes were invoked as authorities to justify and legitimize the conquest, while representing the colonial subjects as an inferior "race," with possibly dangerous mixtures of subjectivities. Within this field, the interrelation between representation and ideology was basic; the discourse about the New World and its subjects was produced through strategies, techniques and manipulations which dominated the field of objectivity justifying the legitimacy of the conquest and colonization. Lévi-Strauss points out that the colonists could not understand the Indians, and commission after commission was sent to inquire if they were descended from the lost tribes of Israel, or Mongols, or Scotsmen; if they had always been pagans; or if they were lapsed Catholics who had once been baptized by Saint Thomas. We can draw two conclusions, he adds, from the differences between the two methods of inquiry:

> the white men invoked the social, and the Indians the natural; and whereas the white men took the Indians for animals, the Indians were content to suspect the white men of being gods. One was as ignorant as the other, but the second of the two did more honour to the human race. (80)

I should like to stress an important component of addressing the question of the colonial subject and the imperial gaze of the conqueror's social imaginary, using as referents colonial historians who have undisputedly established the concept of the "invention" of America: the New World as an imaginary construct of the conqueror. The notion of "invention" (to create from anew) goes back to the early sixteenth century (c. 1510) when the historian Andrés Bernáldez called Columbus the "inventor of the Indies"[3] (*Historia de los Reyes Católicos don Fernando y doña Isabel* 679, qtd. in Maravall, *Estudios de historia del pensamiento español* 2: 426). Shortly afterwards, in an unpublished work whose manuscript is dated 1525, the humanist Fernán Pérez de Oliva specifically addressed the "discovery" as the "invention of the Indies." At the same time, in the first descriptions, the concept of "New World" (*Novus Orbis*), attributed to the historian Pedro Mártir de Anglería in a letter to Cardinal Sforza in 1493, was popularized through its use in the first chronicles, specifically those of Captain Gonzalo Fernández de Oviedo (1526) and Francisco López de Gómara (1552). Although written from differing points of view as to "who" discovered the New World, they both agreed on the different natures of the Indies and Europe. Gómara wrote that those regions were new because "all [their] things are different from ours," emphasizing a newness of nature.[4] By the end of the sixteenth century and especially in the seventeenth, some cosmographers and historians still established homologies between the "new" and cruelty, cannibalism, or human monstrosities: pygmies, giants, beings with no digestive tracts, half-fish half-humans. The image of the human body was the privileged topic of medical discourse, while classification of the savage rested on the notions of multiplication, association, deformation—never static representations (see Le Goff). However, scientific observation gained ground, and the empirical notion of "having witnessed with my own eyes" prevailed in the minute cataloguings and descriptive discourse of the New World.

Invention, imaginary constructs, fantasy and phantasmatic representations were all related to the fabulous tales of the "exotic" East as told by Marco Polo. From a no less negative perspective, as a historical marker the year 1492 represents the conquest of Granada, the expulsion of the Jews and the "discovery" of America—all signs of internal and external imperialism. Political remedies reached a virulent stage in Castile due to the continued existence of Jewish communities after the systematic policy of expulsion and to the prominence of the *conversos* who had attained positions within the executive branch of the government. Their presence in the government instigated the establishment of the Inquisition, whose operations began in Seville (1480). By 1483, the Supreme Council of the Inquisition was placed under the direct control of the Crown, with firm roots in Castile and with the necessary administrative organization to deal with New Christians (those Jews and Moriscos who were suspected of having covertly returned to their old beliefs). After the holy war, or Reconquest, ended in 1492 with the achievement of Spain's territorial unity, the victory was converted into the destruction of the infidel; religious zeal and the process of economic gains strengthened the divine mission. The "colonial subjects" were referred to as "new," juridically speaking, after 1525: the "Old Christians" and the "New Christians." Religious, economic, social, political and racial signifiers converged in the raptures of imperial grandeur.

This imposition of a unity (what will later be called "One Monarch, One Empire, and One Sword," revitalized later by Franco) was supported by technologies of knowledge: judicial, linguistic, cultural. In these circumstances, denotative language redirected representations to a social imaginary based on negative referents. Grammarians, humanists, theologians and politicians concurred in their emphasis of one point: racial marginalization and exclusion based on sexual, moral or physical traits. Cervantes's *Don Quijote* would later reinvert the referents through the device of inscribing various authors, one of them Moorish. Cide Hamete could not possibly be the author, and he "lies" because all Moors are liars (a racial cliché to the present). Within this coherent constitution of an economic program, the opposition between "old" and "new" was indeed an imperial marker (signifier) of colonial identities, specifically as the virulent "purity of blood" (*limpieza de sangre*) legislation was enforced against Jews and Moriscos in the Peninsula, the Society of Castes was imported into the New World, and laws were faithfully enforced in the colonies against miscegenation. The state-based society of estates of late medieval Castile was imposed upon the multiracial colonies. If by royal decree of

1501 the Indians were "people who were far from possessing reason," by the seventeenth and eighteenth centuries
discriminatory policies became stronger against *mestizos*,
and *mulattos*. Illegitimacy and the stigma of slavery placed
the *castas* at the lower end of the scale of classification, as
pointed out by Mörner in his excellent synoptic study of
race relations. Because rhetorical inventions must be
studied within the context of their history and the technologies conditioning ideological formations, we must
analyze the linguistic and institutional representations of
the New World in terms of a cultural text. Within this
concrete historical situation, difference and alterity constituted strategies of exploitation, exclusion and representation with a chain of signifiers: "Old" World/"New"
World; Christian/infidel; purity (*limpieza de sangre*)/
impurity; decadence/vigor; morality/licenciousness; brav-
ery/ cowardice.

These technologies of knowledge historically found
support in the natural sciences and in a representational
(denotative) language theory, subtexts (*pre-texte*) of a mul-
tidirected representation of the colonial subject. As early as
the fifteenth century, Girolamo Fracastoro's poem *Syphilis*
(1530), which coined the name we still use for this sexually
transmitted disease, was soon blamed in the popular
imagination (through a "fictive" control) for the alleged
sexual proclivities of the Indians and the passion of the
sailors commissioned by Ferdinand and Isabelle. Physi-
cians attributed the plague to the New World, and Fracastoro (as Eatough has demonstrated[5]) interwove two
myths—that of the Holy Wood (Guaiacum), and that of
the mercury cure—using as a vehicle the classical myth of
Syphilis, the Shepherd. This strategy directly linked the
epic themes of the Discovery with allusive mirrors of Atlantis and the horrors of human sacrifice by the Aztecs and
island cannibals. Through this mythological "borrowed
language" (to use Marx's term; see *The Eighteenth Brumaire*), Fracastoro puts forward the "American thesis," or
the belief that the Americans were the source of the
scourge. The borrowed language of mythology, which had
been the authoritative support in historical and cos-
mographical discourse to represent newness (the Garden

of Eden, the ancients' Golden Age, the Fountain of Youth, Atlantis, the Gardens of the Hesperides, the pastoral poems, the Spanish Crown equivalent to the greatness of the classical world), could also be manipulated for representations of negative identities. Many intellectuals had worked from narratives of this sort; Fracastoro is not a unique example of fictive manipulation to represent the degeneration of the other in medical science. Such a theory of "degeneration" would later be re-articulated by Cornelius de Pauw, who would give a negative representation of the Conquest (an anti-Spanish discourse) as a result of the sexual plague:

> Man already overwhelmed, found, by the burden of this existence the height of misfortune, the germs of his death in the arms of pleasure and at the breast of joy.

> L'homme déjà accablé du fardeau de son existence, trouva, pour comble d'infortune, les germes de la mort entre le bras du plaisir et au sein de la jouissance. (*Recherches philosophiques sur les Américains ou memoirs intéressants pour servir l'histoire de l'espèce humaine*, 2 vols., Berlin, 1768-69 qtd. in Marchetti I, p.v.)

Such supporting fictions had been worked out previously during the Reconquest and after the fall of Granada. In the same way that the Muslims (derogatively referred to as Moorish, or *moros*) had been frequently represented as licentious, lascivious, and having body odors; both "Indians" and Muslims were often represented through sexual "irregularities" or "aberrant" sexual practices (sodomy), with poignant signifiers inferring impure menstrual blood. Examples of such fictive narratives abound during the seventeenth century. A privileged example would be a pamphlet by Juan de Quiñones (1632) about an *auto de fé* against Francisco de Andrada, who suffered blood discharges. Indians were prone to such a disease, he concluded, for three "logical" reasons: they were lazy, fearful and tired. Their melancholic humors multiplied, which brought on the wrath of God. Such blood discharges from the back are a sign of "perpetual ignominy and disgrace" (una señal perpetua de ignominio y oprobio). Indians "smelled" and were a "rebellious caste." The same author wrote a small treatise in 1631 against the Gypsies in homologous terms. Furthermore, he added the marker of witchcraft and spying, which made them "worse than the Moorish" (see Zavala).

By the eighteenth century such "popular" narratives written not only in erudite prose but also in the popular *romance* meter multiplied. The romance meter indicated a poet's control over mnemotechnic strategies, specific social auditories, and modes of production (learning the rhyme by heart and repeating it to other audiences, quite common in oral cultures). For example, in popular narratives about Jews, there were allusions to mass ritual murders (the killings of six priests and crucifixion of nine children), while others mentioned the burning of religious images. A third case described the romantic experiences of a princess in dialogue with the story of the "Jew with a pound of flesh" (a popularized *Merchant of Venice*? Shylock's pound of flesh?). In all of these cases, the inscribed sociogram utilized the same intertextual signifiers. No less a denotative signifier is that of the black slave during the eighteenth century. An example, again in the form of a *romance* is the story of Pedro de Guzmán, who not only tried to rape the white maids of the household, but, incapable of carrying out his will, finally killed them, while also doing away with three children. The oppositional markers are the unbridled passion of the slave and the triumphant chastity of the women. While the women prefer to die rather than surrender to his lechery, the slave is portrayed as a homicidal psychopath, blinded with lust and rage.

Exclusion as ideological and social practice was frequent in the sixteenth and seventeenth centuries through juridical, economic and cultural representations (see Redondo). The silenced discourses came from minorities: Muslims, Jews, and Gypsies, who were often accused of witchcraft and demonology. Somber colorings frequently fell on women, often represented as having intercourse with the Devil, and other sexual aberrations. This discursive formation inscribed the fears of venereal diseases and combined them with asepsis to claim the moral cleanliness of the social body. As a product of technology, and in the name of the biological and natural sciences, this discourse justified the racism of the State, grounding them in religious and social truths (see Foucault's chapter "Scientia Sexualis" in *History of Sexuality*).

Representation and "mirror" are closely interwoven with the signifier and the technological power of the signifier to impose scientific taxonomies as a vision of the reality it seems to articulate. This representational practice, as appropriation of a narrative, is basic in the often quoted *Eighteenth Brumaire*: "they cannot represent themselves, they must be represented." In terms of our specific colonial signifier and its inscription in the cultural text, it must be read in light of exclusion, exploitation, and marginalization: a silenced discourse. The identity of the colonized subject was thus represented through the power of a borrowed language, introduced by technologies of knowledge: the authorities of myths (as in Fracastoro's poem), the authority of theology, of science and of rhetoric. All of these refer to the manipulation of discourse through narrative strategies. By the eighteenth century, and due to the emergent new sciences and their taxonomies, the colonized American subject would be represented through signifiers from the natural sciences with a borrowed language originating in the popular *Histoire naturelle, générale et particulière, avec la description du Cabinet du Roi*, written by Jean Louis Leclerc, count of Buffon, and widely read in Spain and the colonies. This authority rendered Buffon's pages on America and the Americans the "borrowed language" of the colonizer's signifier. This natural history was a product of the new philosophical, genealogical, and analytical spirit of natural reality and the faith in the methods of empirical observation in the formation of experience: a creative act issuing forth a unique, totalizing, hegemonic form of truth. Empiricism was the philosophical method taken to support scientific inquiry. It also accounted for a conception of knowledge based on "association" (Hume) by resemblance and contiguity in time and space: a study of humankind through the law of association.

Within this conception of knowledge based on the natural sciences, the associations and contiguities led to a technology of observing, dissecting and re-ordering objects (facts) according to mental imaginary constructs, which would then be inserted in the all-encompassing, systematic, ordering of knowledge. Buffon's borrowed language projected an identity of the New World as weak, indifferent, incapable of progress (modernity), because the Americans (Indians) were limited to the satisfaction of immediate needs. In his words:

> all natural Americans were, or still are, savages; Mexicans and Peruvians have been so recently brought under orderly government that they should not be considered an exception. Whatever the origin of these savage nations is, it must be common to all.

> tous les Américains naturels étoient, ou sont encore, sauvages, les Mexicaines et les Péruviens étoient si nouvellement policés qui'ils ne doivent pas faire une exception. Quelle que soit donc l'origine de ces nations sauvages, elle paroit leur être commune à toutes. (VI, 1752 [(5)], 305)

Thus, through the technology of natural science, Buffon constructs the identity of the colonized subject as a *sauvage* or inferior race. This "savage state" is the basic construct of his "racist anthropology," as Gliozzi calls it (see also Hanke, *Aristotle and the American Indian*). He is not the only one. Fontenelle defended European supremacy and was no admirer of primitivism, unlike Rousseau, as Le Goff reminds us.

It is worthwhile to turn to historical semantics to interrelate the concepts of representation and imaginary to the construction of the colonized subject. In a classic article, philologist Leo Spitzer derived the modern concept of "race" (which was introduced by Carl Linnaeus, *Systema natural*) from the Medieval Latin *ratio*. This term had a polysemy of referents in the Medieval reception of Platonism: "idea" (*rationesrerum*) and subsequently "*Ratio*," the creative idea of the universe, the hegemonic unity of humanity (see *Essays in Historical Semantics*). These *rationes* (types) of humankind were the concrete assemblage of Buffon, according to a racial (racist) anthropology. His taxonomical model was based on binary oppositions: *sauvage/policé*, race/nation. His signifier signified as follows: *état sauvage* codified as race; *état policé/état de civilisation* codified as nation (see Marchetti 19). The binary opposition nature/culture denied the possibility of social organization—modernity, technology, knowledge, language, morality—to the state of nature. The *sauvage* was thus a degenerating species, since humankind was originally white, as Buffon asserted in his important empirical taxonomy *Variétés dans l'espèce humaine*.

> thus, white seems to be the primitive color of Nature, that climate, food, and customs alter and change to yellow, brown, or black.

> Le blanc paront donc être la couleur primitive de la Nature, que le climat, la nourriture et les moeurs altèrent et change, et même jusqu'aun jaune, au brun ou au noir. (VI, 1752 [(5)]:293-94)

These images or representations of the colonial subject were popularized at the end of the colonial period in New Spain through "didactic" illustrations which legitimized the construct of the subject. Seen from this angle, illustrations (paintings, woodcuts, engravings) were summoned as impressions of mentality, as "collective memories": the product of an encounter between the natural sciences and the constructions of subjects. Such icons were directly linked as formative experiences in the racist anthropology of the colonizer's signifier; they appear, from our contemporary perspective, as the loci of the violence of the constitution of the colonial subject. They were discourses about the colonial world and its dominant language in which fanciful variations (linguistic imaginings) were introduced wherever possible, breaking scientific frontiers (biological species) and substituting the "real" with bizarre nomenclature. They were a delirious discourse which made abundant use of the grotesque and an official monologism which pretended to possess a ready-made truth. Strengthened since the Conquest by control over language (naming and marking natural species) and through contiguities and correspondences (what modern anthropology calls a system of relationships) with the mythological arcane, the contiguities of human taxonomies produced "trans-species" equivalences for the signified: hybrids, mutations from animals and human beings, genetic drifts or human travesties creating a hierarchical valorizing distance, or cross-markers between peoples.

The signifiers of the colonizer's social imaginary produced phantasmatic beings through the borrowed language of mythologies and theologies and teleologies. This taxonomical science reduced the "other," the "subject," to a common negative denominator, to markers which would account for social behaviors that fell outside the law (both natural and judicial), yet which could then be resolved by the judiciary system. Medical discourse, judicial discourse and cultural discourse distributed and institutionalized the colonial signifier. We are dealing with a multiplicity of discourses produced by a whole series of mechanisms operating in different institutions. As a historical signifier, the date of 1492 had been organized around the theme of (one) religion and (one) social structure and resulted in a discourse which was markedly unitary and monological. Whatever endangered this "relative" uniformity and its reproduction was broken, scattered. Distinct discursivities of control took form in demography, biology, medicine, ethics and pedagogy. They were technologies of knowledge aimed at adjusting tensions or conflicts within a network in order to contain proliferating discourses. The ethnic denominator was the most intense focus of representation; it was under constant surveillance. The non-European population was always questioned, frequently as an "unnatural" (primitive) or savage stage in the field of sexuality, by all the agencies of control and mechanisms of reproducing imaginary representations. The point we will consider is the form of imaginary power that was exercised, which grounded racism in scientific truth.

The most popularized social taxonomy of the New World population was called the *castas*. Etymologically, it referred to "animal species," by 1500 to "race or lineage of men," and by 1513 to "class, type or condition." Originally applied to the Hindu Indian caste hierarchy, the Portuguese expanded its polysemy throughout all modern languages as "a social class deprived of mixture and contact with the others." While in the New World it carried negative connotations, in the Peninsula it connotes Castilian mythologizations: "historical caste"/Castile/ *castizo/casticismo*. Within the taxonomies of the Americans (Indians), it served the purpose of emphasizing the difference between the physiology of reproduction and the scientific theories of "savages," who were outside the laws of civilized society and social behavior, by bringing to light through signifiers the "unnatural," "degenerate" biology of the mixed American population. One such power mechanism of the authoritative carnivalesque that borrowed language from the colonial signifier was a racial model of New Spain conceived as follows (qtd. León).[6]

1. Spaniard and Indian woman = *mestizo*
2. Mestizo and Spanish woman =*castizo*
3. *Castizo* woman and Spaniard = Spaniard
4. Spanish woman and Negro (sic) = Mulatto
5. Spaniard and Mulatto woman = Moorish
6. Morisco woman and Spaniard = Albino
7. Spaniard and Albino woman = a "throwback" (*Torna atrás* or *Salta atrás*)
8. Indian and *Torna atrás* woman = wolf (*Lobo*)
9. Wolf and Indian woman = *Zambayo, Zambaigo, Zambo*
10. *Zambayo* and Indian woman = *Cambujo*
11. *Cambujo* and Mulatto woman = *Albarazado*
12. *Albarazado* and Mulatto woman = *Barcino*
13. *Barcino* and Mulatto woman = coyote (*Coyote*)
14. *Coyote* woman and Indian = *Chamizo*
15. *Chamizo* woman and Mestizo = *Coyote mestizo*
16. *Coyote mestizo* and Mulatto woman = "there you are." (*Allí te estás.*)

Such genealogies of the colonial subject as an ethnic amalgam were frequently portrayed through literary prototypes and visual iconography as didactic representations at the end of Vice-Royalty of New Spain. Special mention should be made of three important Mexican colonial paintings: the octogonal work of Luis de Mena, "Castas"; another by Miguel Cabrera (1763); and sixteen *recuadros* by Andrés de Islas (1774), all in the Museum of America in Madrid. Finally, in the Museum of Man (Paris), another painting illustrates the *apache*. The taxonomy found in such colonial paintings both in the Historical Museum (Mexico) and the Museum of America (Madrid) include a few more signifiers:

17. Wolf and Chinese woman = *Jíbaro*
18. Cambujo and Indian woman = *Zambayo*
19. *Zambayo* and Wolf woman = *Calpamulato*
20. *Calpamulato* and *Cambujo* woman = "suspended in the air" (*Tente en el aire*)
21. *Tente en el aire* and Mulatto woman = "I don't understand you" (*No te entiendo*)
22. *No te entiendo* and Indian woman = a "throwback" (*Torna atrás*)

The paintings respect the hierarchy of the scale of classification as well as the dress legislation. The prototypes emerge as historical inscriptions of the caste system and negatively illustrate the pragmatics of the 1770s directed to prevent socially unequal marriages. The New Spain courts (*audiencia*) asked for special orders to prohibit priests from marrying people belonging to *castas*, especially forbidding mixtures with blacks. In Viceroy Revillagigedo's words in 1794: [Negroes sic] "have disfigured and deteriorated the Indian caste in many ways and have given rise to all ugly castes that can be seen in these kingdoms" (qtd. Mörner, 69). While artificial, the *castas* illustrated by these paintings were representative of the concern with genealogy as a pluridirected monologic discourse.

An etymological explanation is necessary to grasp the carnival images and the significance of these homologies. *Zambayo* means "zambaio" or crossed-eyed, and in the sense of Indian or black is "medically explained" in the sixteenth century by the anatomical singularity of the blacks, portrayed with crossed-legs. Other metonymical freed signifiers, such as "*chamizo*," "*albino*," "*calpamula-to*," "*morisco*" were based on shades of complexion (the "*color quebrado*"); others were zoological, deliberately derogatory—"coyote," "mule," "wolf," "cow"; while yet others directly alluded to the intricate fluctuations of conceived "advances" and "retreats" of the population. Especially where Indian and black blood was dominant, the names denoted scorn, contempt, mockery. Such were the representations of the multiple imperial gaze.

The carnival images of miscegenation acquired a Baroque complexity in the association and fusion of European and Indian, black, and Chinese, creating a visible spectacle of shades and complexions and forming bizarre composites of human types, pigments, languages and psychologies. Beginning with the *Leyes de Indias* of 1680, Spanish laws accepted such an amalgam by creating both prototypes in rudimentary combinations and a maze of designations and gradations within an "imaginary" system of nomenclatures which vary geographically; markers are not homogeneous. Shades of complexion and shape of the nose, lips, head, and body structure served as inspiration for the intended humorous or insulting signifiers of phenotypes resulting from mixtures, captured by the imperial gaze. Fragmentation and carnival images of laughter coincide with messianic overtones by suggesting a simultaneity of systems of control and hierarchization. Representation here is a delirious discourse on power to the authoritative monologue which possesses a ready-made truth. Laughter is here not the freedom of the Bakhtinian carnivalesque but the "madness" of "the infinity of non-nature" (to borrow from Foucault).[7]

In another sense, this "discourse of madness" is the artificial arrangement of reality. This "laughing madness" (the experience of "reasoned unreason," or Goya's "The dream of reason produces monsters," as I would call it) was a method to turn the colonial subject into monological descriptions and prescriptions. Differences were homogenized. We will recall that Orientals in Mexico—as C. R. Boxer emphasizes—were called *chinos*, whether they were Filipino, Japanese, Indonesian, Indochinese, Indian or really Chinese. In other cases, the "borrowed language" used had as referents the prejudiced misnomers used in the Peninsula: *ladino, morisco*. These images were a strange carnival hell; the colonial subject was fragmented, transformed into signifiers of deformities—extremities, protruding organs, enormous noses or humps—as markers of inferior nature (such as in the well-known seventeenth-century satirical sonnet by Quevedo on the nose, a metonymy for Jew). This discourse of laughing madness aims at the decline of the Empire; at what an early economist (*arbitrista*) Martín González de Cellórigo referred to in 1600 as a disoriented society enticed away by false values—a society of "the bewitched, living outside the natural order of things" ("una república de hombres encantados que viven fuera del orden natural"). Madness was the marker for the decline. In terms of the colonial signifier, it is interesting to compare that the "transspecies" combinations in these hybrid populations are normally the product of Indians and blacks with another mixture. A new "metamorphosis" opened up to biological and evolution technologies; this "Scale of Nature" whose project was to distribute all living beings, animal or vegetable, into a hierarchy of collective units, was an artificial classification. However, it had elements in common with classical sources, such as the borrowed language of Ovid's *Metamorphoses*, which was quite influential reading in the seventeenth century, as it was a period acutely aware of the changes and transformations to which all things are subject. The re-creation of the myth within the new natural sciences suited contemporary conventions and social values. There can be no misunderstanding that the freed signifiers convey movement or elocutionary acts while in the atmosphere of a scientific constative statement. Or, put in other terms, these illustrations indicate the problematic nature of rhetoric: how an ideal rhetoric of using words could lose contact with truth, for it could be put to purposes of deception. If we keep in the foreground the canonical Aristotelian discussion of rhetoric, what emerges are the devices of signifiers which point to rhetoric as a power which could be misused at a level of classification.

The borrowed language and the combination of signifiers in the racial models were reinforced by the growing number of *mestizos*, viewed by the Spaniards as a potential threat to their own economic domination. The attempt to pass for a white European became widespread in the expanding number of occupations and in the diversified economy. To be sure, these mocking, derogatory identities of the colonial subject—within the geographical varieties—were to privilege several forms of access to property and occupations: the ownership of mines, land, and cattle, as well as access to professions in trade and the bureaucracy. The criteria of purity of blood and phenotype were reinforced to limit membership in the elite, and the technologies of control were strengthened. From the onset of the conquest, Indians had been either exterminated, or else turned into vassals of inferior state who lacked the faculty of reason.[8] But "passing for" was the problem in this "pigmentocracy" (to use the Chilean historian Alejandro Lipschutz's witty term) in the last years of the colony; policies of segregation and enforcement of dress codes point to the growing assimilation, feared by the *encomenderos* and the Crown. As the royal attorney of the Mexican *audiencia* wrote in 1770: "the liberty with which the plebes have been allowed to choose the class they prefer, insofar as their color permits, has stained the class of natives as well as that of the Spaniards" (qtd. Mörner 69; this book offers ample examples). Privileges and lower tributes as well as social mobilization were the goals.

These images of the "other" obey categories of natural history, which prop up the representation of the colonial subject in terms of artificial "trans-species," trans-conceptual entities, linking animals, geographies and verbal constructs. The lexical categorizations illuminate the imperial (political) motives through which the colonizer sought to represent American society (family structure, social foundation) as simple lawlessness, both from a theological and a judicial angle. These are constructs of the cultural imagination, using a borrowed language to articulate a whole dimension of a signified—the colonial subject—by the manipulation of power through an apt control of scientific technology (natural sciences, grammar). Such fields of knowledge were built into an iconography representing judicial and therefore penal control through imaginary constructs. As such, it was a force aspiring to dominance over colonial society. Such iconographies aimed at capturing the attention of the populace and imposing the views of the European (not only Spanish) signifier on that populace. The collective notions contained by the signifier were devised to legitimate the monopoly of power and the social (and moral) hierarchy because, as was made clear in the fundamental work by Buffon, the stages of culture and civilization belonged to *nations*, not to *races* of the "*état sauvage.*" A devaluation of nature was interwoven into a supporting fiction that argues against humankind and culture(s) in the New World. "New" was linked to a moral and social hierarchy in binary opposition: new/old, imperfect/perfect, primitive/civilized. The elocutionary forces of such a taxonomy were both constative and denotative and were a tactical alliance to introduce order and to establish a principle that would distribute population according to boundaries and a fixed hierarchy, techniques which had been aptly used as an agency of regulation with the *conversos* or New Christians. At work in this taxonomy was a juridical representation which legitimized relations of power and reinforced the consolidation of the social body of the State.

Such taxonomies, popularized in narratives (*historias*), historical accounts (*relaciones*), news, ballads (*romances*), fictional prose and iconography, were based on an imaginary identity (or associative link) between the appropriator and the appropriated to make representation necessary. The result was the polemical cultural text of Francisco Xavier Clavijero, who distinguished New World human types as follows: The Indians or Americans, the Europeans, the Asians, and the Africans residing in those lands. From this plurality, emerge the *Creoles* (children of the Europeans) and the mixed races called *castas* by the Spanish: the descendants of Europeans and Americans, Europeans and Africans, and Africans and Americans (IV [1781] 160 qtd. Marchetti 57).

Such metalanguages on cultural texts were based on binary correspondences (homologies): a shared cultural identity expressed in recognizable symbolic negative language. Language and symbol were employed as political tools to increase power and impose a colonial identity aiming at a political construction of an inferior, enslaved collectivity. The symbolic activity of the discourse aimed at a mythical construction of the colonial subject as a primitive, archetypal difference to be trapped in hierarchies and traditions. The subject was represented by this borrowed language, losing him-/herself like an object; the flow of negative images dissipated subjectivity through derogatory symbols and lexicon. The relation of the subject to the signifier was embodied in a negative enunciation. It was a disjunction of identity which reduced the colonial subject to a common denominator of imaginary social experiments in order to legitimate Imperial hegemony at a time (the end of the Viceroyalties) when the most acute and profound critiques of land tenement—*latifundia*—and its socio-economic deformations were being produced. One such critique came from the Bishopric of Michoacán in 1799. According to Manuel Abad y Queipo, of the four and one-half million inhabitants of New Spain (Spaniards, Indians, castes), the Spanish represented one-tenth of the population "and they alone hold almost all the property and riches of the Crown" (qtd. Florescano 134).[9] The parodic travesties of subjectivities that we enumerated were aimed at subjugating the colonial subject, and ironically, they were created at precisely the time (end of the eighteenth century) when the epic grandeur of the imperial destiny was disintegrating. In 1813, after the War of Independence was finally won, the caste taxonomy was abolished at a time when the laughing madness of social taxonomy was taking hold. The striking image which comes to mind is Marx's *The Eighteenth Brumaire*:

> Men make their own history, but they do not make it just as they please; they do not make it under circumstances chosen by themselves, but under circumstances directly encountered, given and transmitted by the past. The tradition of all the dead generations weighs like a nightmare on the brain of the living.[10]

Thus, after 1813 the colonial signifier and its representations were devoid of a referent. The colonial subject
re-appropriated language; the "subversion of the subject"
brought forth the deliverance of the imprisoned meaning.

NOTES

[1] I refer to a contemporary tendency to use "Third World" as an extremely general and confusing categorization grounded on non-qualified
notions of "nation," "nationalization," "class," as practiced by Jameson
(For critiques of Jameson, see Ahmad). Spivak, and Radakrishnan tend
to use the term "Third World" without geographical qualifications, in
a homogenizing whole. The reader should clearly conclude that I
specifically refer to "Third World" in terms of the following key questions: *who?*, *what?*, *when?*, which are basic to the contextualization of
technologies and utterances.

It is also important to stress within this general problem of subject
representation, the representation of the colonizer in Aztec chronicles
which projects another image. This image alluded to strangeness and
strength, since the teleological projection the Aztecs developed was
grounded in the myth of Quetzalcóatl. Therefore, theirs was a
representation of gods with strange dress and strong armaments, since
the Europeans had superior military technology (see León Portilla).
Prophecy, divination and magic were the sources of the representative
language of the Indian culture (see Todorov's, *La conquête de
l'Amérique: la question de l'autre*, a book which otherwise is a Eurocentric "new invention" of America, and Lévi-Strauss 80).

[2] Incidentally, the texts on the constitution of the subject I am
reconsidering indicate overwhelmingly that Americans lacked the capacity to reason to such an extent that, because of their inferiority, no
Indians were included in the Mexican Inquisitional Tribunal in 1601.
Moreover, they were in fact exempt from the jurisdiction of the Holy
Office, on the grounds that they were too low on the scale of humanity
to receive faith. Such a Eurocentric conceptualization should raise
questions on the contemporary debate over modernity and postmoder-
nity, and the "rational" stand of modernity.

[3] Bernáldez linked the New World with a utopia, since Indians lived in
a "golden age." Incidentally, Bernáldez was a stern defender of the
monarchy's policies towards the Moriscos.

[4] Pérez de Oliva's manuscript was found at Yale University and published by José J. Arrom, ed. *Historia de la invención de Indias*. Bogotá: Instituto Caro y Cuervo, 1965. For an analysis from differing points of view on Fernández de Córdoba and Oviedo, see Maravall, *Antiguos y modernos* (Chapter 5) and O'Gorman, *La idea del descubrimiento de América*, who emphasizes Oviedo's messianic imperialism. O'Gorman's thesis prompted a reply from Marcel Bataillon (see Bataillon and O'Gorman).

The bibliography on colonial history is overwhelming; for basic reading see Elliott, Gerbi, and Chaunu. Needless to say, both the "encounter" and the conquest prompted the development of historiography; some histories embraced derogatory terms while others were grounded in humanism. In the eighteenth century some Spanish *ilustrados* criticized the conquest, and it became a political issue which served as a dividing line between what we would now term "conservatives" and "liberals" (see Hanke, *La lucha española por la justicia en la conquista de América*).

[5] The Brazilian sociologist Gilberto Freyre reinverts the term syphilis and equates "syphilization" and "civilization."

[6] This taxonomy, also found in paintings in Madrid and Mexico, is discussed in Mörner and Vázquez. See the excellent catalogues of the Museo de América, *Mestizaje Americano*, and García Sainz.

Mörner offers another classification from the Peruvian Vice-Royalty not less Baroque, although more *mathematical*: *mestizo, cuarterón de mestizo, quinterón, requinterón, mulatto, cuarterón de mulatto, quinterón, requinterón*, (58). In other places, they were called *pardos* (Venezuela), or else *rayado, jarocho, sambo, prieto, tresalbo*. Mörner also points that in 1700 the term "morisco" was forbidden, as not to confuse the Spanish *morisco* with the New World *casta*. Within this context, it is important to stress that Africans were imported to Perú soon after the conquest to exploit silver mines. By the seventeenth century, there were around 30,000 blacks in Lima integrated into society (see Bowser). Still today, *moreno, prieto, cholo*, and *roto* are derogatory terms in Latin American countries.

[7] It seems pertinent to stress that "carnival laughter" is here the opposite of Bakhtin's seminal term in his analysis of Rabelais, since it is aimed at enslaving, not freeing. This negative inversion of carnival is worth considering. I adapt from Foucault's *Madness and Civilization*. I hope it is clear that I am historizing Foucault's concepts in the context of Cellórigo's perception, closely related to Cervantes's referential model for *Don Quijote*, whose first part was published five years afterwards.

[8] There are obvious patterns which connect racial prejudices in America with the Reconquest, however, it is highly improbable to sustain that

"blood purity" was used to distinguish the orthodoxy of *españolidad* from the infidel, as suggested by Root, who obviously confused *casta/castizo* with *españolidad*. There are important accounts of the *casta* system in works by Leonard, Woodbridge, Diggs, Martínez-Alier (who reproduces a *dictamen* given in Mexico in 1752 on unequal marriages involving a person's class or race or both), Boxer (an essential work about Portuguese colonies in Africa and Brazil), and Stein and Stein (see specifically Chapter 3 of *The Colonial Heritage*).

Boxer reminds us that since few women were taken to the colonies, miscegenation was frequent until it was juridically controlled. It seems that no woman was carried in the first and second voyages, while the 1,500 men who were left behind in the second trip were killed by the Arawaks, a Caribbean population which was soon annihilated because of illnesses, starvation and overwork. West who demonstrates impressively that the Arawak Indian population numbered as many as four million. Most Caribbean islands, however, were virtually abandoned around the 1520s, except as staging posts for the silver fleets, until the early seventeenth century, when northern Europeans settled in some of them, while introducing sugar as a crop and black slaves as the main workforce. Mörner suggests that if the figures of the pre-Colombian Indian population are correct (around fifty million or more), "the demographic disaster that took place in the New World after 1492 is probably without counterpart in the history of mankind" (12).

[9] Abad y Queipo figures among the few who spoke in favor of the *castas* and explained that if they behaved badly, it was due to discrimination and poverty. The truth is that it became progressively harder to distinguish *mestizos* from Spaniards due to assimilation and acculturation in the early nineteenth century.

[10] Indian and mestizo revolts (people of *color quebrado*) were vital before the Wars of Independence and the discriminatory laws were abolished. Venezuela, the first Spanish American nation to declare its independence in 1811, had in its constitution: " [the *Pardos*] are to enjoy the natural and civil reputation and to cover the inalienable rights that correspond to them as to all other citizens" (qtd. Mörner 82).

WORKS CITED

Ahmad, Aijaz. "Jameson's Rhetoric of Otherness and the 'National Allegory.'" *Social Text* 17 (1987): 3-25.

André Thevet's North America: A Sixteenth-Century View. Trans. Roger Schlesinger and Arthur P. Stabler. Toronto: McGill-Queen's Univ. Press, 1987.

Bataillon, Marcel and Edmundo O'Gorman. *Dos concepciones de la tarea histórica con motivo del descubrimiento de América*. México: UNAM, 1955.

Bowser, Frederick P. *El escalvo africano en el Perú colonial: 1524-1650*. México: Siglo XXI, 1977.

Chaunu, Pierre. *Conquista y explotación de los nuevos mundos (siglo XVI)*. Barcelona: Nueva Clío, 1972-73.

Corominas, Joan. *Diccionario crítico etimológico de la lengua castellana*. 4 vols. Bern, 1954.

Eatough, Geoffrey, ed. *Fracastoro's "Syphilis."* Liverpool: Francis Cairns, 1984.

Elliott, John H. *The Old World and the New: 1492-1650*. Cambridge: Cambridge Univ. Press, 1971.

Florescano, Enrique. *Origen del desarrollo de los problemas agrarios de México: 1500-1821*. México: Era, 1971.

Foucault, Michel. *History of Sexuality. Vol. I: An Introduction*. Trans. Robert Hurley. New York: Vintage, 1980.

—. *Madness and Civilization*. Trans. Richard Howard. New York: Pantheon, 1965.

—. *The Order of Things: An Archeology of the Human Sciences*. Trans. of *Les motes et les choses*. New York: Vintage, 1973.

García Saiz, Mª Concepción. *La pintura colonial en el Museo de América (I): La escuela mexicana*. Madrid: Ministerio de Cultura, 1980.

Gerbi, Antonello. *La disputa del nuovo mondo. Storia di una polemica: 1750-1900*. Milano: Ricciardi, 1955.

Gliozzi, Giuliano. *Adamo e il nuovo mondo. La nascita dell'antropologia comme ideologia coloniale: della genealogia bibliche alle teorie razziali (1500-1700)*. Florence: La Nuova Italia, 1977.

Hanke, Lewis. *Aristotle and the American Indian: Study in Race Prejudice in the Modern World*. Chicago: Henry Regnery, 1959.

—. *La lucha española por la justicia en la conquista de América*. Madrid: Tecnos, 1959.

Jameson, Frederic. "Third World Literature in the Era of Multinational Capitalism." *Social Text* 15 (1968): 65-88.

Leclerc, Jean Louis. *Histoire naturelle, générale et particulière, avec la description du Cabinet du Roi.* Fe 44 vols. Paris, 1749-1804.

Le Goff, Jacques. *L'imaginaire médiévale.* Paris: Gallimard, 1985.

León, Nicolás. *Las castas del México colonial.* México, 1924.

León Portilla, Miguel, ed. *Visión de los vencidos. Relaciones indígenas de la Conquista.* México: UNAM, 1959.

Leonard, Irving A. *Baroque Times in Old Mexico.* 1959. Ann Arbor: Univ. of Michigan Press, 1978.

Lévi-Strauss, Claude. *Tristes Tropiques: An Anthropological Study of Primitive Societies in Brazil.* Trans. John Russell. New York: Atheneum, 1969.

Lovejoy, Arthur O. *The Great Chain of Being.* 1936. Cambridge: Harvard Univ. Press, 1976.

Maravall, José Antonio. *Antiguos y modernos.* Madrid: Sociedad de Estudios y Publicaciones, 1966.

—. *Estudios de historia del pensamiento español. La época del Renacimiento.* Madrid: Cultura Hispánica, 1984.

Marchetti, Giovanni. *Cultura indigena e integrazione nazionale. La "Storia antica de Messico" di F.J. Clavijero.* Albano Terme: Piovan Editore, 1980.

Martínez-Alier, Verena. "Elopement and Seduction in 19th Century Cuba." *Past and Present* 55 (1972): 91-129.

Marx, Karl. *The Eighteenth Brumaire of Louis Bonaparte.* New York: International Publishers, 1963.

Mestizaje Americano, Catálogo Museo de América. Madrid, 1985.

Mörner, Magnus. *Race Mixture in the History of Latin America.* Boston: Little, Brown, 1967.

O'Gorman, Edmundo. *La idea del descubrimiento de América.* México: UNAM, 1955.

—. *La invención de América.* México: Fondo de Cultura Económica, 1958.

Radhakrishnan, R. "Ethnic Identity and Post-Structuralist Difference." *Cultural Critique* 6 (1987): 199-220.

Redondo, Agustín, ed. *Les problèmes de l'exclusion en Espagne* (XVI-XVIIe siècles) Paris: Publications la Sorbonne, 1983.

Root, Deborah. "Speaking Christian: Orthodoxy and Difference in Sixteenth-Century Spain." *Representations* 23 (1988): 118-134.

Spitzer, Leo. *Essays in Historical Semantics.* New York: S.F. Vanni, 1948.

Spivak, Gayatri. *In Other Worlds: Essays in Cultural Politics.* New York: Methuen, 1987.

Stein, Stanley J. and Barbara J. Stein. *The Colonial Heritage of Latin America: Essays on Economic Dependence in Perspective.* New York: Oxford University Press, 1970.

Todorov, Tzvetan. *La conquête de l'Amérique: la question de l'autre.* Paris: Seuil, 1982.

Vázquez, Josefina. *La imagen del indio en el español del siglo XVI.* Xalapa: Universidad Veracruzana, 1962.

West, David. *The West Indies: Patterns of Development, Culture and Environmental Change Since 1492.* Cambridge: Cambridge Univ. Press, 1987.

Woodbridge, Hensley C. "Glossary of Names Used in Colonial Latin America for Crosses Among Indians, Negroes and Whites." *Journal of Negro History* 2 (1953): 405-427.

Zavala, Iris M. "Lo imaginario social," en *Rubén Darío, bajo el signo del cisne* (forthcoming).

—. "Viaje a la cara oculta del sietecientos." Iris M. Zavala, ed. *El Siglo XVIII.* Special issue of *Nueva Revista de Filología Hispánica*, 33. 1(1984): 4-33.

—. "The Social Imaginary: The Cultural Sign of Hispanic Modernism." Inaugural Lecture. Utrecht University, February, 1989.

CHAPTER 10:
THE INSCRIPTION OF CREOLE
CONSCIOUSNESS:
FRAY SERVANDO DE MIER

René Jara

(translated by Ahna Bishop-Jara)

In this essay I propose to examine the historical figure of
Fray Servando Teresa de Mier Noriega y Guerra (1763-
1827) and his role in the foundation of Mexican Creole
discourse. By discourse I mean the articulation of the national consciousness which, imbedded in the early period
of Spanish colonization, would become a decisive factor in
the struggle for Latin American independence. Mier was
not alone; others shared his dream throughout the Continent. Yet, his qualities as a projector of national identification through fiction were probably unequaled.

Servando Teresa de Mier was born on October 18, 1763,
to a prominent family of Monterrey. In 1710, his paternal
grandfather, Don Francisco de Mier Noriega, immigrated
from Spain to the New World. Many years later his grandson would claim the right of nobility and true ascendency
based on the bloodline linking his grandfather to the

Dukes of Granada and Altamira. His mother's family, on the other hand, had been one of the first to settle in the region of New León; Servando would argue that through her he had inherited a claim for which there exists no substantive evidence. He would often use this inheritance to substantiate his opinion that in the case of the re-establishment of the Mexican Empire, he would have sufficient right to occupy the throne, as he was the descendant of Cuauhtémoc (Mier, *Escritos inéditos* 39, 349). From the family library he obtained knowledge of the history of New Spain, while from the lips of his father he heard the stories and legends popular at that time. Among them was one which held that Christianity had been brought to the New World well before the arrival of the Spaniards.

While the dominant preoccupation of Fray Servando was the independence of the Spanish colonies of America, that preoccupation did not revolve around the problem of political order, but rather was derived from a natural hierarchy: America pertained to Americans alone; nature itself supported emancipation (Mier, *Memorias* 2: 54). Spain lacked the "natural" title of dominion so that the labor of discovery, the task of civilizing and the concession of territory by the Pope in favor of the Crown were nothing but fallacies and crimes. The Spaniards could not invoke rights to evangelical preaching since that goal had been achieved before they set foot on American land. Such arguments, based on Enlightenment truths, were reinforced by geographical distance and the convenience of political emancipation from the dominion of Spain. The mother country was deemed to be a backward nation, ignorant, without factories or industry, a nation that had been able to survive only at the expense of its colonies, all of which gave Fray Servando a sufficient vantage point from which to formulate a separatist perspective.

Inspired by the writings of Las Casas, Fray Servando sustained that the nations of America had always had an ancient pact with the kings of Spain, which was made explicit in the Laws of the Indies (*Leyes de Indias*). These Laws allowed the Spanish territories to govern themselves according to their own interests since they were considered kingdoms, not colonies, and were called the Magna Carta or the Constitution of America. Underlying Fray Servando's ideas about independence was the rivalry between the Creole Spaniards and the Peninsular Spaniards; he resented the favoritism of the Colonial government toward the former, which in turn was detrimental to the latter's opportunities. The discrimination toward the Creoles in the sphere of power, as well as in the areas of social and economic influence, was in itself justification for separation from Spain.[1]

The war of independence was, in Mier's mind, an attempt at rebellion whose goal was to replace the Peninsular ruling class with a Creole aristocracy. His intention, though, was not to initiate a revolutionary process that would destroy the system; more than destroying the status quo, he wanted to maintain it while replacing its leaders. He fought for a central republican government led by the Creole elite of Mexico City, with the elite of the provinces excluded. Within this framework, the war for independence would allow Mexico to resurrect rights, which up until that point had been violated. Moreover, Spanish legislation, as well as its Indian counterpart, guaranteed not only the legitimacy of the transfer of power, but at same time facilitated the continuity between old and new governments.

On the subject of government, Mier's proposals clearly show a marked repugnance for innovation and experimentation. The fundamental criterion for a new government would be the re-establishment of the Creole aristocracy to positions of power and authority which by deed and right belonged to them. In other words, Fray Servando's proposals were dominated by a vision in which the center of political activity would be transferred from Spain to America, from Madrid to Mexico City (Lombardi, Chapter 4). His image of independence was one of triumphant *criollismo*, thus thrusting the Creoles into the center of power. Such an image coincides with the height of exalted Creole sentiment, which had its origins in the sixteenth century.

During the sixteenth century, Creole patriotism represented the feelings and interests of an upper class whose place of birth denied them the right to govern their own country (Brading, *Los orígenes* 13-14). The term Creole was commonly used to designate the white children of Spaniards or the legitimate children of a Spanish and Indian union (González y González, *En torno a la integración* 407-424). In Mexico, however, the term was applicable only to the children of Peninsular Spaniards and their descendants who were not of mixed blood (Aguirre Beltrán 32). The Creoles formed part of the dominant caste, but unlike the Europeans, they were merely inheritors of the fortunes and adversities of their parents, owners of a vicarious destiny. Their activity was reduced to anguished demands regarding the merits and jurisdiction that they had inherited from their parents.[2]

Towards the end of the sixteenth century, Creole literature is characterized by a mood of bitterness and dislocation. The conqueror's dream of laying the foundations for a seigneurial society had vanished; the gradual disappearance of the indigenous population had diminished the value of the *encomienda* estate. The Creoles had lost all hope of political compensation because the Crown had always doubted that they were capable of filling the posts that their Spanish parents had once held. There was a belief that the American personality was erratic and feeble; despite the rapid growth of the Creoles' intellectual abilities, it was thought that they would begin to decay due to failing fortitude and health when they reached approximately thirty years of age. Meanwhile, the Creole characterized himself as a pilgrim in his own land.[3]

In the beginning of the seventeenth century, Spanish Americans created an image of themselves as dispossessed inheritors. The failure of the Crown to respond to Creole demands requesting a permanent grant of Indians and reserving the administrative posts in the New World for those born in America visibly amplified the hatred towards the *gachupín* (Spanish immigrant to the New World). Throughout the century the animosity between Creoles and Peninsular Spaniards frequently developed into familial feuds (Brading, *Miners and Merchants* 109-113, 209-215).

During the eighteenth century, Spanish prejudice fostered the image of the Creole as a person of weak

personality, a stereotype against which Don Benito Jerónimo Feijoo would react in the seventh volume of his
Teatro crítico universal (1730) (see Feijoo 2: 110-125; also
Crobato and Millares). The continued resurgence of the
topic would provoke in 1755 a new defense of the attitudes
and intellectual successes of the Creoles, put forth in this
case by the Mexican Juan José de Eguiara y Eguren in a bio-
bibliographical dictionary of Mexican authors, the *Bibliotheca Mexicana*. His was the first account of Mexican cultural production; it began before the Spanish conquest and
detailed 250 years of colonial domination. The text was a
reaction to the *Cartas latinas* ("Latin Letters") written by
the Dean of Alicante, Don Manuel Martí, who not only
raised doubts about the Spanish American's capacity to
educate himself through study, but he also emphatically
denied that such an education could take place in the West
Indies. Thus was born the project of writing a *Bibliotheca
Mexicana* ("Mexican Bibliotheca"), in which there would
be room for every Spaniard and every native of septentrional America of any class or race who showed a capacity
for literary production. In the first volume there is a long
preface which presents a wide panorama of Mexican
culture from before the conquest until 1754, the year in
which the book was completed (see notes by Gómez
Orozco). A basic element of Eguiara y Eguren's apology for
the Creole intellectual was the insistence on the accomplishments of the indigenous cultures, the Creole tradition
reflected in Mexican antiquity, and his description of the
Aztecs as equal in wisdom to the ancient Egyptians. From
that point on, Creoles would be equal to their European
brothers. In short, a canon had been formed.

The Creoles could no longer identify themselves with
their Spanish ancestors, so they located the beginnings of
self-identification in the Aztec past. This neo-Aztec association (*neoaztequismo*) had manifested itself with timidity
in the seventeenth century in Franciscan chronicles, especially in texts by Juan de Torquemada. Torquemada's
Monarquía indiana was a defense of the human condition
of Indians, who were considered by the first Spanish
colonists overseeing Indian laborers (*encomenderos*) as
brutes unworthy of rational treatment. In the text, he

demonstrated that the Indian race, had progressed slowly, like all others, from a state of bestiality to a higher state of civilization. At the same time, however, he interpreted the religion of the Mexicans as a product of the direct intervention of the Devil. Torquemada justified the conquest as a means of converting the indigenous world to Catholicism, and from this point of view, his providential interpretation of the conquest as divine punishment and liberating redemption would come to temper the effects of the "black legend" (*leyenda negra*) of the Spaniards' actions in the Indies. Such a legend, projected by the apostolic and literary work of the Dominican Bartolomé de Las Casas, shook the moral foundations of colonial society.[4] Nevertheless, Torquemada undermined the "neo-Aztec" idea comparing Aztec antiquity with that of the Romans. From another angle, if, in the defense of the Indian, Torquemada consecrated the idea of a stammering neo-Aztec comparison between Aztec and Roman antiquity, at the same time he impeded its acceptance because of his theory of demonic intervention in the formulation of the indigenous religious model (Phelan, *The Millenial Kingdom* 17-39, 111-170 and León Portilla's "Introducción" to Torquemada, *Monarquía* XXXIX-XLI). One would have to wait for Boturini and Mier in order to exorcize the Devil from indigenous American culture and religion.

Bartolomé de Las Casas had underscored two facets of the Spanish conquest; on the surface, was the conqueror as a rapacious criminal, and underneath, was the humanitarian zeal of the Christian friar. His denigratory theory concerning the Hispanic enterprise had been balanced thanks to the providential millenarism of the Franciscan Order. For the Dominicans, the war had been rapacious and cruel, but for the Franciscans it had been a necessity and a prerequisite for redemption. The control of the colonizing enterprise passed from the hands of the warrior to those of the saint. The principal occupation of the friar would be the welfare of the tortured, degraded and dispossessed Indian. The Creole, meanwhile, lingered in solitude, digesting the leftovers of the Crown's and the Church's consumption. The Creole had neither destiny nor origin.

The European Enlightenment was to electrify the Creole around the last quarter of the eighteenth century, moving him toward a consciousness of identity and patriotic values. The century of the Enlightenment had a strong impact on America and Spain, further empassioned by Las Casas's theory of the conquest. Franciscan millenarism was revealed as insufficient to explain American reality. Both the zeal of the friar and the heroism of the soldier would no longer be accepted as givens. Divine intervention as a rationalization for Hispanic expansionism was attacked in the name of reason. The granting of territory to Spain and Portugal by Papal authority, and the Church's pronouncement of the savage's irrationality were equally repudiated. The picture formerly painted by the chroniclers, conquerors and missionaries shaped reality to accomodate expansionist interests; they privileged Western discourse over New World reality. Furthermore, the Spanish had not defeated their equals; their victory had been won over new, still primitive and savage nations, ruled by tellurian forces.

The tendency of pseudo-scientific discourse, as instituted first by Buffon, to condemn the influence of nature on the inhabitants of the New World reached spectacular dimensions in Cornelius de Pauw and William Robertson. Both De Pauw and Robertson emphasized the vile character of the American who became weak, cowardly and stupid when exposed to the forces of the environment. This assessment severely affected the Creoles, Indians and *mestizos*, and was to confirm Hispanic racial prejudice (see Gerbi; González y González, "El optimismo nacionalista" and Zavala). Another perspective from the Enlightenment was needed to combat these ideas. That perspective was to come from a conscious patriot who would value the search for Creole origins: the Jesuit Francisco Xavier Clavijero.

It was now clear in the Creole mind that their idea of nationality could not insert itself into the cultural atmosphere of Spain. The desire to establish a national culture found an intellectual locus in the land that they inhabited and in the ideal man that had lived in Mexico since preconquest times: the authentic, uncontaminated and ancient Mexican. In this image they could find themselves and their origin. As a consequence, given the quest for identity and nationality, the Creole would completely renounce formal links to linear kinship and adopt vertical autonomy. For this reason the concept of *criollismo*, or Creole consciousness, took on neo-Aztec characteristics.

In Clavijero's conception, the Aztecs had not been subjected to the tyranny of the environment—as De Pauw and Robertson had claimed—and, moreover, had even managed to establish a culture that was as ancient and prestigious as those of the Old World. In light of Rousseau's perspective, Clavijero discovered the epitome of the noble savage in the Aztec, situated on the border which separated the evils of civilization from the state of natural purity that ignored the values of social life (see Clavijero, 4: *Disertaciones* and Aguirre Beltrán 13-14, 19-20). This Jesuit Creole established in his *Historia antigua de México* a systematic comparison between the Latin American world of the pre-conquest and other civilizations, specifically seen in the volume entitled *Disertaciones*. The formal bases of this comparison rely on the ideas of the Enlightenment which established that nations were, to a great extent, modeled according to their cultural milieu, and that the sins and vices of society were not a result of the anger and punishment of God, but rather a consequence of environmental conditions. From this angle, the enterprise of the conquest was not only unable to create the social conditions for the advancement of Indian talents, but had also impeded Indians from achieving cultural growth.

This point of view implied nothing less than the negation of the effectiveness of the Spanish colonization in America. At the same time, it pointed to the increasing awareness of the Indian's derelict condition at that time (Phelan, "Neo-Aztecism"). For Clavijero as well as Mier, and for all of the spokesmen of Creole patriotism, the image of the contemporary Indian was untenable. They went so far as to accord inferiority to the Indian; deceitfulness, alcoholism and superstition were his most evident characteristics. The Creoles never once considered them to be part of human reality. The image of the Indian was valuable only insofar as it constituted a significant embodiment of the intelligent and cultured Aztec of antiquity. The adoption of the Aztec world as a classical culture augmented the recognition of the deplorable plight of the descendants of the Aztecs. In Clavijero, the idea of Creole responsibility for the improvement of the Indian's social conditions surfaces as a need for rightful positioning of the Indian figure in the Mexican nation. However, the passion for social change in Clavijero, which probably had more to do with his fight for independence than with anything else, did not find its echo in Mier who, for different reasons, would be the legitimate heir of Clavijero's neo-Aztec approach. Although Clavijero continued the Franciscan tradition in which forced enslavement and subjugation of the Indian were a natural retribution for the sins of heresy, he openly criticized the theory of diabolical intervention. On the other hand, his work foreshadowed the insurgent attempt to negate the inmediate past, resorting instead to an idealization of the ancient Indian.

The Creole neo-Aztec idea would imply an appropriation of various symbols of Aztec culture, as well as a thorough assimilation of Christian ideology. This process which was initiated in the seventeenth century with Carlos de Sigüenza y Góngora and would continue into the eighteenth century with the writings of an Italian aristocrat named Don Lorenzo Boturini Benaduci, would find its full resonance in the sermons, letters and memoirs of Mier. In his work *Fénix de Occidente* ("Phoenix of the Western World") Carlos de Sigüenza contended that the priest-god Quetzalcóatl, one of the important figures of the Aztec pantheon, had prophesized the arrival of the Spanish and their subsequent domination of the empire. Quetzalcóatl was none other than St. Thomas, who had come to the New World to preach the Word of God. Thus, the similarities between Christianity and the indigenous religion now had a satisfactory explanation (Leonard, *Ensayo bibliográfico* 16-17).

Sigüenza was successful in introducing an apostle into an epoch and a region that many considered to be a fixed dominion of Satan, from whose control the Spanish Christian conquest was the only salvation (Leonard, *Don Carlos de Sigüenza y Góngora* 97-99). Mier was to continue in the same vein as his predecessor by ridiculing the idea that the Devil had become a catechist and had erected the cross in Mexico. It had not been the Devil but an apostle sent by Christ (*Memorias* 1: 26-28).

Lorenzo Boturini stated in his *Idea de una historia general de América septentrional* ("Idea for a General History of South America") that he could demonstrate that there was an equivalence between St. Thomas and Quetzalcóatl. The documents he possessed permitted him to reconstruct the history of ancient Mexico from the time of the universal "Great Flood" to the years of the conquest. He also claimed the existence of many verified apparitions of Our Lady of Guadalupe, who had been converted into one of the popular myths of New Spain. Thus, the very concept of "New Spain" had to be eliminated (4-7, 104, 150-158).

Toward the end of the eighteenth century, Father Mier denied the validity of the traditions surrounding the apparitions of Guadalupe in order to inscribe a more substantive Creole reading. He contended that the image of the Virgin had already been painted on the cape that Juan Diego brought to Zumárraga and that this same cape belonged to St. Thomas. Simultaneously, he stated that Guadalupe was identical to Tonantzín, a goddess who had been worshipped in Tepeyac since antiquity. In order to understand the function of this new synchronism, we must reconstruct the origins and foundations of the Lady of Guadalupe cult in Mexico.

According to the pious tradition, the Virgin Mary appeared before the Indian Juan Diego on a hill in Tepeyac between the ninth and twelfth days of December in 1531. At that time, She ordered Juan Diego to reveal the apparition to the Bishop of Mexico so that he could erect a temple on the sacred ground where she had appeared. According to the legend, the Bishop did not believe the Indian and asked for a sign from the Virgin. Following Her orders, the Indian collected roses and other flowers from the hill and brought them to the Prelate, after his uncle, Juan Bernardino, had been healed by Her intercession. When the Prelate opened the cape in which the flowers were carried, he was astonished to find the miraculous image of the Virgin painted on it. From a message transmitted to Juan Bernardino and communicated by him to Juan Diego, Mexico was to venerate the Virgin with the name of Our Lady of Guadalupe (see Lazo de la Vega, Fernández de Echeverría y Veytía and Bergoend, 46-58).

Despite the indisputable presence of the Guadalupe cult during the sixteenth century, Guadalupe did not acquire canonical confirmation until at least 1648, when Miguel Sánchez, a lawyer, published his *Imagen de la Virgen María de Dios de Guadalupe* ("Image of the Virgin Mary of God of Guadalupe") (Maza 38). Sánchez adapted his interpretation to the Creole canon of the seventeenth century. According to Sánchez, God had arranged a precise moment for the discovery of America, so that in such an atmosphere the Virgin of Guadalupe, the Mother of God, would later appear. The creation of the world by God prioritized the blessings of faith and redemption given to the human race through the crucifixion of Christ—the second Adam brought into the world—upon the tomb of the first Adam. However, the second Eve was in need of a new paradise—that of Columbus and the chroniclers of America—in which Her appearance would be sure to signal the establishment of a joint redeemer in the New World. Moreover, it would provide faith and redemption for the inhabitants of the second fallen Eden created for Her.

The Spanish justification of the conquest as an opportunity or responsibility for the propagation of the true faith was converted into a pretext to validate the apparition of Guadalupe as a prestigious and sacred Creole identity. Since then the image of Guadalupe has been institutionalized as a Mexican national emblem (Maza 38-50).

In 1649, the following year, Don Luis Lazo de la Vega published in Náhuatl *El gran acontecimiento con que se apareció la Señora Reina del Cielo Santa María* ("The Great Event of the Apparition of Our Lady; the Queen of Heaven, Holy Mary"), which because of its language and correspondence to the indigenous spirit, gave rise to the popularity of Marian tales. Subsequently, this work would be attributed to the knowledgeable Indian Don Valeriano because his own manuscript, which was translated by Fernando de Alva, had passed from Carlos de Sigüenza's hands to those of the Prebendary Lazo (López Beltrán 5-137; Maza 51-55).

The years 1629 and 1737 formed the new solid cornerstones of the Tepeyac cult. Popular opinion annointed the image of Guadalupe as the people's coat of arms in the presumed victory against the floods of 1629-1634. Guadalupe was officially recognized in 1737 as the benefactor of Mexico City when the Virgin was credited with the defeat of the plague which took the lives of 150,000 people in 1736. In light of Guadalupe's miraculous intervention, Cabrera y Quintero published his *Escudo de armas de México* ("Coat of Arms of Mexico") (1738) in which he calculated that the plague occurred exactly two hundred years after the apparition. Such ideas formed the keystone to a Creole mentality which was dominated by fascination with colonial millenarism and marked by an indigenous rationalization of history dominated by a cyclical imaginary (Lafaye 254-263). The process of Creole appropriation and popularization of the myth culminated in 1785 with the book *Estrella del Norte de México* ("Mexico's Star of the North") by the Jesuit Francisco de Florencia in which the biblical quotation *Non fecit taliter omni nationi* is adopted as a chivalresque motto of the Guadalupe legend (Maza 61-66).

At this point, it is worthwhile to emphasize that the extension of this Catholic cult among the indigenous population was due to the equivalence that the Indian saw between Guadalupe and the image of Tonantzín. The same conceptualization was later appropriated by Father Mier who used it as the basis of his argument. The chronicles of missionaries, especially those of Sahagún and Torquemada, concurred in their assertions that Tonantzín was a principal divinity whose name in Spanish signified "our adored mother." Her most important temple was located on the Tepeyac hill one league from Mexico City, and people used to come from all parts of the country to pay her tribute. According to Sahagún, Cihuacóatl was identifiable with Tonantzín because both names had the same connotation in reference to Catholic tradition. Cihuacóatl was the mother serpent, the representation of the earth and

Mother Goddess of the human race. Colonial syncretism assimilated Cihuacóatl into Eve, who was betrayed by the serpent (Robelo 59-136). At the same time, the couple Cihuacóatl/Quetzalcóatl was the personification of Ometéotl, a primary duality, which constituted the origin of life and the material world.

Franciscan zeal against the validation of the Guadalupe cult is easily understood. The acceptance of such a figure by the masses not only verified the vitality of idolatry but also created hideous deviations from the truth. It was inevitable that Guadalupe/Tonantzín, the feminine image of Ometéotl, would be the totalizing image of God for the Indians. Guadalupe meant nothing less than a deconstruction of the patriarchal system of colonization and conversion undertaken by the Europeans in the Indies. She was equal to the Mother Goddess, a symbol of Woman and her generative capacity. Closely associated with Earth, She did not need a masculine counterpart, for She did not feed Herself with death to produce new life in an inexhaustible cycle. Because of Her, the Indians remembered that all cultural constructions, including that of imperial dominion, were only possible thanks to the cultivation of their land and to the womens' participation in the activities surrounding the harvest. Franciscan alacrity for the elimination of idolatrous figures, such as that of the Lady of Guadalupe, combined with the rapid native assimilation of the Virgin as its own produced a cultural ambiguity from which the Guadalupan cult would surge as a dynamic figuration for all Mexicans: the Christian belief in the Inmaculate Conception had been transformed into a Mexican divinity. The perception of the Tepeyac cult as a problematic issue in a number of colonial texts brought about intense opposition to the idea of an Indian Church which could provide a locus for religious syncretism. Nevertheless, the arrival of the Jesuits, the death of the Franciscan pioneers who championed religious purity, and the rapid introduction of the Baroque Counter-Reformation ideology through the secular clergymen who encouraged the figuration of cult images provided the conditions for the acceleration of religious and national syncretism by the 1570s.

In New Spain, the Creole *mestizo* as well as the Indian[5] had been treated with contempt by the *gachupín*. As a result of the grace and dignity afforded to the Virgin Mary by her miraculous apparitions, these censured classes were granted social integrity and justification. The presence of the Mother of Christ denoted the salvation of the New World, an area of the universe which had been chosen as the site for the regeneration of Christianity. Creoles, *mestizos* and Indians united in devotion to Guadalupe under one religious and national denomination against the agents of peninsular domination represented by the image of Nuestra Señora de los Remedios (see Gibson, *The Aztecs Under Spanish Rule* 132-133; Meier, and Ricard). Guadalupe was colored with the hue of an Amerindian origen; at the root of this cultural inscription rested the progression towards a rehabilitation of the indigenous past.

The consideration of the aforementioned image of Guadalupe in her symbolic function permits the conjecture of the following ideas. For the Indians, the image of Guadalupe was a fountain of love, generosity and the recuperation of the primigenial Mother who administered the maternal caretaking lost in adulthood. This religious experience was a return to the vanished road which led to a primitive state of being where physical problems and social difficulties were minimalized. For them, it was a genesis of security and hope for salvation from their present miserable state. For the Creoles, Guadalupe embodied the possibility of revolt against the father figure: the Spanish authority and the domination by the "other". A successful victory over this Spanish presence would be equivalent to a promise of life given by the Mother of God. It was already a given that Guadalupe was a lady who had been triumphant over epidemics and calamities, and it was clear that She could vanquish colonial domination.

One might think that the Indians were only affected by the humiliation of military defeat by the Spanish conquest. However, the consequences of the abolition of traditional religion and indigenous divinities cannot be overlooked in this analysis (see León-Portilla, *The Broken Spears*). In this context, the apparition of Guadalupe represented the return of Tonantzín, the recuperation of faith and the recovery of Indian gods. This recuperation signified that the Indians were capable of receiving salvation and assimilating the doctrines of Christianity. The apparition of Guadalupe confirmed the identity of the Indians as reflective Mexican citizens who were both subject and object of laws that governed and defended them. The plight of the Creoles, on the other hand, was different.

Disinherited without a specific space within the social hierarchy and often without the right to exist as protected citizens, the Creoles, *mestizos* and lower castes were denied social recognition and prestige. While the Creoles had acquired power and influence towards the end of the seventeenth century and through the eighteenth, they were prevented from acquiring higher social status. For the Creoles as well as for the Indians and *mestizos*, Guadalupe signified not only a supernatural and celestial promise, but also the hope of acquiring an inhabitable space in society. From a political angle, the cult of the Virgin Guadalupe generated a desire for a Paradise which the legitimate heirs of the Creoles would control and in which they would mobilize forces to attain a glorious future. They would be responsible for the expulsion of the foreign Spaniards who were culpable for never recognizing or adhering to their social responsibilities (see Wolf).

In the middle of the seventeenth century, Miguel Sánchez justified the discovery of America as a divine decision by which the Virgin Mary could manifest the new nation's providential fate by locating in Mexico a second Paradise. According to Sánchez, Israel had been chosen as the womb of Christ and Mexico was the fountain of Guadalupe. Towards the end of the century, Francisco de Florencia embraced the thesis *non fecit taliter onmi nationi* which established Mexico as the chosen nation, far superior to all others. The genuine miracle of Guadalupe was established. The Hispanic significance of conquest and colonization was in the process of desintegrating; there was no space in America for the Devil; Indians were rational beings worthy of salvation; Creoles, *mestizos* and all other castes who had mixed with the Indians and who had lived under prior conditions of marginalization and desertion were equally entitled to redemption. On the other hand, the historical monuments and legacies of America had articulated the prestige of an ancient civilization. Moreover, the existence of the Saint-God Thomas/Quetzalcóatl who evangelized the New World centuries before the arrival of the Spanish could no longer be denied. Now, all that was needed to synthesize the disperse elements of the Creole sense of national identity into a coherent discourse was the master stroke of Fray Servando Teresa de Mier's pen.

On the twelfth of December 1794, Mier was asked to preach a sermon concerning Guadalupe, and in delivering the message he brought to light new arqueological discoveries. A very important one in the contemporary context presented an allegorical interpretation of the hieroglyphics found on the Aztec stone calendar discovered in Mexico City's Plaza de las Armas in 1790. Mier's reading of the calendar gave a distinct physiognomy to Christian and Indian history in Mexico.

At the same time, his interpretation of history as contained in his "Apuntes para el sermón sobre la Aparición de Nuestra Señora de Guadalupe" ("Notes for the Sermon On the Apparition of Our Lady of Guadalupe") both summarized and attempted to close evident loopholes in the Guadalupean tradition: a) the image of the Virgin Guadalupe was not painted on Juan Diego's cape, but instead it had originally appeared on the Apostle Thomas's cloak; b) the Indians who were already Christians had worshipped the image for at least 1,750 years in Tepeyac, the same location where St. Thomas constructed the church; c) when the Indians had committed apostasy by separating themselves from Christian teachings, the image had already been hidden, and in 1531 when the Virgin revealed herself before Juan Diego, it was with the intention to show the Indians their error; d) the image had been miraculously imprinted on a cloth belonging to St. Thomas in the first century (Hernández Dávalos 3: 7-70).

The sermon rested predominantly on two arguments. The first declared that the preaching of the Gospel in the New World had occurred many centuries before the Conquest by St. Thomas. Servando reinforces his argument by bonding the Christian figure with the religious models of ancient civilizations. In Syria, St. Thomas had been called Tomé, in Chinese he was Chilancambal, and for the Indians of Mexico he was Quetzalcóatl. The second argument sustained that the cult of Mary had been practiced under the name Tonantzín, on the hill in Tepeyac.

The importance of these ideas rested on the elaboration of certain concepts which originated in Sigüenza y Góngora. The sermon confirmed the Franciscan fears advanced by Father Bustamante, which in turn provoked the writing of the document *Información* by Archbishop Montúfar in 1556. Guadalupe was none other than Tonantzín. Mier's exhaustive study of the tradition of the apparitions of 1531 pointed to a growing militant Creole consciousness. Mary had been a presence in the remote Aztec past. She was the actualization of the Mother-Goddess that America needed to justify its existence in modern history. At the same time, the intricate connection between the venerated Guadalupe and St. Thomas would serve as a credible rival to their Spanish equivalents, Pilar de Zaragoza and Santiago. Thus, *neoaztequismo* progressively evolved into a zealous anti-Hispanism.

The *Opúsculo guadalupano* ("Guadalupean Opuscule") (1790) by José Ignacio Bartolache profoundly affected Mier's patriotic spirit (qtd. Brading, *Los orígenes* 160-161). Many of the ideas of Bartolache's text are reflected in Mier's production, although not all are accepted in the body of his ideological construction. Bartolache had contended that there was a separation of 117 years between the original apparition of the Virgin and the first oral account of Guadalupe in 1648 by Sánchez. Also, the original manuscript of the account that had been attributed to the respected Indian Valeriano by Sigüenza y Góngora, had been transcribed some eighty or eighty-two years after the first account by Sánchez. The quality of the cloth upon which the Virgin appeared was another element of the analysis. Bartolache argued that the texture of the *ixcotl* palm leaf, onto which the image was impressed, was of a material which the common Indian did not utilize to make capes. While giving his sermon, Mier denied this last premise saying it was absolutely false, and although he did not have time to prove it, he asserted his authority on the subject (Hernández Dávalos 3: 33). On the other hand, Mier compromised his position in his *Apología* (1817) so that an absolute conclusion could be drawn regarding the mysterious cloak: it did not belong to Juan Diego (*Memorias* 1: 48-49). Mier's erratic criticism of the 1531 apparition operated as an indication of his Creole obsession rather than as a preoccupation of a friar in search of the truth.

Likewise, his ideas concerning the relation between St. Thomas and Quetzalcóatl were extracted to a large extent from his knowledge of the manuscript of the *Clave general de geroglíficos americanos* ("General Key to American Hieroglyphics") by Don Ignacio Borunda, Licenciado de la Audencia. Mier was not an original thinker, but he was conscious of what he was doing. Through a laborious and imaginative exegesis of the arqueological discoveries of 1790, Borunda had managed to date the findings back to the first century of the Christian era. His was a real feat of the imagination. With his gaze focused upon the remnants of the past, Borunda saw St. Thomas cross the ocean in a fragile skiff, arrive on the beaches of Patagonia, penetrate the pampas, climb the Andes and finally rest in Cuzco, where upon converting the Inca, he started the evangelization of the New World. Then, as if retelling the images of a dream sent from God, he saw the Saint continue his pilgrimage through the highlands of Ecuador, Nicaragua and Guatemala. He stopped in Palenque for awhile until he moved to southern Anáhuac. It was in this region that the Saint was converted into Quetzalcóatl. His instruction of Christianity and establishment of the Eucharist had ended the practice of ancient, idolatrous religions. Thus a new tradition replaced the old one; the Aztecs constructed a statue of Christ/Huitzilopochtli with the seeds of wild amaranth which they consumed after worshipping it. The evangelization work by St. Thomas in America had lasted twenty years, and it was during that time that he instructed the Toltecs. This same group, famed for their craftsmanship of silver and gold and knowledge of medicine and hygiene, had founded the city of Tula in the eighth century. Foreseeing the apostasy of the converts, St. Thomas had concealed the images of Mary and Jesus, images that he had painted for the Náhuatl Christians in various caves around the region. These were the same images which the Spaniards found and which had become the focus of veneration in Chalma, Tepeyac and other places. The last part of Borunda's vision extends into an anticipation of Christianity in the New World, St. Thomas departs from the same place that he entered the region. He embarks from Xicallanco and sails to Cozumel, where he places several crosses as a permanent testimony of his presence in a region which many centuries later would become America (Robelo 252).

Mier's response to Borunda in his *Apología* shows a rhetorical displacement by which the image painted on St. Thomas's cape functions as a consolatory remedy "to prevent an emotional or scandalous response from the ignorant" ("para precaver el sentimiento o escándalo de los ignorantes") (*Memorias* 1: 51). The credibility of his conjecture rested on the historical verisimilitude that he could appropriate to the Creole class, in spite of the impossibility that a divine image would have been painted on the cloak of an Indian. It was extremely important to achieve an admirable and glorified self-image for the country he was inventing (*Memorias* 1: 50). The interrogative rhetoric of his *Memorias* seems to ask the questions: Was the cloak of an apostle of Jesus Christ of such importance? If there were vestiges of the presence of St. Thomas in many parts of America, why then did it produce such a scandal that Mexicans possessed his cape upon which Our Lady of Guadalupe was imprinted? Specifically, he states:

> The cloak of the Apostles was Jewish, as was the cape of the Indians. According to Father Calancha, the cloak which St. Thomas wore while he was in America was formed of two fabrics, as was that of Our Lady of Guadalupe. This then is certainly the image of the "Mother of the True God" that the Indians in Tepeyacac worshiped also named Coatlicue which means "her garment is that of Thomas". Here I have spoken sufficiently in order to form an tentative conjecture. As I observed before, the insufficiency of such an hypothesis is what I had predicted from the beginning. If these things appear delirious it is

important to understand that they are not as such for
those of us who have studied our ancient customs.

La capa de los Apóstoles era una capa judía como la
de los indios. La que llevaba en América Santo Tomé,
según el padre Calancha, era de dos lienzos, como la
de Nuestra Señora de Guadalupe, y a ésta, si es la
imagen de la "Madre del Verdadero Dios" que
adoraban los indios en Tepeyacac, llamaban también
Coatlicue, que quiere decir "su vestido es el de Tomé".
He aquí lo suficiente para una conjetura muy débil
como advertí que era la que prediqué. Si estas cosas
parecen delirios, no lo parecen tanto a los que han estudiado nuestras antigüallas. (*Memorias* 1: 52)

Mier's Creole consciousness and neo-Aztec production
is marked by an intensity which, without doubt, was the
result of an inquisitorial reaction against his sermon by
Archbishop Don Alonzo Núñez de Haro y Peralta. Consequently, Mier was placed under house arrest and his writings and notes on Borunda were confiscated. With these
documents he had intended to substantiate a discourse
which would be subjected to the scrutiny of the Creole
prebendaries José Patricio de Uribe and Manuel de Omaña.
Because of his analysis, he was condemned to ten years of
exile and confinement in the Dominican Convent of Las
Caldas in the province of Santander, Spain (see Uribe and
Omaña, "Censura" in Hernández Dávalos 3: 80-122). Ten
years of isolation became two decades of European exile, a
punishment which instead of crushing his defiant
perspective only sharpened it.

On April 18, 1794, Don Juan Bautista Muñoz presented
his *El Discurso histórico-crítico sobre las apariciones y el
culto de Nuestra Señora de Guadalupe de México* ("Histo-
rical-Critical Discourse on the Apparitions and the Cult of
Our Lady of Guadalupe") before the Royal Academy of
History (see Munóz, "Disertación", Hernández Dávalos 3:
132-141). Mier, who was in agreement with the anti-ap-
paritionist document of the Royal Chronicler of the Indies,
wrote a series of six letters supporting this particular point
of view with few variations ("Cartas", Hernández Dávalos
3: 151-223).

Muñoz's discussion of the apparitions in Mexico appropriates the accounts of Mariano Fernández de Echeverría y Veytía as a point of departure. These accounts, entitled *Baluartes de México* ("Bulwarks of Mexico"), were written in 1775 and their publication prohibited until 1820. The Royal Chronicler considered the work of Veytía the most representative synthesis of everything that had been published about the apparitions (Muñoz in Hernández Dávalos 3: 132-135). The silence of previous and contemporary historiographical texts on the subject, especially those by Torquemada and Cisneros, were cited by Muñoz as proof in opposition to the tradition. In addition to published works, he fortified his argument with passages from unpublished books and unedited sections from Sahagún's *Historia general*. In this section Muñoz refers to Sahagún's account concerning the sanctuary of Tonantzín and the letter which Viceroy Martín Enríquez wrote on September 25, 1575. This letter, which refers to a thesis on the apparition, negates its validity in light of some documents which he considered fraudulent, such as the testimony of Juana Martín and the incomplete quotation of Sahagún, which were used to support Miguel Cabrera's argument. In a final analysis, Muñoz ended up with the suspicion that the story of Guadalupe had originated in the indigenous mind as a superstitious response to the floods that occurred between 1629 and 1634.

The *Cartas* ("Letters") of 1797 initiated a combative, apologetic activity in Fray Servando's production. Emphasis was now placed on the ficticious character of the traditional account of the apparitions, negating the miraculous nature of the painting, and addressing the impossibility of the conservation of such an image. On this last point Mier flirted with the theory that the image of Guadalupe had been fabricated in Pedro de Gante's sweatshop. He reasoned that the original Mexican manuscript—that of Valeriano—which appeared eighty years after the supposed apparition, was nothing more than a sacramental play (*auto sacramental*), for young students at the School of Santiago (Colegio de Santiago). Their teacher Valeriano had been the author of a fiction, whose objective was to equate Guadalupe with Tonantzín (Mier

Colección de documentos 3: 197-200). From Mier's perspective, this was a comedy full of anachronisms, contradictions, idolatry and mythological errors (Hernández Dávalos 3: 185-196). Following in the footsteps of Bartolache and Muñoz, he attested to the idea that the tradition had not actually existed during the first 117 years since the apparition and speculated that it had blossomed during the years of the flood. In contrast to Muñoz's conjecture that the tradition was a consequence of popular reaction to disaster, Mier related it to the appearance of Don Fernando de Alva Ixtlixochitl. Mier argued that Guadalupe was never mentioned until five years after the flood subsided. It was at this time that the Indian Ixtlixochitl, a noble ecclesiastical judge of the Indians, paraphrastically translated Don Antonio Valeriano's Mexican novel into Spanish. Then, he argued, the translation fell into the hands of Sánchez who added the adjoining section on the analogy between the "Woman" of the *Apocalipsis* ("Apocalypse"), which he published in 1648 and the apparition of Guadalupe (Mier in Hernández Dávalos 3: 165, 167, 176). All that Mier needed for the substantiation of a Creole legend was proof that Guadalupe/Tonantzín had been worshipped in Tepeyac by the Indians since the time of St. Thomas (Mier, *Memorias* 1: 36-44).

The *Cartas* constructed an argument supporting the rumors that the Apostle brought Christianity to America before the Spanish conquest, even though he did not necessarily appear during the first century of the Christian era. Regarding this point, Mier modified and inserted some considerations which he had previously described in his sermon, especially when the chronological order of events came into conflict with his premises. Such is the case when he proposes the presence of the Apostle in eighth-century Tula where Thomas/Quetzalcóatl supposedly governed and counseled the inhabitants of that city. The miraculous longevity of Christ's disciple had to be explained in enlightened eighteenth century New Spain.

Although the presence of the Gospel in America before the conquest was an indisputed fact—stated Mier—there was doubt as to the definite identity of this messenger. Quoting Boturini and Veytía, Mier affirmed that there had been two messengers in the New World; one established himself sometime during the sixth and eighth centuries and the other appeared twelve years after the great eclipse, which was interpreted by contemporary researchers as a sign of the death of Christ. For Mier the elder messenger could be no other that St. Thomas. The first reason was that throughout the expansion of America the name of "Tomé" was preserved as a religious figure; the second was that the holy scriptures named Thomas as the only Apostle successful in converting unknown, barbarous nations to Christianity.

According to legend, Thomas traveled from Eastern India to China. It was assumed that China communicated regularly with America during the early years of Christianity. For many, the possibility existed that the second messenger appeared during the seventh century, and in that case he was none other than the Jew St. Bartholomew. It was during the seventh century that Bartholomew exercised his apostleship in China and later became the Bishop of Tula where he was martyred. It was also equally plausible that this second messenger could have been St. Brendan who arrived in America with seven companions from Ireland. Before mysteriously returning to Europe, they constructed seven churches in the New World. The establishment of this story corresponded to the history of Quetzalcóatl who, according to Torquemada, during the same period embarked from Pánuco with seven holy disciples. Later, these seven disciples became known as the seven Thomases. Quetzalcóatl had appropriated the title of Grand Priest of Tollán, where he was persecuted by Huemac and forced to flee. On the road to Cholula, he marked his journey with crosses which were later discovered by the Spanish during their expedition through the Yucatán region (Mier in Hernández Dávalos 3: 213-214). Perfectly conscious of his political power, Mier repeatedly returned to this topic, especially in his work *Historia de la revolución de Nueva España, antiguamente Anahuac* and *Apología* ("History of the Revolution of New Spain, Formerly Called Anahuac") (see Mier, *Historia de la revolución* 2: ii-xliii; *Memorias* 1: 20-35; *Escritos inéditos* 39-59).

Mier now inscribes an evident correction in his own discourse which clearly shows that the Dominicans perceived Quetzalcóatl as an image capable of being manipulated, having the potential to promote the spiritual change which the Mexicans needed in order to shake off the colonial yoke and restore the Anahuac empire. For this reason, he concealed problems of chronological inconsistency and explored the possibilities which would permit him to emphasize the inscrutable fact that ancient Mexicans were recipients of Christian grace and salvation independent of Spanish intervention. He stated that there was nothing to doubt the presence of the Gospel in the New World beginning in the tenth century because it was already known that Norman, Danish, Irish and Scottish colonies existed in the New World and believed in the true God and the Christian Faith, saying:

> What I am forced to affirm is that if both messengers did not have the same name, then the most popular was named Thomas. Thus, his name as well as his message are the key to ancient Aztec history, its theology, the foundation of Mexico, its empire and the conquest by the Spanish.

> Lo que yo me atrevo a asegurar es que si ambos predicadores no tuvieron el mismo nombre, el más célebre se llamó Tomé, y su predicación y su nombre son la clave de la historia antigua azteca, de su teología, de la fundación de México, de su imperio y de la conquista de los españoles. (*Memorias* 1: 34-35)

As did his predecessors, Mier followed the ideological line of Creole inscription which underscored a responsibility to revise documents produced by the *gachupines* or Peninsular Spaniards. Creole sentiment attributed their lack of recognition in historical production to blind ignorance as well as to the early missionaries' unwillingness to recognize important Mexican experiences. According to Mier, the Spanish clergy had trapped the Mexican mind within a nightmare in which the Creoles were the target of divine wrath. The idolatrous serpent cult acquired strong symbolic connotations, and the Mexican nation became a slithering, twisted image in the eyes of the world (*Historia de la revolución*, 2: xx-xxi, xxiii-xxiv). After destroying the libraries and museums of Indian art, the Spaniards misrepresented all types of information by relying on the word of the illiterate masses. Corruption and political ramifications had continuously falsified the past of the American territories until any residue of the true destiny of America as a predestined paradise was intentionally erased from historical memory. Any trace of the true legacy of the migration of the Anahuac Mexicans as a sign of their relation to the people of Israel in the desert had been stolen from the national consciousness (*Historia de la Revolución*, 2: xxviii).

Mier's published work *Historia de la revolución de la Nueva España, antiguamente Anahuac* together with his dissertation on Quetzalcóatl, give us considerable insight into his ideas on Creole identity. At the end of Mier's *Historia* he added an *Apéndice de Documentos* ("Appendix of Documents") in which the *Documento No. 1* consisted of a transcription of Don Antonio de Capmany's minutes of the judgment dictated by the Academy of History on his Guadalupean sermon. On this point Mier clearly dismisses himself from all charges, blaming the incident on Bishop Haro (*Historia de la Revolución* 2: i-ii). In the same document, Mier added a section called "An illustrative note of this document which deals with the message of the Gospel in America before the Conquest" ("Nota ilustrativa de este documento, y en que se trata de la predicación del Evangelio en América antes de la Conquista"), in which he developed the theory of Quetzalcóatl/St. Thomas.

Mier wrote in his *Apología*:

> I saw that the (Mexican) fatherland secured an Apostle for itself, a glory that all nations desire. This was especially true for Spain, which, despite being only a fistful of dirt, was not content with less than three Apostles of the highest order even though everyone claims them.

> Vi que la patria se aseguraba un Apóstol, gloria que todas las naciones apetecen, y especialmente España, que siendo un puño de tierra no se contenta menos que con tres apóstoles de primer orden, aunque todos se los disputen. (*Memorias* 1: 8)

Spain's claim to no less than three saints such as James, Peter and Paul was thought to be outrageous. Mier, who viewed America as one third of the physical world, found this was the same Spain that denied America the appropriation of the dubious Apostle Thomas. Such an attitude proved the injustice of the *gachupines* whose pretext for domination and exploitation rested solely on their misunderstanding of the popular tradition which identified Mexico and the New World with the pagan hero-god Quetzalcóatl.

Dormant within the texture of Mier's allegations lies a significant symbolic fight between native gods and the deity of the stranger. In Mier's discourse there is an ongoing rivalry between James, the sacred champion of the Spanish Reconquest, whose adoration spread without difficulty throughout America, and the Mexican champion Quetzalcóatl/Thomas, whose reverence was still prohibited. Mier's pen inscribed a detrimental hagiography that became polemical (Layfaye 200-203).

The construction of the Western World under the ægis of Christianity necessitated the creation of Quetzalcóatl as a Christian missionary and the transformation of the indigenous Tonantzín into the image of the Virgin Mary. Both myths were made necessary by the maturation of Mexican national consciousness.

There was an evident exigency for the institutionalization of equality between Mexico and Spain. For this reason, the linkage between the saint and the Marian episode became essential. In the same fashion, the Mexican figures had to enact an analogous saga in keeping with the relation between the Iberian model of James and the venerated image of Mary as Pilar de Zaragoza.

In congruence with the Spanish model, Mier located a discursive space where the two principal myths of colonial Mexico could comply with a new national consciousness. His confessions embodied an intention none other than to defend the cult of Guadalupe from its critics. Yet, in retrospect, the result of his efforts confirmed the baptism and sanctification of the Aztec civilization as a genuine representation of the ancient Mexicans. At the same time, this movement debilitated the fundamental right of the Spanish monarch as an authority and evangelical force in the New World. Instead of working as an instrument of Divine Providence as the *gachupines* proclaimed, the conquest had been a destructive force of native Christianity. Further justification of the conquest was quickly negated and the given right of the monarchy as a governing power in America was obliterated because Americans had finally rediscovered the identity which was already theirs. The revitalization of the Quetzalcóatl and Guadalupe myths provided the populace with both a meaning of the word "Mexico" and a Christian history, and it gave the Creoles a national destiny and a viable origin.

Now that national discourse was developing, the need for political independence followed closely. Spiritual independence had been won by Fray Servando Teresa de Mier, a Spanish and Aztec nobleman who became a religious and secular hero.

NOTES

[1] For further study on biography and the political and ideological significance of Fray Servando see works by Brading (*Los Orígenes del nacionalismo mexicano*, especially 59-148), Hadley, Lafaye, O'Gorman (59-148) and Lombardi.

[2] For further information, see works by Benítez, Cook, Gibson (*The Aztecs Under Spanish Rule*, especially pages 61-63, 136-141) and Haring (246-257).

[3] I am deliberately using the masculine marker to refer to both Creoles and Peninsular Spaniards throughout this paper. Colonial society was a patriarchal universe in which the behavior of women was strictly prescribed. Women had two choices: to engage in matrimony or enter a religious order. They were to remain virgins until their marriage and had to live separately from men. When married, they could only have close contact with their fathers, husbands, and sons. Women of lower economic stratas could not always follow the model of the virtuous wife and mother set by the upper classes, but they were heavily influenced by it. Moreover, the only viable and respectable alternative for family life provided to women by the Church was not always a result of the woman's will and desire. It was often imposed on her by the patriarch,

or the head of the family, who wanted not only to guard the virginity of a daughter, but also to prevent her from marrying. Marriage involved a dowry consisting of land or capital which the patriarch preferred to pass on to a son. All women had to follow the Law of the Father, and accept his symbolic universe.

4 Regarding the function of the texts of Father Las Casas and the famous "black legend" see the following works: Gibson, "Introduction" to *The Black Legend* (3-27), Hanke, and Carbia.

5 On this point, see works by McAlister, Marshall, Mörner and Gibson.

WORKS CITED

Aguirre Beltrán, Gonzalo. Introducción. *Antología*. By Francisco Javier Clavijero. México: Sepsetentas, 1976.

Benítez, Fernando. *La vida criolla en el siglo XVI*. México: El Colegio de México, 1953.

Bergoend, Bernardo. *La nacionalidad mexicana y la Virgen de Guadalupe*. México: Editorial Jus, 1968.

Boturini Benaduci, Lorenzo. *Idea de una Historia General de la América Septentrional*. Madrid: Imprenta de Juan Zúñiga, 1746.

Brading, David A. *Miners and Merchants in Bourbon Mexico, 1763-1810*. Cambridge: Cambridge Univ. Press, 1971.

—. *Los Orígenes del nacionalismo mexicano*. México: Sepsetentas, 1973.

Carbia, Rómulo. *Historia de la leyenda negra hispanoamericana*. Madrid: Publicaiones del Consejo de Hispanidad, 1944.

Clavijero, Francisco Xavier. *Antología*. Ed. Gonzalo Aguirre Beltrán. México: Sepsetentas, 1976.

—. *Historia Antigua de México*. 4 vols. México: Porrúa, 1958.

Cook, Sherburne. "The Incidence and Significance of Disease Among the Aztecs and Related Tribes." *Hispanic American Historical Review* 26 (1946): 320+.

Corbato, Hermenegildo. "Feijoo y los españoles americanos." *Revista Iberoamericana* 5(1942): 59-70.

Feijoo, Benito Jerónimo. *Teatro crítico universal.* 9 vols. Madrid, 1753.

Fernández de Echeverría y Mariano Veytía. *Baluartes de México: Descripción Histórica de las Cuatro Milagrosas Imágenes de Nuestra Señora, que se veneran en la muy noble, leal e imperial Ciudad de México, Capital de la Nueva España.* México: Alejandro Valdés, 1820. México: Edmundo Aviña Levy Editor, 1967.

Gerbi, Antonello. *La disputa del Nuevo Mundo.* México: Fondo de Cultura Económica, 1960.

Gibson, Charles. *The Aztecs Under Spanish Rule: A History of the Indians of the Valley of Mexico, 1519-1810.* Stanford: Stanford Univ. Press, 1964.

—. *The Black Legend.* New York: Alfred A. Knopf, 1971.

Gómez Orozco, Federico. Nota Preliminar. *Prólogos a la Biblioteca Mexicana.* By Juan José de Eguiara y Eguren. México: Fondo de Cultura Económica, 1944.

González y González, Luis. "En torno a la integración de la realidad mexicana." *Estudios históricos americanos.* Ed. Julio Le Riverend, et al. México: El Colegio de México, 1953. 407-424.

—. "El optimismo nacionalista como factor de la independencia de México." *Estudios de historiografía americana.* Ed. Isabel Gutiérrez del Arroyo, et al. México: El Colegio de México, 1948. 165-188.

Hadley, Bedford K. *The Enigmatic Padre Mier.* Austin: Univ. of Texas Press, 1955.

Hanke, Lewis. "Indians and Spaniards in the New World: A Personal View." *Attitudes of Colonial Powers Toward the American Indian.* Eds. Howard Peckman and Charles Gibson. Salt Lake City: Univ. of Utah Press, 1969. 1-18.

Haring, C.H. *El imperio hispánico en América.* Buenos Aires: Peuser, 1958.

Hernández Dávalos, J.E., ed. *Colección de Documentos para la Guerra de Independencia de México de 1808 a 1821.* 6 vols. México, 1877-1882. Germany: Kraus Reprint, 1968.

Lafaye, Jacques. *Quetzalcóatl and Guadalupe.* Chicago: The Univ. of Chicago Press, 1976.

Lazo de la Vega, Luis. *El Gran Acontecimiento... Historia de la Aparición de Nuestra Señora de Guadalupe*. México: Carreño e Hijo Editores, 1926.

León-Portilla, Miguel. *The Broken Spears: The Aztec Account of the Conquest of Mexico*. Boston: Beacon Press, 1962.

—. Introducción. *Monarquía Indiana*. By Juan de Torquemada. México: Universidad Nacional Autónoma, 1964.

Leonard, Irving. *Don Carlos de Sigüenza y Góngora: A Mexican Savant of the Seventeenth Century*. Berkeley: Univ. of California Press, 1929.

—. *Ensayo bibliográfico de Don Carlos de Sigüenza y Góngora*. México: Monografías Bibliográficas Mexicanas, 1939.

Lombardi, John. *The Political Ideology of Fray Servando Teresa de Mier*. México: Sondeos, 1968.

López Beltrán, Lauro. *La protohistoria guadalupana*. México: Editorial Jus, 1966.

Marshall, C.E. "The Birth of the Mestizo in New Spain." *Hispanic American Historical Review* 19 (1939): 161-184.

Maza, Francisco de. *El guadalupismo mexicano*. México: Porrúa y Obregón, 1953.

McAlister, Lyle. "Social Structure and Social Change in New Spain." *Hispanic American Historical Review* 43 (1963): 349-370.

Meier, Matt. "María Insurgentes." *Historia Mexicana* 23 (1971): 166-480.

Mier, Fray Servando Teresa de. "Apuntes para el Sermón sobre la Aparición de Nuestra Señora de Guadalupe." Hernández Dávalos 3: 7-70.

—. "Cartas del Dr. Mier al Cronista de Indias Doctor D. Juan Bautista Muñoz sobre la tradición de Nuestra Señora de Guadalupe, escritas desde Burgos, año de 1797." Hernández Dávalos 3: 151-223.

—. *Escritos inéditos*. Eds. J.M. Miguel y Verges and Hugo Díaz Thome. México: El Colegio de México, 1944.

—. *Historia de la Revolución de Nueva España, antiguamente Anáhuac o verdadero Orígen y Causa de ella con la Relación de sus Progresos hasta el Presente Año de 1813*. 2 vols. México, 1922.

—. *Memorias*. 2 vols. Ed. Antonio Castro Leal. México: Porrúa, 1946.

Millares, Carlos A. "Feijoo y América." *Cuadernos Americanos* 3 (1944): 139-160.

Mörner, Magnus and Charles Gibson. "Diego Muñoz Camargo and the Segregation Policy of the Spanish Crown." *Hispanic American Historical Review* 42 (1962): 558-569.

Muñoz, Juan Bautista. "Disertación de D. sobre la Aparición de Nuestra Señora de Guadalupe." Hernández Dávalos 3: 132-141.

O'Gorman, Edmundo. "Fray Servando Teresa de Mier." *Seis estudios históricos de tema mexicano*. México: Universidad Veracruzana, 1960. 59-148.

Phelan, John Leddy. *The Millenial Kingdom of the Franciscans in the New World*. Berkeley: Univ. of California Press, 1970.

—. "Neo-Aztecism in the Eighteenth Century and the Genesis of Mexican Nationalism." *Culture in History*. Ed. Stanley Diamond. New York: Columbia Univ. Press, 1960. 760-770.

Ricard, Robert. *La conquista espiritual de México: Ensayo sobre el apostolado y los métodos misioneros de las Ordenes Mendicantes en la Nueva España de 1523-4 a 1572*. Trans. Angel María Garibay. México: Editorial Jus, 1947.

Robelo, Cecilio. *Diccionario de mitología histórica y documental sobre la aparición de la Virgen de Guadalupe de México*. México: Fuente Cultural, 1952.

Torquemada, Juan de. *Monarquía Indiana*. Ed. Miguel León-Portilla. México: Universidad Nacional Autonoma, 1964.

Uribe, Joseph and José Manuel de Omaña. "Censura que sobre dicho Sermón ["Apuntes"] expusieron los Señores Doctores y Maestros." Hernández Dávalos 3: 80-122.

Wolf, Eric R. "The Virgin of Guadalupe: A Mexican National Symbol." *Introduction to Chicano Studies: A Reader*. Eds. Livie Duncan and H. Russell Bernard. New York: Macmillan, 1973. 246-252.

Zavala, Silvio. *La filosofía política en la conquista de América*. México: Fondo de Cultura Económica, 1947.

APPENDIX

DOCUMENTING THE CONQUEST

Dossier Compiled and Edited by
MARIO GOMEZ-MORIANA

Translated into English by Lawrence Mantini
with the assistance of Luis A. Ramos-García

THE CHARTER OF ADMIRAL COLUMBUS
17 APRIL 1492

INSTRUCTION FROM THE SOVEREIGNS
TO COLUMBUS
29 MAY 1493

ARTICLE OF THE TESTAMENT OF THE QUEEN,
OUR LADY DONA ISABELLA

INSTRUCTION THAT DIEGO VELAZQUES
ISSUED TO CORTES
23 OCTOBER 1510

AGAINST THOSE WHO DEPRECATE OR CONTRADICT
THE BULL AND DECREE OF POPE ALEXANDER VI

THE CHARTER OF ADMIRAL COLUMBUS
17 APRIL 1492

[*General Archives of the Indies, General, 418, Book 1, Folio 1-1*]

The Charter of Admiral Columbus

Transcription of the articles adopted by the King and Queen, Our Sovereigns, and Don Christopher Columbus, their Admiral of the ocean sea, in the village of Santa Fe of the region of Granada on the seventeenth of April of 1492. The articles petitioned and which Your Highnesses declare and grant Christopher Columbus as recompense for that which he has discovered in the ocean seas and for the voyage that with the help of God he now is about to undertake in the service of Your Highnesses are as follows:

Article 1. Your Highnesses appoint Christopher Columbus Admiral of the ocean sea.

Firstly, that Your Highnesses as Lords of the said oceans, designate henceforth the aforesaid Don Christopher Columbus their Admiral of all those islands and mainlands that by his efforts and industry may be discovered or obtained in the said ocean seas during his lifetime, and after his death, his heirs and successors in perpetuity, with all those privileges and prerogatives that appertain to that office, similar to those enjoyed by Don Alonso Enrique de Sandoval High Admiral of Castile, and the others, his predecessors in the aforesaid office which they hold in their regions. So may it please Their Highnesses. Juan de Coloma.

Article 2. Your Highnesses name Don Christopher Columbus Viceroy of the Indies and for those appointments that are to be made he should choose three for each office and Your Highnesses one.

Likewise, that Your Highnesses name the aforementioned Christopher Columbus Viceroy and Governor General of all the said mainlands and islands that as has been stated, he may discover or acquire in the said seas; and that for the government of each one and whichever of them, he may select three persons for each office, and that Your Highnesses should take or choose one who would be most suitable to you and thus the lands that God our Lord will permit him to gain and find in the service of Your Highnesses will be better governed. So may it please Your Highnesses. Juan de Coloma.

Article 3. Admiral Columbus may take the tenth part of all that which the lands may hold, less the costs incurred.

Also, that all and any goods, whether they be pearls, precious stones, gold or silver, spices and whatever other goods and things of whatsoever sort, name and manner they may be that might be bought, traded, discovered, gained or obtained within the limits of the said Admiralty that Your Highnesses heretofore have granted the said Don Christopher [Columbus] and wish that he shall have and take for himself the tenth part of all of that, deducting all the costs that may be encountered thereto, so that of the clear remainder he may have and keep the tenth part for himself and do with it as he may wish, the other nine parts remaining for Your Highnesses. May it please Your Highnesses. Juan de Coloma.

Article 4. That if he should bring here goods that might be contested there and a suit should arise, it should be brought before the appropriate judge.

Moreover, if because of the goods that he may bring from said islands and mainlands which, as has been stated, might be gained or discovered or taken in trade there from other merchants, any lawsuit should arise in the place where said commerce and trade should be held, and so that always and in perpetuity such a suit should pertain to the Admiral and his office, may it please Your Highnesses that he or his designate and no other judge should be made aware of such a suit and thus should oversee it from then on. So may it please Their Highnesses, if it pertains to the said office of Admiral which he accordingly held the aforementioned Admiral Don Alonso Enriquez being deceased, and the others his predecessors in their districts, and it being just. Juan de Coloma. [signed]

Article 5. About which the aforementioned Columbus, if he so wishes, may be able to contribute one eighth toward the equipping of the ships and receive the corresponding profit.

Likewise, that in all the ships which may be equipped for the aforementioned trade and negotiation, as many times as desired, the said Columbus, if he should wish, he may contribute and pay one eighth of all that such equipping may cost, and also that he should have and take for himself one eighth of all the profit that may result from such an outfitted fleet. May it please Your Highnesses.

*These Articles of Agreement are transacted and dispatched with the replies of Your Highnesses at the end of each Article in the village of Santa Fe of the region of Granada, the seventeenth of April in the year of 1492 after the birth of Our Savior Jesus Christ. I, the King. I, the Queen. By order of The King and The Queen. Juan de Coloma.

[*General Archive of the Indies, General Index 418, Folio 1-4*]

Instruction from the King and the Queen, Our Sovereigns, to Don Christopher Columbus, Their Highnesses' Admiral of the Islands and mainlands discovered and to be discovered on the ocean sea in the area of the Indies, and their Viceroy and Governor over them and likewise their Captain General of the fleet that Their Highnesses now send to the aforesaid islands and mainlands, as to the manner in which he should carry out this voyage on which he now embarks by order of Their Highnesses, as much in his departure and that of the fleet as in his journey and after he shall have arrived, God willing, is this that follows:

Instruction of Admiral Columbus

1. To the effect that the indians be treated with kindness, and brought into our Holy Catholic Faith for which Father Bartolomé and other clergy are delegated.

Firstly, since it pleased Our Lord God in His blessed mercy to discover the aforesaid islands and mainlands, and Our Highnesses, the King and the Queen by the efforts of the aforesaid Christopher Columbus, their Admiral, Viceroy and Governor of the lands, who has made known to Their Highnesses that the inhabitants of them whom he encountered, he observed them to be very disposed to be converted to Our Holy Catholic Faith since they have neither law nor faith which has pleased and pleases Their Highnesses; for in everything, it is right that it be done primarily in the service of God Our Lord and the exaltation of Our Holy Catholic Faith. Therefore, Their Highnesses, wishing that Our Holy Catholic Faith be increased and expanded, mandate and charge the aforesaid Admiral, Viceroy and Governor that by all ways and means possible he shall seek and endeavor to attract the inhabitants of the aforesaid islands and mainlands so that they be converted to Our Holy Catholic Faith and to help in this, they send the Reverend Father Buil, together with other clergy whom the aforesaid Admiral is to take with him. The clergy, with the help and industry of the indians who came here, shall endeavor that they be well informed on the beliefs of Our Holy Faith for they will already know and understand much of our language and shall be trying to teach them in it in the best way possible. In order that this may be best carried out after the fleet has arrived safely, the aforesaid Admiral shall undertake and ensure that all who sail in it and, as shall others henceforth, treat the aforementioned indians gently and well without causing them any annoyance and endeavor that they have much conversation and friendliness with one another, doing the best possible work that they can. Furthermore, the aforesaid Admiral should graciously give them gifts of Their Highnesses' goods carried on board for barter and treat them with much respect. In the event it should occur that someone or some persons should mistreat the aforesaid indians in whatever manner, that the aforesaid Admiral, as Viceroy and Governor of Their Highnesses, punish him severely by virtue of the powers of Their Highnesses that are vested in him for that purpose, because spiritual matters without the temporal cannot long endure. The aforementioned Admiral, Viceroy and Governor is directed on the other matters as follows:

2. To the effect that the aforesaid Admiral be provided with the best caravels, pilots and sailors for the fleet.

Firstly, for the voyage he must seek the best caravels that can be found in Andalusia and that the sailors and pilots be those who best know their craft and are most trustworthy, so that with the authority that Their Highnesses conferred upon the Admiral and upon Don Juan de Fonseca in order to prepare this fleet, it is understood that he may choose the ships that he may want for it, selecting at his will those that the Admiral shall feel are suitable.

3. To the effect that all those persons who shall be sailing shall present themselves before the aforesaid Don Christopher Columbus and bring their purser's voucher and their assigned pay allotment.

All persons who are to go on the ships, if it shall be possible, should be known and trustworthy persons and all are to present themselves before the said Juan de Fonseca and before Juan García de Soria, chosen by the chief pursers as their deputy for this fleet, before whom the aforementioned presentation is to be made, as well as before the deputy of the said chief pursers, and he is to record it in his book, and the paymaster is to disburse the pay that they are to receive, in accordance with the payroll and vouchers authorized by the aforesaid Admiral and Don Juan de Fonseca and of the said Juan García de Soria, and not in any other way.

4. In order that all purchase agreements and contracts that are made shall be executed before a senior notary, the Admiral and Don Juan de Fonseca.

All the contracts that are transacted with whatsoever captains and sailors and officers and other persons who shall be in the said fleet, and likewise, all the procurement that shall have to be made of ships as well as of provisions and stores and supplies and whatsoever other things for the said fleet, and the ships that shall set sail with the aforesaid Admiral and Don Juan de Fonseca and with the persons that shall be appointed and in the presence of the aforesaid Juan García de Soria as deputy [endorsed] of the said chief pursers in order that he record this fact, and likewise in the presence of another notary if the aforesaid Admiral shall want this to be done. And the procurements that shall be transacted in the places where they shall land

and those which shall have to be made in other places shall be discharged by the persons who the aforesaid Admiral and Don Juan de Fonseca consign to it and before a public notary. And he who shall be charged with disbursing the pay for this fleet shall pay the monies that in all the above mentioned shall reach the amount authorized in the payroll and vouchers by the said Admiral and Don Juan de Fonseca and by the said Juan García de Soria as purser.

5. To the effect that Juan García [de Soria] keep a record book in which the stores and provisions that shall be carried will be recorded.

The aforesaid stores and provisions and supplies and goods and other things that shall be bought and shall be consigned to the persons that the aforesaid Admiral shall name, and the aforesaid Juan García de Soria will be in charge of them and will keep a record and account of it, one to submit to Their Highnesses and another to send to the purser who is to remain in the said islands with the authorization of the said senior accountants.

6. So that the aforesaid man and aforesaid men certify those who shall come on board, and that these make a pledge of homage to defend Their Highnesses in all.

At the time that the aforesaid fleet is to depart in favorable conditions, all the captains and pilots and sailors and cavalrymen and foot soldiers and officers and other persons that shall sail on it shall record all that which they carry before the aforesaid Admiral, Don Juan de Fonseca and before the persons that they designate and before the said Juan García de Soria as deputy purser so that the persons that sail be known and the qualifications and occupation of each of them, and all are to take an oath and pledge homage to the King and to the Queen, Our Sovereigns, to serve them faithfully on this voyage, on the voyage at sea as well as upon arrival at the islands and mainlands. And on the return voyage, whatever may befall, they should keep guard in word or deed or in council in the service of Their Highnesses and over their possessions as faithful and loyal vassals, subjects of Their Highnesses, and wherever they see their duty to lie they should adhere to it, and if they should see the contrary, they would reject it with all their might, and they should make it known to the aforesaid Admiral Captain General so that he may remedy it. Likewise, in all things and whatever may befall they will remain loyal to the aforesaid Admiral as Admiral of Their Highnesses on sea and on land, as Viceroy and Governor of Their Highnesses, so that all may be in compliance with him in this instruction, and no one may do the contrary, which Their Highnesses require be done and fulfilled according to this present instruction, and that they shall act accordingly, under the penalty which befalls those who break similar pledges and homages.

7. That no person who shall come on board may carry goods for barter.

Furthermore, Their Highnesses order that no one nor any person of those that shall sail on the said fleet in whatsoever state or condition they may be, they shall not bring nor may they carry goods of any kind on the said fleet, nor on other ships, for barter of any kind on the said islands and mainlands, since no one is to do so except as agents of Their Highnesses, as will be specified later.

8. That goods and commodities that shall be carried upon disembarkation will be set out and displayed for inspection.

At the time when, with good fortune, they shall arrive at the islands and mainlands where they are to disembark, the aforesaid Admiral and Governor for Their Highnesses is to order that all the captains and crew and ships set out and present for inspection of persons, as well as ships and arms and supplies and provisions and other things they shall be carrying, so that no ship nor anyone whosoever may carry any goods to barter in any way, be it gold nor other things, on all of the said islands and mainlands without an order from Their Highnesses as is stated. If any shall be found to carry more than that which they declared at the time they shall have left Castile, as was entered in the record book of the one who went as a deputy of the said chief pursers, who is to be stationed on the said islands, that he surrender it and that the aforesaid Admiral Viceroy, or whoever may be empowered by him, and he shall give it to the person who, by authority of Their Highnesses, should receive the goods there which Their Highnesses shall send, in the presence of the said deputy of the said pursers so that he may take charge of it.

9. So that any trading shall take place in the presence of the treasurer or whosoever he shall name.

Also, that whatsoever trading might be done, the Admiral should do it, or the person that may be named by him, together with the treasurer of Their Highnesses who is to be there, and no other person whatsoever, and he should do it in the presence of the said deputy of the aforesaid pursers or before the official who will be placed there for that purpose, so that he may take charge of it and enter it in the book which he is to keep on said trading. And because it could happen that this trading might be done in various places where the treasurer may not be able to go, he should send another in his place, together with the persons that the aforesaid Admiral will name, and in the presence of the aforesaid deputy of the pursers or of their official, and not in any other manner.

10. That the Viceroy have or send for and name magistrates, constables, and that these be qualified in civil and criminal matters.

After the aforesaid Admiral Viceroy Governor shall arrive, he shall, by virtue of the powers vested in him for that purpose by Their Highnesses, appoint magistrates and constables on the islands and lands where he shall be. And the persons that sail with him and on whatsoever other islands where there may be people, any of those persons that sail with the said Admiral and on his fleet may preside over lawsuits be they civil as well as criminal, just as are others likewise appointed by the other Viceroys and Governors wheresoever Their Highnesses may delegate them, and the aforesaid Viceroy may hear and be advised of the appellate or first instance courts, as he considers that more is needed and as other governors and viceroys of Their Highnesses are accustomed to do. [signed]

11. That the Viceroy name, if it shall be necessary, three subjects as councilmen and jurymen.

Furthermore, that if it shall be necessary to name councilmen and jurymen and other officials for the administration of the people or of whatsoever community that shall have to be established, the aforesaid Admiral Viceroy and Governor shall name three persons for each office as has been set forth by Their Highnesses, and from these Their Highnesses shall choose one for each office, and thus by the order of Their Highnesses they shall be provided. But since on the voyage the said officials cannot be obtained in this way, therefore, in this instance, the aforesaid Admiral and Viceroy and Governor of Their Highnesses shall name them.

12. Concerning the form in which proclamations are to be made.

Moreover, whatever justice that shall be carried out, let it be declared that this is the justice that the King and Queen, Our Lords, order to be done.

13. That all decrees be signed by Their Highnesses, by the Viceroy, and their notary.

Also, that all the authorized provisos and orders which the aforesaid Admiral and Viceroy shall have to execute shall be written by Ferdinand and Isabella, the King and the Queen each one signed by the aforesaid Don Christopher Columbus as Viceroy and endorsed by the notary who shall follow the practice utilized by the other notaries who sign the other Viceroys' letters, and shall be sealed on the back with the seal which Their Highnesses place in their viceroyalties.

14. That a customs house shall be erected where all the goods may be stored.

Also, God willing, as soon as the aforesaid Admiral arrives, he should erect a customs house where shall be placed all the goods of Their Highnesses, those that shall be here as well as those that shall be sent elsewhere. And at the time they unload said stores, these should be placed in the aforesaid customs house in the presence of those persons whom the said Admiral Viceroy shall name for that duty, and before the aforementioned deputy of the said chief pursers who is to be present, and before another officer who will be placed there by the said Admiral so that the books will be kept and all will be written down, and that duty will be entrusted to the treasurer whom Their Highnesses will send there, so that all payments may be made, as aforesaid, and if something should be missing he should make them pay forthwith.

15. So that all shall present themselves before the Viceroy in order that they shall be paid their wages.

Moreover, that whenever the aforesaid Admiral shall see that the appointed time has come that notification be made to all the personnel that are in service, that they are obliged to present themselves before the persons that he shall named for that purpose, and before the deputy of the said chief purser who are to be present there, and when it shall be required to pay the wages of the said personnel they are to be paid by way of the said notification and by the payroll and voucher of the aforesaid Viceroy and of the said purser and in no other way.

16. To the effect that all captains and sailors be subject to the orders of the Viceroy if it should be necessary, and that ships be sent to other places to trade or explore.

Likewise, if the aforesaid Admiral, after he shall have arrived at the islands, shall see that it is necessary to send whatever ships with whatever crew to whatever place to discover whatever has not been discovered up to this point, whether for trade, or to send them here or to any other place whatsoever, all captains and sailors who are assigned to do so shall comply with the order, subject to the penalties that shall be applied to them. These penalties in this case, Their Highnesses empower the aforesaid Admiral and Governor General to enforce them on persons and property of those concerned.

17. That if Juan García [de Soria], as deputy treasurer shall want to appoint another in his place who may keep the record book, he may do so.

Likewise, in order that there may be a customs house in Cádiz where are to be loaded and unloaded all the goods, and arms, and supplies and provisions which shall be shipped, those that go on the said fleet as well as those that remain on the aforementioned islands and mainlands, likewise those that shall be brought from there. All of which is to be loaded in the said customs house and nowhere else.This customs house is to have the person whom Their Highnesses shall send, or Juan García de Soria as deputy of the said chief pursers, is to keep a record of all that shall be loaded and unloaded there, so that by his book the charges and settlements of it shall be made, so that if the aforesaid Admiral shall want to place any other official there so that he himself may keep a record of it, he may do so and let him do it.

18. That the Admiral retain the eighth part of that which shall be found, paying likewise for one eighth of the goods.

Furthermore, it pleases Their Highnesses that the aforesaid Admiral shall keep one eighth part of all that shall be gained of whatsoever there shall be of gold or other things in the said islands and mainlands, the aforesaid Admiral paying one eighth part of the cost of the goods, so that the said trade shall be done taking out first the tenth part of it that the said Admiral is to have in accordance with the letter of the charter which Their Highnesses have ordered to be set forth with the said Admiral.

19. To the effect that the aforesaid Admiral keep and comply with the letter of this instruction or be subject to the penalties provided by law.

We the King and the Queen, with this document, direct you Don Christopher Columbus, our Admiral and Viceroy and Governor of the islands and mainlands, which by our command have been discovered in the ocean sea in the region of the Indies, and our Captain General of our fleet which we send there, order that you examine the decree written here above, and keep it and comply with it according to its provisions, and that you will not go, nor pass beyond, nor consent to do so, nor exceed the intent of it in any manner whatsoever. Decreed in the city of Valencia on the 29th day of the month of May of the year 1493 of the birth of Our Savior Jesus Christ. (signed) [I the King, I the Queen. By order of the King and the Queen. Fernando Alvarez.]

ARTICLE OF THE TESTAMENT OF THE QUEEN, OUR LADY DONA ISABELLA

[General Archive of the Indies, Seville, Royal Patronage, Parcel 1, Number 5]

And also, since at the time we were granted by the Holy Apostolic See the islands and mainlands of the ocean sea already discovered or yet to be discovered, our principal intention at the time that we made this request to His Holiness, Pope Alexander VI, and he granted us the concession to procure and induce and attract the people of these lands was to convert them to our holy Catholic faith and to send to the said islands and mainlands prelates and religious and clerics and other learned and God-fearing people to instruct the natives and inhabitants of the islands and mainlands in the Catholic faith, and to teach them and endow them with good customs and to teach them diligence, due to and according to the terms contained in the aforementioned concession, therefore I request the King, my lord, most affectionately, and I entrust and command the aforementioned princess my daughter and the aforementioned prince her husband that they should do so, and ensure that this should be their principal aim, and that they should be very diligent and not allow nor give any opportunity that the indians, who are the natives and inhabitants of said islands and mainlands already gained or about to be gained, should receive any harm to their persons or their property, but they should order that they be well and justly treated, and if they have received any harm that they should remedy it and provide that nothing be done in excess of what is enjoined and commanded by the apostolic mandate of the aforementioned concession.

[General Archive of the Indies, Seville, Royal Patronage, File 15, Number 7]

Transcript of the Instruction that Diego Velazques issued to the captains whom he sent for exploration.

Authorized.

Instruction that Diego Velazques issued in the name of Their Highnesses to Hernando Cortes who will go as captain of the fleet which God Our Lord may guide to the islands and lands newly discovered in the ocean sea.

1518 + Instruction from Diego Velazques to Cortes.

Inasmuch as I, Diego Velazques, Governor and Captain General and Director of the chieftains and indians of this island Fernandina for Their Highnesses, etc.
I ordered recently, in the name and service of Their Highnesses a voyage to explore and to go around the Yucatan island, Santa Maria de los Remedios, which had newly been discovered, and to discover however much more that may please God our Lord and in the name of Their Highnesses to take possession of it all, a fleet with the necessary crew, on which was its captain by name Juan de Grijalva of the town of Trinidad of this island, who sent me a caravel from among those he had, because it was shipping water, and on it some men that the indians on the said Santa Maria de los Remedios had wounded and others who were sick and because of all that had happened to it, even to these newly discovered islands and land, of which one is an island called Cozumel and he gave it the name of Santa Cruz, and the other is a large territory, part of which is called (...) that he gave the name Santa Maria de las Nieves, from which he sent me the said caravel and

crew and wrote to me about how he was continuing to seek the answer to his primary question, if that territory was an island or a mainland, and that after many days when with reason one was to have obtained news concerning what is presumed, but such news from him has not been received to this date and it is not known if he must be or is in some extreme need of help and also because a caravel which I sent to the aforementioned Juan de Grijalva from the port of this city of Santiago, so that it should join with the fleet he was leading at the port of Saint Christopher of Havana, because it was much better provisioned and thus this was suitable to serve their Majesties, it so happened that when it arrived where it planned to find him, the aforementioned Juan de Grijalva had set sail and had left with the entire fleet. Since he left a message about the voyage that the aforementioned caravel was to make, and since the said caravel on which sailed 80 or 90 men did not find the said fleet, it took the said message and went following after the aforesaid Juan de Grijalva. And as it seems, and has been learned by means of information from the wounded and sick that the said Juan de Grijalva sent me, it had not joined up with the fleet, nor had there been any news of it, nor of the said wounded and sick. They learned of it on the return since for a great part of the trip they came along the shores of the island of Santa Maria de los Remedios along which they had gone, and it is presumed that with bad weather, they could be driven toward the mainland or arrive at some place where the said 80 or 90 men might run some risk, whether because of the ship, or because of being so few in number or because of being lost while searching for the aforesaid Juan de Grijalva, although they were very well supplied with all that was necessary and even more. Because after I sent the said fleet with the said Juan de Grijalva, I have been informed almost certainly, by an indian from the said island of Yucatan, Santa Maria de los Remedios, of how some Christian beings are in the power of certain head chiefs there, and they have them as slaves and they are using them on their estates, and that they took them many days ago and from a caravel that was said to be for some time at Porto Perdido. It is believed that one of them is Nicuesa, the captain whom the Catholic King, His Highness Ferdinand, ordered to go to the mainland and redeem them. It would be a great service to Our Lord God and to Their Highnesses, for all of which it seems to me that, in the service of God Our Lord and of His Highness, as I have said, it would be suitable to send, in pursuit of and to aid the said fleet which the said Juan de Grijalva led, and in search of the caravel which went in pursuit after him, to rescue, if it may be possible, the aforementioned Christians who are captives in the power of the indians. Having many times thought about it, and weighed it, and discussed it with responsible people about sending, as I am now sending, another such fleet, also supplied and made ready with ships and provisions as well as the crew and all else for such an important undertaking, so that just in case the crew of the other first fleet or of the said caravel that was following it encounters a large band of infidels, there may be enough to help them and disarm them in that way. And if they should not find them, it can by itself safely sail and land in its search of all those islands and lands and learn about them and do all else that should be done in the service of God Our Lord and is proper in the service of Their Highnesses. And to the end, I was reminded of the command offered to you, Fernando Cortes, to appoint you fleet captain, in view of your long experience, having served Their Highnesses with me on this island, with confidence that you are a responsible person, showing prudence and diligence in every way, that you will give a good account of all that which you would be ordered to do for me in the name of Their Highnesses, I give you a letter of the agreement, stating that you shall lead and command as is deemed appropriate in the service of Our Lord God and Their Highnesses. And in order that all that is agreed upon be better guided, go and take command, and do that which you have to do and oversee with all vigilance and diligence, inquire and learn, complying fully with the instruction that you have from your patrons, which they directed to me and to the lieutenants and captains that I would send to the islands where you might go.

And in keeping with the instruction and its subject and form, not withholding anything before carrying it out, in everything and for all according to what is contained in it, guiding you and accompanying you in accordance with the following.

1. Firstly, the primary purpose which you and all those in your company are to carry out is, and must be, in order that God Our Lord be served and praised on this voyage and our Holy Catholic Faith be spread, that you shall not permit, in any manner or means, that anyone shall speak ill of God Our Lord, nor His Mother Mary, nor His Saints, nor utter blasphemy against His Name, in any way whatsoever. Above all, you shall admonish everyone, and for those who commit similar offenses, punish them with all possible rigor.

2. Also, in order that you may serve God Our Lord in many ways, you shall not permit any public sin such as cohabitation in public nor that any of the Spanish Christians of your company engage in an excess or casual coitus with any woman outside of our law, because it is a very odious sin against God, and divine and human laws prohibit it, and you shall proceed with great vigor against him who shall commit such a sin and offense, and you shall punish him in conformity with the laws that apply and are provided for such cases.

3. Also, because in similar situations, full agreement is very useful and beneficial, and on the contrary, disputes and disagreements are damaging, and out of dice and card games much scandal and cursing of God and of His Saints tend to ensue, you shall strive not to take nor accept in your company any person who is believed to be suspicious of service to God Our Lord and to Their Highnesses, and take heed if he is rebellious, and frivolous, and rowdy. And you shall forbid bringing dice and playing cards on board any ship and you shall announce it to the ships' crews as well as to the shore crews, imposing severe penalties on them, which you shall administer to the persons who disobey.

4. Also, after the departure of the fleet from the port of this city of Santiago, take every precaution and care that at the ports of this island of Fernandina where you shall go

ashore, you do not allow that your crew shall bother anyone on it, nor take anything from the inhabitants or resi-
dents, or indians. And each time you go ashore at the said
ports, you shall remind them of it with the warning that
those who shall disobey and violate it shall be severely
punished in accordance with the law.

5. Also, after you shall have received, with the help of
God, the provisions and other things you are to put on
board at the said ports, and have presented and set out for
inspection the crew and arms you are carrying on each
ship, watching carefully that in the inspection of arms that
there shall not be the deceptions which in similar cases are
frequently carried out, lending them to one another for
the said inspection. And given that all is in good order in
the said ships and crew, in the shortest time possible you
shall leave, in the name of God, to continue your voyage,

6. Also, before you set sail again, you shall look over very
diligently all the ships of your command, and you will inquire and search, in all possible ways, to see if they might
carrying some indian man or woman native of these islands, and if you should find one, hand him over to the
authorities, so that when the persons leave, in whose
charge they have been left in the name of Their Highnesses, they shall return them, and not in any way will
you consent that any indian may go on said ships.

7. Also, after the ships have gone out to sea, and the small
boats are brought in, you shall go on the small boat
belonging to the ship on which you are sailing, to each one
of the ships, and by taking with you a notary and on the
basis of his records, you shall send back to sea the crews
that each ship may be carrying so that you may learn of
anything that is missing from its contents from the said
copies that each ship will have made, so that you shall
know with more certainty the crew that you are taking.
And from each copy you shall give a transcript to the captain that you shall put on each ship, and concerning the
persons whom you shall decide on and who have con-
tracted with you and to whom you have given payments,
it is agreed that you shall send me a statement so that this
shall be known here.

8. Also, at the same time as this previous occasion when you visit the said ships, you shall order and notify the captains whom you shall place on each ship, and the masters and pilots who are going or might go on them, and to each one separately and to all of them together, that they should take special care to follow and accompany the ship on which you shall be going. And in no way or form shall they separate from you, so that each day they shall all speak to you or at least be within sight of your ship, so that with the help of Our Lord, you shall all arrive together at the island of Cozumel St. Augustine which is your proper goal and destination, taking each of them concerning this matter before your notary, demanding their pledge and placing large and severe penalties upon them. And if that which, God forbid, should happen, that because of bad weather or because a storm should overtake them on the sea, and the ships should be forced to separate and not go together in formation, if the aforesaid happens and they should arrive at the aforesaid island before you, you shall assure and order, under the aforesaid penalty, that no captain, nor master, nor any other person who may be on those ships should dare to leave them and go onto the land in any way or manner. But rather, they should remain under sail and fully alert until you shall arrive, and because it could be that you or those who might have eventually become separated from you might arrive at the island at night, you shall order and advise all of them that if any ship is missing at night, they should set out lanterns so that they should see and be aware of each other, and you will do the same also if you arrive first or wherever you may be at sea, so that all may follow you and see you and know where you are going. And at the time when you disembark on this island, you will order and see that all take part in the sacking that is to be carried out, and that you shall give them advice and orders in this so that all shall be in good order.

9. Also, you shall advise and command the said captains and masters and all the other persons who might be on the said ships that if they should arrive before you at any of the ports of the aforementioned island, and some indians might come to the said ships, that the indians should

be very well treated and received, and that in no way
should any person in any way, nor under any conditions,
dare to cause them any annoyance or say anything to them
that might be unpleasant to them nor tell them where you
are going. Except that since they are waiting, you should
tell them the purpose of your going; nor should you demand of them or question them if they know anything
about the Christians who are captives on the island of
Santa Maria de los Remedios in the power of the indians,
so that they shall not warn them and kill them, and on
this you must place very great and severe penalties.

10. Also, after you shall arrive in due course at the said island of Santa Cruz, being informed that this is the island
by information from the pilots or by Melchor, an indian
who is a native of Santa Maria de los Remedios, and
whom you shall take with you, you shall endeavor to see
and sound the depths of all the other ports and entrances
and waterways that you can, wherever you may go on the
said island as well as on Santa Maria de los Remedios and
Punta Llana, Santa Maria de las Nieves, and everything
that you shall find in the said ports you shall cause to be
recorded on the charts of the pilots, and by your notary all
that has to do with the said islands and mainlands,
indicating by name each one of the said ports and waterways, and where each of the provinces may be, so that you
shall have made a full and complete report of everything.

11. Also, when you shall have arrived, with the aid of God
Our Lord, at the said island of Cozumel Santa Cruz, you
shall speak to the chieftains and indians of it and of all the
other islands and lands wherever you may go, telling
them how you, by order of the King our Lord, have come
to visit them and to give them to understand that he is a
very powerful king, whose vassals we and they are, and
whom many of the peoples of this world must obey, and
who has subjugated and subjugates many parts and lands
of the world, some of which are these parts of the ocean
sea where they and many others dwell. And you will relate to them the names of the lands and islands. It is best to
know all the coast of the mainland up to where they are
located, in Española and San Juan and Jamaica and this island of Fernandina, and however many more you may

know. And that he the King has granted them and grants them many favors, and for this purpose he has on each island his captains and crews, and I am on this island by his command, and having information about them and the places where they are, I send you in his name so that you may speak to them and demand that they subject themselves under his yoke of servitude and royal protection, and that they may be certain that having done so and signed it legally and properly they shall be, by His Highness and by me in his name, very well repaid and favored and compared against his enemies. And you are to tell them how all the natives of these islands are doing likewise, and as a sign of servitude they are giving and sending a great quantity of gold, precious stones, pearls and other things they have, and likewise Their Highness are granting them many favors. And you are to tell them that they should do likewise, and should give him some of the aforementioned things and other things they may have, so that His Highness may know their willingness to serve him. And so that it may gratify them you also shall tell them how, having learned how the battle that Captain Francisco Hernandez had with them there had turned out, it made me very sad, because His Highness does not wish that on his account, nor that of you his vassals, any of them should be mistreated, and I in his name send you so that you should speak to them and pacify them and assure them of the great power of the King our Lord, and that from this point on, if they should wish to peacefully dedicate themselves to his service, that the Spaniards shall not engage them in battles or wars, in the face of such conformity and peace, and that they shall be aided against their enemies, and all the other things that you feel that you should say to them to attract them to this our purpose.
12. And also, because on many parts of the said island of Santa Cruz there have been found, on top of certain tombs and burials, certain crosses which tell us that they have among themselves a great deal of veneration, you shall seek to inquire, by all possible means and much diligence and care, to learn the reason why they have it, and if they have it because they might have had or have some news of Our Lord God and whether any man has suffered for

this cause. And on this subject you shall be very vigilant, and by means of your notary you shall take down the entire story, whether on the aforesaid island or on any other islands to which you may go where you happen to find this said cross.

13. Also, you shall take great care to inquire and learn, by all ways and means that you can, whether the natives of said islands or any one of them may have any sect or belief or rite or ceremony in which they may believe, or in which they may worship, or if they have any mosques, or any houses of prayer and idols or other similar things, and if they have people who administer their ceremonies like ulemas [Moslem scholars] or other ministers, and for all of this you shall bring your notary a very complete account of how their faith is carried out.

14. Also, since you know the principal reason why Their Highnesses allow new lands to be discovered is so that, for the great number of souls as well as the innumerable land that may have been or is in these lost places outside of Our Holy Faith, for lack of anyone who would give them any true knowledge, you should try very hard, if by any chance you have sufficient conversation with the natives of the islands and lands where you shall go, to be able to inform them about it so that they shall be acquainted with it, at least making them understand, in the best way you can. And you shall give time and place for this, in the way that seems best to you, which may be suitable to the service of Our Lord God and Their Highnesses.

15. Also, once you have arrived at the said island of Santa Cruz, and in any other lands where you may go, you shall work, in any way that you can, to inquire and learn some news of the fleet which Juan de Grijalva led, because it could be that the said Juan de Grijalva might have returned to this island. And if they should have any news of him, or if they might know for certain whether he might be in some area or port of the said island. And likewise, by this same order, you shall try to learn some news of the caravel which Cristobal de Oliva took charge of, and which went in pursuit of the said Juan de Grijalva, you shall learn if he arrived at the said island and if they know that

he suffered some defeat, and if they have or know any news of where he is and how he is.

16. Also, if they should provide any news about whether they know anything of the said fleet which is in the vicinity, you shall try to join up with it, and after joining it, if you might have been able to have learned any news about the aforesaid caravel, you shall issue the order and agreement so that, everything being agreed upon and all informed of where you shall be waiting and to follow so that you shall not be once again scattered and separated, you shall specifically state how they shall go in search of the said caravel and bring it to where you agreed.

17. Also, if on the said island of Santa Cruz you shall have no news that the caravel may have returned here or is nearby, and you might learn some news about said caravel, you shall go in search of it. And once you have found it, you shall try to search for and learn some news of the said fleet which Juan de Grijalva led.

18. Also, given that you have done all the above things, as the time and opportunity to do so shall have been offered you, if you still have learned no news of the said fleet or the caravel that went in pursuit of it, you shall then go along the coast of the island of Yucatan Santa Maria de los Remedios on which there are six Christians in the power of certain head chiefs, according to what Melchor, a native indian of the said island says and will tell you, and you shall attempt by all ways and means possible to have the said Christians rescued through love or any other way that shall not be a detriment to them, nor to the Spaniards you have with you, nor to the indians. And because Melchor, the native indian from the said island whom you are bringing with you, knows the chieftains who are holding the captives, you shall make sure that said Melchor shall be treated very well by all, and you shall not allow that anyone should harm him or show anger toward him, nor that anyone should speak to him except you alone, and you shall show much love toward him and you shall do everything good that you can for him, so that he may find out and tell you the truth about all that you may ask and command, and that he may point out and show you the said chieftains. Because, since these said indians in case of

war are very clever, it could be that they might name as chieftains other indians who are not so clever, so that the latter might speak for them and that from them they might learn by experience what they should do or what they might tell them, and since said Melchor shall have great fondness for you, he shall not allow them to deceive you, without advising you beforehand, or on the contrary if anyone deals with him in any other manner.

19. Also, you shall take great notice and care that all the indians of all the places where you may go on the sea or wherever you may be on land, who come to see you or speak to you, whether about the rescue or anything else, shall be very well received and treated by you and by all others, showing them much friendship and love, and encouraging them as it shall seem to you to be required, according to the occasion or the people who may come to you, and you shall not allow, under severe penalties which you shall impose on such behavior, that any annoyance nor any unpleasant thing be done to them, but rather you shall endeavor, by all ways and means possible, that when they leave you they shall go very happy and content and satisfied with your conversation and with all those of your company, because doing otherwise would be a great disservice to Our Lord and to Their Highnesses, because our demand would not have any effect.

20. Also, if before you join up with the said Juan de Grijalva, some indians should wish to trade with you some things of theirs for things that you have, because trade shall be better received in all ways, and from the things that are there, you shall take a chest with two or three locks and you shall designate from among the good men of your company, those that seem to you to be the most zealous in the service of Their Highnesses and who are trustworthy persons, one to be overseer and one to be treasurer for the trading that shall be done, and you shall trade in gold, pearls, precious stones, metals and whatever other things there may be. And if for that chest of three locks there is a key for each lock, you shall give one key to the said overseer and the other to the treasurer, and the third shall be kept by you yourself or by whoever you command, and all shall be placed in the aforesaid chest,

and the trading shall be done in the presence of your notary who shall certify it.

21. Also, if it should become necessary to make landings several times, whether to take on firewood or other things that may be necessary, when such a necessity should arise, so that the Spaniards can do so without danger, you shall send with the people who are going for wood or for water a person in whom you have a great deal of confidence and it shall be well understood that he is a sensible person whom you command and all shall obey, and you shall see to it that all those you send with him shall be the most peaceful, and quiet, and trustworthy and sensible that you can find, and the best armed, and you shall command them that in their comings and goings, there should not be scandal nor brawling with the natives of the said island, and you shall see that there shall be no danger and that in no way shall they sleep on land even one night, nor should they go so far from the shore that they cannot return quickly to it, so that if something should happen in regard to the indians, they can be aided by the men on the ships.

22. Also, if by chance there should be a town near the sea coast, and if you should discern among its people such good will that it seems to you that by their wishes and with no great disturbance to them, nor any danger to the Spaniards, you can go to see them, you shall be sure to take with you the most peaceful and sensible and well-armed men that you can find, and you will command them before your notary, under penalties that you shall impose on them, that no one should dare to take anything from the said indians, whether it may be of small or great value, nor in any way or manner should they dare to enter their houses or trifle with their women nor should they take them, nor approach them, nor speak to them, nor say or do anything else that might be presumed to cause any annoyance. And they should not stray too far from you nor separate from you in any way or manner nor for anything that might be offered to them, even if the indians come out to meet you, until you order them what they should and must do, according to the time and necessity in which you find yourself or that you may see.

23. Also, because it might happen that the indians might show good will toward you in order to deceive you and kill you and force you to go to their towns, you shall exercise much care and vigilance in the way in which you regard them, and if you go you must always go very much on the alert, taking with you the people described above and with the arms at the ready. And you shall not allow the indians to intermingle with the Spaniards, at least not many of them, unless you go to them first and make them understand that you are doing so because you do not want any Spaniard to do or say anything which might anger them, because if many indians intermingle with you they could set up a trap whereby while all were embracing one another others could leave, and since there are many of them you could run into danger and perish, and you shall leave the ships readied, so that they are well prepared, so that if the need should arise you can be aided by the crews that you left behind on them, and you shall leave with them a certain signal as to what they should do if they should find themselves in need of doing it for you if you need it.

24. Also, may it please Our Lord God, when you have found the Christians on the said island of Santa Maria de los Remedios who are captives, and you have searched all around the island for the said fleet and the said caravel, you shall continue your voyage to Punta Llana, which is the principal port of the mainland which said Juan de Grijalva recently discovered, and you shall continue on in search of him up along the coast, searching all the rivers and ports until you arrive at the bay of San Juan and Santa Maria de las Nieves, which is the place from which the said Juan de Grijalva sent me the wounded and the sick, and he wrote to me what had happened to him up to that point. And if you find him there, you are to join up with him, and so that there should be no differences or divisions between the Spaniards you bring with you and those that are already there, each one shall be responsible for the crew he brings with him, and both of you together and in agreement shall consult about everything that may occur, be it good or bad, so that everything in the service of Our Lord God and of Their Highnesses will be agreed upon and

according to the instruction that Juan de Grijalva received from his patrons and mine, and this which in the name of Their Highnesses I now give to you, and, may it please Our Lord God if there should be some trading or gift of any value, it should be received by both of you together in the presence of Francisco de Peñalosa, the overseer appointed by his patrons.

25. Also, you shall attempt with great diligence and solicitude, to inquire and learn the secret of the said islands and mainlands and all the others adjoining them, and, Our Lord God having been served, that might also be discovered, and you are to discover from the actions and conversation of all the people, and each one of them in particular, all that you can learn about the trees, springs, plants, animals, gold, precious stones, pearls and other metals, spices, and anything else whatsoever that you can learn and obtain from the said islands and mainlands. And you shall make a complete account before a notary. Once it is known that there is gold on the said islands and mainlands, you shall learn where it is from and what it is like, and if you should have to look for it some place where you can see it, you shall work to obtain a sample of it so that you can give a more accurate account of it, especially on Santa Maria de los Remedios from where the said Juan de Grijalva sent me certain grains of gold to be melted down and some already cast, and if those articles of worked gold are made there or if they bring them from, and trade for them in, other places.

26. Also, on all the islands which may be discovered, you shall disembark, and in the presence of your notary and many witnesses and in the name of Their Highnesses you shall take possession of the lands with all possible solemnity, carrying out all the acts and procedures that are required in such cases and are usually done. And in all these things you shall attempt, in every way that you can and in a proper and orderly way, to speak to whoever might inform you of other islands and mainlands, and of the ways and character of the people of these lands, because it is said that there are big-eared people and many who have faces like dogs, and likewise where might be found the Ama-

zons who, according to the indians you are taking with
you, are near that place.

27. And also because, besides the things stated above and
those that have been given and entrusted to you by my orders, you may be offered many other things which I, not
being there, cannot anticipate either the means or resolution of them, and which you, being present and a person
of whom I have had experience and in whom I have
confidence, shall take great care and diligence to safeguard
these things and look after them and administer them in
such a way that shall be most suitable in the service of Our
Lord God and of Their Highnesses. You shall provide for
all of these as wisely as you can and should do so, according to the circumstances in which you find yourself, con-
forming in every way that you can with the said instructions cited above, and those of some wise and prudent
persons chosen from among those you are taking with you
in whom you have trust and confidence, and whom you
from experience to be zealous in the service of Our Lord
God and of Their Highnesses, and who shall know how to
give you their opinions.

28. Also, because it might be that among the people who
might go with you from this island of Fernandina there
might be some who might owe money to Their Highnesses. You shall endeavor, in every way that you can in
all the ports that you come to on this island where people
wish to go with you, to learn if any one of them owes in
any way on this island any monies to Their Highnesses,
and if they do owe monies, you shall make them pay it,
and if they cannot pay, then enough people are to remain
on the island and shall serve as security for the debt of
such a person, and if they shall not pay it and leave others
as security to pay it for them, then you shall not in any
way or manner take them into your company.

29. Also, you shall endeavor, after you have arrived at
Santa Maria de las Nieves, or before that if it seems better
to you, and after you have found the fleet and the caravel,
to send to me as quickly as possible, in a ship which is a
good one and which you have the least need of, an account of all that has happened to you and what you have
done and plan to do, and you shall also send me all the

things of gold, pearls and precious stones, spices, animals and fruits and birds and all the other things that you might have, so that I may make a full and complete report to the King Our Lord, and so that I may send it to him so that His Highness may see it and have a very full and complete account of all that there is in these said lands and territories, or that you have heard is there or might be there.

30. Also, in all civil or criminal cases that between persons or in any other way might arise there, you shall learn of them and all concerning them in accordance with law and justice, and in no other manner, since for each single matter and part of it and for all that is added and connected to it, I, in the name of Their Highnesses do give and grant to you full and complete authority, the same as I have received from Their Highnesses, with all of the particulars and conditions added and connected to it. And in the name of Their Highnesses, I command all and whatever persons, of whatever status, quality and condition, whether they may be noblemen, senior pilots and master pilots, boatswains, and sailors, and good men of the sea and of the land who are going or may go or might be in your company, that they should hold and keep you, the said Hernando Cortes, as their captain, and as such, they must obey you and carry out your orders and appear before you at your summons and consultations. And in all other necessary things and concerning your aforesaid responsibility, and for any and all purposes, they should join you and carry out and obey your commands, and give you all assistance and help in any and all things, under the penalty or penalties that you might impose upon them in the name of Their Highnesses. Which penalties, any and all of them that you might impose on them, either in written form or orally, and, from now on and from that time to the present, I do impose these penalties and hold them to be already imposed, and they shall be carried out upon the persons and properties of those who have incurred such penalties and might go against what has been written above, or who might come forward and consent to go against or evade or give help and aid for that purpose. And you can carry out these penalties and order them car-

ried out against their persons and properties, *dated in this city of Santiago, port on this island of Fernandina, the 23rd day of the month of October in the year one thousand five hundred and ten after the birth of Our Lord and Savior Jesus Christ.*

Against Those Who Deprecate or Contradict the Bull and Decree of Pope Alexander VI

[*General Archive of the Indies, Royal Patronage, Parcel 1, Number 1, Roll 1*]

Against those who deprecate or contradict the Bull and Decree of Pope Alexander VI in which he grants the right to their Catholic Majesties and to their successors, and exhorts that they conquer the Indies, subjugating those savages and afterwards converting them to the Christian religion, and submitting them to their rule and jurisdiction, it is contended:

Firstly, according to Deuteronomy, Chapter 17, where, by authority of divine law, the church determines that in dubious causes dealing with conscience, there being differing opinions in some town or city, it is necessary to refer to the Apostolic See, as was done at the beginning of this conquest of the Indies, and it must be decided by the Pope. And whoever shall contradict it should die on this account, i.e., be excommunicated.

And also, according to Chapter 25, where grave penalties are imposed on those who disobey or contradict or deprecate the decrees of the Roman Popes, and one who does so will be deemed a heretic and excommunicated, as in the intent of the aforesaid text, and so declares the passage of the chapter on violators.

Likewise that Saint Thomas, in Book Nine final article, says that the Pope can err in certain cases which are based on an uncertain medium, which is the testimony of men, but not in universal cases that deal with customs. The Pope also could err as a man, but not when he is upheld by the Holy Spirit which governs the church, such was the judgment of John Neapolis, according to Book 11, as well as Sylvester q.v. But given that, in some decree pertaining to the mores and universal state of the church, like this one of Alexander, the Pope could err, one should not think for that reason that he erred, nor is it the right of any particular persons to judge this, even though they may be

very learned, nor of any judge, if it is not another Pope or
General Council, because as Saint Augustine says in his
book of true religion, according to Chapter 4, [on these
temporal laws, although men may base judgments about
them at the moment of instituting them, nevertheless,
once ratified and signed, it is wrong for the judge to judge
the laws themselves, but rather to judge according to
them] because this decree and rescript law is like a
pontifical epistle, [given that the writings of princes have
the force of laws], especially such a rescript law as this one,
dealing with the universal conversion of the infidels, how
it is to be done and by what means. Because, as St. Thomas
says, q.v., [one must give greater faith to a Pope when he is
defining or making a judgment regarding human affairs
in the church than to an assemblage of learned men], and
St. Bernard in his book of dispensations speaking of Pope
Agatho says, q.v., [who has better reason to receive Divine
assistance than he who has taken upon himself the
administration of the mysteries of God? And him, whom
we should regard as God, we should likewise hear him as
God in those things that are not blatantly against God], and
so much more so in a decree such as this one, which is in
complete agreement with the decree of Pope Saint
Gregory, Book 23, Chapter 4, not to mention with the
pronouncements and testimonies of the holy doctors
Augustine, Gregory, Ambrose and Thomas, and the
ancient act of the church by the emperors who are faithful
members of it, and praised by all Christians, and in
accordance with the Holy Scripture both old and new
testaments as we hold to be well proved, and not only not
contradicted by any Pope, but rather previously confirmed
by all the other Pontiffs who followed after Alexander
through graces and indults for bishoprics and churches
which have been founded by this conquest in those
subjugated and converted lands, and founded in the
power and command which Christ gave to his vicar to
preach the gospel throughout the whole world. And in
order to accomplish this easily, the subjugation of the
infidels to the Christians is necessary, and consequently
he, the Pope, was given the power for this subjugation,
having temporal forces for it through the rights given to

him by Chapters q.v., from which it is stated that he who is
entrusted with the principal responsibility is also jointly
considered to be entrusted with anything additional which
may be necessary toward accomplishing that end. And as
St. Thomas says, Chapter 22, Part 40, articles 2 to 3. [*The
authority who is entrusted with a certain end should be
able to do whatever is required to achieve that end*] or, as
he says, speaking on the same occasion of just wars, to
which the Popes exhort the Christian monarchs so they
will come to a holy and spiritual end, which is the
conversion of the infidels. Because, as he himself says in
Book 3 of his Rules for Princes, [*the power of the Pope,
even though it is seen to deal principally with spiritual
things, is not excluded from temporal matters, given that
the temporal is governed by the spiritual.*] Thus being that
the conquest is just, as is more extensively proven by the
pamphlet printed in Rome with the approval of the vicar
of the Pope and the prelate of the Holy Office and all the
learned mentors of the Roman Court, to whom the
emperor will justly give more credit than to all the
remaining theologians and canonists and universities of
Christendom, if they should greatly contradict one
another, this being as it is in his favor and confirmation of
the decree and apostolic indult of Pope Alexander.
Therefore, the truth being as it is that it is such a holy
thing to pursue this conquest having the strength and will
for it, since to obstruct it would be a very great sin [*against
the charity owed to God and to mankind*], what could be
more contrary to this charity than to act against the
expressed will of Him [*who wants all men to be saved and
to become aware of the truth*], or than to tolerate the
injuries to God and the blasphemies that are done in the
name of idolatry, as St. Thomas says, when these can be
eliminated by subjugating the idolaters. And what could
be more contrary to charity toward humanity than to
impede the way to their conversation and salvation,
which man cannot achieve without faith and without
believing in Christ. [*But how will they believe without
having heard of him? How will they hear without
someone to preach? How will they preach if they are not
sent?* (Romans 10) *How will they be sent if the barbarians*

are not subdued and, once the impediments are eliminated, the way made smooth for preaching? Let us send preachers (he says) as Christ sent the Apostles, as lambs among wolves.] This is to return to the first point and condemn the conquest through works and indirect ways *[without realizing, as St. Augustine says, that those were other times and that everything is carried out in its own moment. Who would then have given credit to the emperors?]* Because subjugation is just, since it is very useful for preaching? Because, once the barbarians are subjugated, there is not danger to the preachers, and each one of the barbarians can freely convert without fearing his chieftain or his priest, which would be totally the opposite if they were not subjugated, and in 100 years not so many would be converted as would be converted in two weeks by doing it this other way. For then all can come together voluntarily to be baptized, and God, through the sacrament of baptism, will impress upon them good character and give them a deep faith which is a great help and assistance to the recipient. Also it is very much against the principle of charity toward humanity not to prevent, if one can, the injuries to the innocents whom the barbarians sacrifice to the devils, as was done in New Spain, and to the women whom they bury alive with their husbands the chieftains when they die, as is done in Peru. And finally, to prohibit this conquest whose purpose is to preach the gospel is against that precept of Christ, *[going throughout the whole world, preach the gospel to all creatures]*. And if they say that, although the conquest is just, it should be abandoned because of all the evil and the injuries done because of it to the barbarians, to this it is already responded and proved that the benefit that comes to these barbarians from this conquest, spiritual as well as temporal, is far greater than the damage done to them. So that, in conclusion, I say that if our rulers can do this and meet the costs, it would be better to do so *[for, as St. Paul says, hypocritically or sincerely, Christ must be proclaimed]*. And to advise that it should not be done and that we should stop doing it, though we are still able to do so, would be, as it has been said, a very grave sin.

APENDICE

DOCUMENTANDO LA CONQUISTA

Dossier compilado y transcripción paleográfica por
MARIO GOMEZ-MORIANA

Transliteración por Luis A. Ramos-García

Asistencia editorial por Oscar Pereira

CAPITULACION DEL ALMIRANTE COLON, 1492
ABRIL 17 DE 1492

INSTRUCCIONES DE LOS REYES A COLON
MAYO 29 DE 1493

CLAUSULA DEL TESTAMENTO DE LA REYNA NUESTRA SEÑORA DOÑA YSABEL

TRASLADO DE LA INSTRUÇION QUE DIEGO VELAZQUES DIO A LOS CAPITANES QUE ENBIO AL DESCUBRIMIENTO
OCTUBRE 23 DE 1510

CONTRA LOS QUE MENOSPRECIAN O CONTRADICEN LA BULLA Y DECRETO DEL PAPA ALEXANDRO SEXTO

Capitulacion del Almirante Colon, 1492

[*Archivo General de Indias, Ind. Gral. 418, libro I, Folios 1-1*]

Treslado de las cosas capituladas entre el Rey e la Reyna nuestros señores y don Xristoval Colon su almyrante del mar oceano en la villa de Santa Fee vega de Granada a XVII de 92.

Las cosas suplicadas y que vuestras altezas danle o pagan a don Cristoval Colon en alguna satisfacion de lo que a descubierto en los mares oceanos e del viaje que con ayuda de Dios agora a de hacer por ellos en servicio de vuestras altezas son las que se syguen:

Capitulo 1. *Sus altezas hazen almirante del mar oceano a don Xristoval Colon.*

Primeramente que a vuestras altezas como señores que son de los dichos mares oceanos fazen dende agora al dicho don Xristoval Colon su almyrante en todas aquellas yslas e tierras firmes que por su mano o yndustria se descubriran o ganaran en los dichos mares oceanos para durante su vida e despues del muerto a sus herederos y subscesores perpetuamente con todas aquellas preminencias e prerrogatyvas pertenecientes al tal oficio e segund que don Alonso Enrrique de Sandoval almyrante mayor de Castilla e los otros sus predescesores en el dicho oficio lo tenyan en sus distritos. plaze a sus Altezas. Juan de Coloma.

Capitulo 2. *Sus altezas hazen birrey a don Xristoval Colon en las Indias e que los oficios que se ovieren de poner escoja el de cada oficio tres e vuestras altezas escojan uno.*

Otro sy que vuestras altezas fazen al dicho don Xristoval Colon su visorrey e governador general en todas las dichas tyerras firmes e yslas que como dicho es el descubriere o ganare en las dichas mares e que p[ara] e regimyento de cada una e qual quier dellas faga el elecion de tres personas para cada oficio e que vuestras altezas tomen e escojan uno el que mas fuere a su servicio y asi seran mejor regidas las tyerras que Dios nuestro Señor le dexare ganar e hallar a servicio de vuestras altezas. [plaze] a sus Altezas. Juan de Coloma.

Capitulo 3. *El almirante Colon lleve la decima parte de todo lo que oviere quitadas las costas. costas asy.*

Yten que de todas e quales quier mercaderias sy quier sean perlas piedras preciosas oro o plata especieria e otras quales quier cosas e mercaderias de quales quyer especie nonbre e manera que sea que se conpraren trocaren hallaren ganaren e ovieren dentro en los limites del dicho almyrantasgo que dende agora vuestras altezas hasen merced al dicho don Xristoval e quieren que aya e lleve para sy la decima parte de todo ello. quitadas las costas todas que se hisieren en ello por manera que de lo que quedare limpio e libre aya e tome la dicha decima parte para sy mismo e haga della su voluntad quedando las otras nueve partes para vuestras altezas. plaze a Sus Altezas. Juan de Coloma.

Capitulo 4. *Que si traxere aca las mercaderias que alla grageare y se moviere pleito se conosca ante el Juez que le corresponde.*

Otro sy que sy a causa de las mercaderias quel traera de las dichas yslas e tyerras que asy como dicho es se ganaren o descubrieren o de las que en trueque de las aquellas se tomaren aca de otros mercaderes naciere pleito alguno. en el lugar donde el dicho comercio e trato se terna e fara que syenpre la premynencia de almirante e su oficio le pertenecera del tal pleito. plega a vuestras altezas quel o su tenyente e no [otro] juez conozcan del tal pleito e asy lo provean dende agora. p[laze] a sus Altezas. sy pertenece al dicho oficio de almyrante segund que lo t[enia]

(rubricado)

el dicho almyrante don Alonso Enrriquez defunto e los otros sus antecesores en sus destritos e syendo justo. Juan de Coloma.

Capitulo 5. *Sobre que el dicho Colon, si quisiere pueda en los navios que se armaren contribuir con la octaba parte y tirar de la ganancia correspondiente.*

Yten que en todos los navios que se armaren para el dicho trato e negociacion cada e quando e quantas vezes se armaren que pueda el dicho don Xristoval Colon sy quisyere contribuyr e pagar la ochaba parte de todo lo que se gastare en la armazon e tanbien aya e lleve el provecho de la ochaba parte de lo que resultare de la tal armada. plaze a Sus Altezas. Juan de Coloma. Son otorgados y despachados con las respuestas de vuestras altezas en fyn de cada un capitulo en la villa de Santa Fee de la vega de Granada a diez e siete de abril año del nacimiento de nuestro salvador Yhesuscristo de mill e quatrocientos e noventa e dos años. Yo el Rey. Yo la Reyna. por mandado del rey e de la reyna. Juan de Coloma.

INSTRUCCIONES DE LOS REYES A COLON
MAYO 29 DE 1493

[Archivo General de Indias, Ind. Gral. 418, folio, 4]

Instruycion del rey e de la reyna nuestros señores para don Xristoval Colon almyrante de sus altezas de las yslas y tyerra firme descubiertas y por descubrir en el mar oceano a la parte de las Yndias y su visorrey e governador dellas y otro sy capitan general desta armada que sus altezas agora embian a las dichas yslas y tierra firme para la forma que a de tener en este viaje que agora faze por mandado de sus altezas asy en su partida e de la armada que lleva como en su camyno y despues que alla sea llegado Dios [que]riendo es esta que se sygue:

Ynstrucion del almirante Colon

1. *Sobre que los indios sean tratados con agrado, y atraidos a nuestra Santa Fe Catolica para lo qual se enbia con otros religiosos a Fray Bartolome.*

Primeramente pues a Dios nuestro señor plugo por su santa mysericordia descobrir las dichas yslas e tierra firme al rey e a la reyna nuestros señores por yndustria del dicho don Xristobal Colon su almyrante bisorrey e governador dellas el qual a hecho relacion a sus altezas que las gentes que en ellas hallo pobladas conocio dellas ser gentes muy aparejadas para se covertyr a nuestra santa fee catolica porque no tyenen nynguna ley ny seta de lo qual a plazido e plaze a sus altezas porque en todo es razon se haga principalmente respeto al servicio de Dios nuestro señor y ensal[za]myento de nuestra santa fe catolica. por ende sus altezas deseando que nuestra santa fee catolica sea aumentada y crecida, mandan y encargan al dicho almyrante bisorrey governador que por todas las vias y maneras que pudiere procure y trabaje a traer a los moradores de las dichas yslas e tyerra firme a que se convyertan a nuestra santa fee catolica y para ayudar a ello enbian alla al devoto padre fray Buyl, juntamente con otros religiosos quel dicho almyrante consygo a de llevar. los quales [por] mano e yndustria de los yndios que aca binyeron procuren que sean bien ynformados de las cosas de nuestra santa fee pues ellos sabran ya e entenderan mucho de nuestra lengua y procurando de los ynstruyr en ella lo mejor que ser pueda. e porque esto mejor se puede poner en obra despues que en buen ora alla sea llegada el armada procure e haga el dicho almyrante que todos los que en ella van e mas fueren de aquy adelante traten muy bien e amorosamente a los dichos yndios syn que les hagan enojo alguno e procurando que tengan los unos con los otros mucha conversacion e famyliaridad hasiendose las mejores obras que ser pueda e asy mismo el dicho almyrante les de algunas dadivas graciosamente, de las cosas de mercaderias de sus altezas que lleva para el rescate, e los honrre mucho, e sy acaso fuere que alguno o algunas personas trataren mal a los dichos yndios en qualquier manera que sea que el dicho almyrante como bisrrey e governador de sus altezas lo castigue mucho por virtud de los poderes de sus altezas que para ello lleva, e porque las cosas espirituales syn las tenporales no pueden luengamen[te] durar, el dicho almyrante, visrrey e governador en las otras cosas la horden syguyente:

2. *Sobre que el dicho almirante lleve las mexores caravelas, pilotos y marineros, para esta armada.*

Primeramente para su camyno deve buscar las mejores caravelas que halle en el Andalusya y los marineros e pilotos sean los que mas saben de los oficios e mas fiables y pues que en el poder que sus altezas die[ron] al almyrante e a don Juan de Fonseca para haser esta armada se contiene [que] pueda tomar los nabios que quysiere para ella escojalos a su vo[luntad] los que mas viere el almyrante que conbienen.

3. *Sobre que todas las personas, que bayan se presenten ante dicho don Christobal Colon, y lleben certificazion de los contadores, y sueldo que lleban.*

Toda la gente que fuere en los navios sy ser pudiere sean personas co[noci]das e fieles y todos se an de presentar ante el dicho don Juan de Fonseca e por ante Juan de Soria que los contadores mayores enbian alla por su lugartenyente para esta armada. ante el qual se a de haser la dicha presentacion como ante lugartenyente de los dichos contadores mayores e a la de asentar en su libro. e el pagador a les de pagar el sueldo que obi[eren] de aver por las nomynas e libramyento firmado de los dichos almyrante e don Juan de Fonseca e del dicho Juan de Soria e no en otra manera.

4. *Para que todos los asientos, y contratos, que se hacen se celebren ante escrivano mayor, almirante y don Juan de Fonseca.*

Todos los asyentos que se fisyeren con quales quier capitanes e marineros e oficiales e otras personas que fueren en la dicha armada e o[tro] sy todas las conpras que se ovyeren de faser asy de nabios como de mantenymientos e de pertrechos e armas y mercaderias e otras quales quier cosas para la dicha armada y los nabios que se fletaren por los dichos almyrante e don Juan de Fonseca y por las personas que para ello nonbraren e en presencia del dicho Juan de Soria como lugartenyente (rubricado). de los dichos contadores mayores para que haga libro dello. e otro sy en presencia de otro escribano sy quisyere poner por sy el dicho almirante. esto y las conpras que se hisyeren en los lugares do ellos estovyeren e las que se ovyeren de haser en otros lugares se fagan por las personas que los dichos almyrante e don Juan de Fonseca enbiaren para ello y por ante escrivano publico. e el que tubiere cargo de haser la paga para esta armada pague los maravedies que en todo lo susodicho montare por nomynas e libramyentos firmadas de los dichos almyrante e don Juan de Fonseca y del dicho Juan de Soria como contador.

5. *Sobre que Juan Garcia haga un libro donde siente las armas y mantenimientos que se llevare.*

Las quales dichas armas e mantenymientos e pertrechos y mercaderias e otras cosas que se conpraren se entreguen a las personas que el dicho al[myrante] nonbrare e a aquellos haga cargo el dicho Juan de Soria e haga libro e cuenta dello uno para traer a sus altezas otro para enbiar al conta[dor] que a destar en las dichas yslas con poder de los dichos nuestros contadores mayores.

6. *Para que el dicho, y dichos tomen razon de los que se embarcaren y que estos hagan pleyto omenage de defender en todo a sus Altezas.*

Al tienpo que la dicha armada aya de partir en buen ora. Todos los capi[ta]nes y pilotos e marineros e gente de cavallo e de pie e oficia[les] e otras personas que fueren en ella ayan de registrar todo lo que llevaren por ante el dicho almyrante el don Juan de Fonseca y ante las personas que ellos nonbraren e por ante el dicho Juan de Soria como lugartenyente de conta[dor] por que se sepa las personas que ban e de que calidad e oficio son cada una dellas e todos ayan de hacer e fagan juramento e pleito omenaje al [rey] e a la reyna nuestros señores para los servir en este viaje fielmente y que a[sy] en el camyno a la yda como despues llegados a las yslas e tierra fir[me] e a la buelta en todo lo que se ofresciere en dicho o en hecho o en conse[jo] guardaran el servicio de sus altezas y pro de su hasyenda como fie[les] e leales vasallos subditos de sus altezas y donde bieren su ser[vicio] allegaran e sy el contrario bieren lo arredraran a todo su po[der] e lo faran saver al dicho almyrante capitan general para que lo remedie. Asy mismo que en todo e por todo estaran a obediencia del dicho a[lmyrante] como almyrante de sus altezas en la mar e en la tyerra como bis[rrey] e governador de sus altezas. de manera que todos esten confor[mes] con el para lo susodicho e nynguno pueda faser lo contrario. lo qual to[do sus] altezas los mandan que fagan e cunplan por esta presente ynstru[cion] que fagan y cunplan asy so las penas en que quebranta [sic] caen los [que] quebrantan semejantes pleitos e omenajes.

7. *Que ninguna persona, que se enbarcare pueda llebar para rescate mercadurias.*

Otro sy sus altezas mandan que nynguna ny algunas personas de las que fueren en la dicha armada de qualquier estado o condicion que sean. no lleven ny puedan llevar en la dicha armada ny en otros navios mercaderias algunas para haser rescate alguno en las dichas yslas e tierra firme porque nynguno lo a de haser salvo para sus altezas como adelante sera contenydo.

8. *Que se haga alarde luego que se desembarquen, y manifiesten las mercadurias y pertrechos que llevaren.*

Al tienpo que en buen ora llegaren a las dichas yslas e tierra firme donde an de desenvarcar, el dicho almyrante como bisrrey e governador por sus altezas de las dichas yslas e tierra firme a de mandar que todos los capitanes e gente e navios hagan alarde y presentacion asy de las personas como de nabios e armas e pertrechos e mantenymientos e otras cosas que llevaren y porque nynguno ny algunas personas no an de llevar mercaderias algunas para haser rescate alguno de oro ny de otras cosas en todas las dichas yslas e tyerra firme syn mandamyento de sus altezas como dicho es e sy acaeciere llevar mas de lo que manyfestaren al tienpo que de Castilla partieren segund fueren asentados en el libro del que fue por tenyente de los dichos contadores mayores que a de residir en las dichas yslas que lo pierda e que lo faga tomar el dicho almyrante bisorrey o quien su poder ovyere e lo entregue a la persona que por sus altezas ovyera de tener alla las mercaderias que sus altezas enbien en presencia del dicho tenyente de los dichos contadores porque el le haga cargo dello.

9. *Sobre que en presencia del thesorero o quien el nombrare se celebre todo rescate.*

Yten que qualquier rescate que se fisyere lo haga el almyrante o la perso[na] que por sy nonbrare e el thesorero de sus altezas que alla a de estar e non otra persona alguna y que lo haga en presencia del dicho tenyen[te] de los dichos contadores o ante el oficial que para ello el pusyera porque les haga cargo dello e lo asyente en el libro que a de tener de los dichos rescates. e porque podra ser que el rescate se aya de faser en divers[as] partes que donde no pudiere yr el thesorero enbie otro en su lugar juntamente con las personas que el dicho almyrante nonbrare e en presencia del dicho tenyente de los contadores o de su oficial e no en otra manera.

10. *Que el virrey ha o[rden] por que llegue nombre alcaldes, e alguaciles, y conoscan estos civil y criminal-mente.*

Despues que llegare el dicho almyrante bisorrey governador por virtud de los poderes de sus altezas que para ello lleva a de poner alcalde e alguasyles en las yslas e tierras donde el estubiere y las gentes que lleva e en otras quales quier yslas donde obiere quales quier gentes de las que ban con el dicho almyrante e en su armada p[ara] que bean los pleitos que ovyere asy cebiles como cremynales como l[os] acostumbran poner los otros visorreyes y governadores donde [quier] que sus altezas los tyenen e el dicho visorrey e governador oya [y] conozca de las apelaciones o de primera ynstancia como enten[diere] que mas conbiene y segund lo acostunbran de haser los otros gover[na]dores e bisorreyes de sus altezas. (rubricado)

11. *Que el virrey nombre si fuese necesario tres sugetos para regidores o jurados.*

Yten que sy fuere menester de nonbrar regidores e jurados e otros oficiales para admynystracion de la gente o de quales quier poblacion que se ovyere de haser el dicho almyrante bisorrey e governador nonbre tres personas para cada oficio como esta asentado con sus altezas y dellas tomen sus altezas una para cada oficio e asy por probisyon de sus altezas sean probeydos pero porque en este camyno no se pueden probeer los dichos oficiales desta manera que por esta vez los nonbre el dicho almyrante e bisorrey e governador de sus altezas.

12. *Sobre la forma en que se ha de pregonar.*

Yten que qualquier justicia que se ovyere de haser diga el pregon esta es la justicia que mandan haser el rey e la reyna nuestro señores.

13. *Que todas las provisiones sean firmadas de Sus Altezas, del virrey, y su escrivano.*

Yten que todas las probysiones e mandamientos patentes que el dicho almyrante bisorrey e governador ovyere de dar bayan escritos por don Fernando y doña Isabel rey e reyna etc. e firmados del dicho don Xristoval Colon como bisorrey e sobre escritos e firmados del escrivano que tubiere en la forma que lo acostunbran los otros escrivanos que firman cartas de los otros bisorreyes e soldados en las espaldas con [el] sello de sus altezas como lo acostunbran faser los otros bisorrey[es] que ponen sus altezas en sus reynos.

14. *Que se labre una casa de aduana donde se guarden todas las mercadurias.*

Yten que luego en llegando Dios queriendo mande el dicho almyrante bisorrey que se haga una casa de aduana donde se pongan todas las mercaderias de sus altezas asy de las que aca fueren como las que a[lla] se ovyeren para enbiar aca y al tienpo que descargaren las dichas mercad[erias] se pongan en la dicha casa en presencia de las personas que para ello el dicho almyrante bisorrey para ello nonbrare y ante el dicho oficial de los dichos contadores mayores que alla a de estar e ante otro oficial que ponga por sy el dicho almyrante para que se hagaan dos libros en que todo se escriva y por ello se cargue al thesorero que sus altezas alla enbian para que se hagan los rescates segund desuso dise e sy algo falta[re] de lo que aca les fuere entregado que lo hagan luego pagar.

15. *Para que todos se presenten ante el virrey para que se les paguen sus sueldos.*

Yten que cada que el dicho almyrante visorrey viere que cunple que fagan alarde de todas las gentes que alla estovieren sean tenidos de lo faser e se presenten ante el o ante las personas que para ello el nonbrare e ante el lugartenyente de los dichos contadores mayores que alla an de estar e quando se ovyere de pagar el sueldo a la dicha gente se pague por el dicho alarde y por nomynas e libramyentos del dicho al[myrante] e visorrey e del dicho contador y no de otra manera.

16. *Sobre que todos los capitanes y marineros se sujeten al virrei si se necesitase i que vayan navios a otras partes a rescatar o descubrir.*

Yten que sy el dicho almyrante despues que fuere llegado a las yslas biere que cunple enbiar quales quier navios con quales quier gentes a quales quier partes para descubrir lo que hasta aqui no se a descubierto o para rescates o para enbiarlos aca o a otras quales quier partes que sean tenidos de lo faser e conplir todos los capitanes e marineros a quien lo mandare so las penas que les pusyeren. las quales por la presente sus altezas dan poder al dicho almyrante e visorrey e governador general para la esecutar en las personas e bienes de los que en ellas cayeren.

17. *Que si Juan Garcia como theniente de thesorero quisiere poner otro en su lugar que escriva el libro de asiento lo pueda hacer.*

Otro sy porque en Cadis aya de aver una casa de aduana donde se an de cargar e descargar todas las mercaderias y armas e pertrechos e mantenymyentos que se ovyeren de llevar asy para yr en la dicha armada como para quedar en las yslas e tyerra firme como para lo que de alla se traxere lo qual todo se a de cargar e descargar en la dicha casa y non en otra parte alguna la qual a de tener la persona que sus altezas mandaren e el dicho Juan de Soria como thenyente de los dichos contadores mayores a de escrevir todo lo que alla se cargare y descargare para que por su libro se haga cargo e descargo dello que sy el dicho almyrante quysyere poner alli otro oficial alguno para que asy mismo lo escriva que lo pueda haser e faga.

18. *Que el almirante goze de la octava parte de lo que se hallare pagando tambien la octaba de las mercadurias.*

Otro sy a sus altezas plaze que aya el dicho almyrante la ocha[va] parte de lo que se ganare en lo que se ovyere de oro e otras cosas en dichas yslas e tyerra firme pagando el dicho almyrante el ochava parte de costo de la mercaderia porque se fisyere el dicho rescate sacando primeramente la decima parte que dello a de aver al dicho almyrante segund e por la forma que se contyene en la capitulacion que sus altezas tyenen mandado asentar con el dicho almyrante.

19. *Sobre que el dicho almirante guarde lo contenido en esta instruccion bajo las penas impuestas.*

Nos el Rey e la Reyna por la presente mandamos a vos
don Xristoval Colon nuestro almyrante e visorrey e
governador de las yslas e tyerra firme y por nuestro
manda[do] se an descubierto en el mar oceano a la parte de
las Indias y nuestro ca[pi]tan general de la nuestra armada
que para alla mandamos haser que beades esta ynstrucion
suso escrita y la guardades y cunplades segund que en ell[a]
se contyene y contra el thenor della no bayades ny pasades
ny consyntades yr ny pasar en manera alguna fecha en la
cibdad de Varcelona a veynte y nueve dias del mes de
mayo año del nacimiento de nuestro salvador Yhesucristo
de myll quatrocientos y noventa y tres años.

(rubricado)

Yo el Rey. Yo la Reyna. Por mandado del rey e la reina.
Fernando Alvares.

CLAUSULA DEL TESTAMENTO DE LA REYNA NUESTRA SEÑORA DOÑA YSABEL

[*Archivo General de Indias, Sevilla, Patronato Real, Legajo 1, número 5*]

Yten por quanto al tiempo que nos fueron concedidas por la Santa Sede apostolica las yslas y tierra firme del mar oceano descubiertas e por descubrir nuestra principal intencion fue al tiempo que lo suplicamos al papa Sesto Alexandro de buena memoria que nos hizo la dicha concesion de procurar de ynducir e atraer los pueblos dellas e los convertir a nuestra sancta fe chatolica y embiar a las dichas yslas e tierra firme perlados e religiosos e clerigos e otras personas doctas e temerosas de Dios para instruir los vecinos e moradores dellas en la fe chatolica e los enseñar e dotar de buenas costumbres e poner en ellos la diligencia devida segun mas largamente en las letras de la dicha concesion se contiene por ende suplico al rei mi señor muy afectuosamente y encargo e mando a la dicha princesa mi hija e al dicho principe su marido que asi lo hagan e cumplan e que este sea su principal fin e que en ello pongan mucha diligencia e no consientan ni den lugar que los yndios vecinos e moradores de las dichas yndias e tierra firme ganadas e por ganar reciban agravio alguno en sus personas ni bienes mas manden que sean bien e justamente tratados e si algun agravio an recebido lo remedien e provean por manera que no excedan cosa alguna de lo que por las letras apostolicas de la dicha concesion no es ynjungido e mandado.

TRASLADO DE LA INSTRUÇION QUE DIEGO VELAZQUES DIO A LOS CAPITANES QUE ENBIO AL DESCUBRIMIENTO

[*Archivo General de Indias, Sevilla, Patronato Real, Legajo 15, número 7*]

Visto

Instruçion que Diego Velazques dio en nonbre de sus altezas a Hernando Cortes que va por capitan del armada que Dios nuestro Señor guie a las yslas e tierras nuevamente descubiertas en el mar oceano.

1518 + Instruçion de Diego Velazquez a Cortes.

Por quanto yo Diego Velazquez alcalde e capitan general e repartidor de los caciques e yndios desta ysla Fernandina por sus altezas etc. enbie los dias pasados en nonbre e servicio de sus altezas a ver e bojar la ysla de Yucatan, Santa Maria de los Remedios, que nuevamente avia descubierto e a descubrir lo demas que Dios nuestro Señor fuese servido e en nonbre de sus altezas tomar la posesion de todo un armada con la gente necesaria, en que fue en nonbre por capitan della a Juan de Grijalva de la villa de la Trinidad desta isla, el qual me enbio una caravela de las que llevava, porque haçia mucha agua e en ella cierta gente que los yndios en la dicha Santa Maria de los Remedios, se avian herido e otros adolecido y con la raçon de todo lo que le avia ocurrido hasta estas yslas e tierra que de nuevo descubrio, que la una es una ysla que se diçe Cozumel e la puso por nonbre Santa Cruz, e la otra es una tierra grande que parte della se llama Ulua que puso por nonbre Santa Maria de las Nieves desde donde me enbio la dicha caravela e gente e me escrivio como yva syguiendo su demanda pricipalmente a saber, si aquella tierra hera ysla o tierra firme e a muchos dias que de razon avia de aver sabido nueva desde que se presume, pues tan nueva del hasta oy no se sabe que deve de tener o estar en

alguna estrema necesidad de socorro e asymismo porque
una caravela que yo enbie al dicho Juan de Grijalva desdel
puerto desta cibdad de Santiago, para que con el armada
que llevava se juntase en el puerto de San Cristoval de la
Habana, porque muy mas proveydo de todo e como a
servicio de sus altezas convenia, fuesle, quando llego a
donde penso hallarle el dicho Juan de Grijalva se avia
hecho a la vela y hera ydo con toda la dicha armada,
puesto que dexo aviso del viage que la dicha caravela avia
de llevar y como la dicha caravela en que yban ochenta o
nobenta honbres no hallo dicha armada, tomo el dicho
aviso e fue en seguimiento del dicho Juan de Grijalva e
segun parece y se ha sabido por ynformacion de las
personas heridas o dolientes que el dicho Juan de Grijalva
me enbio no se avia juntado con el ni della avia avido
ninguna nueva ni los dichos dolientes ni heridos, la
supieron a la buelta, puesto que vinieron mucha parte del
viage costa a costa de la ysla de Santa Maria de los
Remedios por donde avian ydo de que se presume que
con tiempo forçoso podrian decaer hasia tierra firme o
llegar a alguna parte donde los dichos ochenta o noventa
españoles corren detrimento por el navio o por ser pocos
o por andar perdidos en busca del dicho Juan de Grijalva
puesto que yvan muy bien pertrechados de todo lo
neçesario e demas desto, porque despues que con el dicho
Juan de Grijalva envie la dicha armada, he sydo
ynformado de muy cierto por un yndio de los de la dicha
ysla de Yucatan, Santa Maria de los Remedios como en
poder de ciertos caçiques priçipales della, estan seys
cristianos cativos y los tienen por esclavos e se syrven
dellos en sus haçiendas que los tomaron muchos dias a de
una caravela que con tienpo por alli deçian a porto
perdido, que se cree que alguno dellos deve ser Nicuesa,
capitan que el Catolico Rey don Fernando de glorisa
memoria mando yr a tierra firme e redemirlos, seria
grandisymo servicio de Dios nuestro Señor e de sus
altezas por todo lo qual, pareçiendome que al servicio de
Dios nuestro Señor e de su alteza como he dicho convenia
enbiar en seguimiento y socorro de la dicha armada que el
dicho Juan de Grijalva llevo y en busca de la caravela que
tras el, en su seguimiento fue, como a redemir, sy posible

fuese los dichos cristianos que en poder de los dichos yndios, estan cativos. Aver de aviendolo muchas veçes pensado y pesado y platicado, con personas cuerdas de enbiar como enbio otra armada tal e tanbien bastecida y aparejada asy de navios e mantenimientos como de gente e de todo lo demas, para semejante negocio necesario que sy por caso a la gente de la otra primera armada o de la dicha caravela que fue en su seguimiento hallase en alguna parte cercada de ynfieles, sea bastante para los socorrer e desarmar asy ep sy no los hallasen, por sy sola pueda, seguramente andar e calar, en su busca todas aquellas yslas, e tierras e saber el secreto dellas, e hazer todo lo demas que al servicio de Dios nuestro Señor cunpla y al de sus altezas convenga y para ello he acordado de la encomienda a vos, Fernando Cortes, y os enbiar por capitan della por la esperiencia que de vos tengo del tienpo, que a que en esta ysla en mi conpañia aveys servido a sus alteças, confiando que soys persona cuerda, que con toda prudencia y çelo, de su real servicio dareys buena raçon e quento de todo lo que por mi en nonbre de sus alteças vos fuese mandado, carta de la dicha negociacion, la que guiareys y encomendareys como mas al servicio de Dios nuestro Señor e de sus alteças convenga, y porque mejor guiada la negociacion de todo, vaya, lo que aveis de hazer y mirar que con mucha vigilancia e diligencia, ynquerir e saber cunpliendo en todo la ynstrucion que llevays de sus paternidades, la qual, condieron para mi e para los tenientes y capitanes que yo enbiase a las yslas donde vos ys, y de aquella y de su tema y forma no escondiendo en cosa alguna antes la cunpliendo, en todo e por todo segun que en ella se contiene guiandoos y siguiendoos por lo que sygue:

1. Primeramente, el principal motivo que vos y todos los de vuestra conpañia, aveys de llevar es, y a de ser, para que en este viage sea Dios nuestro Señor servido, e alabado y nuestra santa fee catolica anpliadla que no consyntyreys que ninguna forma de qualquiera calidad e condino que sea, diga mal a Dios nuestro Señor, ni a Santa Maria su madre, ni a sus santos, ni diga otras blasfemias contra su santisymo nonbre, por ninguna ni alguna manera, lo qual ante todas cosas, les amonestareys a todos, y a los que

semejantes delito cometieren castigallos eys conforme a derecho con toda la mas rigurosidad que se pueda.

2. Iten, porque mas conplidamente en este viage podays servir a Dios nuestro Señor no consyntyreys ningun pecado publico asy como amançebados publicamente ni que ninguno de los cristianos españoles de vuestra conpañia aya exceso ni cuyto casual con ninguna muger fuera de nuestra ley, porque es pecado a Dios muy odioso y las leyes divinas e umanas lo proyben, y procedereys con todo rigor contra el que tal pecado o delito cometiere, e castigarlo eys conforme a de ser por las leyes que en tal caso hablan y disponen.

3. Iten, porque en semejantes negocios, toda concordia es muy utile e provechosa y por contrario las discusiones y discordias son dañosas y de los juegos de dados e naipes suelen resultar muchos escandalos y blasfemias de Dios e de sus santos trabajareys de no llevar ni lleveys en vuestra conpañia, persona ninguna que se crea que es muy çelosa del servicio de Dios nuestro Señor e de sus alteças y se tenga noticia, que en bullicioso e amigo de novedades y alborotador y defendereys que en ninguno de los navios que llevays aya dados ni naipes, y avisareys dello asy a la gente de la mar como de la tierra ynponiendoles sobrello reçias penas, las quales executareys en las personas que lo contrario fyçieren.

4. Iten, despues de salida el armada del puerto desta cibdad de Santiago terneys mucho aviso e cuydado de que en los puertos que en esta ysla Fernandina saltaredes, no haga la gente que con vos fuere enojo alguno ni tomen cosa contra su voluntad a los vecinos e moradores e yndios della y todas las vezes que en los dichos puertos saltaredes, los avisareys dello, con apercibimiento que seran muy bien castigados los que lo contrahiçieren, y si lo hiçieren castigarlos eys conforme a justicia.

5. Iten, despues que con la ayuda de Dios nuestro Señor ayays recibido los bastimentos e otras cosas que en los dichos puertos aveys de tomar e hecho el alarde de la gente e armas que llevays de cada navio por sy, mirando mucho en el registro de las armas no aya, los fraudes que en semejantes casos se suele hazer prestandoselas los unos a los otros para el dicho alarde e dada toda buena horden

en los dichos navios e gente, con la mayor brevedad que se pueda, os partireys, en el nonbre de Dios a seguir vuestro viage.

6. Iten, antes que os sigays a la vela con mucha diligencia mirareys todos los navios de vuestra conserva, e ynquerireys e hareys busca por todas las vias que pudierdes, sy llevan en ellos, algun yndio o yndia, de los naturales desta isla e sy alguno hallardes lo entregad a las justiçias para que salidas las personas en que nonbre de sus altezas estan deposytados se los buelvan y en ninguna manera consentireys que en los dichos navios vaya ningun yndio.

7. Iten, despues de aver salido a la mar los navios e metidas las barcas yreys con la barca del navio donde vos fuerdes, a cada uno dellos, por sy llevando con vos un escribano e por las copias, tornareys alla mar la gente que cada navio llevase para que sepays sy falta alguno de los contenidos en las dichas copias que de cada navio ovierdes fecho porque mas çierto sepays la gente que llevays y de cada copia dareys un treslado al capitan que pusyerdes en cada navio y de las personas que fallardes que se asentaron con vos y le aveys dado dineros y quedasen me enviad una memoria para que aca se sepa.

8. Iten, al tienpo que esta postrera vez, visitaredes, los dichos navios mandareys e apercebireys a los capitanes que en cada uno dellos ponsyerdes, e a los maestres e pilotos que en ellos van o fueren y a cada uno por sy y a todos juntos tengan especial cuydado de seguir e aconpañar el navio en que vos fuerdes, y que por ninguna via e forma se aparten de vos en manera que cada dia todos os hablen o a lo menos, lleguen a vista e conpas de vuestro navio porque con ayuda de nuestro Señor llegueys todos juntos a la ysla de Cozumel Sant Agustin donde sera vuestra derecha derrota y viage, tomandoles sobre ello ante vuestro escribano, juramento e poniendoles grandes e graves penas, y sy por caso lo que Dios no permita acaesciese que por tienpo forçoso o tormenta de la mar que sobreviniese, fuese forzado que los navios se apartasen, y no pudiesen yr en la conserva, arriba dicha y llegasen primero que vos a la dicha ysla, apercibirles eys e mandareys so la dicha pena que ningun

capitan ni maestre ni otra persona alguna de los que en los
dichos navios fueren, sea osado de salir dellos ni saltar en
tierra por ninguna via ni manera sy no que antes syenpre
se velen y esten a buen recabdo hasta que vos llegueys
porque podria ser que vos o los que de vos apartasen con
tienpo y llegasen de noche a la ysla, mandarles eys e
avisareys a todos que a las noches faltando algund navio
hagan sus faroles para que se vean e sepan los unos de los
otros e asymismo vos lo hareys sy primero llegardes e por
donde por la mar fuerdes porque todos os sygan e vean e
sepan por donde vays e al tienpo que desta ysla os
desabrarcardes mandareys e hareys que todos tomen curso
de la derrota que han de llevar e para ello se les de su
yntruçion e aviso porque en todo aya buena horden.

9. Iten, avisareys e mandareys a los dichos capitanes e
maestres e a todas las otras personas que en los dichos
navios fueren que sy primero que vos llegaren a alguno
de los puertos de la dicha ysla e algunos yndios fueren a
los dichos navios, que sean dellos muy bien tratados e
resçevidos que por nynguna via nynguna persona de
nynguna manera ni condiçion que sea, sea osado de les
hazer agravyo ny les dezir cosa de que puedan resçebir
synsabor ni a lo que vays, salvo como estan esperando que
vos les direys a ellos la cabsa de vuestra yda ny les
demanden ni ynterrogen sy saben de los cristianos que en
la ysla de Santa Maria de los Remedios estan cabtivados en
poder de los yndios, porque no los avisen e los maten e
sobrello porneys muy rezias e grandes penas.

10. Iten, despues que en buen dia llegueys a la dicha ysla de
Santa Cruz syendo ynformado que es ella asy por
ynformacion de los pilotos o por Melchor yndio natural
de Santa Maria de los Remedios que con vos llevays,
trabajareys de ver y sondar todos los mas puertos e
entradas e aguadas que pudierdes por donde fuerdes asy
en la dicha ysla como en la de Santa Maria de los
Remedios e Punta Llana Santa Maria de las Nyeves e todo
lo que hallardes en los dichos puertos hareys asentar en
las cartas de los pilotos e a vuestro escrivano en la relacion
que de las dichas yslas e tierras aves de hazer, señalando el
nonbre de cada uno de los dichos puertos e aguadas de las

provinçias de cada uno estovyere por manera que de todo hagays muy cunplida e entera relaçion.

11. Iten, llegado que con ayuda de Dios nuestro Señor seays a la dicha ysla de Cozumel Santa Cruz hablareys a los caciques e yndios que pudierdes della e de todas las otras yslas e tierras por donde fuerdes diziendoles como vos ys por mandado del Rey nuestro señor a los ver e bisytar e darles heys a entender como es un rey muy poderoso cuyos vasallos o subdittos nosotros e ellos somos e a quien obedesçan muchas de las generaçiones deste mundo e que a sojuzgado e sojuzga muchas partidas e tierras del, unas de las quales son estas partes del mar oçeano donde ellos e otros muchos estan e relatarles heys los nonbres de las tierras e yslas conbiene a saber toda la costa de tierra firme hasta donde ellos estan en la Española e San Juan e Jamayca a esta Fernandina e las que mas supierdes, e que a todos los naturales a hecho e haze muchas mercedes, e para esto en cada una de ellas tiene sus capitanes e gente e yo por su mandado estoy en esta ysla, e abido ynformaçion de aquellas en donde ellos estan, en su nonbre os enbio para que les hableys e requyrays se sometan debajo de su yugo servidunbre e anparo real e que sean çiertos que haziendolo asy e firmandole bien e legalmente seran de su alteza e de mi en su nonbre muy remunerados e favoresçidos e conparados contra sus enemigos e dezirles heys como todos los naturales destas yslas asy lo hazen e en señal de serviçio le dan e enbian mucha cantidad de oro piedras perlas e otras cosas que ellos tienen e asy mismo sus altezas les hazen muchas mercedes e dezirles heys que ellos asymismo lo hagan e le den algunas cosas de las susodichas e de otras que ellos tengan para que su alteza conozca la boluntad que ellos tienen de servirle e para ello los gratifiquen, tanbien les direys como sabida la batalla que el capitan Françisco Hernandez que alla fue con ellos obo que a mi me peso mucho porque su alteza no quyere que por el ny por sus basallos ellos sean maltratados e yo en su nonbre os enbio para que los hableys e apacigueys e los hagays çiertos del gran poder del Rey nuestro señor e que sy de aqui adelante ellos paçificamente quisyeren darse a su servicio que los españoles no ternan con ellos batallas ni guerras ante

mucha conformidad e paz e seran en ayudarlos contra sus enemigos e todas las otras cosas que a vos paresçiere que se le deven dezir para los atraer a este proposyto.

12. Iten, porque en la dicha ysla de Santa Cruz se a hallado en muchas partes della e ençima de çiertas sepolturas e enterramientos cruces las quales dizen que tienen entre sy en mucha beneraçion travajareys de inquirirles saber por todas las vias que ser pudiere con mucha diligencia e cuydado las significaçion porque la tiene e sy la tienen porque ayan tenido o tengan notiçia de Dios nuestro Señor e que en ella padesçio honbre alguno e sobre esto porneys mucha vigilançia e de todo por arte vuestro escrivano tomareys muy entera relaçion asy en la dicha ysla como en qualesquier otras que la dicha cruz hallardes por donde fuerdes,

13. Iten, terneys mucho cuydado de ynquirir e saber por todas las vias e formas que pudierdes sy los naturales de las dichas yslas o de alguna dellas tengan alguna seta o creençia o rrito o cerimonia en que ellos crean o en que adoren o sy tienen mezquitas o algunas casas de oraçion o ydolos o otras cosas semejantes e sy tienen personas que administren sus çeremonias asy como alfaquies o otros mynistros que de todo muy por estenso traereys ante nuestro escrivano muy entera relación en manera que haga fee.

14. Iten, pues sabeys que la prinçipal cosa para que sus altezas permiten que se descubran tierras nuevas es para que tanto numero de animas como de innumerable tierra ayan estado e estan en estas partes perdidas fuera de nuestra santa fee por falta de quien della les diese verdadero conosçimiento travajareys por todas las maneras del mundo sy por caso tanta conbersaçion con los naturales de las yslas e tierra donde vays tuvierdes para les poder ynformar della como conozcan a lo menos haziendoselo entender por la mejor buena via que pudierdes como sy un solo Dios creador del çielo e de la tierra e de todas las otras cossas que en el çielo e en el mundo son e dezirles heys todo lo demas que en este caso pudierdes e el tienpo diere para ello lugar todo lo que mas e mejor os paresçiere que al servicio de Dios nuestro Señor e de sus altezas conbiene.

15. Iten, llegado que seays a la dicha ysla de Santa Cruz e por todas las otras tierras por donde fuerdes trabajareys por todas las vias que pudierdes de ynquerir e saber alguna nueva del armada que Juan de Grijalva llevo porque podria ser que el dicho Juan de Grijalva se oviese buelto a esta ysla y tuvyesen ellos e dello nueva e lo supiesen de çierto o que estuviese en alguna parte o puerto de la dicha ysla e asy mysmo por la mysma horden travajareis de saber nueva de la caravela que llevo a cargo Cristoval de Oli va que fue enseguimyento del dicho Juan de Grijalva sabres sy llego a la dicha ysla e sy saben que derrota llevo o sy tienen o saben alguna nueva de adonde esta y como.

16. Iten, sy dieren nuevas o supieredes de la dicha armada que esta por alli travajareys de juntaros con ella e despues de juntos sy se puediere aver sabido dar nueva de la dicha caravela dareys horden e conçierto para que quedando todo a buen recabdo avisados los unos de los otros de donde os podreys esperar e ymitar porque no os torneys a derramar e concretareys con mucha prudençia como se vaya a buscar la dicha caravela e se trayga donde conçertardes.

17. Iten, sy en la dicha ysla de Santa Cruz no supierdes nueva que la armada aya buelto por alli o esta çerca e supierdes dar nueva de la dicha caravela yreis en su busca e hallado que la ayays travajareys de buscar e saber nueva de la dicha armada que Juan de Grijalva llevo.

18. Iten, fecho que ayays todo lo arriba dicho segund e como la oportunydad del tienpo para ello os diere lugar sy no supierdes nueva de la dicha armada ny caravela que en su seguimiento fue yreys por la costa de la ysla de Yucatan Santa Maria de los Remedios en la qual estan en poder de çiertos caçiques prinçipales della seys cristianos segund e como Melchor yndio natural de la dicha ysla que con vos llevays dize e os dira e travajareys por todas las vias e maneras que ser pudiere por aver los dichos cristinaos por rescate o por amor o por otra qualquyer via donde no yntervenga detrimento dellos ny de los españoles que llevays ny de los yndios e porque el dicho Melchor yndio natural de la dicha ysla que con vos llevays conosçe a los caçiques que los tienen cabtivos hareys que el dicho Melchor sea de todos muy bien tratado e no consentireys

que por nynguna via se le haga mal ny enojo ny que nadie hable con el sy no vos solo e mostrarle heys mucho amor e hazerle eys todas las buenas obras que pudierdes porque el obtenga e os diga la verdad de todo lo que le preguntaredes e mandaredes e os enseñe e muestre los dichos caçiques porque como los dichos yndios en casos de guerras son mañosos podria ser que nonbrasen por caçiques a otros yndios de poca maña para que por ellos hablasen y en ellos tomasen espirençia de lo que devian hazer por lo que ellos les dixesen e tenyendo os el dicho Melchor buen amor no consentiria que se os haga engaño sy no antes os avisara lo que biere e por el contrario sy de otra manera con el se hiziese.

19. Iten, terneys mucho aviso e cuydado de que a todos los yndios de aquellas partes que a vos binyeren asy en la mar como en la tierra donde estuvierdes a veros y hablaros o a rescatar o a otra qualquyer cosa, sean de vos y de todos muy bien tratados e resçebidos mostrandoles mucha amystad e amor e anymandoles segund que os paresçiere que al caso e a las personas que a vos binyeren lo demandan e no consentireys so grandes penas que para ello porneys que les sea fecho agravyo ny desaguisado ninguno sy no antes travajareys por todas las vias e maneras que pudierdes como quando de vos se partieren vayan muy alegres e contentos e satisfechos de vuestra conbersaçion e de todos los de vuestra conpañia porque de hazerse otra cosa nuestro Señor e sus altezas podrian ser muy desservidos porque no podria aver efetto vuestra demanda.

20. Iten, sy antes que con el dicho Juan de Grijalba os juntaredes algunos yndios quysyeren rescatar con vos algunas cosas suyas por otras de las que vos llevays, porque mejor recebid aya en todas las cosas del rescate e de los que de alli se oviere llevareys un arca de dos o tres çerraduras e señalareys entre los ombres de bien de vuestra conpañia los que os paresçiere que mas zelosos son del servicio de sus altezas e que sean personas de confiança uno para veedor e otro para thesorero del rescate que se ovyere e rescatareys asy de oro como de perlas e piedras preçiosas metales e otras qualesquyer cossas que ovyere e sy fuere el arca de tres çerraduras la

una llave dareys que tenga el dicho veedor e la otra el thesorero e la otra terneys vos o vuestro mandado y todo se metera dentro de la dicha arca, e se rescatara por ante vuestro escrivano que dello de fee.

21. Iten, porque se ofresçiera nesçesidad de saltar en tierra algunas vezes asy a tomar alguna leña como a otras cosas que podrian ser menester, quando la tal nesçesidad se ofreçiere para que syn peligro de los españoles mejor se pueda hazer enbiareys con la gente que a tomar la dicha agua e leña fuere, una persona que sea de quyen tengays mucha confiança e buen conçebtto que es persona cuerda al qual mandareys que todos obedezcan, e mirareys que la gente que asy con el enbiardes sea la mas paçifica e quyeta de mas confiança e cordura que vos pudierdes e la mejor armada e mandarles heys que en su salida e entrada no aya escandalo ny alboroto con los naturales de la dicha ysla e mirareys que sea e vayan muy syn peligro e que en ninguna manera duerma en tierra ninguna noche ny se alexen tanto de la costa de la mar que en breve no puedan bolver a ella porque sy algo les acaesçiere con los yndios puedan de la gente de los navios, ser socorridos.

22. Iten, que sy por caso algund pueblo estovyere cerca de la mar e en la gente del vierdes tal boluntad que os parezcan que seguramente por su boluntad e syn escandalo dellos e peligro de los españoles podeys yr a berle e os determynaredes a ello llevareys con vos la gente mas paçifica e cuerda e bien armada que pudierdes e mandarles eys ante vuestro escrivano con pena que para ello les porneys que nynguno sea osado de tomar cosa ninguna a los dichos yndios de poco ni mucho valor ni por ninguna via ny manera ny sean osados de entrar en ninguna casa dellos ni de burlas con sus mugeres ni tomar ny llegar a ellas ny las hablar ny dezir ny hazer otra cosa de que se presuma que se pueden resabiar ny se desmanden ni aparten de vos por ninguna via ny manera ny por cosa que se les ofrezcan aunque los yndios salgan a vos asta que vos les mandeys lo que deven e an de hazer segund el tienpo e nesçesidad en que os fallardes e vierdes.

23. Iten, porque podria ser que los yndios por os engañar e matar os mostrasen buena boluntad e os ynçitasen que fuesedes a sus pueblos, terneys mucho estudio e vigilançia

de la manera que en ellos veys e sy fuerdes yreys syenpre muy sobre aviso llevando con vos la gente arriba dicha e las armas muy a recabdo e no consyntireys que los yndios se entremetan entre los españoles a lo menos muchos sy no que antes vayan e esten por su parte haziendoles entender que lo fazeys porque no quereys que nyngund español les haga ny diga cosa de que resçiban enojo porque metiendose entre vosotros muchos yndios pueden tener çelada para en abraçandose los unos con vosotros salir otros e como son muchos podriades correr peligro e peresçer, e dexareys muy aperçebidos los navios asy para que ellos esten a buen recabdo como sy para que nesçesidad se ofresçiere podays ser socorrido de la gente que en ellos dexays e dexarles heys çierta seña asy para que ellos fagan sy en nesçesidad se vieren como para que vos la hagays sy la tuvyerdes.

24. Iten, avido que plaçiendo a Dios nuestro Señor ayays los cristianos que en la dicha ysla de Santa Maria de los Remedios estan cabtivos y buscado que por ella ayays en la dicha armada y la dicha caravela seguyreys vuestro viaje a la Punta Llana que es el principio de la tierra grande que agora nuevamente el dicho Juan de Grijalva descubrio e correreys en su busca por la costa della adelante buscando todos los rios e puertos della fasta llegar a la baya de San Juan e Santa Maria de las Nyeves que es desde donde el dicho Juan de Grijalva me enbio los heridos e dolientes e me iscrivyo lo que hasta alli le avia ocurrido e sy ally le hallardes juntaros heys con el e porque entre los españoles que llevays e alla estan no ayan diferencias ny divisyones quando juntos seays cada uno tenga cargo de la gente que consygo lleva e entrambos juntamente e muy conforme consultareys todo aquello que obiedes que mal e mejor al servicio de Dios nuestro Señor e de sus altezas sea conforme e a las ynstruçiones que de sus paternydades e myas el dicho Juan de Grijalva llevo e esta que en nonbre de sus altezas agora yo os doy e juntos que plaziendo a Dios nuestro Señor seays sy algund rescate o presente ovyeren de valor por qualquyer via resçibase en presençia de Francisco de Peñalosa veedor nonbrado por sus paternidades.

25. Iten, trabajareys con mucha diligencia e soliçitud de ynquerir e sabe el secreto de las dichas yslas e tierras e de las demas a ellas comarcanas y que Dios nuestro Señor aya sydo servido que se descubran e descubrieren asy de la manera e conbersaçion de la gente e de cada una dellas en particular como de los arboles fontas yervas aves anymales oro piedras preçiosas perlas e otros metales espeçieria e otras qualesquyer cosas que de las dichas yslas e tierras pudierdes saber e alcançar e de todo traed entera relaçion por ante escribano sabido que en las dichas yslas e tierras ay oro sabreys de donde e como lo ay e sy lo ovyere de myrar en parte que vos lo podays ver travajad de lo catar e ber para que mas çierta relaçion dello podays fazer ispecialmente en Santa Maria de las Nyeves de donde el dicho Juan de Grijalva me enbio çiertos granos de oro por fundir e fundidos e sabreys sy aquellas cosas de oro labradas se labran alli entre ellos o las traen e rescatan de otras partes.

26. Iten, en todas las yslas que se descubrieren saltareys en tierra ante vuestro escrivano e muchos testigos e en nonbre de sus altezas tomareys e aprehendereys la posesion dellas con toda la mas solegnydad que ser pueda faziendo todos los actos e diligençias que en tal caso se requyeren e se suelen hazer e en todas ellas travajareys por todas las vias que pudierdes e con buena manera e horden de aver lengua de quien os podays ynformar de otras yslas e tierras e de la manera e calidad de la gente de ellas porque diz que ay gentes de orejas grandes e muchos que tienen las caras como perros e asy mysmo donde e a que parte estan las amazonas que dizen estos yndios que con vos llevays que estan çerca de alli.

27. Iten, porque demas de las cosas de suso contenydas e que se os an encargado e dado por my ynstruçion se os pueden ofresçer otras muchas a que yo como absente no podria prevenyr en el medio y remedio dellas a las quales vos como presente e persona de quyen yo tengo ysperiençia e confiança e con todo estudio e diligencia terneys el cuydado so cuydado que con bien para dellas guiar y myrar e encamynar e proveer como mas al servicio de Dios nuestro Señor e de sus altezas convenga proveereys en todas segund e como mas sabiamente se

pueda e deva hazer en oportunidad de tienpo en que os hallaredes para ello os diere lugar conformandoos en todo lo que ser pudiere con las dichas ynstruçiones arriba contenydas e de algunas personas sabias e prudentes de las que con vos llevays de quyen tengays credito e confiança por espirençia seays çierto que son zelosos del servicio de Dios nuestro Señor e de sus altezas e que os sabran dar su paresçer.

28. Iten, porque podria ser que entre las personas que con vos fuesen desta ysla Fernandina oviese algunas que devyesen dineros a sus altezas travajareys por todas las vias que pudierdes que en todos los puertos que en esta ysla tocaredes e gente quysyere yr con vos sy alguna della debe por qualquyer via en esta ysla dineros algunos a sus altezas e sy los deviere hagays que los paguen e sy no los pudieren pagar luego queden fianças en la ysla bastantes que los pagara por la tal persona e sy no los pagaren e dieren fianças que por ellos paguen no le llevareys en vuestra conpañia por nynguna via ny manera.

29. Iten, travajareys despues que ayays llegado a Santa Maria de las Nieves e antes sy antes os paresçiere e ovyerdes fallado la armada e caravela de con toda la mas brevedad que fuere posyble de me enbiar en un navio del que menos nesçesidad tuvyerdes e que bueno sea la razon de todo lo que os ovyere ocurrido e de lo que aveys fecho e pensays fazer e enbiarme heys todas las cosas de oro perlas e piedras preçiosas espeçieria anymalias e frutas e aves e todas las otras cosas que pudierdes aber avido para que de todo yo pueda hazer entera e verdadera relaçion al rey nuestro señor e gelo enbie para que su alteza lo vea e tenga muy entera e cunplida relaçion de todo lo que ay en las dichas tierras e partes o tengays notiçia que ay o puede aver.

30. Iten, en todas las cabsas asy çeviles como crimynales que alla entre unas personas con otras o en otra qualquyer manera se ofresçiere o acaesçieren conosçereys dellas e en ellas conforme a derecho e justicia e no en otra manera que para todo lo suso dicho e para cada una cosa e parte dello e para todo lo a ello anexo e conexo e dependiente yo en nonbre de sus altezas vos do e otorgo poder cunplido bastante como e segund que yo de sus altezas lo tengo con

todas sus ynçidençias e dependençias anexidades e
conexidades e en nonbre de sus altezas mando a todos e
qualesquyer personas de qualquyer estado calidad e
condicion que sean cavalleros hidalgos pilotos mayores e
maestres pilotos e contramaestres e marineros e hombres
buenos asy de la mar como de la tierra que van o fueren o
estovyeren en vuestra conpañia que ayan e tengan a vos el
dicho Hernando Cortes por su capitan e como a tal os
obedezcan e cunplan vuestros mandamientos e parezcan
ante vos a vuestros llamamientos e consultas e a todas las
otras cosas nesçesarias e conçernyentes al dicho vuestro
cargo e que en todo e para todo se junten con vos e
cunplan e obedezcan vuestro mandamyentos e os den
todo favor e ayuda en todo e para todo so la pena o penas
que vos en nonbre de sus altezas les pusyerdes las quales e
cada una dellas vos las ponyendo agora por iscrito como
por palabra yo desde agora para entonçes e desde entonçes
para agora las pongo e he por puestas e seran ejecutadas en
sus personas e bienes de los que en ellas yncurrieren e
contra lo susodicho fueren o vinyeren e consyntieren yr o
pasar e dieren favor e ayuda para ello e las podades
ejecutar le mandar ejecutar en sus personas e bienes, *fecha
en esta çibdad de Santiago puerto desta ysla Fernandina a
veynte e tress dias del mes de otubre año del nasçemento
de nuestro Señor e Salvador Yhesu Cristo de mill e
quinientos e diez e ocho años.*

CONTRA LOS QUE MENOSPRECIAN O CONTRADICEN LA BULLA Y DECRETO DEL PAPA ALEXANDRO SEXTO

[*Archivo General de Indias, Patron 1, No.1, Ro.2*]

Contra los que menosprecian o contradicen la bulla y decreto del Papa Alexandro Sexto en que da facultad a los Reyes Chatholicos y los successores y exhorta que hagan la conquista de Yndias subiectando aquellos barbaros y tras esto reduziendolos a la Religion Christiana e los somete a su imperio e jurisdicion se oppone.

Primeramente el *c. per venerabilem qui fil. sint leg.* donde por la auctoridad de la ley divina deut. 17 determina la iglesia que en las causas dubdosas tocantes a la consciencia aviendo diversos pareçeres en algun pueblo o çibdad se a de recurrir a la sede apostolica como se hizo al principio desta conquista de Yndias y se a de estar al juicio del Papa y quien lo contradixere que muera por ello (*id est*) que sea excomulgado.

Yten el *c. nulli c. violatores c. generali 25 q. 1* donde se ponen graves penas a los que no obedecen o contradizen y menosprecian los decretos de los Romanos Pontifices y se da por heretico y excomulgado el que lo haze como significa el dicho *c. generali* y lo declara la glosa del *cap. violatores.*

Yten que Santo Tomas *quodl(iveto) nono.* articulo ultimo dize que el papa puede errar en las causas particulares que van fundadas sobre medio inçierto que es el testimonio de los ombres, pero en las causas universales tocantes a la fee y al estado universal de la iglesia como son tambien las que tocan a las costumbres, el papa tambien podria errar en quanto ombre, pero no en quanto es enderezado del Spiritu Santo que goviena la iglesia, en la qual sentencia fue Jo(an) de Nea(polis) *quod li(veto) 11 et Sylvestre in verbo canonizatio,* pero dado que en algun decreto pertinente *ad mores et statum universalem ecclesiae* como este de Alexandro pudiese errar el Papa no por esso se a de pensar que erro, ni juzgar esto toca a personas particulares

aunque sean doctissimas ni a ningun juez, si no es otro
Papa o Conçilio general porque como dize S. Augustin *in
libro de vera religione, et habetu c. in istis dist(intione) 4.
in istis temporalibus legibus quam quam der homines
iudicent, cum eas instituunt, tamen cum fuerint institutae
et firmatae non icet iudici de ipsis iudicare, sed
solummodo ipsas* porque este decreto y rescripto ley es
como una decretal extravagante, *cum rescripta principum
vim habeant legum* mayormente tal rescripto como este
tocante a la universal conversion de los infieles como se a
de hazer y porque medios, porque como dize Santo Tomas
en el *quod(liveto) allegado maior fides adhibenda est uni
papae aliquid in humanis seu causis in ecclesia dicernenti
vel iudicanti quam multis simul sapientibus* y S. Bernardo
en el libro de *dispensatione* hablando del Papa Aduo
*(inquit) potius divina consilia requiruntur quam abillo cui
credita est dispensatio mysteriorum dei ipsum pro inde
quem pro deo habemus tanquam deum in ijs, quae non
sunt aperte contradeum audire debemus*, quanto mas en
un decreto como este conforme en todo al decreto de S.
Gregorio Papa. 23. q. 4.c. *si non* y a las sententias y
testimonios de los sanctos doctores Aug(ustin), Gregorio,
Ambrosio, Thomas y hecho antiguo de la iglesia por los
emperadores fieles miembros della y alabado de todos los
christianos. *c. non invenitur.23. q. 4.* y conforme a la
Sagrada Scriptura testamento viejo y nuevo como
tenemos muy provado y no solamente no contradicho por
algun Papa mas antes confirmado por todos los otros
Pontifices que se siguieron despues de Alexandro por
gracias e indultos para obispados e iglesias que por esta
conquista se an fundado en aquellas partes soiuzgadas y
convertidas y fundado en el poder y mandamiento que
Christo dio a su vicario de predicar el evangelio en todo el
mundo, para lo qual haserse comodamente es necessaria la
subiection de los infieles a los christianos y por
consiguiente le fue dado poder para la subiection teniendo
fuerzas temporales para ello por los derechos allegados. *c.
praeterea c. prudentia c. suspicionis de off(itium)* del
donde se declara que a quien se comete el principal
negocio iuntamente se entiende ser cometido lo accessorio
y necessario para aquel fin y como dize Santo Thomas. 22.

q.40.ar.2.ad. 3.(tium) potestas ad quam pertinet finis, debet disponere de ijs, qui pertinent ad finem, lo qual dize hablando en el mesmo caso de las guerras iustas a que exhortan los papas a los reyes christianos por venir al fin divino y spiritual como es la conversion de los infieles, porque como dize el mismo libro 3 *de Regimine principis, potestas papae quamquam vis potissimum versetur in spiritualibus tamen non excluditur a temporalibus, quatenus temporalia diriguntur ad spiritalia.* Pues siendo asi que la conquista es justa como esta mas largamente provado por el librito impresso en Roma con approbation del vicario del Papa y del maestro del Sacro palacio y todos los doctos de Corte Romana a quien el emperador dara como es razon mas credito que a todo el resto de theologos y canonistas y universidades de la Christiandad, si contradixesen, maiormente siendo esto como es en su favor y confirmacion del decreto e indulto apostolico de Alexandro Papa. Asi que si siendo como es esta la verdad es cosa tan sancta proseguir esta conquista aviendo fuerzas y comodidad para ello, que impedirla seria grandissimo *peccado* contra *Charitatem dei et proximi.* Que cosa puede ser mas contra *charitatem dei* que hazer contra su expressa voluntad *qui vult omnes homines salvos fieri, et ad veritatis agnitionem venirem* que tolerar las injurias de Dios y blasfemias que se hazen por la idolatria, como dize Santo Thomas, pudiendolas quitar subiectando los idolatras. Que cosa ay mas contra *charitatem proximi* que impedir la via de su conversion y salvacion la qual los ombres no pueden alcanzar sin la fee y sin creer en Christo, *quo modo autem credent in eum quem non audierunt, quo modo audient sine predicante, quo modo predicabunt, nisi mittantur Rom. 10. quo modo mittentur, nisi barbaris subijciantur, et sublatis impedimentis via praedicationis muniatur! mittamus (inquit) praedicatores ut Christus misit apostolos tanquam agnos inter lupos.* Esto es tornar a lo primero y reprovar la conquista por obras e vias indirectas *non animadvertentes ut ait Aug. aliud tunc fuisse tempus et omnia suis temporibus agi, quis enim tunc crediderat imperatorum.* Por que si la subiection es iusta porque se a de dexar siendo como es utilissima para la predication. Porque subiectados los barbaros no ay peligro para los predicadores y de los barbaros cada uno se puede convertir libremente no tiniendo temor del cazique ni del sacerdote, lo qual es todo al contrario no estando subiectos y no se convierten tantos en cien años como destotra manera en quinze dias que luego todos en comun voluntariamente se baptizan y Dios por el sacramento del baptismo les imprime el character y da la fee infusa que es grande ayuda y disposiçion para la adquisita. Tambien es mucho contra la charidad del proximo no repeller, pudiendo, las injurias de los innocentes que sacrifican los barbaros a los demonios como se hazia en la Nueva España y de las mugeres que entierran bivas con los caziques sus maridos quando mueren como en el Peru. E finalmente prohibir esta conquista cuyo fin es la predication del evangelio es contra aquel precepto evangelico de Christo *euntes in universum mundum predicate evangelium omni criaturae Mar.16.* E si dizen que aunque la conquista es justa se a de dexar por los males e injurias que se hazen por ella a los barbaros a esto ya esta respondido y provado que el bien que viene a los barbaros desta conquista ansi spiritual como temporal es infinito maior quel daño. Asi que concluiendo digo que si estas conquistas pueden hazer nuestros Reyes a su costa seria mejor por muchas razones mas sino que todavia se deven hazer *dum modo ut Paulus ait, sive per occassionem sive per veritatem Christus annuntietur Eph. 1.* y aconsejar que no se haga o dexarlo de hazer pudiendo como esta dicho seria gravissimo peccado.

CONTRIBUTORS

ROLENA ADORNO. Professor of Latin American Literature at the University of Michigan. She is the author of *Guaman Poma: Writing and Resistance in Colonial Peru* (1986), a critical edition of the *Nueva coronica y buen gobierno*, 3 vols. (with John V. Murra, 1980, 1987), an edited volume *From Oral to Written Expression: Native Andean Chronicles of the Early Colonial Period* (1982), and numerous articles on colonial Spanish American literature, including an essay for Volume I of the *Cambridge History of Latin American Literature*. She is currently at work on a study of Renaissance humanism in early colonial Mexico.

TOM CONLEY. Professor of French at the University of Minnesota, recently of the Ph.D. Program in French at the City University of New York and currently on the Faculty at Miami University of Ohio. Specializing in problems of text and image in French and Comparative Literatures, he has published on Montaigne in *Oeuvres et critiques, MLN,* and other journals. Work in Hispanic areas includes *Surrealismo documental: lectura de 'Tierra sin pan'* (1988) and "Broken Blockage: notas sobre la guerra civil en el cine de Hollywood," *Revista de Occidente* (1987). *Ensayos sobre el cine* is promised to appear through Hyperion editions.

ANTONIO GOMEZ-MORIANA. Professor of Comparative Literature and Hispanic Studies, and Director of the Comparative Literature Program at the Université de Montréal. Director of the monographic series "L'univers des discours". He has written on a wide range of topics including *Lazarillo de Tormes* and the picaresque novel, Cervantes, the Spanish "comedia," Unamuno, Ortega, text and discourse theory. His most recent books are: *La subversion du discours rituel* (1985) and *El Quijote, juego semiótico* (forthcoming).

BEATRIZ GONZALEZ STEPHAN. Professor of Literary Theory and Latin American and Venezuelan Literature at the Universidad Simón Bolívar in Caracas, Venezuela. Her research has focused on problems of Latin American literary historiography, the nineteenth century, modernism, the Avant Garde and the contemporary period. Her publications include the following: *La historiografía literaria del liberalismo hispanoamericano del siglo XIX* (1987); *Contribución al estudio de la historiografía literaria hispanoamericana* (1985); *Problemas de historiografía literaria latinoamericana: una puesta al día* (1989); *La duda del escorpión: la tradición heterodoxa en la narrativa latinoamericana* (forthcoming).

RENE JARA. Professor of Spanish-American Literature at the University of Minnesota. He has written extensively in the areas of literary theory and criticism. His latest books are *Farabeuf: Estrategias de la inscripción narrativa* (1982), *Los límites de la representación* (1985), and *El revés de la arpillera: Perfil literario de Chile* (1988).

STEPHANIE MERRIM. Associate Professor of Hispanic Studies at Brown University. She has published widely on modern and colonial Latin American topics, including *Logos and the Word* (1983) and the forthcoming *Towards a Feminist Understanding of Sor Juana Inés de la Cruz*. A long-standing focus of her research is the early historiography of the New World.

WALTER D. MIGNOLO. Professor of Latin American Literature, Semiotics and Literary Theory at the University of Michigan. Founder and editor of *Dispositio. Revista Hispánica de Semiótica Literaria*. Author of several books and articles among them *Textos, modelos y metáforas* (1984); *Teoría del texto e interpretación de textos* (1986); "Teorías literarias o de la literatura ¿Que son y para qué sirven?", in *Teorías de la literatura en la actualidad*, G. Reyes ed. (forthcoming). He is currently finishing a book on the Latin American colonial period, *Representing the New World: Literacy, Territoriality and Colonization.*

BEATRIZ PASTOR. Professor of Spanish-American Literature at Dartmouth College. She has written extensively on the Colonial and Modern periods. Her publications include *Roberto Arlt y la rebelión alienada* (1980) and the prize-winning *Discurso narrativo sobre la conquista de América: Ensayo* (1983).

JOSE RABASA. Assistant Professor of Spanish at the University of Maryland, College Park. He has published articles on colonial discourse in Mercator's *Atlas*, Cortés's representation of Tenochtitlan, and the scriptural economy in Columbus's writings. *Fantasy, Errancy and Symbolism in New World Motifs: An Essay on Sixteenth Century Spanish Historiography* is the title of his recently completed book.

NICHOLAS SPADACCINI. Professor of Hispanic Studies and Comparative Literature at the University of Minnesota. He has written especially on Cervantes, the picaresque novel, and Spanish Golden Age drama, edited several Spanish classics and co-edited books of literary theory and criticism, among them *Literature Among Discourses, The Spanish Golden Age* (1986), *The Institutionalization of Literature in Spain* (1987), *Autobiography in Early Modern Spain* (1988) and, *The Crisis of Institutionalized Literature in Spain* (1988).

IRIS M. ZAVALA. Professor of Spanish and Literary Theory at Rijksuniversiteit, Utrecht. She is the author of some twenty books on Unamuno, Valle-Inclán, Darío, modernism and post-modernism, literary theory, utopian socialism, ideology, Romanticism, the nineteenth century, and eighteenth-century narrative. Among her books are: *Masones, comuneros y carbonarios* (1970), *Fin de siglo, modernismo, 98, bohemia* (1974), *Clandestinidad y libertinaje erudito en los albores del siglo XVIII* (1978), *El texto en la historia* (1981), *Women, Feminist Identity and Society in the 1980's* (1985). She has also published four books of poetry and two novels. The Spanish government recently awarded her the *Lazo de Dama de la Orden del Mérito Civil* for her contributions to Hispanic studies.

CONTRIBUTING EDITORS TO THE APPENDIX

MARIO GOMEZ-MORIANA. Educational advisor at the Junta de Andalucía and Director of the Pedagogic Section of the Museo de Bellas Artes, Seville.

LAWRENCE C. MANTINI. Associate Professor of Hispanic and Romance Linguistics at the University of Minnesota. His areas of specialization are Ibero-Romance historical linguistics and dialectology. He is Review Editor of *Hispanic Linguistics*, a publication of the Prisma Institute, Department of Spanish and Portuguese, University of Minnesota.

OSCAR PEREIRA. Doctoral Candidate, Dept. of Spanish and Portuguese, University of Minnesota. His areas of interest include nineteenth- and twentieth-century Spanish philosophy. He has recently published an article entitled "Desintegración social y sensibilidad pastoril bajo el régimen fascista chileno" in *Poética de la población marginal: Sensibilidades determinantes* (1988).

LUIS A. RAMOS-GARCIA. Program Director of the Quin-centennial Fellowships and Summer Program for Spanish Teachers at the University of Minnesota. He received his Ph.D. in Spanish Literature from the University of Texas at Austin. His research has focused on eighteenth-century Spanish Literature and Latin American fiction. He is a translator, lecturer, and Editor-in-Chief of Studia Hispanica Editors, a U.S. publisher of bilingual books and critical editions from Spain, Latin America and the United States.

INDEX

468

470